S0-ARO-091

Enterprise Knowledge Portals

Enterprise Knowledge Portals

Next-Generation Portal Solutions for Dynamic Information Access, Better Decision Making, and Maximum Results

HEIDI COLLINS

AMACOM

American Management Association

New York • Atlanta • Brussels • Buenos Aires • Chicago • London • Mexico City
San Francisco • Shanghai • Tokyo • Toronto • Washington, D.C.

*Special discounts on bulk quantities of AMACOM books are available to corporations, professional associations, and other organizations. For details, contact Special Sales Department, AMACOM, a division of American Management Association, 1601 Broadway, New York, NY 10019.
Tel.: 212-903-8316. Fax: 212-903-8083.
Web site: www.amacombooks.org*

Library of Congress Cataloging-in-Publication Data

Collins, Heidi.
Enterprise knowledge portals : next generation portal solutions for dynamic information access, better decision making, and maximum results / Heidi Collins.
p. cm.
Includes bibliographical references and index.
ISBN 0-8144-0708-0
1. Business enterprises—Computer networks. 2. Management information systems. 3. Knowledge management. 4. Electronic commerce. 5. Web portals. 6. World Wide Web. 7. Internet. I. Title.

HD30.37 .C657 2002
658.4'038'011—dc21 *2002009989*

Printing number

10 9 8 7 6 5 4 3 2 1

For the glory of God alone

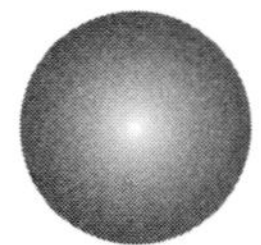

CONTENTS

Introduction xi

PART I: ENTERPRISE KNOWLEDGE PORTAL DEFINITION 1

CHAPTER 1: WHAT YOU NEED TO KNOW ABOUT KNOWLEDGE MANAGEMENT 3

- Be Organized Around Work Processes 6
- Maintain Knowledge and Facilitate Communication 10
- Focus on the Future 15
- Support Your Organization's Business Objectives 18
- Promote Innovations 20
- Maintain a Knowledge-Creating Organization 22
- Key Points 23

CHAPTER 2: ENTERPRISE PORTALS OVERVIEW 26

- Enterprise Portals for Your Knowledge Management Objectives 29
- Types of Enterprise Portals 32
- User Communities 35
- Enterprise Portal Services 37
- Enterprise Portal Functionality 41
- Enterprise Portal Integration Features 66
- Key Points 74

CHAPTER 3: CREATE YOUR ENTERPRISE KNOWLEDGE PORTAL 77

- MyCompany Case Study Introduction 80
- Enterprise Portal Market Overview 82

Document Your Knowledge Management Objectives 86
Enterprise Knowledge Portal IT–Enabling Framework 114
Enterprise Knowledge Portal Map 140
Key Points 161

PART II: THE ENTERPRISE KNOWLEDGE PORTAL PROGRAM **169**

CHAPTER 4: OUTLINE THE ENTERPRISE KNOWLEDGE PORTAL PROGRAM 171
Enterprise Knowledge Portal Value Proposition 172
Enterprise Knowledge Portal Program Charter 175
Enterprise Knowledge Portal Requirements 201
Enterprise Knowledge Portal Strategy 209
Enterprise Knowledge Portal Architecture and Infrastructure 225
Enterprise Knowledge Portal Program Plan 235
Executive Approval 249
Key Points 255

CHAPTER 5: THE ENTERPRISE KNOWLEDGE PORTAL ORGANIZATION 259
Process and Governance 261
Culture and Behavior 275
Key Points 277

PART III: THE ENTERPRISE KNOWLEDGE PORTAL PROJECTS **281**

CHAPTER 6: THE ENTERPRISE KNOWLEDGE PORTAL METHODOLOGY 283
MyCompany Case Study Introduction 288
Business Objects 289
Content Elements 301
Business Object Context 310
Storyboards and Scripts 317
Key Points 334

CHAPTER 7: FINANCIAL METRICS 341
Human Resources Information 343
Labor Savings 345
Cost Savings 347
Revenue 349
Project Costs 350

Return on Investment 353
Key Points 359

PART IV: THE ENTERPRISE KNOWLEDGE PORTAL INFRASTRUCTURE AND ENVIRONMENT **363**

CHAPTER 8: ENTERPRISE KNOWLEDGE PORTAL TECHNICAL ARCHITECTURE 365
Enterprise Knowledge Portal Information Technology Environment 367
Enterprise Knowledge Portal Information Technology Staff 377
Key Points 381

CHAPTER 9: SUPPORT AND COMPETENCY CENTER SERVICES 384
Enterprise Knowledge Portal Support and Competency Center Services 384
Enterprise Knowledge Portal Support and Competency Center Staff 393
Key Points 400

PART V: APPENDIXES **405**

APPENDIX A: KNOWLEDGE MANAGEMENT RESOURCES 407

APPENDIX B: ENTERPRISE KNOWLEDGE PORTAL RESOURCES 409

APPENDIX C: RECOMMENDED READING 411

BIBLIOGRAPHY 413

INDEX 417

INTRODUCTION

"A corporation's success today lies more in its intellectual and systems capabilities than in its physical assets. Managing human intellect—and converting it into useful products and services —is fast becoming the critical executive skill of the age."

JAMES BRIAN QUINN, PHILIP ANDERSON, AND SYDNEY FINKELSTEIN, *MANAGING PROFESSIONAL INTELLECT: MAKING THE MOST OF THE BEST*

The enterprise knowledge portal is the intersection between knowledge management and the enterprise portal. The components that make up knowledge management strategies include locating information, learning by doing, capturing human expertise, and reusing information and human expertise. Implementing a knowledge management initiative is challenging. Your knowledge management efforts will work best when integrated as part of other corporate initiatives. The return on investment (ROI), benefits, and value proposition of your knowledge management initiative blends into your business strategy and cannot be easily segregated. Enterprise portals, however, allow companies to implement their knowledge management initiatives straight into their business strategies. The resulting enterprise knowledge portal solution brings people, work processes, content, and technology into a single solution. For example, even if your company was not founded on the Web, you are continuing to create new strategies and initiatives that will allow you to take advantage of knowledge management techniques and tools in order to be more competitive in the new Web-enabled market. Thus, your enterprise knowledge portal initiative will be focused on e-business and e-commerce opportunities. The enterprise knowledge portal will provide opportunities in almost every aspect of your organization. Think about how your knowledge management objectives delivered through the Web will help in business-to-employee, business-to-business, or business-to-consumer work efforts.

This book offers detailed instructions on how to create an enterprise knowledge portal solution to implement knowledge management initiatives for the twenty-first century. In it, you will find answers to several questions:

- What are knowledge management opportunities and which particular opportunities should you pursue?
- What is the best way to integrate knowledge management strategies and initiatives with existing work processes?
- How do you measure return on investment?
- How do you define an enterprise knowledge portal for your specific business needs?
- How do you need to be organized to manage an enterprise knowledge portal solution?
- What skills and capabilities will you need to successfully design, develop, implement, and maintain an enterprise knowledge portal solution?
- How will knowledge management impact your existing work processes?
- How will the enterprise knowledge portal be able to adopt and change as your work processes improve?

The enterprise knowledge portal will assist you in identifying the most valuable information assets of your organization. You will find your most valuable information assets scattered among people, processes, and content. The ultimate goal is to create an enterprise-wide environment that seamlessly connects these people, processes, and content assets together. This book will provide details on how to:

- Determine the structure of your enterprise intellectual capital in relationship to your strategic goals and objectives.
- Put in place the organization that will manage knowledge assets in a way that satisfies customers, increases profits, and decreases costs.
- Learn how to multiply the value of knowledge from inside and outside your organization.
- Create a successful knowledge management infrastructure that minimizes technical, cultural, and logistical barriers.

- Know what information is essential to make sure people have the knowledge they need to succeed.
- Distribute knowledge, employing personalization techniques that meet the needs of business processes within and across organizational boundaries.

Your enterprise knowledge portal, the next-generation enterprise portal design, offers improved benefits and features that your organization can take advantage of in a Web-based software solution. Knowledge management and enterprise portal solutions are driven by e-business and corporate initiatives that are never done, never static, and always changing. The goal is to recognize what knowledge management successes look like, realize when your enterprise knowledge portal offering has achieved some success, and launch the next phase of the enterprise knowledge portal. Your enterprise knowledge portal program will be implemented as a cohesive collection of development and infrastructure projects. Each project is a succinct effort that can be delivered in six to nine months and is tied directly into the overall enterprise knowledge portal program for your organization.

The enterprise knowledge portal provides several opportunities for your organization to achieve your corporate objectives. It is designed to leverage Web-based technologies to connect people, work processes, and the data they need using the Internet, intranet, and extranet. Your enterprise knowledge portal must support the following structure to meet the definition of a complete solution. It must:

- *Dynamically build content into the enterprise knowledge portal when the user opens the portal page.* The information the user has requested will continue to reside and be maintained in the data source it originates from. The portal object will attach to the data source, retrieve the content requested, and present the information as the user has configured it to be presented. This process guarantees that every user has access to the same single source of information, provided he has the security rights to interact with the information.
- *Dynamically retrieve content that is relevant, timely, and accurate.* This structure makes the enterprise knowledge portal an actionable environment for users. Providing a user interface that brings content from legacy systems, Enterprise Resource Planning (ERP) solutions, Customer Relationship Management (CRM) solutions, Supply Chain Management (SCM) solutions, selected screens from applications, Web sites, documents, reports, and spreadsheets into a unified view for users will bring significant value and return on investment to your organization.

Knowledge management has often been defined in terms of the nature of knowledge. For the purposes of this book, the definition of knowledge management will be *the ability to locate and bring together people and relevant information to individuals that need it so that they can take effective action when doing their jobs*. You will be able to use the book in several ways. These include:

- *Enterprise Knowledge Portal Reference.* This book may be used as a broad foundation of information of knowledge management and enterprise portals and how to use them in your organization.
- *Enterprise Knowledge Portal Design and Architecture Reference.* This book contains the information needed to design and diagram an enterprise knowledge portal solution. The skills and staffing requirements you should consider can be referenced for future use.
- *Enterprise Knowledge Portal Methodology.* This book contains specific steps you can follow to identify, track, and assign ownership for the information needed to implement your enterprise knowledge portal. You can use this material as it exists or modify the steps to more closely fit your organization's best practices and procedures.
- *Guide to Other Information Sources.* This book collects several resources available on knowledge management, enterprise portals, and other technologies required to support an enterprise knowledge portal. Additional reading material that includes books and articles is provided in the appendixes to gain future knowledge on topics that you might want to investigate.

Part I: Enterprise Knowledge Portal Definition

To design an effective enterprise knowledge portal, you are going to have to gain some perspective of your whole organization. You can complete this work as an individual or as a small team. The enterprise knowledge portal team will need additional human expertise from a small community of knowledge experts with a broad and deep understanding of your organization. The enterprise knowledge portal team and the knowledge expert community will work together to complete several templates designed to give you an overview of where you are today. The template collection is used to map your knowledge management objectives into the enterprise portal features and functions and will provide the details needed to outline a logical path forward for the enterprise knowledge portal.

The ability to map your knowledge management objectives and the enterprise portal functionality together will require a basic understanding as well as the definitions of knowledge management and the enterprise portal. Chapter 1 provides a definition and overview of knowledge management that is broken down to address all aspects of the organization. These include:

- ❒ Knowledge workers
- ❒ End-to-end work processes
- ❒ Management
- ❒ Resource and work process management
- ❒ Vision and strategy
- ❒ Planning and forecasting
- ❒ Corporate mission and objectives
- ❒ Human resources

Chapter 2 is focused on enterprise portals and why they are much more than a browser interface to a website or Web page. The enterprise portal is reviewed as a cohesive architecture that supports a broad collection of features and functions creating a single-user interface to information, services, and applications throughout the organization. It is important to look at these features individually for the purposes of selecting the appropriate vendor and software solutions that address your specific knowledge management objectives. Chapter 3 is an overview of how to quickly identify the communities and the work processes that your knowledge management effort will target to maximize the benefits of the enterprise portal. An equally important benefit will be the prioritization of the features and functionality that will be critical to deliver as part of the enterprise knowledge portal. Your goal is to weave knowledge management best practices into the enterprise portal implementation to create an enterprise knowledge portal vision. The result is the ability for your company to locate, learn, capture, and reuse in a way that is proactively embedded into knowledge workers doing their jobs.

Part II: The Enterprise Knowledge Portal Program

You can get started creating the enterprise knowledge portal program as a small cross-functional team. The extended team members will be a community of knowledge experts with a broad and deep understanding of your work processes. The template collection presented here is used to provide the details needed to describe how the enterprise knowledge portal ties into your existing business strategy, what the scope will be, and when you expect to complete several identified activities. The enterprise knowledge portal program will provide the details needed to deploy a cohesive and consistent enterprise knowledge portal through a cross-functional organizational structure that will manage the work processes and governance to remain successful.

Once your initial research is complete and several key knowledge experts in your organization have approved moving forward to define an enterprise knowledge portal, the next phase of the enterprise knowledge portal is to create a program. A program outlines a "what, who, how, and when" frame for the enterprise knowledge portal. The enterprise knowledge portal program is what bridges your enterprise knowledge portal map (created in Part I) to your organizational structure to manage the resources to build and the methodology to deploy and maintain the enterprise knowledge portal.

You are going to need an enterprise knowledge portal program that provides a well-understood path forward for the project teams to be able to deliver a cohesive and comprehensive solution. Chapter 4 identifies a series of activities and tasks, as well as templates you can use or modify, to create your knowledge management portal program. Chapter 5 provides suggestions for an organizational structure, team membership, and associated skills that you should consider to create and continue to expand to design, build, and successfully support your enterprise knowledge portal initiative.

Part III: The Enterprise Knowledge Portal Projects

The template collection presented here is used to provide the details needed to capture the information critical to design a logical enterprise knowledge portal based on integrating your work processes and personalized content. The enterprise knowledge portal methodology will be integrated into the execution of your enterprise knowledge portal projects. The enterprise knowledge portal methodology will provide the details to design a work process-centric solution. Your project management and system development life cycle systems are not represented in this material but are necessary to deploy a cohesive and consistent enterprise knowledge portal for users.

The enterprise knowledge portal program will be implemented in your organization as a series of enterprise knowledge portal development projects and infrastructure projects. You will want to include or modify the enterprise knowledge portal design methodology presented here to deploy a consistent and cohesive solution. Chapter 6 identifies a series of activities and tasks as well as templates for the design methodology used to successfully implement your knowledge management objectives, business strategy, and work processes directly into each of your enterprise knowledge portal releases. Once you have completed the design of the enterprise knowledge portal for the scope outlined in the enterprise knowledge portal project charter, the next effort is to establish the associated financial metrics. Chapter 7 provides a spreadsheet for establishing a return on investment for the enterprise knowledge portal project.

Part IV: The Enterprise Knowledge Portal Infrastructure and Environment

The purpose of the enterprise knowledge portal technical architecture analysis is to organize your infrastructure planning and documentation activities for the enterprise knowledge portal. The information collected will allow you to clarify the technologies common to your infrastructure environment and identify the information technology personnel that will be necessary to plan, design, develop, and maintain an enterprise knowledge portal in your organization. Overviews of the list of possible technologies you will utilize in your enterprise knowledge portal are described. Technology is constantly evolving. The information presented here is a good introduction to the most common technologies included in enterprise knowledge portal solutions.

You are going to need a centralized infrastructure and architecture to deliver consistent enterprise knowledge portal hardware, software, administration, and security that will support a decentralized collection of work processes and content. Chapter 8 describes common enterprise knowledge portal technologies to be supported in your infrastructure environment and identifies the information technology personnel that will be necessary to plan, design, develop, and maintain an enterprise knowledge portal in your organization.

Once the enterprise knowledge portal has been deployed, the support and competency center will take over the day-to-day maintenance of services. The maintainability issues of the enterprise knowledge portal are covered in detail as a collection of services. This type of organization allows you to break up the enterprise knowledge portal solution into subsets of activities, best practices, and guidelines for more effective management, support, and maintenance. The enterprise knowledge portal services are owned by the support and competency center.

The support and competency center team is responsible for the success of a long-term enterprise knowledge portal in your organization. There are several services that the support and competency center will establish to effectively manage and maintain the enterprise knowledge portal. Chapter 9 describes common enterprise knowledge portal services that will need to be defined and supported. This includes the organizational structure that will be necessary to manage problem resolution work processes, maintain the enterprise knowledge portal library of reusable development objects and documentation, and other activities associated with your enterprise knowledge portal's continued success.

I

Enterprise Knowledge Portal Definition

1

What You Need to Know About Knowledge Management

"A learning organization is an organization skilled at creating, acquiring, and transferring knowledge, and at modifying its behavior to reflect new knowledge and insights."

David A. Garvin, *Building a Learning Organization*

You have probably heard many definitions of knowledge management. The standard theme of these definitions incorporates the ability to define and manage intellectual prowess. Your knowledge management activities and strategies are designed to capture intellectual capital. Technology is used to support these knowledge management activities by incorporating collaboration, just-in-case learning components, and other helpful features into your systems and work processes. Most knowledge management initiatives are integrated into the organizational efforts that are designed to pursue continuous growth where being able to adapt to changing markets and environments is critical. Your ability to quickly learn, adapt, and communicate the introduction of a new product, enhancements to an existing product, or the status of a shipment can make a significant impact on customer satisfaction and future sales. Optimizing the value of knowledge in your organization can only be accomplished if you know where knowledge assets are and how they are being used.

Knowledge management is unique to every organization. Our definition will be generic and outlined in terms of the nature of knowledge. For the purposes of this book, the definition of knowledge management will be *the ability to locate and bring together people and relevant information to individuals that need it so that they can take effective action when doing their jobs*.

Your knowledge management solution should:

- *Be organized around work processes.* Divide your organization's programs and operations into defined units or work processes. These work processes involve the repetition of the same patterns and relationships. This enables the same series of defined steps to be mapped through different levels of your organization and refined for awareness, understanding, consistency, and completeness.
- *Maintain knowledge and facilitate communication.* Every business unit in your organization is unique and responsible for critical activities and deliverables. Your company will require some enterprise coordination and communication to share the same strategy, focus on corporate initiatives, use the same information technology or accounting applications, and complete cross-functional work processes. The task is to define consistency and coordinate activities across business units and throughout your organization. The results of this effort will provide the structure required for you to communicate around and share work processes.
- *Focus on the future.* Continuously broaden human capital, learning, communication networks, and future goals or plans. The expansion of these efforts in your organization will create shorter product cycles as changing market conditions make it critical to create innovations in work processes and product offerings. Your proactive acknowledgement of the future will empower your organization to manage intellectual capital. What you know about your organization, your strategies, your market, your contribution to these changing environments, and how they affect your customers will become the intellectual capital and differentiating quality that sets you and your organization apart from your competitors. Your knowledge management efforts should include some number of defined knowledge documents that are delivered each planning, budgeting, and forecasting cycle to plan for the future by capturing the past.
- *Support your organization's business objectives.* People, information, and content have relative value in terms of the organization's goals and objectives. Once you understand the business objectives, you need to be able to allocate time, attention, and money among the different priorities and work process teams in support of your business objectives.
- *Promote innovation.* Improve results or efficiencies including improvements in normal business (products, services, processes, and exchange of cash) and online business (knowledge and information) to directly

improve the bottom line. Improvements in skills, career opportunities, and personal objectives and commitments for knowledge workers are critical to successfully improve results and achieve efficiencies.

- *Maintain a knowledge-creating organization.* The corporate knowledge structure that is created in a knowledge management initiative should combine the best of the previously existing unwired knowledge hierarchy and blend it with new, online delivery of content and interaction of knowledge workers in your organization. The enterprise knowledge portal framework you create should capture and deliver online information to meet the needs of managers, employees, clients, customers, and suppliers.

The type of knowledge that is maintained by organizations includes content and work processes, general and particular, linear and relational, timeless and timely. In many organizations, knowledge workers have shifted from focusing on trying to understand the best practices for their job functions to focusing on continuous learning and problem solving. Workers in your organization are, no doubt, required to continually redefine best practices based on the current situation, and then to reconfigure tasks and activities, and communicate their knowledge to others so that improvements or changes are constantly recognized and implemented. The individuals that contain and manage this knowledge create a value network for your organization. To perform their responsibilities effectively, each individual must understand her specific role in work processes and how to manage, perform, and improve the completion of activities and tasks.

The value of intellectual capital of an individual's knowledge is difficult to measure. Individuals evolve, change, and gain experience by bringing a wide variety of assets and strengths to a networked group. Knowledge workers have to recognize and continue to grow a sense of priority and importance around the information they manage. Individuals acquire and maintain this knowledge largely on their own. To be successful, every individual needs to have a sense of how different aspects of his knowledge fit together and to find ways to add value working alone, in small groups, or on large teams.

Today, knowledge is increasingly being recognized as the most important asset of organizations. Your organization might already be approaching knowledge management as a set of principles, practices, and technologies focused on innovation and optimization of work processes, supply chains, and customer relationships. This clarification and identification of specific knowledge management opportunities in vertical markets like supply chain management and customer relationship management are making organizations consider browser solutions like enterprise portals to provide an entry point or desktop to functionality for collaboration, content supply chains, search and retrieval, taxonomy or category construction and management, analytics, application integration, personalization, and performance-based metrics. The need for this hybrid of functionality, content, and applications that gives each individual using the enterprise portal a unique perspective and view of the organization is in demand by knowledge workers at every level in your company. With more access and control of information and knowledge, and with a work environment that provides flexibility for each knowledge worker, individuals are better able to create, execute, and be accountable for the underlying business processes they are responsible for. Since lesser-skilled and repetitive activities are being automated, your organization requires highly skilled employees who can manage complex processes while participating in and creating constant improvement or change.

The enterprise portal is an information technology–enabling platform to implement your knowledge management initiatives. If you design the enterprise portal around your knowledge management strategy, you will have built an enterprise knowledge portal. To begin to envision a knowledge management solution that can be implemented to deliver the type of features and services that you want to have available for the enterprise, you have to establish an appropriate knowledge and information-sharing strategy. Your organization, like many organizations, wants a knowledge management solution that lets employees know what information is available to them and allows them to interact seamlessly with the multiple sources of data and applications they need to use while performing their daily tasks at any time of day or night. Knowledge workers need to be able to get documents and understand processes. They want to see their mail, projects, customer updates, and any other critical information in a single intranet or extranet window. They need to be able to collaborate with the appropriate people in your organization if they have questions or knowledge to share with each other, or if they have to get answers or provide insight. Elements to consider and incorporate in your knowledge management strategy and resulting solution are described in more detail in the following sections.

Be Organized Around Work Processes

Your knowledge management solution will shift the emphasis from the actual product and service components of your business transactions to the work processes that enable your products and services. Engrained within your work processes are assumptions, inefficiencies, and redundancies that your knowledge management strategy can redefine, transform, or eliminate. People or knowledge workers in your organization perform work processes. You should map out your work processes to realize how the organization actually works. Walking through every step of the targeted business object from start to finish, ignoring how the work process is supposed to work, creates actual work-process diagrams.

Knowledge workers will have specific relationships or roles and a defined set of responsibilities as they are engaged in and complete these work processes. In each case, each step of a business object will be completed automatically by a system or manually by a user. The collections of steps that are completed by individuals with the same job description or responsibilities define a role. These roles and their associated job descriptions allow the individual knowledge worker to accept some restraints and autonomy. Individuals in any organization often have several roles as they perform their work processes. Knowledge workers with their defined roles have a unique view of the organization. Because roles are unique, work processes are unique. Work processes in the organization exist depending on the role of the individual and the perspective the role has in the work process. Every work process is viewed and perceived slightly differently by every knowledge worker within your organization. The knowledge workers and their understanding of your work processes are collectively your organization. (See Figure 1-1.)

Figure 1-1. Knowledge management conceptual model: knowledge worker.

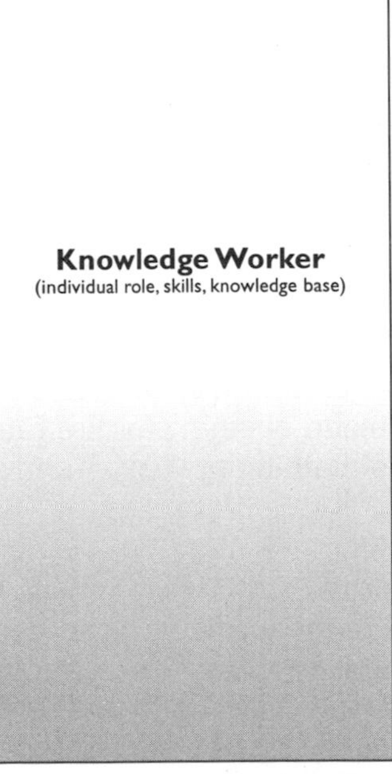

The knowledge of individuals within your organization establishes the range of possibilities your company will choose from when designing your knowledge management strategy and supporting solution. The culture and language in your meetings, written materials, and business discussions will determine the purpose and direction of your knowledge management solution. Often knowledge management project teams focus on your organization's core competencies, how the culture and management policies maintain work processes and practices, and how to affect learning to make behavior in the organization coherent and consistent. Knowledge management is how your company makes the most of the social and technical resources available to it. The goal of your knowledge management initiative should be to maximize the accessibility of assets and how they are used, and minimize the risk of missed opportunities and threats.

With too much information usually available to employees in multiple systems, archives, and stored only within the brains of specific individuals, a road map that would help employees determine available information and how exactly to locate it when they need it is required to effectively and efficiently complete complicated and sequential work processes. This road map would exist in the form of filters, content categorization, and navigation schemes that allow knowledge workers to select the information that is important to them.

In order to maintain your organization's competitiveness, your knowledge workers must be able to change their work processes and their supporting information systems to meet the changing needs of your customers. Enabling the ability of employees to select the information they need, as well as the ability to change the work processes and systems they work with, has a unique set of challenges. Creating a knowledge management system that combines these efforts is an even more difficult management problem. To be successful with this knowledge management initiative, your organization must manage the different activities together, interface with each other without interfering with each other, and be focused on the future. This must be done within the unique context of your organization where the operational activities and strategic initiatives are considered equally over time. Your organization's ability to balance the activities of your knowledge workers between planning for the future and running the business is important for maintaining and expanding shareholder value. (See Figure 1-2.)

When you are creating knowledge management systems, one of the first steps is to describe your business systems in terms of work processes. You then need to represent the individual work processes as flows of activities, such as the fulfillment process from submitting a packing slip to the warehouse, to the delivery of the product to the customer. You then determine which applications and systems are used to perform the activities and which people are responsible for the activities.

Figure 1-2. Knowledge management conceptual model: work processes.

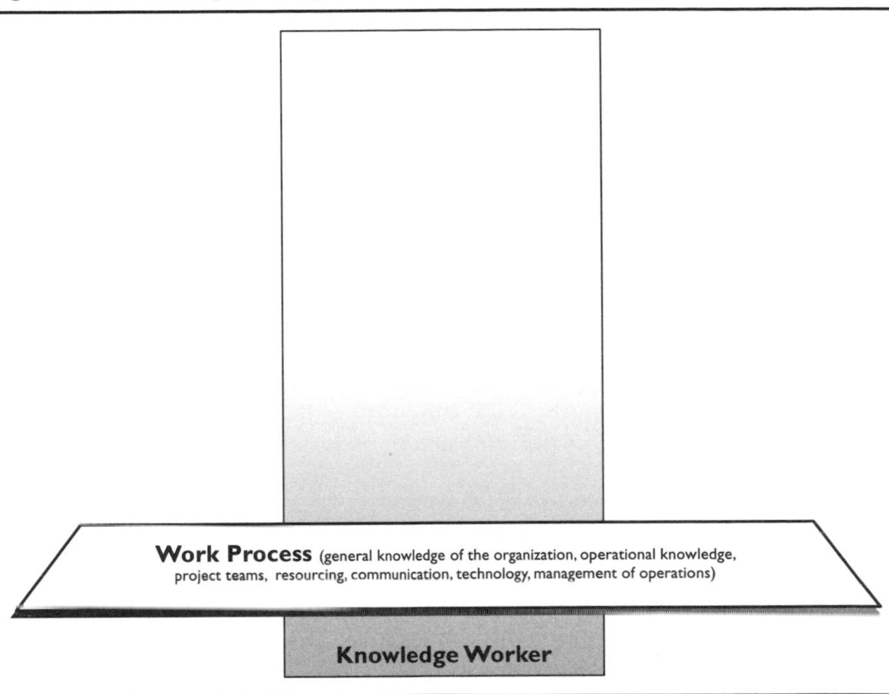

Work processes are repeatable and occur at different levels, individual or workgroup, throughout your organization and create unique structures and challenges at every level of management. For example, planning and forecasting work processes, performance management work processes, and project management work processes should be understood and applied consistently for every business unit. Work processes have relationships and dependencies on each other, so they cannot be considered islands that can be bridged. Individual work processes are integrated to cooperate with each other and need to be supported as part of your knowledge management efforts.

Be Organized Around Work Processes Discussion Questions

- ☐ Do knowledge workers and managers follow a consistent work process where common goals are defined? Are major areas of responsibility in terms of expected results outlined?
- ☐ Do business units have defined measures as guides for assessing their overall performance? Do individual knowledge workers have defined measures for their contribution to the business units' metrics?

- ☐ Do knowledge workers and managers understand the results to be accomplished? Do these objectives tie into the organization's mission or purpose?
- ☐ Do the performance metrics of the individual business units support and complement each other?
- ☐ Are success indicators or change measurements for accomplishments understood? Are quantity, quality, time, and cost represented in these measurements?
- ☐ Are work processes and other defined activities by knowledge workers and managers well defined and understood?
- ☐ Are the resources or other requirements and equipment needed to do work available for knowledge workers and managers when they need them?
- ☐ Are accomplishments or the outcome of the work-process efforts by knowledge workers and managers well defined and understood?

Maintain Knowledge and Facilitate Communication

Your organization is structured in business units and management layers. Your organization chart represents an overview of the management and leadership hierarchy that drives your business units. There are messages, content, and work processes shared throughout and across these business units. Your organization is filled with managers and leaders in all of these business units. At the highest level of your organization, and in each of the business units, consistent messages and objectives need to be coordinated. They should be clear, obvious, and easy to relate to each other. This coordination effort in your organization determines the level of knowledge you will be able to maintain and effectively communicate.

Several management solutions will exist in your organization to audit and improve the performance of knowledge workers and their work processes. (See Figure 1-3.) There will be a defined set of relationships among employees that outline the structure used within a defined business unit to create a productive operation. There will be additional relationships and structures that define how the management of an individual business unit maps into the larger organization. The communication and relationships within business units throughout your company will be unique to those business units. Close cooperation and fixed scheduling can be required to succeed, or high level of controls for safety and security considerations might be necessary. All of these elements will define the formal and informal conversations and productivity of people.

Knowledge workers are most productive when they have the autonomy to complete their work processes and meet the objectives of their

Figure 1-3. Knowledge management conceptual model: management.

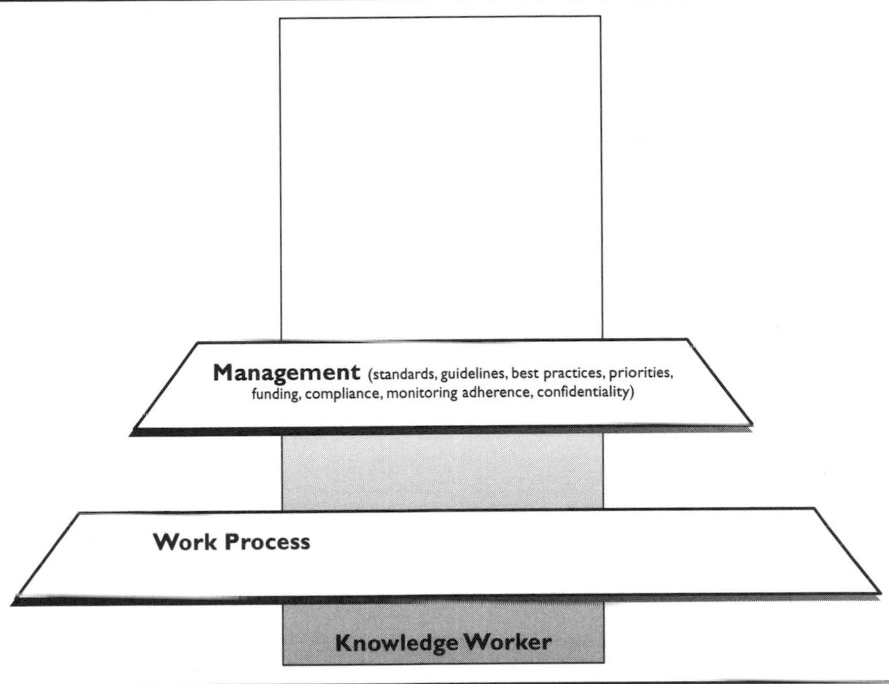

business unit. Workers are not productive when intervention or directives from management interfere or are inconsistent with their work processes and objectives. The relationship between managers and knowledge workers outlined in this book is based on the roles individuals are assigned within the organization. Most knowledge workers are often assigned several roles in the networked structures of organizations today. For example, they will function in the employee role or manager role when interacting with human resources. Each person will have several job-specific roles like sales representative, account manager, and marketing liaison. Each role needs to have well-defined work processes with specified deliverables to remain creative and autonomous within known and understood boundaries of its assigned responsibilities. The relationship between management and work processes is a collection of audit activities that support the combined objectives of the business units involved. The focus is on the management of information that has to be formally shared with knowledge workers to effectively audit the performance of current work processes while knowledge workers continue to function independently within their assigned work processes.

For individual business units to be successful, knowledge workers will share private and public information with other knowledge workers, contractors, suppliers, competitors, outside experts, and others. Work processes will be most effective when knowledge worker roles can dynamically enter and exit the work processes they are involved in. In customer relationship activities a customer will submit an order, review the status of a delivery, and pay invoices by entering and exiting your organization's work processes without a complete understanding of the work process details. It is critical that your work processes allow roles to interact sequentially among the collection of activities that define the work process. You will need business analysts throughout your organization who understand work processes and how work gets done, even though the people actually performing the work might not. Keep in mind that knowledge workers and work processes are continuously changing. Activities will be added, updated, or removed from a work process based on the current performance or feedback to improve performance or achieve a more desired result. The network of individuals and roles involved in a single work process will usually operate with a minimum of organizational structure. The exchanges among the roles in a work process are usually designed to create joint learning opportunities and a shared sense of significance and understanding around work processes. Of course these exchanges are not always successful depending on the understanding, attitude, and agendas of the individual roles and business units involved.

Management is designed to add value to the transactions or activities in a work process or to the environment. The managers in your organization must develop skills to select or filter the information they need to change or to reduce the instability within a work process. Operational managers focus on the most effective way of meeting routine requirements or deploying resources to complete assigned objectives. Your operational managers will divide or share their work processes across several business units to optimize available resources and reduce inefficiencies in work processes. The division of work processes can be by projects, components of projects, clients, types of customers or users, technology, language, problem focus, product cycle time, distribution channel, or pricing structure. For example, if business units in your organization are project-based, there will be product managers, project managers, developers, quality assurance experts, training coordinators, and support roles or resources throughout your organization. Managers will be able to allocate knowledge workers or resources by the roles they are qualified to perform to projects from multiple business units. Training coordinators are often centralized as members of the human resources department and are allocated to projects for specific activities and work processes at the appropriate time. Your organization will want to incorporate specific activities into the enterprise knowledge portal for managers to audit, analyze, and continuously improve the effectiveness of how work processes and knowledge workers are shared across business units.

It is important that managers and employees understand the appropriate level of operational knowledge about how to perform the work processes they participate in. A lot of this knowledge is gained through experience and by reviewing how well your work processes support actual business scenarios and then are revised to solve the issues that arise. As work processes evolve, the individual roles that enter and exit different activities need to be able to work effectively without having to know the details of every work process. Managers and knowledge workers make assumptions about work processes they might only have minimal involvement in through conversations and meetings. These interactions with work processes and the slices of knowledge contained within managers and employees create a broad picture and perception of your organization. To facilitate the necessary foundation of information needed by managers and employees to work together, there are formal communications that include communities of practice, documented procedures, and training courses. The success of these communications can be constrained by groupthink, internal competition, high levels of risk aversion, and intolerance of failures.

Management is responsible for continually auditing work processes to provide regulation between business units. (See Figure 1-4.) The choices made by managers around audit work processes reflect policy even though

Figure 1-4. Knowledge management conceptual model: audit.

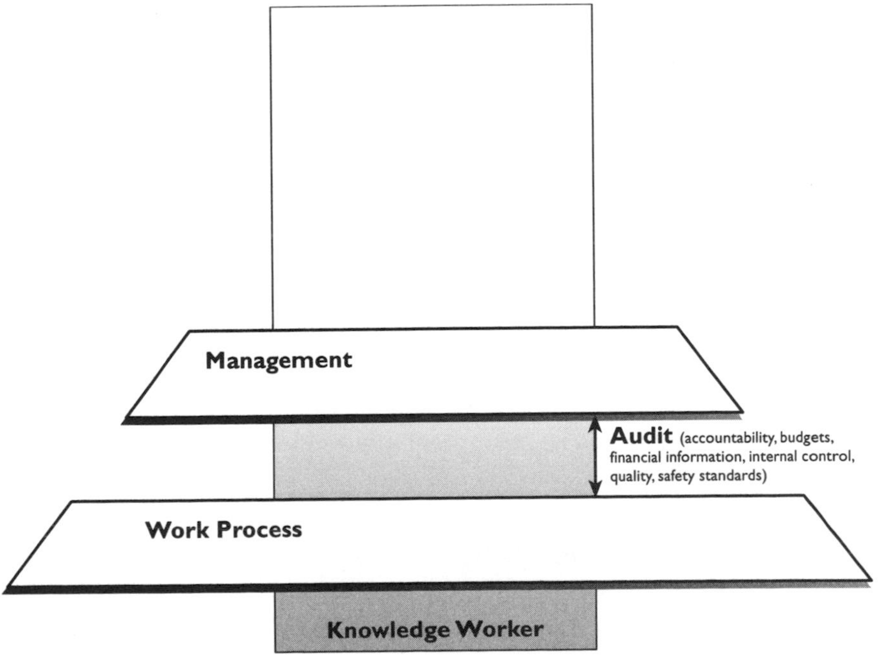

they are not policy decisions. The purpose of these audits is to align the objectives of different business units and coordinate their activities. The work processes that support these audit activities are focused on implementing decisions around common services and resources that must be shared effectively and efficiently. These decisions are made by managers throughout your organization and will occur at different hierarchical levels. It is important that the objectives driving these decisions provide enough consistency for the knowledge workers within different business units to autonomously complete their assigned work processes.

The information needed by managers and knowledge workers to complete work processes must be easily accessible to be used. Individuals rely on filing systems, personal information management systems, group calendars, global address books, and personal organization skills to keep their information in order. Every knowledge worker in your organization has a unique approach to understanding how these individual information systems fit into each other, their work processes, and daily work routines. The organization's network infrastructure will focus on schedules, protocols, certifications, licenses, websites, content, and other applications or information to support your work processes activities. The coordination of knowledge workers, work processes, and technology is extremely challenging when functions are disbursed, work processes are not compatible within your organization, and the volume and variety of the complete collection of work processes is extensive.

Work process best practices contain proprietary information and need to be effectively distributed and available to knowledge workers. Other critical documents that need to be widely available due to the sensitive information they contain include patents and patent applications, qualifications of professional and technical workers, market research results, customer information, project documentation, market opportunities, and many more. These documents contain proprietary information that requires controlled levels of access for different individuals and purposes. Since knowledge workers are exposed and have access to different documents and details of information, your organization will continually have to clarify information delivered through conversations that is paraphrased or interpreted inaccurately. Decisions will have to be made regarding access requirements for security and protection of confidentiality issues balanced against knowledge workers being overwhelmed by information that is insufficiently filtered.

Maintain Knowledge and Facilitate Communication Discussion Questions

- ☐ What were the results of the performance metrics evaluation of your current work processes?

- ☐ What is the analysis process to determine what future work processes and performance metrics should be?
- ☐ Did you accomplish your defined objectives for the organization? For individual knowledge workers and managers?
- ☐ Who was responsible and accountable for the defined objectives? How were these managers and knowledge workers rewarded?
- ☐ How were the defined objectives for the organization met? For individual knowledge workers and managers?
- ☐ How is continuous improvement built into work processes?
- ☐ What changes will be implemented to work processes for managers and knowledge workers?

Focus on the Future

The strategy and vision work processes in your organization focus on the future. Strategic managers prepare for your organization's future, analyzing the successes and failures of goals, and adopting policies to improve results while making certain the organization is optimized based on known strengths. (See Figure 1-5.) Knowledge workers and leaders who coordinate your organization's strategy must have an effective way to communicate, share, or exchange information. The exchange to establish what the additions or enhancements to the corporate vision need to be begins as a brainstorming session with several strategic and operational managers participating. These ideas are usually narrowed down to less than twelve selected topics. There will then be a series of meetings on each topic. To successfully draw on the knowledge, experience, theory, and talent of participants, 90 percent or more of the information made available will need to be shared. The objective is to create an environment where everyone participates equally to define several levels of detail on selected topics and to integrate multiple perspectives.

The topics reviewed will define the short-term and long-term vision for new and existing products, work process improvements, identification of market segments, improvements to the social and physical environment, and evaluation of the recruitment and succession requirements for leadership and other skills needed in your organization. The work processes to select strategic initiatives must effectively set context, build on or maintain the existing corporate identity, foster coherence among competing objectives, and provide final decisions for closure on internal dialogues. Without the work processes to establish this type of definition around your corporate strategies, the result will be a vision and resulting strategy that managers and knowledge workers will have difficulty aligning into business units in order to remain cohesive and autonomous in their day-to-day activities.

Figure 1-5. Knowledge management conceptual model: strategy and vision.

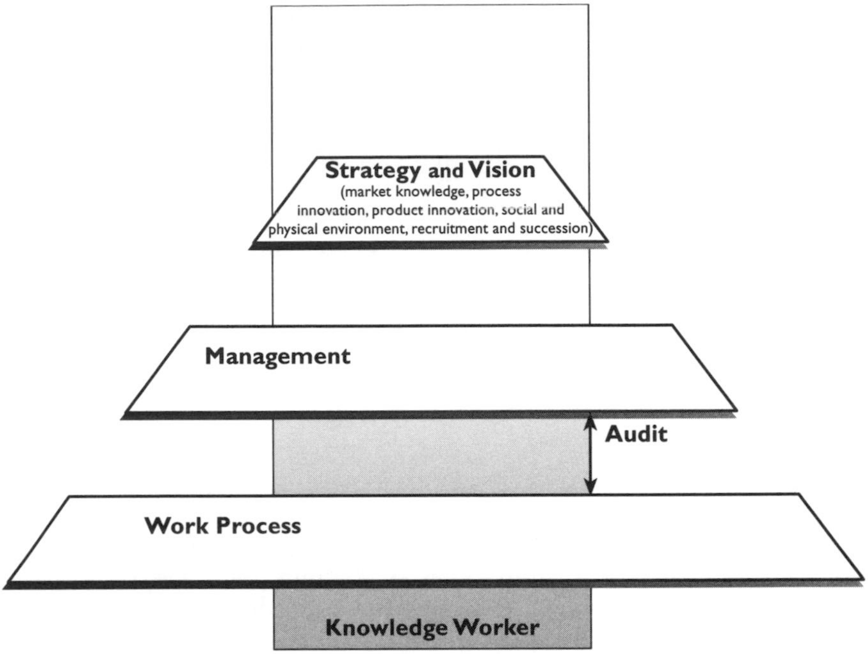

Work processes must be updated and improved to support the mission and objectives of your organization.

Once the core team of strategic and operational managers understands the vision, a strategic plan is created that will outline specific information to include in the planning and forecasting activities for the year. (See Figure 1-6.) These strategic plans will be integrated into the business units as updated or new projects and work processes. Clear strategic initiatives provide the focus that makes it possible for managers and knowledge workers to have choices and follow a direction. For example, sales representatives will be most effective if they have the level of knowledge required to identify the opportunities to pursue (and those not to pursue) based on your organization's vision and targeted market segment.

Managers and knowledge workers can be effective with conflicting priorities and multiple objectives. Managers, knowledge workers, networks of individuals, and organizations all make choices about the division of time, attention, and money for their different initiatives and priorities. These decisions are about the daily tasks and activities that will be completed. These choices define the specific mix of work processes supported by your organization at the current time. It is important that these priorities are aligned and that there is synergy among the work processes and objectives of the

Figure 1-6. Knowledge management conceptual model: planning and forecasting.

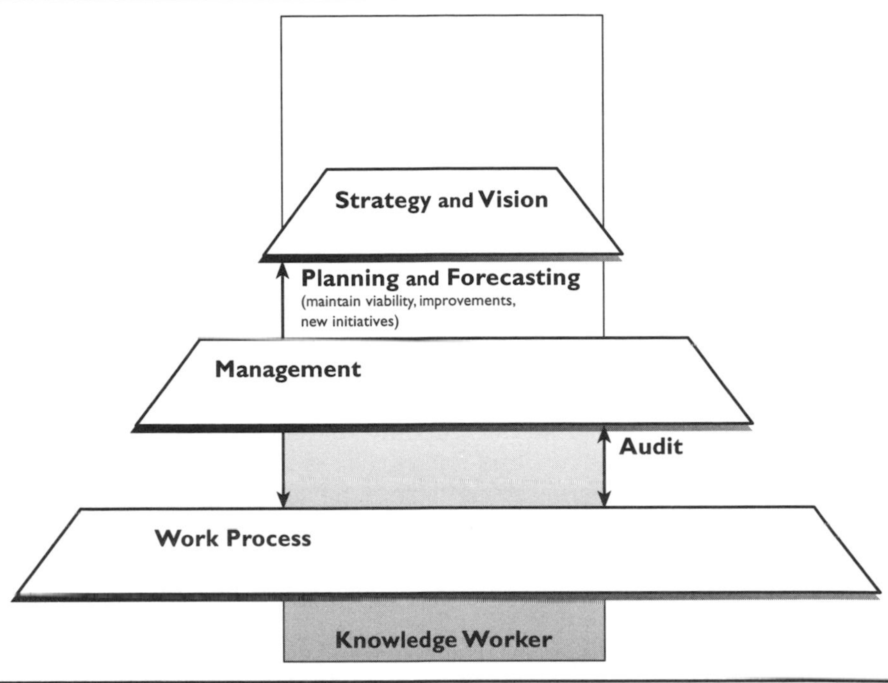

business units. Part of your knowledge management challenge is to ensure that information differences and communications failures are minimized or avoided.

Focus on the Future Discussion Questions

- ☐ Does your organization have a plan for identifying future opportunities and incorporating them into the planning and forecasting of work processes?
- ☐ Do you have checkpoints for monitoring work in progress and using that information to plan for future programs, products, and projects?
- ☐ Does your organization have a clear understanding of the work being done by your collective business units?
- ☐ Does your organization grasp the issues involved in making changes in existing work processes?
- ☐ Does your organization meet its assigned performance metrics?
- ☐ Do business units successfully coordinate shared work responsibilities?
- ☐ Do any business units indicate excessive complaints, serious schedule overruns, or other quality and performance issues?

- ☐ Does your organization have recent unexplainable crises?
- ☐ Do you have resources with the appropriate skills to continue to maintain the business as knowledge workers change positions or leave the organization?
- ☐ Can your organization accurately evaluate its potential and limitations?

Support Your Organization's Business Objectives

The general and specific manifestations of individual and organizational culture are inherent in the mission and objectives of your organization. (See Figure 1-7.) Your mission and objectives must effectively set context to support the existing corporate identity. Culture and identity are powerful and necessary for knowledge workers and networks of individuals within your organization. They will define acceptable behavior. Reward systems need to be aligned and give credit for building an environment that encourages your strategic initiatives and sharing knowledge. The values and morale of your organization are directly related to having sufficient resources avail-

Figure 1-7. Knowledge management conceptual model: mission and objectives.

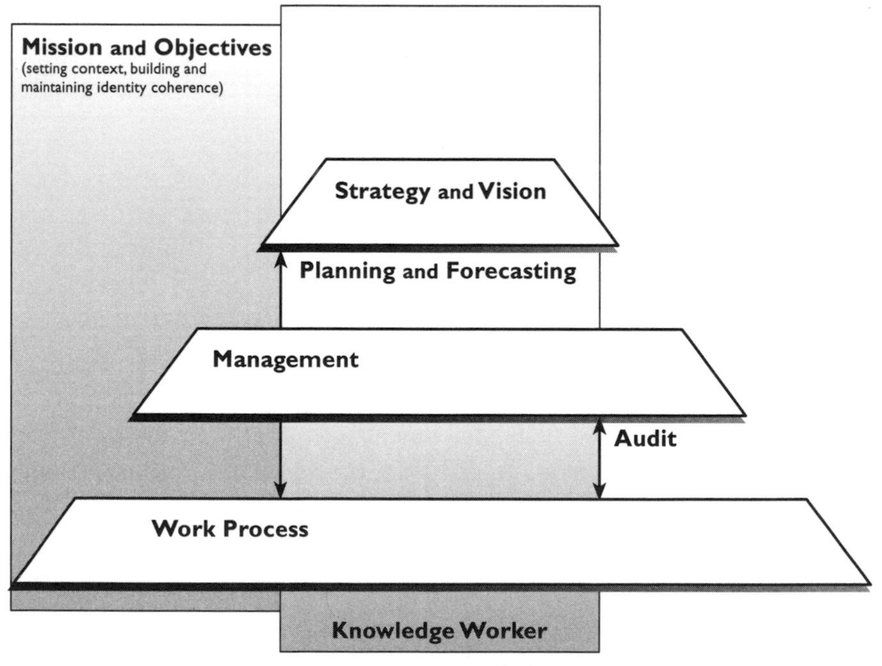

able to build and maintain existing initiatives and to begin new ones. Your organization will be much more effective correcting problems through audit work processes when risks and other issues are integrated into these processes. The destructive behavior of hiding or avoiding risks will result in ineffective work processes throughout your organization. The culture that drives your organization's mission and objectives will define the effectiveness of your knowledge management initiatives.

Individuals throughout your organization will benefit from the short-term and long-term vision that executives, managers, and other responsible individuals use to define and document your corporate strategy. It is critical to review your organization's mission statement to validate how new initiatives will assist in the execution of the overall corporate mission. You can write down the reasons in a short narrative statement that reflects the motivation [illegible] that will be realized. One statement should describe the reasons for the initiative in your organization, the philosophy, and the guidance principles of how the new changes will help the organization. These benefits should be integrated into the planning and forecasting work processes to determine the programs, projects, and performance measurements that will be used to implement the strategy.

Establishing performance-based metrics and maintaining control are critical elements for all relationships within your organization. Identifying your organization's key performance indicators and measuring their success or failure allows accountability to be widely dispersed within the company and with strategic partners, suppliers, and other outside constituencies. To successfully understand and promote your business objectives, knowledge workers and work processes must be effective while being geographically dispersed, and you must ensure that individuals understand their roles and responsibilities. A knowledge management initiative that includes performance-based metrics provides a way for managers and knowledge workers to quickly evaluate the status of their specific organizational and business unit objectives and quickly react when adjustments to existing work processes are required.

Support Your Organization's Business Objectives Discussion Questions

- ☐ Does your chief executive officer (CEO) and top management have the appropriate commitment to communicating and enforcing your organization's mission and objectives?
- ☐ Does your organization set objectives autocratically or participatively?
- ☐ Do you successfully negotiate on acceptable ranges for performance metrics between managers and knowledge workers?
- ☐ Does management explain to knowledge workers the full responsi-

bility of their assigned performance metrics and necessary resources?

- ☐ Does your organization use performance-based metrics as a management system for decision making and problem solving?
- ☐ Does your organization experience any resistance at different or lower levels of management?
- ☐ Does your organization fear that at different or lower management levels performance-based metrics will jeopardize existing management information systems or at least not be compatible with existing operational data?
- ☐ Does your organization have a plan to introduce performance-based metrics? What is the time frame and effort anticipated?
- ☐ Is a performance-based metrics program supported at all levels of management and with all knowledge workers?
- ☐ Is there an appropriate amount of training opportunities, feedback, reviews, and commensurate compensation in your organization?

Promote Innovations

Knowledge workers, networks of individuals, and organizations are all faced with the need to constantly reinvent themselves to adapt to their environments. (See Figure 1-8.) Your human resources effort will focus on the improvement in distribution and management of knowledge to promote the innovation of people and work processes. Work processes must be performed in shorter cycle times and are at risk if knowledge workers cannot effectively incorporate decisions they make into the work process to take the next step.

Improving results and efficiencies in work processes often evolve with changes in team membership of business units or through trends in project work. They can also evolve through focused analysis and review of the process to include continuous improvement activities and tasks. These changes are implemented formally or informally by managers and knowledge workers and are evaluated for how they affect work processes. Innovative changes should be added formally into work process and associated best practices should be updated and communicated to other knowledge workers and business units affected by the change.

There are several human resource aspects that drive your organization. Personal relationships among individuals and members of a network are the most influential on corporate identity and coherence. These networks of people are likely to include some rituals to maintain their sense of identity and will keep individuals who might not be currently working together

Figure 1-8. Knowledge management conceptual model: human resources.

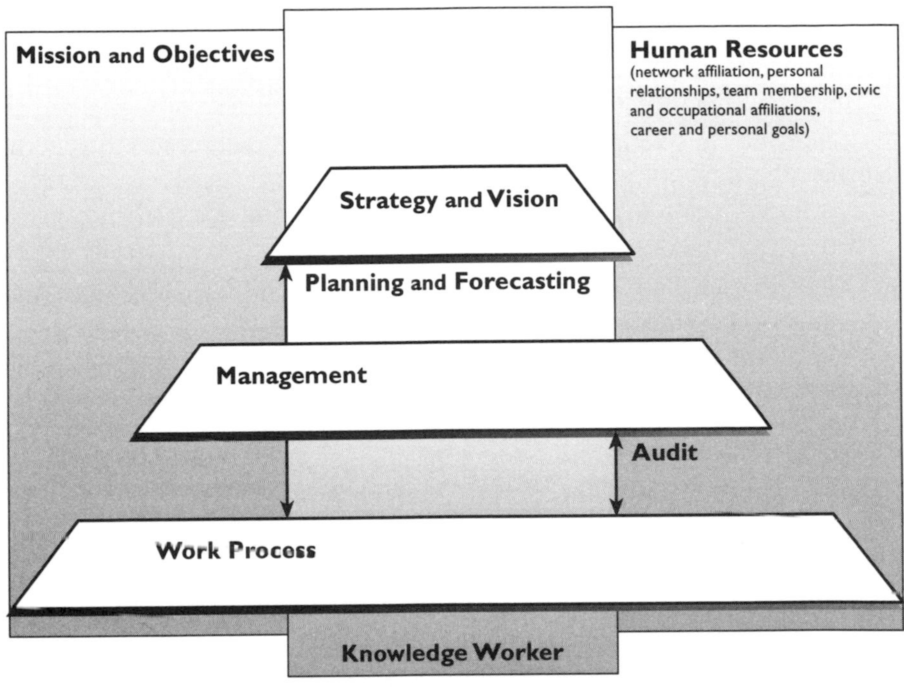

informed about aspects of the business they are not directly involved in. Most of the aspects of intellectual capital and knowledge management must be considered and managed as a whole by your organization. The goal is to balance the attention to detail with attention to relationships while integrating alignment to your business objectives and strategic initiatives.

Relationships and communities can be followed through all levels of your organization and a determination made about how they are affected by particular objectives and work processes. Your organization should have a general knowledge of how enhancing their coordination will benefit their effectiveness. If the right level of communication and cooperation is available, any gaps or duplications in existing work processes should be revealed and appropriately resolved.

The performance enhancement and performance management programs are designed to create a partnership between your organization and individual knowledge workers. These programs and tools are designed to promote innovation by defining agreements between people working together on projects and between groups of people cooperatively focused on a common set of objectives. They create an effective way to clarify and manage expectations of knowledge workers. The following five elements are included in some format and delivered as part of the performance management processes:

1. Performance results that identify what needs to be done and when it needs to be completed
2. Guidelines to specify the principles, policies, and parameters to accomplish the desired performance results
3. Resource requirements to support the human, financial, technical, or organizational objectives
4. Accountability to establish the standards of performance and the schedule for evaluation of these standards
5. Consequences specified to outline what to expect as the result of the evaluation

Promote Innovations Discussion Questions

- ☐ Do you encourage managers and knowledge workers to be self-starters?
- ☐ Do your managers and knowledge workers plan for "what if" scenarios?
- ☐ Do knowledge workers give their best efforts every day?
- ☐ Are managers and knowledge workers allowed to determine what is best and then implement the changes?
- ☐ Are managers and knowledge workers empowered to make their own decisions?

Maintain a Knowledge-Creating Organization

Individuals in your organization are all responsible for participating in the knowledge economy and continuous improvement of their ability, autonomy, and control of their environments. The knowledge management conceptual model in Figure 1-9 identifies the components of your organization that need to be integrated together to create a relevant knowledge management strategy.

The purpose of *Enterprise Knowledge Portals* is to approach knowledge management as a set of principles, practices, and technologies that are focused on innovation and continuous improvement of business-to-employee, business-to-consumer, and business-to-business work processes and relationships. The knowledge management efforts outlined will be delivered as an enterprise knowledge portal that integrates all your organiza-

Figure 1-9. Knowledge management conceptual model.

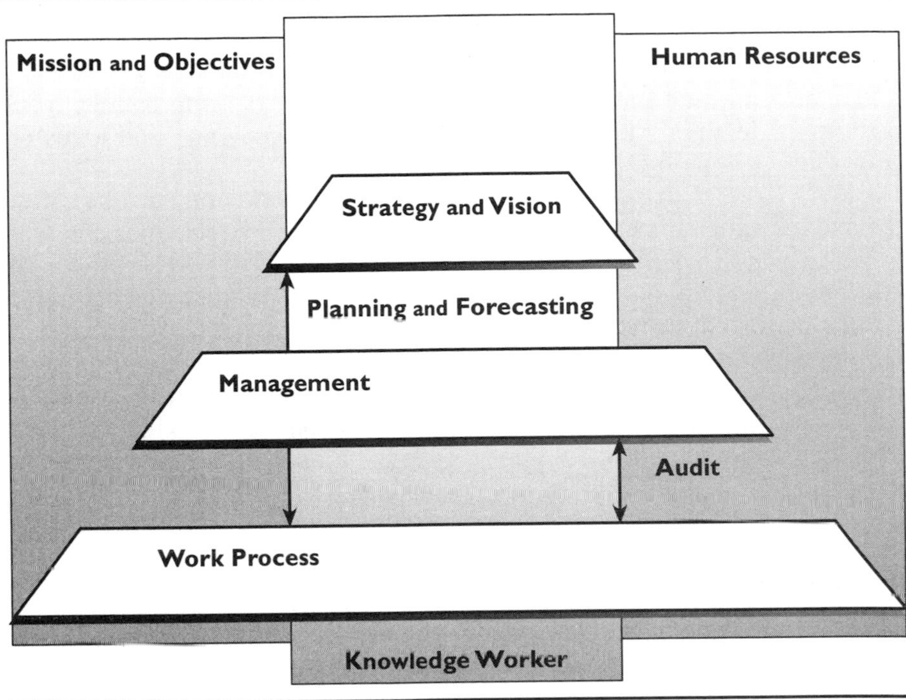

tion's knowledge management targeted elements into the delivered solution.

Maintain a Knowledge-Creating Organization Discussion Questions

- ☐ Does your organization support ideas and negotiate for results?
- ☐ Does your organization plan before doing?
- ☐ Do you have a mentoring organization?
- ☐ Are your managers and knowledge workers self-disciplined?
- ☐ Does your organization have a good balance between building and maintaining?

Key Points

Your organization will use performance-based measurements within its daily work processes for planning, performance monitoring, and communication. The collections of analytics available display an overview of your organization's objectives and its performance against identified measurements. Your business objectives and associated performance of knowledge workers and business units can be reviewed and considered from several different perspectives or dimensions. These measurements allow knowledge workers to understand and participate in the organization's strategy and at any time see the value they are adding. The goal is to connect your business objectives with your work processes to accelerate and focus on your strategy implementations.

Knowledge management is the ability to locate and bring together people and relevant information to individuals that need it so that they can take effective action when doing their jobs. Focusing on the work processes that are critical to your organization will ensure alignment between your corporate objectives, managers, and knowledge workers. There will always be objectives to achieve and work processes to improve. The purpose of your organizational structure and the defined areas of responsibilities within your organization is to make certain that goals are specific, but ways of getting there are left open. The knowledge management considerations to consider in your strategy are:

Be Organized Around Work Processes

- ❒ *Knowledge Worker.* This term defines individual roles, skills, and knowledge base.
- ❒ *Work Process.* This term implies possession of a general knowledge of the organization, operational knowledge, project teams, resource management, communication, technology, management of operations.

Maintain Knowledge and Facilitate Communication

- ❒ *Management.* Management encompasses standards, guidelines, best practices, priorities, funding, compliance, monitoring adherence, confidentiality.
- ❒ *Auditing.* Auditing encompasses accountability, budgets, financial information, internal control, quality, and safety standards.

Focus on the Future

- ❒ *Strategy and Vision.* This term encompasses market knowledge, process innovation, product innovation, social and physical environment, recruitment and succession.
- ❒ *Planning and Forecasting.* Planning and forecasting maintains viability, improvements, new initiatives.

Support Your Organization's Business Objectives

- *Mission and Objectives.* Mission and objectives sets context and builds and maintains identity coherence.

Promote Innovations

- *Human Resources.* This term covers network affiliation, personal relationships, team membership, civic and occupational affiliations, career and personal goals.

Maintain a Knowledge-Creating Organization

- *Enterprise Knowledge Portal.* This is defined as the technology to bring people, process, and content together.

The *Enterprise Knowledge Portal* outlines how to bring an organization that is focused on work processes and continuous improvement into the enterprise portal software solution. The resulting enterprise knowledge portal allows your organization to implement and maintain a knowledge-creating and continuous-learning organization. A methodology and approach on what to consider and steps on how to get started are outlined and presented in the following chapters.

2

Enterprise Portals Overview

"Enterprise Portals enable companies to *unlock* internally stored information, and provide users with a single gateway to *personalized* information and knowledge to make informed business *decisions*."

Shilakes and Tyleman, *Merrill Lynch, Inc.*

Whether you are just beginning or you have a well-defined knowledge management initiative, you have spent a lot of time thinking about what your organization knows and making this knowledge available to people who need to know, when they need to know. At the core of your knowledge management objectives is capturing knowledge and expertise as employees go about their jobs so that a larger community can reuse the information. Our focus here will be on the corporate environment around the people, processes, and content your knowledge management objectives are centered on.

Employees throughout your organization are responsible for making operational and strategic decisions every day. In many situations there are several data sources, systems, and applications that need to be combined. For example, to place an order for a customer an employee might be working in two or three applications. There might be an enterprise resource planning (ERP) system used to check inventory status of a particular part. The employee will have to review or interact with several screens to complete a single part of the process. To review the purchase order, a Web-based application that the customer will see might have to be launched to enter or review the purchase order. If any issues are encountered, a customer relationship management (CRM) system will need to be opened and additional activities completed to finish the task. You can think of dozens of situations in your organization where employees spend an enormous amount of time traversing disconnected applications and systems to find an answer to a question, make a decision, or take some action.

The difficulty employees have navigating this information is only part of the knowledge management problem. Enterprise systems are complex and designed for a specific purpose and function. An incredible amount of training and coaching is needed for a single employee to learn how to effectively complete all of the processes and steps involved to accomplish her assigned responsibilities. In reality only a small fraction of your knowledge workers know how to use all of the functions of one system, and no one person understands all of the systems, databases, and applications that affects his job.

Understanding these issues and adjusting for them in your organization will allow you to recognize and categorize your knowledge management problems so that you can build an enterprise knowledge portal solution to improve information access, knowledge sharing, and decision making. Here are some of the challenges to consider when developing your knowledge management initiatives:

- Employees need to make more informed and consistent decisions
- Employees are asked to complete more activities online and store more information electronically
- Content, applications, and complexity of information continues to grow
- Employees must access information from multiple sources
- Information is difficult to find, navigate, understand, and use

The enterprise portal will help. For example, gathering and distributing document information, indexing and text search, and categorization can be identified as critical knowledge management objectives for your organization and prioritized as critical features to be integrated into the enterprise portal. If your knowledge management objectives are focused on employees making better decisions, then promoting self-help functionality is important. You should concentrate on how employees can help themselves find a doctor, complete expense reports, receive notifications when new information is available, review project status, complete customer updates, and perform activities on any other requested information. Employee self-service will require collaboration with the appropriate experts in your organization if employees have questions, knowledge to share, or insight to contribute. In addition, employees need to be able to easily organize and personalize any information available according to the categories defined for your organization and categories they define for themselves.

Enterprise portals have evolved over time to improve productivity and remove complexity. These solutions are designed to create a bridge between the different and often disconnected applications and systems to make work processes and finding information more intuitive for employees. They are designed to empower employees to access corporate information, find forms, open applications to perform their jobs, review a customer's project status, and perform many other activities from a single browser solution.

The enterprise portal is a key technology in implementing an effective knowledge management program. The enterprise portal concept is to create a "window" that presents information to users and a "door" that allows users to pass through to reach selected destinations and data sources. The enterprise portal defines the central location where navigation services are available for employees to find information, launch applications, interact with corporate data, identify collaborators, share knowledge, and make decisions. The enterprise portal combined with your knowledge management initiatives creates an enterprise knowledge portal with several features that are focused on your business objectives. Several of the benefits of the enterprise knowledge portal include:

- A consistent view of your organization
- Information organization and search capabilities
- Direct access to corporate information and resources
- Direct links to reports, analysis, and queries
- Direct links to relative data and human expertise
- Individual identity and personalized access to content

The enterprise portal is designed to present and share information across your organization. Using the enterprise portal, employees are able to access corporate information using a Web browser such as Microsoft Internet Explorer or Netscape Communicator. The enterprise portal provides a user interface to a multitude of applications and an exponential growing number of documents. It provides a central location to access specific screens or reports from applications, documents relative to the work process at hand, and seamless integration to several enterprise systems at the same time. Using expense reporting as an example, an employee could immediately access a report about his last three submitted expense reports. If he is curious about the status of the latest expense report, he can select the expense report in question and drill into the detail surrounding the current status and work process tasks that have been completed. The employee can submit a question to the accounting department from the same screen and know that the question will be routed to the appropriate person. The employee could provide clarification to the process or additional information from the same screen and know that several applications or systems will be updated with the new information when the submit button is clicked. The enterprise portal is an excellent solution for you, if your organization is looking for improved information access, information organization, and knowledge sharing.

The remaining sections in this chapter are dedicated to understanding the enterprise portal. An overview of the types of enterprise portals available, the user communities and their work processes that can be integrated into the enterprise portal, the services you will need to understand and support as part of an enterprise portal implementation, and the functionality you should expect it to deliver are outlined in detail. As you gain additional understanding of the enterprise portal, you will want to consider how these benefits will improve knowledge management in your company.

Enterprise Portals for Your Knowledge Management Objectives

Our knowledge management definition is the ability to locate and bring together people and deliver relevant information to individuals who need it so that they can take effective action when doing their jobs. We are going to establish a collection of knowledge management objectives that create a working environment to implement our vision. Our example is focused on the business objectives found in our knowledge management definition categories outlined in Chapter 1. The business objectives include:

- *Be organized around work processes.* These knowledge management objectives will concentrate on improving work processes for the general knowledge and performance of the organization. The objectives will specifically focus on knowledge workers and their individual roles, skills, and knowledge base.
- *Maintain knowledge and facilitate communication.* There are two areas of focus associated with these knowledge management objectives. The one collection of knowledge management objectives relates to management standards, guidelines, priorities, and best practices, and the second collection is the audit and quality of these management standards.
- *Focus on the future.* These knowledge management objectives are associated with strategy and vision. They include market knowledge, process innovation, and recruitment, as well as planning and forecasting objectives to maintain viability and implement new initiatives.
- *Support your organization's business objectives.* These are the knowledge management objectives to meet the organization's mission and

objectives. They focus on setting context within the current culture of the organization and driving the change required to modify the culture.

- *Promote innovations.* The relationships your employees have with your organization, teams, each other, and within the community are encapsulated in these work, life, and human resource–related knowledge management objectives.
- *Maintain a knowledge-creating organization.* These knowledge management objectives concentrate on how to bring continuous learning and improvement into work processes, management best practices, strategy, planning, vision, and change management activities.

There are several knowledge management objectives that your organization can take advantage of in an enterprise portal solution. The benefits are incorporated into the enterprise knowledge portal as major elements or software functions and built into the browser-based desktop used by your knowledge workers. These software functions work together in different combinations to achieve the enterprise knowledge portal benefits classified as important by your organization. Knowledge workers effectively complete work processes and make consistent decisions throughout your organization through the enterprise knowledge portal desktop in a way that encourages locating, learning, capturing, and reusing information found in several applications and data sources. The decision cycle consists of:

1. Gathering information
2. Research and collaboration
3. Taking action

The enterprise knowledge portal will need to provide functionality and content for each step in your work processes. There will be boundaries that will limit and define exactly what can and should be accomplished. The enterprise knowledge portal is a facilitator designed to draw your employees, managers, customers, and networks of people into a common community. It is a tool to exchange information and improve your relationship with your employees and your customers. The goal of the enterprise knowledge portal desktop is to implement self-service, self-help, and self-discovery in aspects of your business where it makes sense. For example, knowledge workers who are experts using a specific application or spend most of their day using many aspects of a specific system to complete their assigned responsibilities will continue using these applications and systems. Your organization might decide that the enterprise knowledge portal desktop can provide two separate and distinct benefits to this role of knowledge workers. First, it can provide access to information, applications, and interactions in your organization that they are often not aware of or familiar with. Second, it can provide a format for them to publish their expertise, be recognized as the experts, and be actively involved in improving work processes directly or indirectly related to their responsibilities.

Merging knowledge management objectives and enterprise portal technologies creates the enterprise knowledge portal. Creating this partnership requires effective leadership. The enterprise knowledge portal effort requires leaders with a clear vision, a sense of direction, and a willingness to be the first to model desired behaviors. The enterprise knowledge portal provides a solution that allows leaders to engage directly in the change process, making their role visible in existing work processes, and coaches them to use their communication skills and personal influence to add momentum to your change management plan. The leadership effort will require that you concentrate on at least four critical success factors:

1. Context and content
2. Culture and behavior
3. Process and governance
4. Infrastructure and environment

Communication is what connects people to their organization. It is important to improve communication to increase profit and positively influence business results. Communication work processes are equally as important as other work processes and require the same degree of planning. Business communication requires your organization to become proficient at several technologies to help employees maintain and enhance their interpersonal interactions and connections. Some examples of these technologies are instant messaging, audio- and videoconferencing, taking meeting minutes electronically, webcast presentations that are live or requested on demand, and sharing of your desktop in order to allow team members to interact and walk through activities or issues together. The Web provides an avenue to create new strategies to manage multidirectional information flows. Some communication opportunities include:

- Developing communication strategies that deliver improved business results
- Assessing communication effectiveness and efficiency
- Branding for the organization, employees, knowledge management, and the enterprise portal
- Delivering communication messages across a broad array of media that include the Web, video and audio communications, and electronic delivery of information

- ❒ Aligning the communication function as an integrated part of the enterprise portal
- ❒ Facilitating team meetings and multimedia delivery of scheduled events

Improving involvement moves you closer to a high-performing organization. Engaged employees feel challenged and stimulated to perform their jobs. They understand how their individual efforts contribute to broader organizational goals. The enterprise knowledge portal provides opportunities to improve levels of involvement in understanding corporate objectives and the details of shared work processes. The first step is to gain input by getting employees to express their point of view and provide feedback. The second step is encouraging participation where employees identify issues and then contribute to change and implement the solutions to improve them. The third step is to enable decision making by encouraging employees to take responsibility for their actions. Several employee involvement features include:

- ❒ Gaining employee input through focus groups, customized surveys, and other research tools
- ❒ Encouraging employee participation through suggestions and learning trees
- ❒ Enabling employee decision making through the enterprise portal and team collaboration

You will want to implement performance-based metrics into your enterprise knowledge portal. Measurement helps pinpoint the results your business wants to achieve and the potential obstacles to achieving them. The key performance indicator information is used to obtain qualitative and quantitative metrics that will keep knowledge workers focused on the issues that impact business performance. The enterprise knowledge portal is based on the premise that people deliver results, and you will need to establish a return on investment (ROI) model that supports your enterprise knowledge portal efforts.

Types of Enterprise Portals

The enterprise portal is a personalized browser-based application that allows knowledge workers to gain access to information, collaborate with each other, make decisions in every aspect of their jobs, and take action on all business-related information regardless of the users' virtual location or business unit affiliations, the location of the information, or the format in which the information is stored. The portal concept and technology is rapidly emerging and changing, making it important to focus on the types of portals available and their appropriate role and application. An enterprise knowledge portal implementation will be comprised of multiple types of portals blended into a composite solution. The enterprise knowledge portal must be able to federate the various types of enterprise portals together as a single integrated solution. The four portal categories are briefly described as follows:

- Enterprise information portals
- E-business and e-commerce portals
- Mobile commerce portals
- Internet portals

Enterprise Information Portals

Enterprise information portals are designed for work processes, activities, and user communities to improve the access, workflow, and sharing of content within and across the organization. The enterprise information portal incorporates roles, work processes, work flow, collaboration, content management, data warehouses, learning, enterprise applications, and business intelligence. Additional complications are associated with large scopes, new technology, lack of resources, untrained staff, nonparticipation of users, and few standards or common methods. To encompass all your knowledge management objectives, a complex cross-organizational focus will be required. The federated enterprise information portal is developed and managed as an integrated and reconciled set of technologies, content, and work processes. The enterprise knowledge portal will fail as a collection of stand-alone workgroup or department enterprise information portals. The interrelationships among the technologies, content, and work processes included in the federated solution make the enterprise information portal a single initiative for the enterprise that needs a centralized infrastructure that supports a decentralized collection of work processes and content. Examples of enterprise information portals to consider for your organization include:

- *Horizontal Portals.* These portal solutions are generic in nature and cut across the organization. They provide personalized information for employees, as well as employee self-service. They are designed to support information flow, business activities, and processes across your corporation, suppliers, partners, and supply chain. The horizontal portal will support the following:

1. *Business Intelligence.* The functionality required for specific business objectives supporting data warehousing, routine data analysis, standard report writing, ad hoc querying, analytical processing, and data mining.
2. *Collaboration and Communities.* The ability to facilitate group collaboration, the creation of communities of interest, and best practices. These technologies enable virtual workspaces and workrooms that allow employees, vendors, partners, suppliers, and customers to share documents, e-mails, schedules, and collaborative document creation.
3. *Content Management.* This is the ability to organize, manage, and search across all available structured (databases) and unstructured (documents, records, e-mails, video, and audio files) information sources. This is a seminal enabling technology that facilitates discovery of internal, intranet, and Internet information and data sources.
4. *Learning.* The ability to bring electronic training, mentoring, performance improvement, wizards, and help assistance for the content and work processes available in the enterprise information portal.

❒ *Vertical Portals.* These portal solutions are designed to support specific functions, processes, and applications within the enterprise. They can be considered a subcategory of the horizontal portal and are designed using the same enterprise portal architecture and features. The vertical enterprise portal allows your organization to group individual users into specific roles with objectives that target screens, transactions, and other elements of a work process to be the focus of the enterprise portal user interface. Vertical portals are usually associated with packaged applications for enterprise resource planning (ERP), customer relationship management (CRM), sales force automation (SFA), or supply chain management (SCM). For example, if the vertical portal solution includes various participants in the supply chain, then marketing, retailers, supplies, designers, buyers, and merchandisers will all be able to track materials and products through the work process focusing on the content and information that is relevant to their role in the work process.

E-Business and E-Commerce Portals

The e-business and e-commerce portals can also be referenced as extranet portals. They are enterprise portal solutions that are designed to extend the organization to the people outside the company by including customers, suppliers, and partners in the ordering, billing, customer service, self-service, and business-to-business work processes. Another example of an e-commerce portal is companies that provide commerce-related services to their community of customers, sellers, and vendors. Many companies are extending their e-business opportunities by connecting buyers and suppliers to industry-specific news and related product and service information. Buyers can find the information they need to quickly locate, source, and purchase products and services online using your organization's enterprise portal as the on ramp. Suppliers are able to generate leads and showcase their products and services across multiple marketplaces to find qualified buyers.

Mobile Commerce Portals

Portals that are used for mobile commerce are enterprise portal solutions delivered through Web phones, cellular phones, wireless personal data assistants (PDA), pagers, and other handheld devices. Personal or mobile commerce portals are very important and continue to gain popularity with consumers and employees that need product and service information, prices, discounts, availability, order status, payment status, shipping status, scheduling and installation information, and other critical information from any location. The same content that is delivered to the enterprise information portal can be delivered to the mobile commerce portal. The user presentation that makes the same amount of information available for a wireless device will span several screens or menu options. Icons and drop-down menus are used to save screen space and might require that additional help assistance be made available from each mobile commerce portal screen.

Internet Portals

Internet portals are focused on building large online audiences that span across several demographics and professional orientations. There are two categories of Internet portals: the entire Internet community, and specific communities of interest. Yahoo, Google, AOL, MSN, and Excite are examples of Internet portals designed to meet the needs of the Internet audience and provide the starting point to find products, services, and information across the Internet. Vertical portals focus on specific communities such as consumer goods, computers, banking, or insurance and are designed to provide services to a broad demographic audience. Internet portals have become widely accepted media sources for online information, services, and products.

User Communities

The enterprise knowledge portal will be focused on bringing work processes to users based on their unique roles and functions that they perform in the work process. Each work process is broken into the specific activities that include multiple tasks to be successfully completed. The activities and tasks are assigned to the individual roles or people with the skills to complete each identified task. Depending on the skills and responsibilities of employees in your organization, an individual will be assigned to different roles. In turn, these roles are assigned to work processes. There will be hundreds of work processes defined and added to the enterprise knowledge portal over time. This means that there can be hundreds of roles that complete the individual tasks that compose a work process. It is also fair to assume that there could be hundreds of individuals assigned to each role.

The enterprise portal has a unique object-oriented design. Each page is a composition of several elements that are individually developed and dynamically generated for the user when they access an enterprise portal page. In addition, applying the user's unique role and security rights to the content being loaded into the enterprise portal page guarantees each user will see something different in the user interface. The navigation scheme will only reflect the work processes the user has access to, and content windows on the screen will only reflect information specific to the roles and tasks the user is responsible for in the work process. The information within the content windows will be based on the user's security and access to the application or data source that is presented in the content window. You can begin to visualize why a strong and well-designed work process and associated work flow is critical to facilitate the distribution of only the content to the individuals who need to do their jobs and be guaranteed that work processes are successfully completed.

As you review the remaining enterprise portal functionality, you should consider the work processes and user communities that your initial or continuing enterprise knowledge portal solution will integrate first and continue to integrate in different project releases. Consider the work that is assigned to different user communities and focus on the value and benefits that they will gain through an enterprise knowledge portal solution. The four user communities you might want to focus on initially include:

1. *The Employee Community.* Focus on improvements that can be made in categorizing information that is shared in work processes for:
   - ❒ Human resources
   - ❒ Recruiting
   - ❒ Training
   - ❒ Accounting
   - ❒ Financial planning and analysis
   - ❒ Legal
   - ❒ Information technology

- ❒ Project management
- ❒ Research and development

2. *The Customer Community.* Focus on accessing internal information with external users in shared work processes for:
   - ❒ Marketing
   - ❒ Prospecting
   - ❒ Sales
   - ❒ Field services
   - ❒ Relationship management
   - ❒ Ordering
   - ❒ Customer service
   - ❒ Support
3. *The Supplier Community.* Focus on improved information flow in shared work processes for:
   - ❒ Order and fulfillment
   - ❒ Procurement
   - ❒ Planning
   - ❒ Sourcing
   - ❒ Inventory control
   - ❒ Logistics and distribution
   - ❒ Manufacturing
4. *The Partner Community.* Focus on sharing experience and information in work processes for:
   - ❒ Marketing documents and product release schedules
   - ❒ Lead sharing
   - ❒ Multiple channel partner forecasts management
   - ❒ Partner profile information
   - ❒ Joint-selling opportunities
   - ❒ Knowledge base sharing
   - ❒ Product training and documents
   - ❒ Resource schedules
   - ❒ Feedback collection and analysis

Enterprise Portal Services

The enterprise knowledge portal will always be evolving. Content and services will expand and change. Your enterprise knowledge portal solution needs to encompass what it takes to start and implement your first portal project, how you expect it to grow, and how that growth will be managed. Many enterprise portals begin as a business unit solution to support a small number of users and grow to require several full-time experts to develop, manage, and maintain the solution and the infrastructure. A strategy that predicts upgrades in servers, browsers, and application software is required. As the enterprise knowledge portal solution expands to include additional systems and applications that are presented in content windows, a greater demand is created for incorporating new and existing services that include additional testing and planning requirements to meet the growing need. Managing this growth is a task of your information technology department and enterprise knowledge portal team.

This growth continuum affects the development, system integration, and maintenance of the enterprise knowledge portal solution. The integration of the different technologies, applications, services, and system support is necessary for providing individual working environments to employees through the enterprise portal. Determining how to support and enhance user roles and personalization requirements while the enterprise knowledge portal matures is an important planning requirement. Several aspects of the enterprise portal technical architecture you need to be aware of include:

❐ *Enterprise Portal Architecture.* There are several layers of your organization's infrastructure working together to provide a complete enterprise knowledge portal set of functions. The architecture layers are the Internet, a firewall or demilitarized zone (DMZ), the intranet, portal services, application services, and back-end systems. These are outlined in Figure 2-1. The portal server is a collection of servers that provide several services. These include:

1. *Directory and Security Services.* These services support authentication and allowing users to sign on to the enterprise knowledge portal system once and have access to all information available in the enterprise portal without having to sign on to the individual systems that are being accessed.
2. *The Rules Server.* The rules server manages content and provides work flow as the information is streamed from back-end systems to the desktop or streamed between two different back-end systems.
3. *The Portal Component Server.* This provides a collection of objects for application services, connectivity, and the enterprise portal to present information to the user.
4. *The Personalization Server.* The personalization server maintains user configuration information allowing users to sign on to the enter-

Figure 2-1. Enterprise portal system landscape.

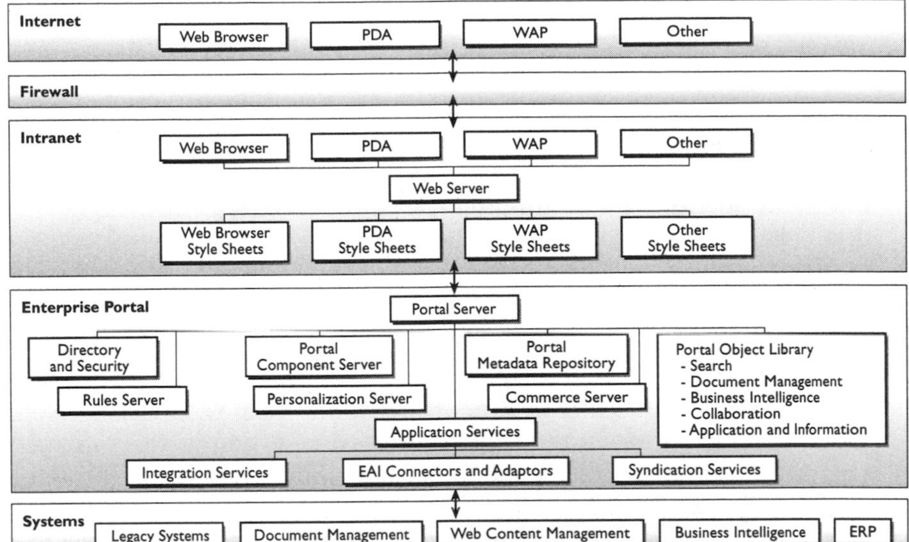

prise knowledge portal from any location and see the enterprise knowledge portal desktop with the content page and content window settings they saved.

5. *The Portal Metadata Repository.* This maintains attributes used by the enterprise portal solution.
6. *The Commerce Server.* This provides role-based templates and other e-business work process elements.
7. *The Portal Object Library.* The library maintains a collection of content windows and other objects purchased or developed within your organization that provide information and functionality in the enterprise knowledge portal.

- *Server Platforms.* The hardware, software, and open standard requirements to effectively deliver the enterprise knowledge portal functions to users in your organization. Your requirements need to be compared to the platforms and standards supported by enterprise portal software vendors. The goal is to clarify the technologies, hardware, software, and information technology personnel that will be necessary to plan, design, develop, deploy, and maintain an enterprise knowledge portal solution. Single sign-on and advanced search features require several unique configuration and installation requirements to be reviewed as part of the enterprise portal software evaluation.
- *Installation.* The enterprise knowledge portal solution requires a platform to manage portal servers and services, application servers, and

integration services. There will be separate servers and configuration requirements for portal servers and services. These include Web servers, metadata repository servers, search servers, index servers, and others depending on the services to be installed and supported. The enterprise portal server and systems or data sources accessed must support open standards to integrate the functionality required. It is important that the application servers and content management tools can be easily integrated to work with the enterprise portal solution. The Web clients and collaboration features must be supported by the browser version and other software installed on client workstations, laptops, and other personal data assistant (PDA) devices that access the portal server.

- *Performance.* To implement an enterprise portal solution that will provide the service levels required is dependent on the existing intranet and Internet infrastructure in your organization. On the basis of the work processes and information needs analysis you will complete, combined with the assessment of your intranet and Internet, you can evaluate whether the existing infrastructure in your organization can support the proposed enterprise knowledge portal solution, or whether additional upgrades must be made as part of the project.
- *Scalability.* Enterprise knowledge portals grow from a single work process to a collection of work processes that work together to provide a browser-based working environment to support knowledge workers throughout your organization. During the first phase of the enterprise knowledge portal project, the primary objective is to deliver different data sources and types of content to the enterprise knowledge portal desktop. Your goal, as additional phases of the project are implemented, is to enable the enterprise knowledge portal to become a universal front-end used to access and manipulate diverse data sources and applications that remain stored on application servers in their native formats. The enterprise knowledge portal provides a browser interface that will require the appropriate capacity and network bandwidth to support this growing number of users.
- *Standards.* There will be several measures or models that will consistently be applied to guarantee the quality of the enterprise knowledge portal solution. These metrics will be used for productivity, quality, and maintainability of the infrastructure and application development environments supporting the enterprise knowledge portal solution. Enterprise portal software vendors use a combination of several programming interfaces and software functions to implement the portal functionality in their products. Each of these portal software applications implements and supports portal features differently. The best process to select the appropriate enterprise portal software solution is to determine the objectives and requirements of your enterprise portal solution and evaluate

which product vendor's solution most appropriately matches your needs.

- *Security.* The security element provides a description of the levels of access each user and roles of users are allowed for each report, document, portal application, and software function included in the enterprise knowledge portal. The types of access allowed include no access, reader, editor, delete, or other. Your organization's information technology security requirements for intranet applications need to be addressed and supported by the enterprise knowledge portal solution implemented in your organization. You should research and review the security models of enterprise portal software application vendors to make certain the security model included in the enterprise portal software application meets the information technology standards defined for your organization.
- *Administration.* The administration element provides two services. The first is the deployment and maintenance activities and tasks associated with the enterprise knowledge portal solution. The second is what can be uniquely configured (a) by an administrator for the enterprise portal system and (b) by each user through enterprise portal personalization.

Enterprise Portal Functionality

The enterprise portal provides a wide collection of services, content, and functionality to knowledge workers. Your business intelligence, collaboration and communities, managed content, and learning considerations are all integrated together using the functionality provided by the enterprise portal. An illustration of how these solutions might be incorporated into the enterprise knowledge portal user interface is shown in several supporting figures. These include:

- *Business Intelligence.* The work processes, performance-based metrics, summary reports, and ability to drill into reports can all be pulled together into the enterprise knowledge portal user interface. An example of available work processes and a specific account payable report used by an employee in Accounting is available for review in Figure 2-2.
- *Collaboration and Communities.* Event calendars, discussion forums, feedback forms, frequently asked questions, knowledge base information, and white papers are available for knowledge workers, managers, and networks of users to find and use. You will want to dedicate entire content pages for community activities and add navigation links throughout the enterprise portal to easily access collaboration and communities activities and tasks. Figure 2-3 shows the ability to access communities

Figure 2-2. Enterprise portal user interface: business intelligence.

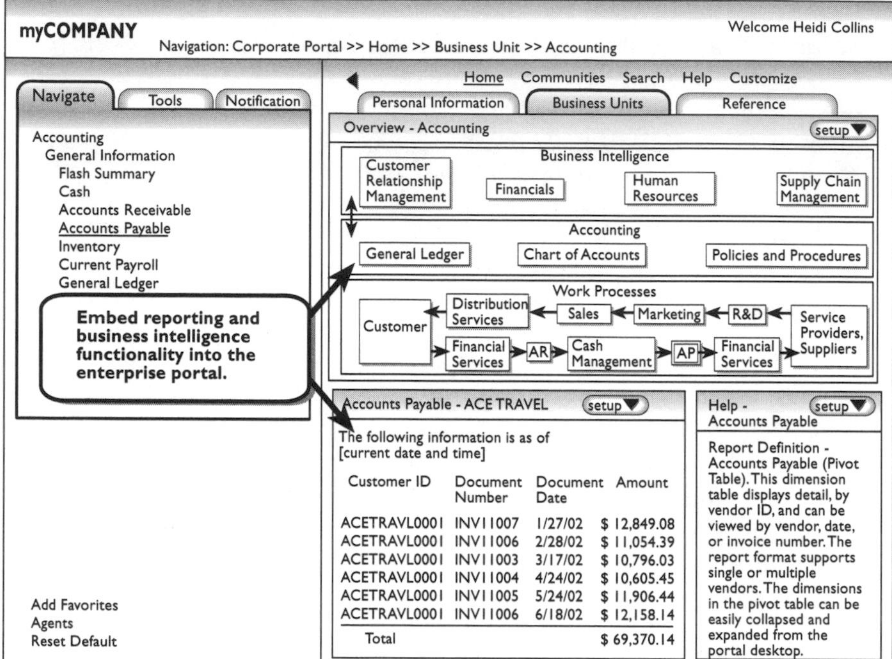

from a pervasive menu in the enterprise knowledge portal and a publications content window where users can subscribe or request content in your organization on specific topics to be sent or published to a content window in their enterprise knowledge portal when it is posted.

- *Content Management.* The ability to quickly find any type of document, transaction, or report is the key objective of your content management solution. Search and taxonomy and the categorization of information are the two most popular functions being deployed by organizations to meet this objective. The enterprise portal user interface allows users to personalize how content is arranged, organized, and displayed. Figure 2-4 demonstrates how content from a document management solution can be integrated into an enterprise knowledge portal.
- *Learning.* Creating an intuitive environment for working and learning simultaneously is the goal to embedding e-learning features into the enterprise knowledge portal. Learning features are built into the enterprise portal as simulations, online wizards, automated business rules, glossaries, and other learning job aids to help employees be productive and efficient. If implemented effectively, help will be a frequently used feature that will need to be easily available for users to access. An example

Figure 2-3. Enterprise portal user interface: collaboration and communities.

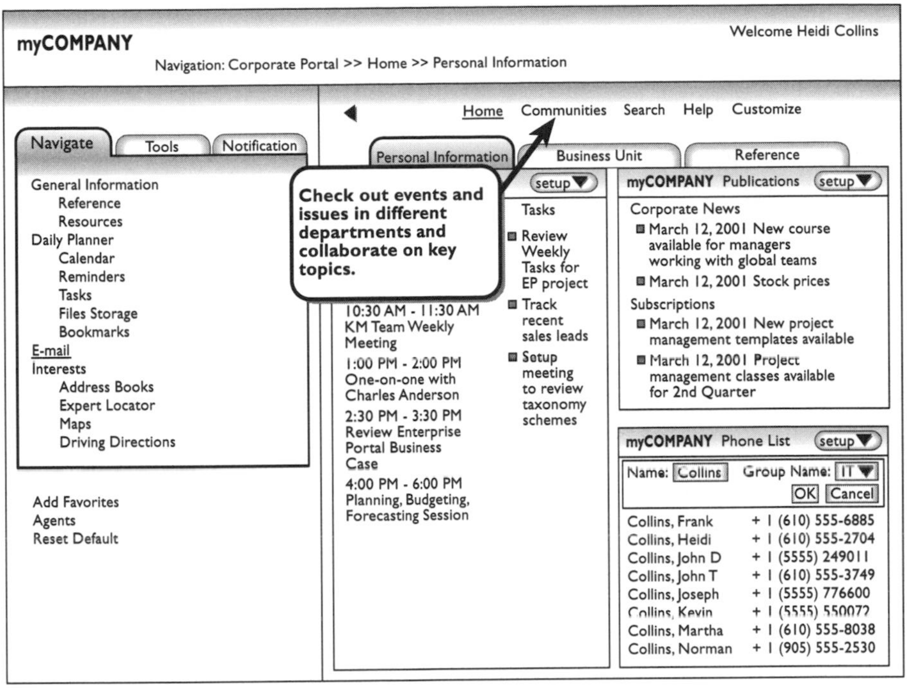

of using help features from the enterprise knowledge portal pervasive menu can be seen in Figure 2-5.

The enterprise portal functionality that your knowledge management objectives require will specifically define the software and implementation requirements of your enterprise portal solution. The software features that have become synonymous with enterprise portals are discussed in detail throughout this section. These include:

- Presentation
- Knowledge organization systems
- Search and index
- Personalization and roles

Presentation

The presentation feature provides the visual experience to the user and encapsulates all the enterprise knowledge portal's functionality. The user experience is designed to be flexible and allow intuitive interaction and

Figure 2-4. Enterprise portal user interface: content management.

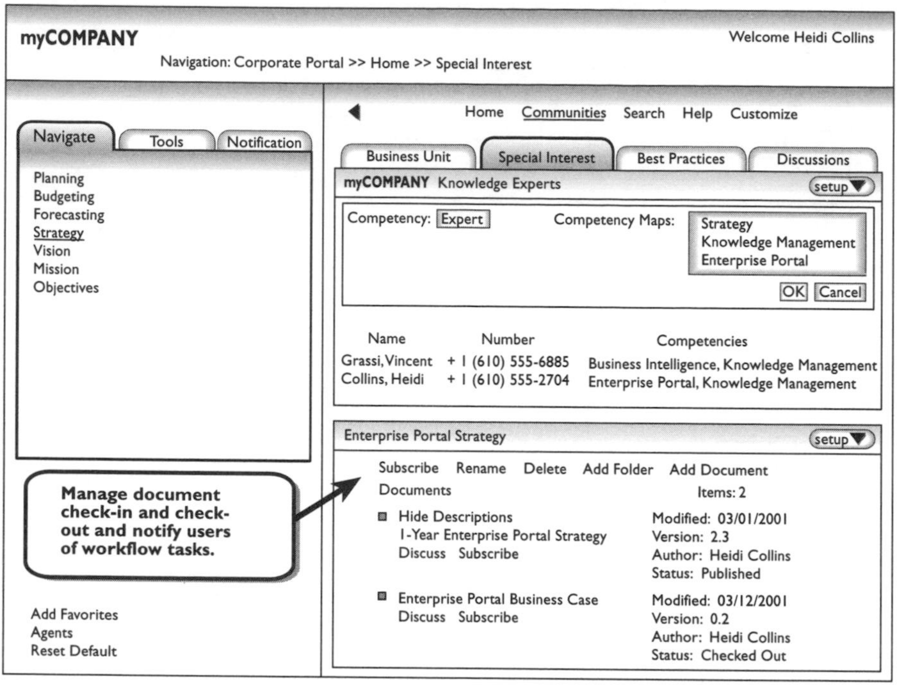

easy navigation throughout. The objects contained in a sample enterprise knowledge portal user interface are shown in Figure 2-6.

The presentation layer of the enterprise portal provides clarity for the information and features presented to the knowledge worker. The content provided will be designed to demonstrate a complete decision support and collaborative environment. The content will focus on the context of information presented to the user from an organizational, functional, or work process–oriented perspective. The enterprise portal is constructed of several layers of portal pages. The highest-level portal pages are used to describe corporate information. They will incorporate messages regarding company news, industry news, and specific information about your business and organization. Additional layers of portal pages will be federated into additional levels of detail. These federated content pages exist for each identified function or work process supported in your enterprise portal solution. The user interface is managed through several presentation elements that include:

- *The Portal Banner.* The portal banner is fixed in the same location on every enterprise portal page. It provides company logos, icons, and labeling that will be consistent throughout the enterprise portal solution.

Figure 2-5. Enterprise portal user interface: e-learning.

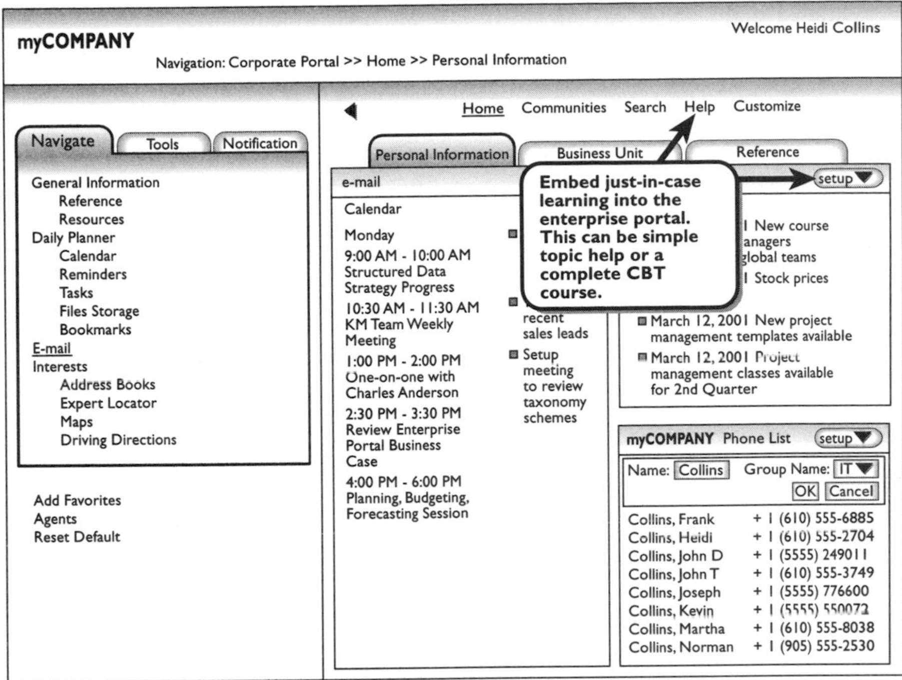

Figure 2-6. Enterprise portal user interface: presentation.

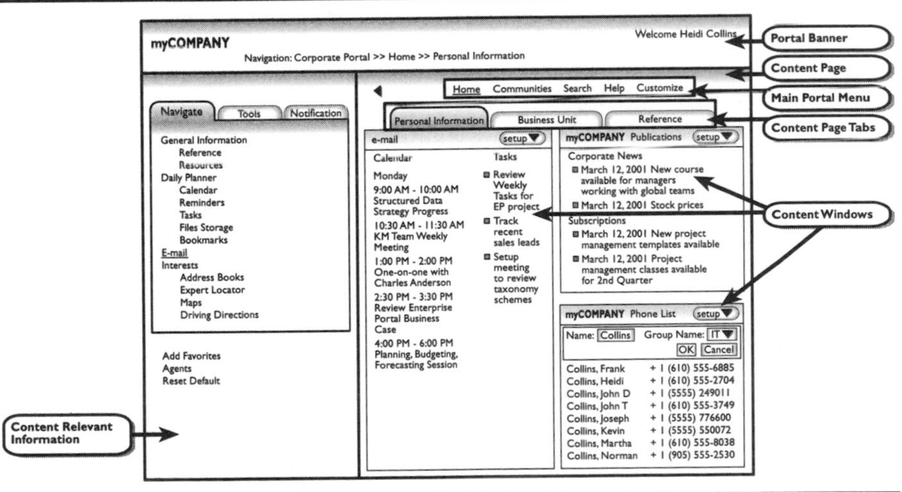

These consistent features are included in the user interface as a banner across the top or in the corner of each page, icons that perform the same function in every place that they are used, and common words or labels that are found on other presentation elements that are interpreted consistently throughout the enterprise portal.

- *The Portal Menus.* Portal menus have two implementations. The first is as a static or fixed set of defined menu options that provide a specific set of services for enterprise portal features that are used frequently and need to be made permanently available to users as they work. The second is a dynamic set of menu options that are context-sensitive to the organizational, functional, or work process content presented on the current enterprise portal page in front of the user.
- *Personalization.* Personalization or customization is available as a portal menu option. In Figure 2-6 the personalization element is available from the static portal menu option labeled "customize." This collection of enterprise portal pages and features allows users to add, delete, or move content windows on and off of individual content pages. Users can create or delete entire content pages. There are global settings that can be configured by users. For example, a user can subscribe to information that can then be pulled from throughout the organization and presented to users in content windows that perform queries to collect the information requested. The same request might be created through a global setting that allows the user to create an intelligent agent that will be executed to present the subscribed content when the user executes the agent from the enterprise portal user interface.
- *The Content Page Tab(s).* The content page tabs are part of the content page and used to create secondary portal pages or subsets of portal pages that are related to the organizational, functional, or work process focus of the main portal content page. In Figure 2-6 the content page tabs available on the primary content page include personal information, business unit, and reference. The complete collection of content windows is distributed between the content pages to organize the information available in a way that makes the most sense to the user.
- *The Content Window(s).* An individual content window is the object used to present data or information. Content windows have several consistent elements associated with them. See Figure 2-6 to view these content window elements. The content window elements include a title bar, a title, and several other features available in the setup option. To view the setup drop-down options, see Figure 2-7. In this example the setup option is a drop-down menu that will include options to:

    - Collapse—Present the content window as a title bar only.
    - Expand—Present the content window as a title bar and the associated content.

Figure 2-7. Content window—setup options.

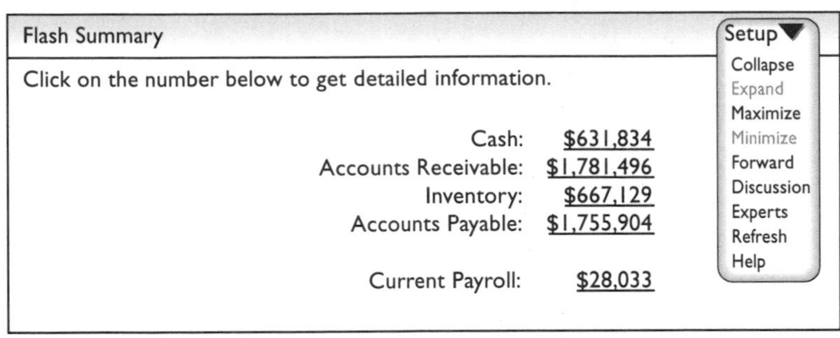

- ❒ Maximize—Open the content window to fill the entire screen. This option might open a new browser window to present a full screen of the information.
- ❒ Minimize—Present the information in the content window framework.
- ❒ Forward—Provide e-mail features that include a link to the content window or an image of the content window in the body of the message.
- ❒ Discussion—Open a discussion thread that includes a link to the content window or an image of the content window in the body of the document.
- ❒ Experts—Contact a list of knowledge workers who are specialists or owners of the content presented.
- ❒ Refresh—Update the content with the latest information available from the data source.

Users can add, delete, or move content windows using the personalization features available in the enterprise portal. There are administration features that will override or lock content windows from all or some of the personalization features allowed by users. This is important to maintain the integrity of the organizational, functional, or work process effort presented in the enterprise portal if removing, moving, or changing content windows would invalidate the activities and tasks users need to complete.

- ❒ *The Content Page.* The content page is the largest frame available in the presentation layer. It contains one or many content windows and content page tabs. The content page is essentially the highest-level view of information required to give an overview of the organizational, functional, or work process effort the user is involved in. The user can select to focus into the content provided by clicking into the content window and drilling into the information presented. The user can focus on a subset of the content by clicking onto another content page tab. The user can select to focus away from the content page presented by clicking on another menu option or using a specific enterprise portal feature like search or help to gather peripheral information.

- *Content-Relevant Information.* The content-relevant information section is a secondary menu option that dynamically reflects information that is indirectly related to the primary focus of the content page facing the user. This relevant information is a general collection of corporate tools, applications, links, reference material, corporate resources, business unit websites, e-mail, discussions, instant messaging, training materials, and other information. The collection of links presented in the content-relevant information section of the enterprise portal should be limited to having some relationship to the focus of the content page. The purpose of the content-relevant information element is to categorize and organize collections of information that provide a balance between the context of information in the content page and the links to additional portal pages or functions the user will need when working with the current portal page.

For example, there may be several items that would be relevant or useful for a user to know about in the right circumstances. The groups or categories selected here include navigate, tools, and notification. The navigate tab or category was selected to provide navigation to other portal pages relevant to personal information management functionality. The tools tab will provide access to standard collaboration and communication applications and can be used to create feedback or discussion documents, interact in work flow procedures, or submit queries and other requests inside your organization. The notifications tab was designed to push and emphasize important messages related to the context of the content page. This includes notifications about new policies and procedures available in your organization, new training events, or information specific to work processes the user is involved in.

To provide additional user-focused functionality, several personalization functions are provided at the bottom of the content-relevant information section. This includes "add favorites" to create hyperlinks that are accessed frequently by the individual user, "agents" that can perform queries or other user-defined activities that are created using the customize option and executed when the user selects this option, and "reset default" to reconfigure selected portal pages back to the organization's default settings.

Portal vendors have established libraries of objects that are used to quickly create content windows for your enterprise portal solution. Your organization will establish the vital information needed to make your enterprise knowledge portal useful. Typical content pages are comprised of a number of content windows. Each content window is responsible for capturing and delivering information back to the portal page from one or more specified data sources. The collections of content windows are displayed on one or many content pages to create the enterprise portal solution. The most significant task of building and maintaining your enterprise knowledge portal will be building and maintaining individual content windows. These objects support several formats and uses for how information is presented. In most cases hyperlinks are contained within content windows to perform an action, get available help, or locate additional information. The types of content windows you might consider include those that involve:

- *Drilling into Reports.* Content windows contain report summaries and key performance indicator information with hyperlinks to drill into more detailed information. See Figure 2-8. There can be several levels of hyperlinks built into these reports. When designing reports, determine the levels of detail required during the design of the content window. It is important that knowledge workers using the reports can easily read the report details in the screens provided to perform their responsibilities.
- *Submitting a Request.* Content windows allow knowledge workers and employees to request additional information. A request form is completed and the results are returned to the user. See Figure 2-9. Activities that require user input, such as completing corporate forms and submitting search requires, benefit from wizards that help complete the form or help topics that define the fields that need to be completed before the form can be submitted.
- *Selecting a Link.* Content windows contain hyperlinks to other sections in the same document or open new content windows with new information. The example presented in Figure 2-10 opens a second content window with the requested tax form displayed on the screen.

Knowledge Organization Systems

The taxonomy or categorization element of the enterprise portal provides information context. The term knowledge organization system is used to define all types of schemes for organizing information and creating relationships to promote content management. It includes classification models that organize material into general categories, subject headings that provide more detailed access, and association tables or authority files that control variations of key information. This includes your organization-specific categories that reflect and support your organization's business. The knowledge organization system provides rapid recognition of common terminol-

Figure 2-8. Content window—drilling into reports.

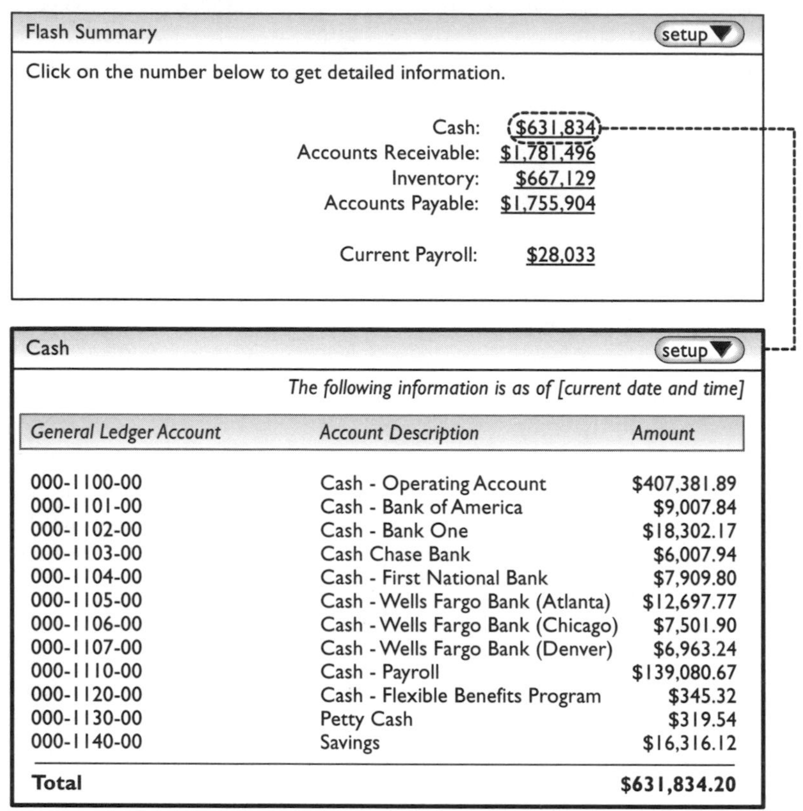

Flash Summary (setup▼)

Click on the number below to get detailed information.

Cash:	$631,834
Accounts Receivable:	$1,781,496
Inventory:	$667,129
Accounts Payable:	$1,755,904
Current Payroll:	$28,033

Cash (setup▼)

The following information is as of [current date and time]

General Ledger Account	*Account Description*	*Amount*
000-1100-00	Cash - Operating Account	$407,381.89
000-1101-00	Cash - Bank of America	$9,007.84
000-1102-00	Cash - Bank One	$18,302.17
000-1103-00	Cash Chase Bank	$6,007.94
000-1104-00	Cash - First National Bank	$7,909.80
000-1105-00	Cash - Wells Fargo Bank (Atlanta)	$12,697.77
000-1106-00	Cash - Wells Fargo Bank (Chicago)	$7,501.90
000-1107-00	Cash - Wells Fargo Bank (Denver)	$6,963.24
000-1110-00	Cash - Payroll	$139,080.67
000-1120-00	Cash - Flexible Benefits Program	$345.32
000-1130-00	Petty Cash	$319.54
000-1140-00	Savings	$16,316.12
Total		**$631,834.20**

ogy used in your company and improves semantics for users of the enterprise knowledge portal solution. When evaluating enterprise portal software solutions you will need to verify that your organization's naming and categorization standards can easily be implemented and maintained.

Knowledge organization systems are used to organize content for the purpose of retrieval and managing collections. It creates a map to build a bridge between the roles of a knowledge worker, the content she needs, and the information available in the collection. Users are presented and are able to easily locate content that they might not have realized existed. A digital library that consists of one or more knowledge organization systems supports the enterprise knowledge portal. This knowledge organization system uses a digital library that can be thought of as a new repository of pointers to information used to provide an overview of the content available throughout your organization and supports retrieval of that information when users need it. A knowledge organization system has the following common characteristics:

Figure 2-9. Content window—submitting a request.

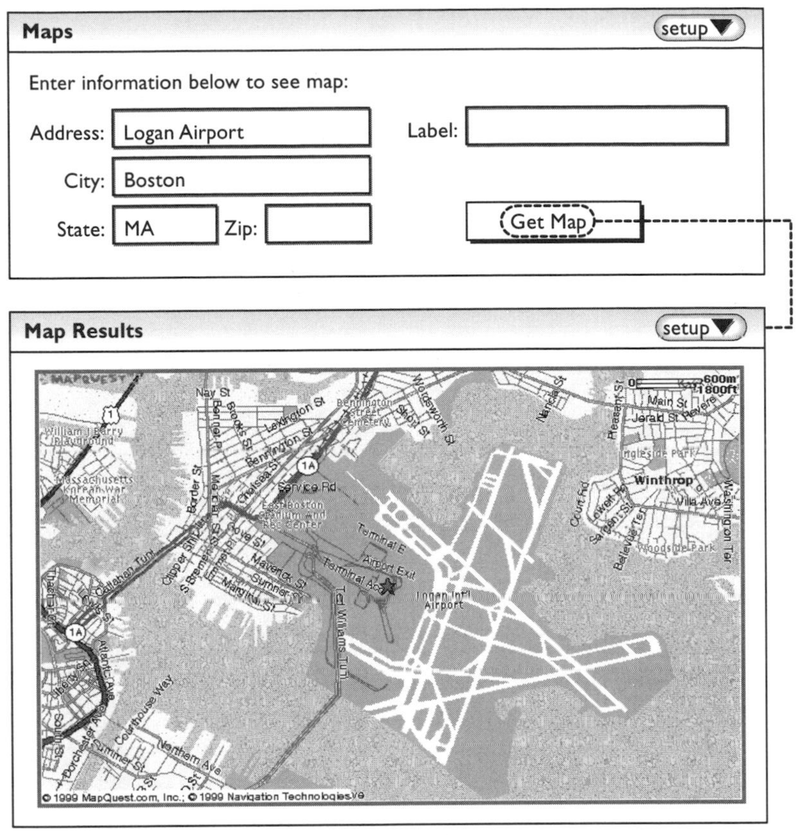

- It imposes a particular view of your organization or enterprise on the content collection.
- Individual content items are characterized in different ways depending on the knowledge organization system used.
- Relationships must exist between the knowledge organization scheme and the content collection so that a knowledge worker or system can apply the scheme to the content collection with reasonable reliability.

There are several ways to make resources accessible to your user communities. The most direct method is to apply and provide multiple subject access to your content collections by classifying or indexing the content items with multiple schemes. This approach overlays multiple layers of terms used to classify one piece of information in different ways in the

Figure 2-10. Content window—selecting a link.

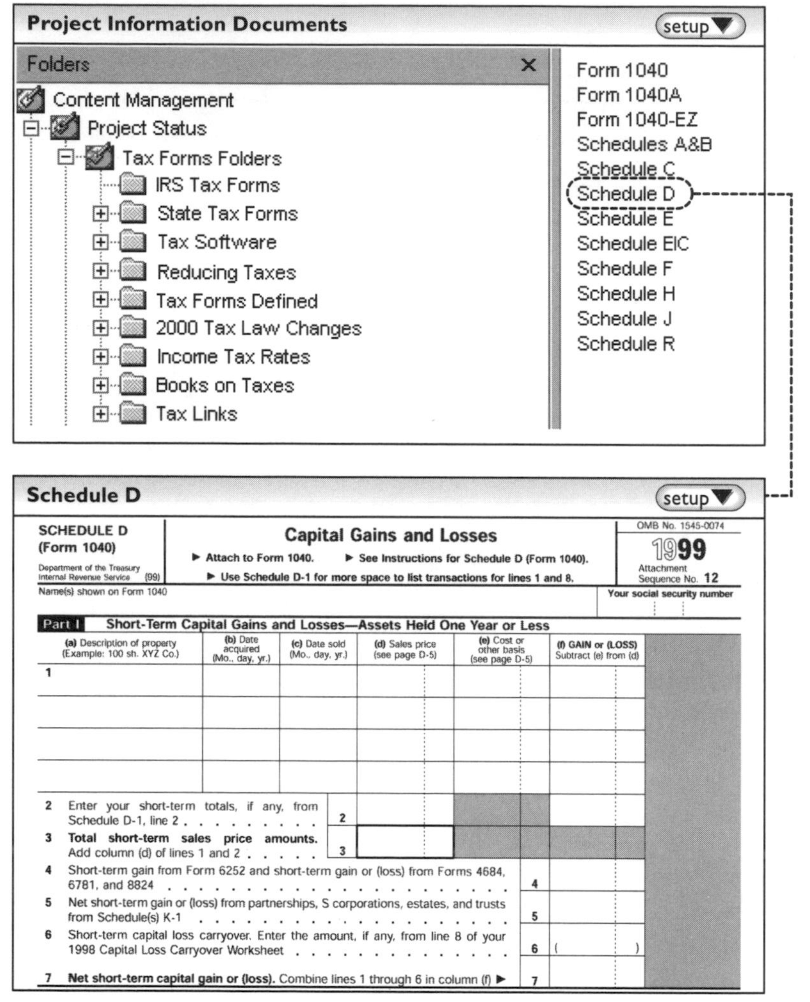

digital library. This allows the knowledge organization system to bring new dimensions to content collections in the digital library. These dimensions are viewed as layers that can be added as attributes to the digital library. A variety of applications and services can be developed to focus on a specific dimension. One of the benefits of the Internet and digital libraries is the degree to which content or information can be made available to broader audiences. The technology facilitates the connection of disparate knowledge communities at the network level. Knowledge organization systems provide alternate subject access; facilitate adding multiple dimensions;

support multilingual access; and supply terms for extensive free-text searching to allow communities to interact in new ways.

All types of knowledge organization systems provide structure and increased access to digital libraries. They provide different degrees of complexity, organization, and function. The enterprise knowledge portal digital library will use the knowledge organization system to link electronic resources together. Knowledge organization systems fall into three general categories. These include term lists, classifications and categories, and relationship lists.

Term Lists

- *Authority Files.* Authority files are lists of terms that are used to create the key words used in search indexes and digital libraries. These key words are linked as pointers into fields and variables available in documents, websites, audio files, and other content items identified in your organization. This type of knowledge organization system will not include a deep organization or complex structure. The presentation may be alphabetical or organized by a high-level classification scheme. A limited hierarchy may be applied to allow for simple navigation. This is important when the authority file is being accessed manually or is extremely large.
- *Glossaries.* A glossary is a list of terms that usually contain definitions. The terms may be from a specific subject field. The terms are relative to the environment they are created in and rarely include variant or alternate meanings.
- *Dictionaries.* Dictionaries are alphabetical lists of words and their definitions. Dictionaries are more general in scope than glossaries. A dictionary may provide synonyms and related words. No explicit hierarchical structure is applied and there is no attempt to group the lists of words by concept.
- *Gazetteers.* A gazetteer is a list of place names. Traditional gazetteers have been published as books or have appeared as indexes to atlases. Each entry may also be identified by feature type like rivers, cities, or schools.

Classifications and Categories

- *Subject Headings.* This scheme provides a set of controlled terms to represent the subjects of items in a collection. Subject heading lists can be extensive and cover a broad range of subjects. The subject heading structure is shallow with a limited hierarchical structure. Subject headings are coordinated with rules on how they can be joined to provide concepts that are more specific when knowledge users need them.

- *Classification Schemes, Taxonomies, and Categorization Schemes.* These types of knowledge organization systems provide ways to separate content items into categories or broad topic levels. Taxonomies are expanding their use for use in object-oriented design and knowledge management systems to indicate any grouping of objects based on a particular characteristic.

Relationship Lists

- *Thesauri.* Thesauri are based on concepts and represent relationships among terms. Relationships commonly expressed in a thesaurus include hierarchy, equivalence (synonyms), and association or relatedness. Associative relationships may be detailed in some schemes. Preferred terms for indexing and retrieval are identified. Nonpreferred terms point to the preferred terms to be used for each concept.
- *Semantic Networks.* Natural language processing has allowed for significant developments in semantic networks. These knowledge organization systems structure concepts and terms not as hierarchies but as a network or a mesh of connections. Concepts are thought of as nodes and relationships branch out from them. They may include cause-effect or parent-child relationships. Semantic networks are used in a variety of search engines.
- *Ontology.* Ontology models represent complex relationships among objects and include the rules and axioms missing from semantic networks. Ontology models describe knowledge in a specific area and are often used in data mining and knowledge management systems.

The term lists, classification and categories, and relationship lists used in your organization are reflected in the enterprise knowledge portal to build connections between structured content, unstructured content, and user profiles. The knowledge organization system is used to bridge all these elements together to provide context and integration in the enterprise knowledge portal. The benefits include:

- *Navigation Schemes.* This is the ability to build dynamic menus on each content page within the enterprise knowledge portal. Navigation schemes can be located in several locations throughout the user interface. An example of this is presented in Figure 2-11.
- *Data Filtering and Analysis.* This is the ability to present summarized reports and information that is clarified or focused for an identified purpose by user role or other attributes.

- *Information Brokering.* This is the ability to provide middleman or negotiator services that deliver the material and data requested by the enterprise knowledge portal user.
- *Work Flow Management.* Work flow management refers to the ability to evaluate and improve work processes or work flow activities by linking content collections to each other for the purpose of maintaining information and making sure all related or linked systems are aware.
- *Information Mining.* This is the ability to locate content items across multiple data sources in the organization using search and query features.
- *Content Management.* This refers to the ability to facilitate guidance, control, and structure for unstructured information.
- *Mission and Task Management.* This is the ability to support the creation of a series of activities that are tracked from inception to resolution regardless of the systems, applications, and repositories used to manage the process.
- *Communication and Collaboration Integration.* This is the ability to foster team activities and promote knowledge workers to share ideas and information.
- *Team Information Management.* Team information management is the ability to provide features for maintaining group schedules, calendars, tasks, address books, and other personal assistance features.
- *Risk Management.* This is the ability to identify, promote, prioritize, and provide assistance in removing issues or concerns that need to controlled or resolved.

Search and Index

There are several common search features your organization will want to include in the search software function of your enterprise knowledge portal solution. Most organizations consider search the most enabling feature of the enterprise portal solution. If your organization considers this feature extremely significant, you will want to consider making this feature pervasive by adding it to the primary menu that is static and constantly available for knowledge workers. See Figure 2-12 to review an example of search as a primary menu option. The standard search features that are available from Internet sites include:

1. *Exact Phrase Search.* In exact phrase search the query returns results that contain at least one occurrence of the string of words entered in the search box.
2. *Keyword Search.* In keyword search the query returns results that contain at least one occurrence of at least one of the words entered in the search box.

Figure 2-11. Enterprise portal user interface: knowledge organization systems.

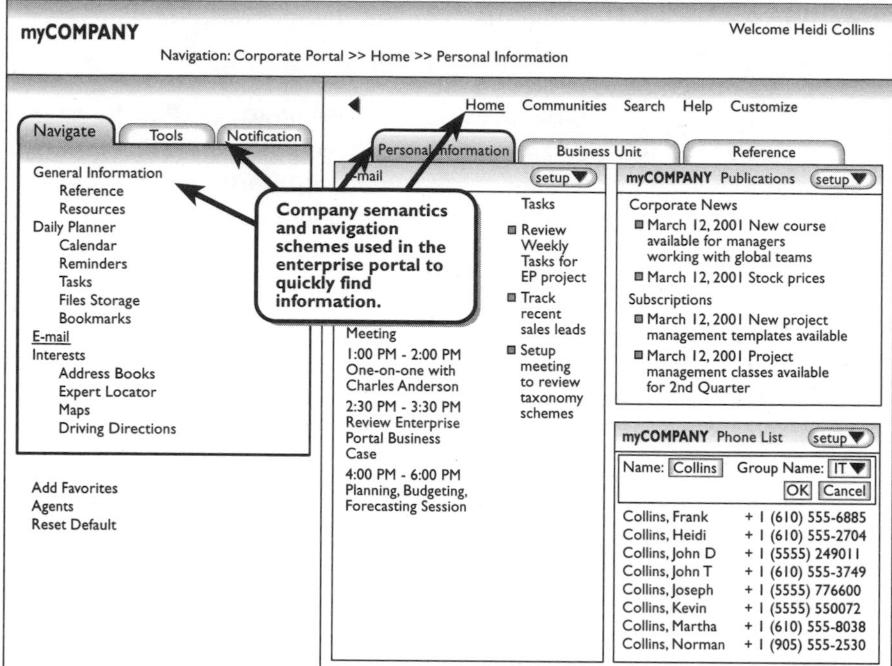

3. *Boolean Search.* In Boolean search the query returns results that use Boolean operators and syntax to perform advanced searches.
4. *Category Search.* In category search the query returns results that are associated with the type of information the user is interested in.

There are currently several types of search functionality available from third-party search products that should be evaluated and considered to be implemented in an enterprise portal solution. These include:

1. *Standard Search Features.* These are guided approaches (exact phrase search, keyword search, Boolean search, category search) to locate the occurrences of a specific target string.
2. *Concept-Based Search.* These are statistical and other guided approaches to locate small clusters or networks of related word occurrences.
3. *Metadata Search.* These reflect stored relationships of structured and unstructured information sources to locate data points that are directly and indirectly related to the specific channel or context in focus.

The results or presentation of search elements in the enterprise knowledge portal solution can be in the form of ad hoc requested searches and

Figure 2-12. Enterprise portal user interface: search and index.

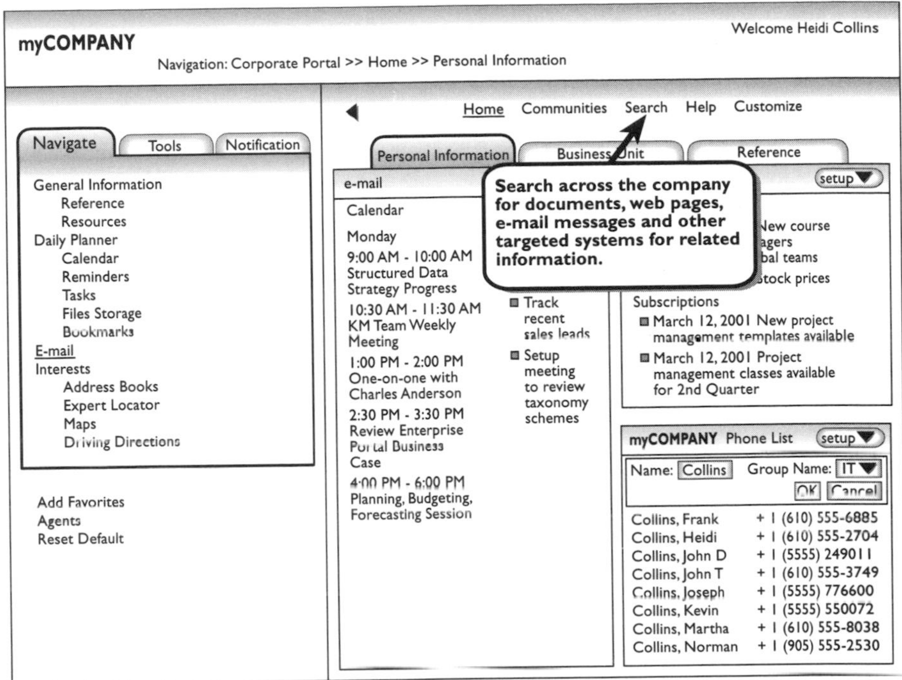

predefined searches. Query screens and search options available to knowledge workers for ad hoc searches need to be incorporated into the presentation layer or interface of the enterprise knowledge portal. Predefined search features and results can appear in many different forms in the enterprise portal interface. These include:

- ❒ Predefined reports containing search results
- ❒ Hyperlinks to related information

It is likely that third-party search tools will need to be incorporated into the enterprise portal solution. There are several advantages for using third-party products to provide search functionality to your enterprise portal solution. Some of these include providing consistent results and services to all enterprise portal users, providing equivalent search features and services for all data sources available in your organization, and providing administration and wizard tools to simplify and accelerate query creation and management.

The enterprise portal can easily be leveraged to present the results of predefined or on-request queries that return results from data sources inside and outside your organization. The ability to have access to information that is necessary or advantageous to making better decisions or obtaining additional knowledge about a knowledge worker's responsibilities can provide the edge your organization needs to stay ahead of your competitors. Knowledge workers should be able to access any kind of information without taking the time to research or locate unknown data points and sources. The enterprise portal solution will provide the knowledge desktop that can continuously grab data and extend and expand the experience and expertise of your knowledge workers with data points and related information relevant to their job requirements and their interests.

The enterprise knowledge portal methodology is used to determine the information required by knowledge workers throughout your organization. The enterprise portal solution will make this information easily available. If implemented effectively this will allow knowledge workers to get information they need without even knowing it existed. To accomplish this, you need to build a query system that will meet the needs of the enterprise knowledge portal users. Query results should be presented in the best time frame possible. This means that some queries will be predefined and scheduled to run automatically presenting updated information to portal users. Other queries will be predefined and only run when executed by an enterprise knowledge portal user. The results are returned to the enterprise portal desktop for immediate review. An additional query feature is to allow users to define their own queries and review the results from the enterprise knowledge portal desktop. An example of a search result set can be seen in Figure 2-13.

The importance of the search feature is to find and filter the information available to users in your organization. This software function will turn large quantities of documents and data sources into knowledge by focusing and categorizing exactly what users need to know into a single location. Enterprise portal solutions or third-party search engines provide services to execute predefined queries that return the data points or information from multiple or identified sources that match the criteria in the query. These matches are stored in an index or catalog by the search application. The index or catalog is used to provide reports or information in content windows presented to the user. The data points and information returned to the enterprise portal from the search catalog can be available in several formats. Some of these formats include:

- A link to an Internet website
- A link to a report inside your organization
- A listing of available reports within your organization for review or research purposes
- A collection of hyperlinks that might provide relevant information related to the content page

Figure 2-13. Enterprise portal search results.

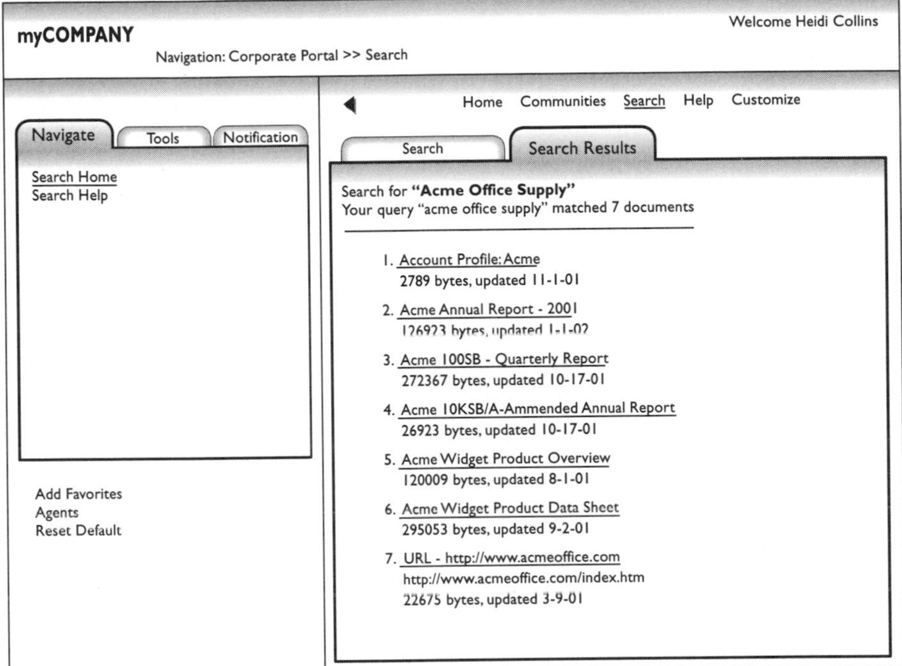

There is a broad set of requirements that your organization needs to implement to provide the searching features needed to quickly find information in your organization and on the Internet. When users create and submit their own search requests they fall into three basic categories:

1. Standard search features
2. Concept-based search
3. Metadata search

Standard Search Features

Search engines have a variety of standard ways to control the results returned by the query agent. There are several searching commands available for basic search requirements that you will need for your enterprise portal. Some of these include:

- *Match Any.* This locates any of the keywords or phrases in the search query.

- *Match All.* This locates all of the keywords or phrases in the search query.
- *Exclude.* This feature is used to submit a keyword or phrase that will be used to narrow a search result set.
- *Title Search.* This allows a search request to be submitted against the HTML title of a Web page.
- *Site Search.* This provides the ability to control what websites are included or excluded from a search query.
- *URL Search.* This provides the ability to search the text contents of a URL.
- *Link Search.* This feature offers the ability to search for all the pages linking to a particular page or domain.
- *Wildcards.* This allows a search for plurals or variations of words by using a wildcard character (usually *).
- *Proximity.* This allows the search query to include information about how close words should appear to each other to be included in the results set.

These types of searches will return the largest number of document and articles. These standard approaches can be effective for basic searches across several types of data sources that a user might need to complete an online query. See Figure 2-14.

To provide much more accurate and complete search results to users from data sources within your organization, more sophisticated search features will need to be considered as part of the enterprise portal solution. In most cases the results of a search query will be predefined and executed to present the results to the user when the content page is opened. These predefined search agents cross-reference data throughout your organization to push information to the user based on cross-references and relationships about knowledge workers and data included in the enterprise portal. There are several different approaches or technologies used to establish these relationships. Your information technology department will need to be able to support the third-party search engine and the relationships throughout your organization that are required to implement search requirements for the portal solution.

Concept-Based Search

A topic or idea can be described using different words or phrases. For this reason, standard search features may be too limiting when you are required to research a topic or subject area. Concept-based searching allows

Figure 2-14. Enterprise portal online search query.

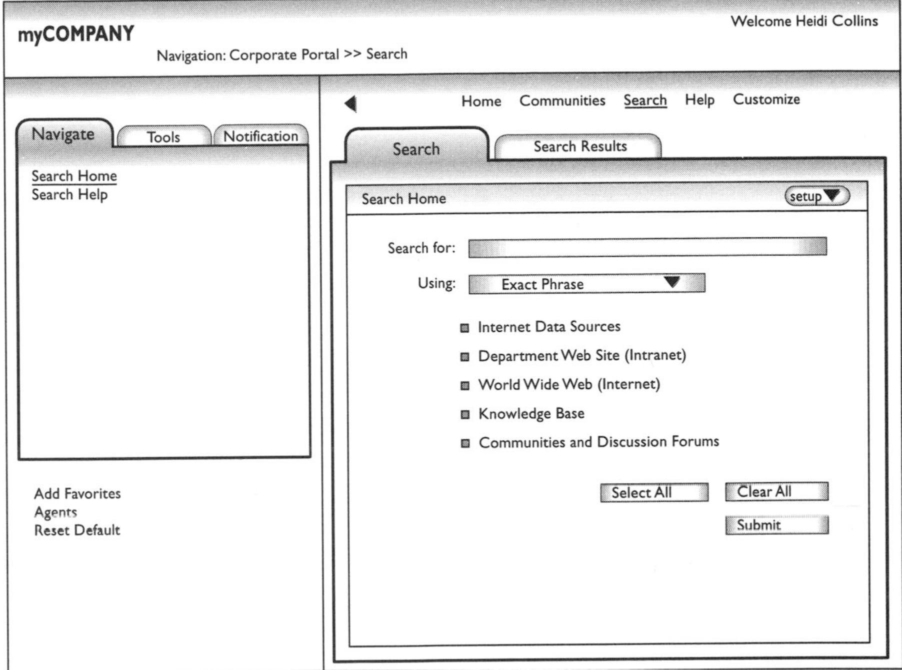

information to be collected by relationship or relevance rather than by exact phrases or keywords. For example, with a concept-based search query of "project management," the search software will return two types of results: a first set that explicitly mentions project management in the text and a second set about project management that references "system development lifecycle" or "software engagements." Concept-based searching can retrieve documents and articles on system development lifecycle and software engagements even if these documents or articles contain none of the original query words of project or management.

There are two approaches to implement concept-based searching:

1. *The Thesaurus Approach.* You will need to have a knowledge organization system to use this approach. This knowledge base is a dictionary of terms and additional details about grammar and punctuation. The search software reads the submitted text, transforming or enhancing the original query with the information contained in the knowledge base. This creates a cross-referenced collection of related phrases that are submitted to the search software to generate the results set.
2. *The Statistical Approach.* The search software begins the process by accepting the submitted text and generating a list of terms that are re-

lated statistically to the words in the original query. The added terms are known to have a significant degree of co-occurrence and are selected to be cross-referenced with the original terms requested. The concept-based search request is complete and all the results are returned to the user. You will find that many of the documents and articles in the results set do not contain occurrences of the original query words but should contain information relevant to the requested search.

If information in your organization is dispersed through multiple systems and data sources with multiple indexing or naming patterns, then concept-based search features might be very useful to cross-reference or establish relationships between data sources, data points, and employees. Enterprise portal users who are searching for information throughout the organization do not need to be familiar with all the naming and categorizing patterns to locate the information they are looking for. To implement the thesaurus approach, the knowledge organization system has to be developed. The knowledge base design and creation can be a time-consuming task that will require continued maintenance. Implementing the statistical approach does not require additional planning but will not be as accurate or relevant as the thesaurus approach in most cases.

Metadata Search

Metadata describes a data point or helps provide access to the data point. These collections of metadata items or elements are used to describe one or many information resources in your organization. There must be an association between the data point and the metadata element to be able to use this type of search to locate information. With respect to the Internet, this metadata relationship exists between the information stored in the "META" field and the HTML Web page it is stored in. The purpose of a metadata search is to improve the recall (identifying all the information available on the topic) and precision (quality of accuracy of the information returned) retrieval of information.

Search software often returns irrelevant information because the query agent cannot distinguish between important and insignificant words in documents and articles. The goal of a metadata search is to target the words that are significant terms in the document or article to achieve precision in the results that are returned by the query agent. Metadata is used to achieve this by classifying the information resource characteristics. For example, you need to locate data points or resources where "crest" refers to a family coat of arms and avoid resources about a mountain crest or toothpaste. Retrieving or recalling as many of the appropriate resources as possible will be critical for the enterprise portal to be completely effective. This is difficult when the relevant information is stored in databases, images, or pdf documents and can be easily missed by standard search queries. Metadata searches can support retrieval of these resources by identifying them through the metadata tags and not the content of the documents or articles.

In larger and more complex sites indexing or cataloging information is limited to only the top levels of the sites hierarchy. If a metadata repository of the information available about the site existed, then the query agent could create an index or catalog for a much larger collection of resources. There are a variety of metadata standards available to (a) access specific types of data sources and (b) provide a standard way of describing a variety of information resources and data sources that can be returned from a single query agent or search process.

Personalization and Roles

Your enterprise portal solution must offer user management and role management to enable personalization of content provided. The personalization and roles features provide a streamlined user experience while accessing and interacting with content. Access to the content has to be managed and the enterprise knowledge portal has to recognize or know the users and the roles these users act in. This information has to be shared and synchronized with the environment, specifically the features that integrate with components that manage the delivery, interaction, and saving of content. The accessed content has to be built and rendered within the enterprise knowledge portal presentation features.

The personalization and roles features are focused on access. Access includes everything needed to get the job done. This is dependent on two things: the role a knowledge worker is acting in and the knowledge worker's preferences and responsibilities. The enterprise knowledge portal manages both roles and users. These are two separate concepts. A role defines how the enterprise knowledge portal is populated with content. It defines the cross-functional interactions required to collect and share corporate knowledge about jobs and work processes. Roles represent the content offered from throughout the enterprise to users. Roles do not provide personalization features. Personalization is a complementary set of features. Personalization is how users organize the content made available in the user interface.

Each enterprise knowledge portal user has a record that provides the basis for authentication to the enterprise portal. This feature allows users to log on to the enterprise knowledge portal once and have access to content and applications throughout the organization. When users access portal pages, content windows are presented in the user interface. Each content window will complete authorization or security requirements to the data source or system accesses displaying the content items that the role and ultimately the user has the right to view. It is critical that this low-level authentication be managed by the logic in the content window to create a focused or role-based view of content in your organization, otherwise business logic would be mirrored or the same for all user roles accessing content through the enterprise knowledge portal.

One of the most popular personalization features is favorites or bookmarks. Favorites enable users to create their own order and hierarchy of content access that suits their personal needs. The enterprise knowledge portal stores all personalization information on a server. This makes favorites accessible from any workstation or device that the enterprise knowledge portal user works from. This allows users to have the same personalized working environment regardless of where they work. The enterprise knowledge portal maintains the definition of the properties used to define the structure of the supporting relational database. You will typically find the following types of information in the data dictionary:

- Definitions of the attributes that comprise each entity
- Integrity constraints placed on the relationships of the entities
- Security information regarding the rights users have or what operations a role is allowed to perform on each entity (read, edit, no access, other)
- Definitions of other structural elements associated with the identity schema

The digital identity is a table in a relational database that documents all the data about the identity entities (tables), the columns (attributes), the keys (unique identifiers), and other details. You will want to establish the attribute definitions that define roles in your organization. This information will provide the enterprise knowledge portal project teams with the details to determine the scope of activities that will need to be completed so that the data required is available for the enterprise knowledge portal solution.

Many users want to personalize the way content windows within the enterprise knowledge portal display information. For example, if a stock ticker is used, users want to determine which stocks are displayed. This is an example of content personalization. The user might also want to indicate where the stock ticker appears on the screen. This is called representation personalization. The content personalization features are managed by the enterprise knowledge portal or by the customization features within the content window.

The summary information and additional levels of detail available to knowledge workers throughout your organization will primarily be presented in content pages and content windows in the enterprise knowledge portal. The second most common location for information is in the content-relevant information sections of the enterprise knowledge portal. It is beneficial to flatten access to information by presenting it to the enterprise knowledge portal user in the fewest number of navigation clicks or tasks as possible. Given that users can add, move, and remove content windows throughout the enterprise knowledge portal, users can organize their own content pages by creating content page tabs and assigning individual content windows to the content page tabs. With rich personalization features that allow knowledge workers to organize content in a way that makes sense to them, the more likely users will continue to access and use the enterprise knowledge portal as a knowledge management tool.

Try to make content windows short and factual and provide links to additional information needed that provides background or training knowledge to less-experienced knowledge workers. For the enterprise knowledge portal to be extremely effective, the content windows and content-relevant information will need to be updated frequently and provide notification to knowledge workers regarding how current the information represented within the content pages is. There needs to be some visual representation that indicates to enterprise knowledge portal users if there is additional content below the information that can be seen on a single screen. Knowledge workers might not realize at first glance that additional information is available below the edge of the browser window. Scrolling the browser window represents a flow in data content where following a link creates a break in the content flow. Be careful how much information is contained in a content page; users will get lost in the page if it is too long. A page length of one and a half screens can be relatively easy for a knowledge worker to keep track of information on the page. If there are doubts regarding how long content pages should be, ask for feedback from the knowledge workers who will be using the enterprise knowledge portal content.

For multipart documents it is important to include document and chapter headings. If content pages are consistently longer than one and a half screens, then building additional navigation features into the content page to help quickly focus the key points or sections of the page would be helpful. Here are some suggestions:

1. Create a shortlist of the distinct sections of the document as links. Knowledge workers will be able to know at first glance what information is contained in the document and navigate quickly to the section of the document they need.
2. Be careful when creating a collection of graphic navigation buttons. Make sure they are widely accepted, well understood, and combined with other textual navigation features that make them easy for users to decode.

3. For large collections of sizeable documents or smaller collections that are not well categorized, use search features to improve retrieval and accessibility of information in your organization.
4. Be sure to include links to improve the utility of your content pages. They need to be worded in a way that prevents them from distracting with the material presented in the enterprise portal. Links provide connections to other information resources, organizational markers (anchors), and a way to provide reference terms to the current document context.

The most important quality aspects of the enterprise knowledge portal solution are that the information available is accurate and up-to-date. The operational and strategic decisions made by enterprise knowledge portal users are only going to be as effective and informed as the information made available to them to make those decisions. If the information is accurate and timely, but users are not able to find information or need different information to work effectively, then the content presented in the enterprise knowledge portal needs to be reevaluated for usefulness. The issue might be that the information available in the enterprise knowledge portal is relevant but additional work processes or functions need to be added to complete or enhance the usability of the enterprise knowledge portal.

Navigation throughout the enterprise knowledge portal needs to be well organized, intuitive, and accurate. Be sure that all the links referenced throughout the enterprise knowledge portal work correctly. Having a site map of your enterprise knowledge portal can be very useful to provide a visual representation of the information resources available. This visual representation can also be used as another navigation resource to find information throughout the enterprise knowledge portal. The site map can provide a high-level knowledge map for users who are having trouble locating information or it can be used as a training tool to help employees recognize the business process owners and relationships of the information available. This is especially helpful when an enterprise knowledge portal site becomes very large. An example of a site map can be seen in Figure 2-15. You might want to consider and evaluate a third-party software package that can create site maps and help verify that links are working correctly to minimize maintenance tasks and ensure the quality of your enterprise knowledge portal.

Enterprise Portal Integration Features

Integrating applications, structured data, and unstructured content into the enterprise portal is one of the fundamental functions to be supported by

Figure 2-15. Example site map.

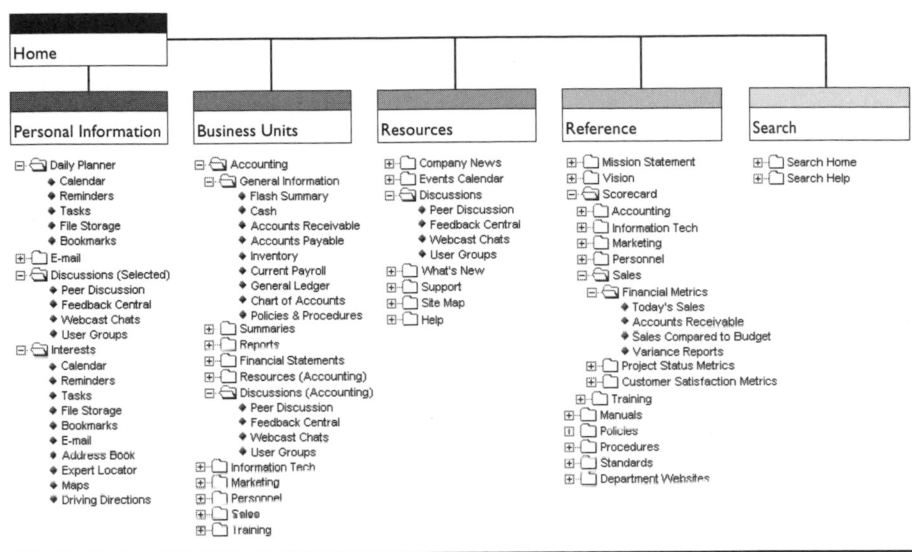

the enterprise knowledge portal. A wide range of internal and external information sources need to work together, interact with each other, and provide the appropriate context to users. The enterprise knowledge portal needs to allow users to initiate and participate in work processes that span across the data and applications used throughout the enterprise. These integration features are designed for knowledge workers to complete their assigned responsibilities more interactively with the systems and other knowledge workers in the organization. The enterprise knowledge portal integration features to consider include:

- ❐ Multi-repository support
- ❐ Application integration
- ❐ Process integration
- ❐ Web services
- ❐ Peer-to-peer computing

Multi-Repository Support

A common mission or objective for the enterprise knowledge portal is to integrate and transparently deliver targeted and actionable information from the full range of data sources available to knowledge workers in the organization. The enterprise knowledge portal must present the information focused on the role of the user accessing the content and relate the information in an understandable format for knowledge workers. This collection of related and disparate information should create new insights for innovative decisions.

Your enterprise knowledge portal will display many kinds of information and data elements on a single content page. From the point of view of the knowledge worker trying to make a decision, there needs to be a way to directly infer relationships between the different sources of information presented. The goal is to interrelate the information content of multiple content windows. For example, a manager can discover overdue receivables in one content window and in another window, using data from a different data source or from a different set of screens in the same data source, this manager can discover that several of the top overdue items are related to sales activity among customers in a specific sales region.

Using the personalization features of the enterprise knowledge portal, an employee can subscribe to content based on areas of interest or categories that are specific to their roles in the organization. A query is executed on a scheduled basis that updates the appropriate content windows with new and updated content items that are specific to the subscription request defined by the knowledge worker. Figure 2-16 shows the main portal menu with hyperlinks from several different data sources to compile the informa-

Figure 2-16. Enterprise portal user interface: multi-repository support.

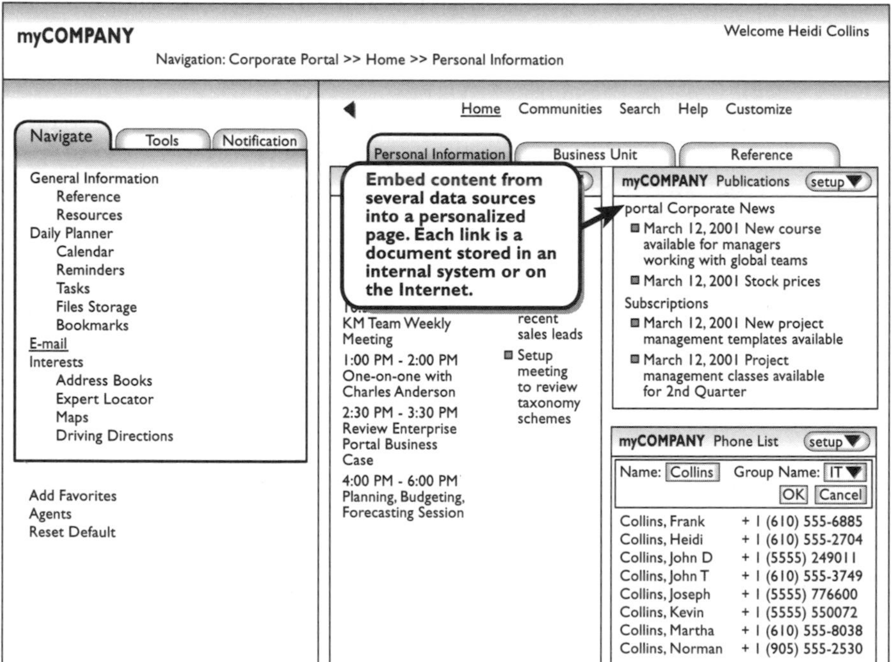

tion the knowledge worker has subscribed to using configuration options available through personalization.

Application Integration

The advantage of bringing aspects of applications into the enterprise knowledge portal desktop is to create knowledge using information that is all related to the specific task being completed at any one time. A successful information environment reflects the details and specific operating and strategic requirements of a function or work process. The best approach is to create a series of enterprise portal templates that focus the subset of information needed by the user roles working together to complete a specific set of activities or tasks. These templates are designed to capture the working climate of knowledge workers and bring the information streams at the appropriate time in the work process from applications that mirror the work environment. These enterprise portal templates that map out information requirements by role have the potential to compress the time period required to implement your enterprise knowledge portal by several weeks or months.

There are many applications that might be represented in the enterprise knowledge portal desktop through multiple content windows. The corporate messaging system is a good example. Notifications are often forwarded to electronic messaging applications like e-mail to let users know the status of certain work processes. Figure 2-17 is an example of bringing calendar and tasks content items into a content window for a knowledge worker.

Process Integration

The role-based approach embedded into your enterprise knowledge portal brings entire work processes, step by step, into a single desktop. Enterprise knowledge portal capabilities that will enhance the user experience include the ability to support alert mechanisms, announcements, and other forms of information that stream important content used to support your work processes into the enterprise knowledge portal. You will want to consider and support these types of features in your enterprise knowledge portal solution. Employees can access and create a collection of predefined intelligent agents that make requests to applications and post the results into specified content pages or content windows throughout the enterprise knowledge portal. Figure 2-18 demonstrates where knowledge workers can configure agents in the enterprise knowledge portal desktop. This same functionality can be integrated into content windows that are added

Figure 2-17. Enterprise portal user interface: application integration.

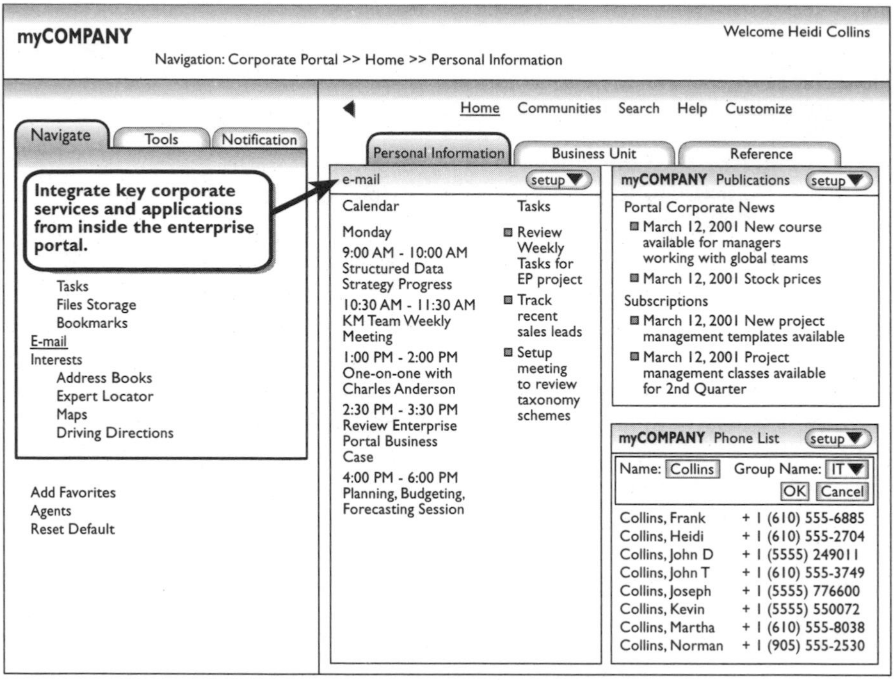

to content pages by knowledge workers using personalization features available in the enterprise knowledge portal.

Vendors and partners have created collections of specialized content windows that can be purchased or downloaded. The specialized content windows provided are often designed to work with specific applications or services in your organization. The development of these application-specific content windows provides several benefits that include the speed of implementation for targeted user roles and a programming code library to be used as a resource to develop customized content windows for your enterprise knowledge portal.

Web Services

There are business-specific work processes being supported by many business units and systems throughout your enterprise. These networks of users and systems provide the overall framework and links that bring your organization and your business community together to exchange information or services. The development and modification of the enterprise knowledge portal over time establishes a collection of data points that describe in de-

Figure 2-18. Enterprise portal user interface: process integration.

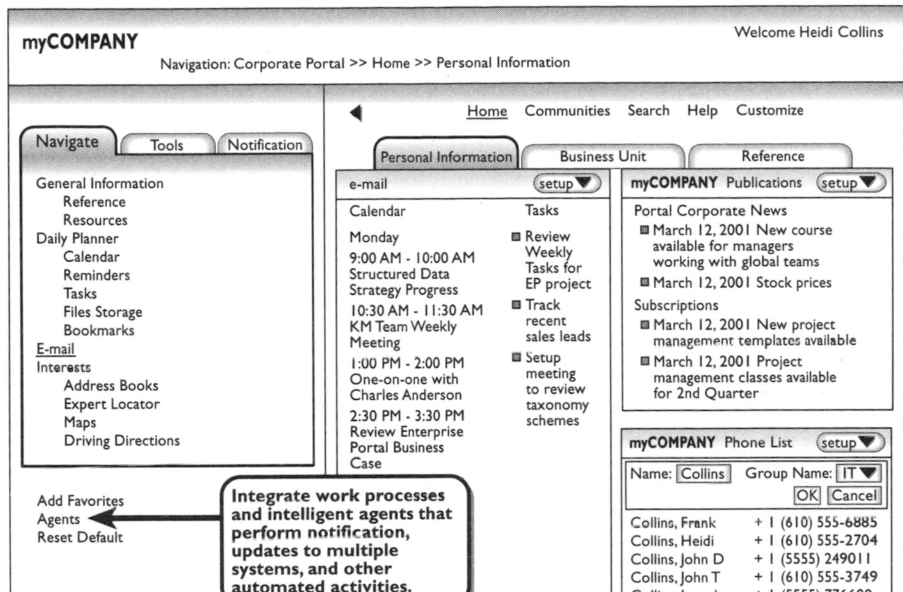

tail aspects of your organization's work process, how work gets accomplished, what the key performance indicators are for individual jobs and business units, and what constitutes the best practices of your organization at a specific point in time.

An effective enterprise knowledge portal will improve the extended enterprise. The ability to manage and publish accurate and reliable Web content becomes mission-critical in this environment. The objective is to leverage the same tools that personalize information streams for internal constituencies and extend them to your enterprise knowledge portal services. This allows specific groups of customers, partners, or suppliers to interact with tailored enterprise knowledge portal content windows. These Web services and e-business portals are becoming a growing proportion of business interactions. The integration is seamless to the user. The features available from the enterprise knowledge portal can all take advantage of the Web services offered by companies to find one another on the Web and make their systems interoperable for e-commerce. Figure 2-19 illustrates how Web services provided to knowledge workers can be easily accessed as hyperlinks from menu options in the enterprise knowledge portal.

Figure 2-19. Enterprise portal user interface: Web services.

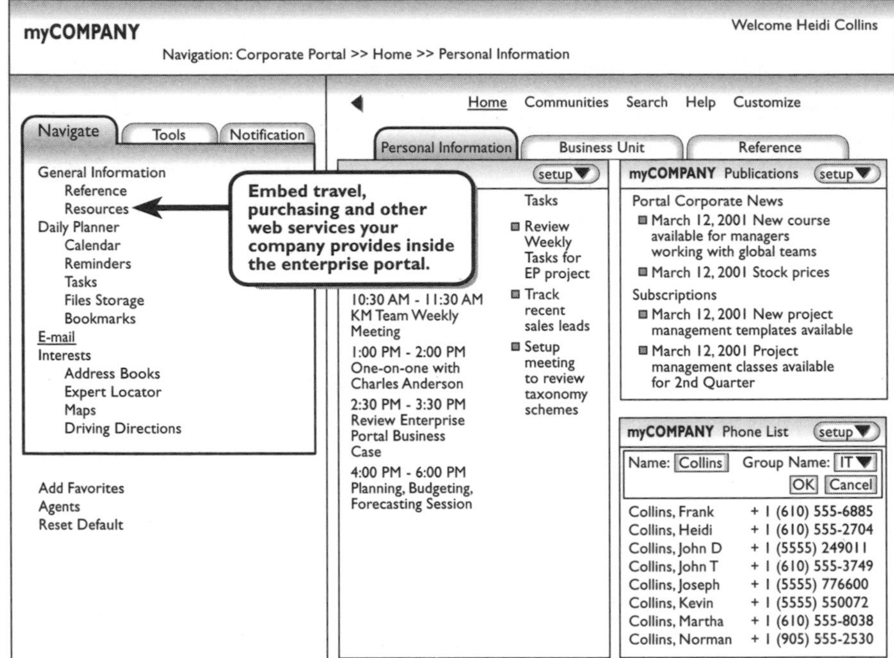

Peer-to-Peer Computing

Peer computing makes a wide array of new capabilities and applications possible. The objective is to allow the Web to serve as a person-to-person or small group communications platform. The concept is to support private spaces for people to meet, share content, and talk. Peer computing may be more adaptable for person-to-person communication. There are several specific ways that widespread use of peer-to-peer communications for small groups can be more effective. These include:

❐ *Reduced Centralized Administrative Resources.* If a small team of knowledge workers and contractors need to meet regularly, make decisions, share documents, and update information, they could use a shared website space or create a shared space on a peer network. For the website to accommodate hundreds of these teams concurrently, the website would need to expand capacity. The shared space on a peer network allows each team member to use his local computing resources to meet his needs. There is no need to have additional bandwidth, processing capacity, or storage. Administrators are not required to manage access to services or maintain the system.

- *Reduced Storage Resources.* Peer-to-peer file transfer can minimize network traffic while eliminating redundant storage. This means the appropriate use of peer computing will naturally lead to a reduction in server-based storage requirements.
- *Optimized Network and Computing Resources.* Peer computing will make direct use of local computing resources in business-to-business and business-to-consumer interactions. The network of users will connect directly with each other instead of requiring applications to move content to the personal desktops of all the team members.
- *Personal Efficiency.* Individual users will make a connection to another person to begin the shared peer computing session. The personal control and ability to initiate sharing work easily with one or two additional team members can be an effective and productive working environment for users.

Figure 2-20 demonstrates locating a knowledge worker in your organization to open a peer computing session for the purpose of gaining additional information needed to complete a work process.

Figure 2-20. Enterprise portal user interface: peer-to-peer computing.

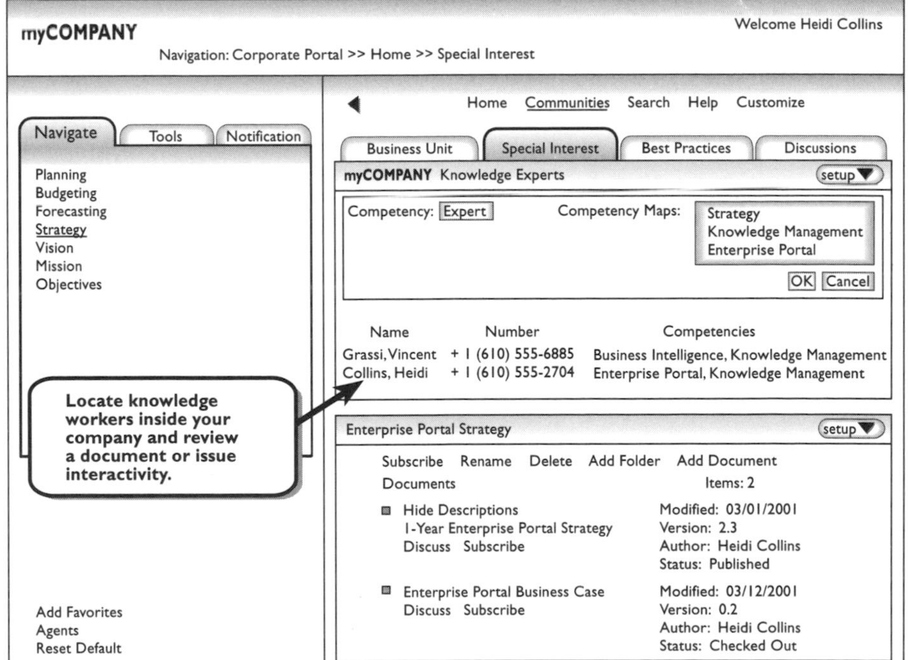

Key Points

The enterprise portal is an intuitive user interface with a whole lot of middleware integrated to work with your existing infrastructure applications and services. The enterprise knowledge portal is a collection of technologies working together rather than a single product you can purchase from a vendor. The types of enterprise portals available include:

- Enterprise information portals
- E-business and e-commerce portals
- Mobile commerce portals
- Internet portals

The knowledge worker's value is created through the transformation of several loosely defined data sources and work processes into a single, cohesive electronic workplace. Your challenge is to create an effective user interface that provides unified work processes that cut across a multitude of information technology systems. The result is an enterprise knowledge portal that provides services like single sign-on, comprehensive search, application access and integration, personalization, deployment, administration, collaboration, content management, business intelligence, learning, metrics, and security. Think about opportunities the enterprise knowledge portal will provide to improve work processes for employees, customers, suppliers, and partners.

The enterprise knowledge portal has evolved from a way to locate content to a platform to execute multiple transactions, implement end-to-end work processes, and collaborate with internal and external knowledge workers. Your enterprise knowledge portal must be easy to deploy with broad configuration capabilities that incorporate diverse content and applications. The result is an electronic workplace for knowledge workers to function cross-functionally in well-managed roles and as networks of users. There are several categories of functionality available in the enterprise knowledge portal that will be essential to supporting knowledge management in your organization. These include:

- *Presentation.* Presentation is the complete set of technologies and services used to provide the visual experience to users. It encapsulates all of the enterprise knowledge portal functionality. The underlying infrastructure environment will outline the enterprise knowledge portal architecture, server and operating system platforms, installation and configuration, performance, scalability, standards, security, and administration. The collection of services, content and functionality integrates business intelligence, collaboration and communities, managed content, and learning considerations integrated together through the enterprise knowledge portal. The user interface of the enterprise knowledge portal provides continuity of the information and features presented to the knowledge worker.

- *Knowledge Organization Systems.* This collection of technologies is a key component to bringing meaning and focus to the information users use. Your taxonomies and categorization schemes can be automatically linked to structured and unstructured content in your organization to present a comprehensive list of concepts or categories throughout the enterprise knowledge portal. The knowledge organization system is used to group related information into similar themes or concepts. The contextual maps that are presented to users provide an intuitive table of contents to find information or provide a logical structure to search results.
- *Search and Index.* Full-featured advanced search technology are required to access, manage, and organize information stored in many and varied sources throughout your organization. Search capabilities that enable users to look for mission-critical information and have it presented in several formats that are designed to meet individual needs and preferences are critical.
- *Personalization and Roles.* The personalization and role functionality is dependent on the roles a knowledge worker is acting in and preferences and responsibilities the same knowledge worker is responsible for. The enterprise knowledge portal maintains information about users to authenticate the system and gain access to all the data sources accessed. Users will need to interact with screens to enter and submit information. They will need to easily navigate and link to additional content pages and content windows. An individual content window needs to be able to expand to take over the entire content page, the content needs to reformat to fit the screen, and the content window needs to be able to be minimized back to the original size. Content windows need to be able to be collapsed to a title bar and expanded back to their default size. When the user selects a specific set of values from the corporate taxonomy and submits the request, the information on the content page and in the content windows will be filtered to present the information relative to the values selected. Users need to be able to configure content windows to different formats or different slices and dices of information by default when they are dynamically built to the page. Users need to be able to rearrange content windows on the same portal page or move to additional portal pages that they add. Users will need to add or remove content windows from portal pages. The user needs to be able to set notification and alert parameters, subscribe to information that is delivered at some regular interval to content windows, and have

access to other customization functionality designed into the enterprise knowledge portal. The user will require a broad and narrow navigation scheme to get to content pages and content windows. There are additional features you might want to include in your enterprise knowledge portal or features that the vendor provides as part of their enterprise portal software solution.

To effectively use the collection of enterprise knowledge portal functionality, you will need to directly link a wide range of internal and external information sources together. The enterprise knowledge portal allows users to initiate and participate in work processes that span across your entire organization without having to search for screens in applications or understand the entire work process. Several integration features to include in your enterprise knowledge portal solution include:

- ❐ Multi-repository support
- ❐ Application integration
- ❐ Process integration
- ❐ Web services
- ❐ Peer-to-peer computing

The enterprise knowledge portal is reviewed as a cohesive architecture that supports a broad collection of features and functions creating a single user interface to information, services, and applications throughout your organization. Taking your knowledge management priorities from Chapter 1, it is important to look at the enterprise portal features individually for the purposes of selecting the appropriate vendor and software solutions that address your specific knowledge management objectives. Chapter 3 outlines a series of steps to create an overview of how to quickly identify the communities and the work processes your knowledge management effort will target to maximize the benefits of the enterprise portal. You will need to tie your specific priorities to the enterprise portal features and functionality that will be critical to deliver as part of the enterprise knowledge portal. Your goal is to weave knowledge management best practices into the enterprise portal implementation to create an enterprise knowledge portal vision. The result is the ability for your company to locate, learn, capture, and reuse in a way that is proactively embedded into knowledge workers doing their jobs.

3

Create Your Enterprise Knowledge Portal

"Ultimately, all differences between companies in cost and price derive from the hundreds of activities required to create, produce, sell, and deliver their products or services . . . differentiation arises from both the choice of activities and how they are performed."

Michael Porter, *Harvard Business Review*

An enterprise portal can be implemented to deliver the features and services you need to coordinate the work processes and objectives of your knowledge management initiative. The enterprise knowledge portal is a "window" that allows users to pass through to reach selected destinations. The enterprise knowledge portal creates a central location where navigation services are available for managers and knowledge workers to find content, launch applications, interact with multiple applications and systems, identify collaborators, share knowledge, and make decisions. The enterprise knowledge portal is:

> A personalized interface to online resources for knowledge workers to organize and integrate applications and data. The solution allows knowledge workers to access information, collaborate with each other, make decisions, and take action on a wide variety of business-related work processes regardless of the knowledge worker's virtual location or business unit affiliation, the location of the information, or the format in which the information is stored.

Enterprise knowledge portals can provide the technology needed to implement a successful knowledge management strategy for your organization. Enterprise knowledge portals provide features that focus on meeting the objectives of your knowledge management initiatives.

Knowledge management is simple enough to think about in general. Every activity employees are involved in is explored to include or improve the ability to locate, learn, capture, and reuse information. One scenario is a knowledge worker looking for information and expertise in the organization to help them resolve a customer complaint. If the issue is complex and requires some unique answer, you want to encourage the experts in your organization to share their knowledge or their sources of information to generate the most appropriate response. The overall objective is to produce continuity and quality in your customer responses. You want knowledge workers to learn from the experts to one day become and be recognized as the new generation of experts. If you are successful you will have an organization that knows how to capture experience for future reuse.

You will need to think from a slightly different perspective to gain a better understanding of what an enterprise knowledge portal offers and how to take advantage of this new paradigm. Maybe you have a best practice sharing application to promote how information can be located, learned, captured, and reused. Before you review the latest user-requested improvements in work flow or search for your best practice sharing application, how can an enterprise knowledge portal help? Consider each requirement separately and not as a single application, but as a collection of functional components. Do you have an application or other solution in your organization that already has a similar work flow and approval process or an application that allows you to dynamically define and implement work flow and approval processes? Do you have a search engine that catalogs content from several data sources to return a search result set that contains a collection of information from across your organization? The enterprise knowledge portal is going to be able to bring the existing best practice sharing application, work flow and approval, and enterprise search results into a single user interface. There are a number of benefits in this solution. You are reusing the work flow and approval process without duplicating the programming effort and trying to keep these separate implementations aligned over time. You are managing content through an enterprise categorization scheme to share a constantly growing content store within your organization. In addition, the enterprise knowledge portal will provide additional features to present knowledge workers with personalized content to match their assigned responsibilities when they are working in the best practice sharing application screens through the enterprise knowledge portal. Links to applications, services, content, and access to human expertise are easily integrated into the enterprise knowledge portal pages. Communication with people anywhere within the company or at a customer site would be a logical next step for our best practice sharing solution, and is possible. At some point you might want to consider dynamic formation of communities that can be successfully implemented without information technology involvement. Make sure the information generated by these dynamic communities is captured and cataloged as part of the personalized work experience for future retrieval and reuse.

As you think about your possible enterprise knowledge portal opportunities, you should target a cross-functional collection of features that provide a basic set of functionality to get started. This approach will give knowledge workers the best opportunity to integrate all or part of the available knowledge management functionality into their jobs and changing how work gets done. The concept is that by providing a starting point for each of your selected knowledge management objectives, a larger number of employees will be able to experience knowledge management in your organization. This initial community of enterprise knowledge portal users can quickly begin to provide feedback into your knowledge management initiative, leading to a better-defined direction for your enterprise knowledge portal program and a better chance for approval and acceptance by your user communities. This approach will mean that technologies to support the depth of knowledge management functionality your company will need might not always be available in your infrastructure. This situation is an opportunity for knowledge workers to define a collection of well-understood end-to-end work processes that incorporate locate, learn, capture, and reuse components. Future deployment of the enterprise knowledge portal will enhance functionality and infrastructure to meet user demand. If you map your knowledge management objectives into a well-designed and centrally supported enterprise knowledge portal architecture, your company should be able to take full advantage of what technology can bring to your knowledge management efforts.

To complete the enterprise knowledge portal definition, you will want to create a map of how knowledge management and enterprise portals will work together for you. The result is a picture of how your unique knowledge management objectives can be delivered as an enterprise knowledge portal using as much of your existing information technology architecture as possible. If the enterprise knowledge portal solution can give you a better way to locate, learn, capture, and reuse work processes, resources, and information, then the enterprise knowledge portal functionality requirements you complete will give you an initial perspective about where your enterprise knowledge portal initiative might start and a vision around what the enterprise knowledge portal might look like in one, three, or five years.

To design an effective enterprise knowledge portal, you are going to have to gain some perspective of your whole organization. You can complete this work as an individual or a small team. The enterprise knowledge portal team will need additional human expertise from a small community of knowledge experts with a broad and deep understanding of your organization. The enterprise knowledge portal team and the knowledge expert community will work together to complete several templates designed to give you an overview of where you are today. The template collection is used to map your knowledge management objectives into the enterprise portal features and functions and will provide the details needed to outline a logical path forward to implement your enterprise knowledge portal. This information will feed into the enterprise knowledge portal program included in Part II of this book. The program will formally outline the plan to implement your enterprise knowledge portal. The enterprise activities and deliverables to determine what an enterprise knowledge portal will need to do to meet your organization's knowledge objectives are presented in Figure 3-1 and covered in detail throughout the remaining sections.

MyCompany Case Study Introduction

MyCompany is a case study of a fictitious consulting organization that provides information technology services to other companies. It is a company dedicated to matching successful, talented, proven chief information officer and chief technology officer skills with your need to capitalize on information technology. MyCompany brings the technology expertise to turn your business initiatives and supporting strategies from a vision to a reality. The services offered range from a review of your current information technology architecture and infrastructure environment to contracting a CIO or CTO to work in your organization to design, architect, and implement enhancements to the existing information technology environment.

MyCompany has established a knowledge management initiative to improve all aspects of what they do and how they do it. They have reviewed the organization and have decided to focus on a complete set of knowledge management objectives. They are going to identify these objectives from every aspect of their organization and prioritize at least one or two objectives from each category to implement in the first phase of their knowledge management initiative. The initial effort will be to gain some perspective of the myCompany organization and use this information to create an enterprise knowledge portal program. The enterprise knowledge portal program will be implemented as a combined series of application development projects and infrastructure projects. They realize that the appropriate organization governance, change management effort, methodology, measurements, technical architecture, and support services will need to be established as part of a successful enterprise knowledge portal program.

The first set of activities will be to create an overview of myCompany by mapping their knowledge management objectives into an enterprise portal. They are going to complete the following activities:

Figure 3-1. Enterprise knowledge portal map activities and deliverables.

Activities	Deliverables
Document Your Knowledge Management Objectives	• Organization Mission and Initiatives Questionnaire (Optional) • Knowledge Management Objectives Questionnaire ▪ Be Organized Around Work Processes Section ▪ Maintain Knowledge and Facilitate Communication Section ▪ Focus on the Future Section ▪ Support Your Organization's Business Objectives Section ▪ Promote Innovations Section ▪ Maintain a Knowledge-Creating Organization Section • Knowledge Management Objectives Template ▪ Summarize Results of the Knowledge Management Objectives Questionnaire
Enterprise Knowledge Portal IT–Enabling Framework	• Enterprise Knowledge Portal IT–Enabling Framework Template ▪ Identify Primary Enterprise Knowledge Portal Technologies ▪ Add Features to the Enterprise Knowledge Portal Technologies ▪ Document Existing Applications, Systems, and Services • Enterprise Knowledge Portal IT–Enabling Framework Spreadsheet ▪ Spreadsheet Format of the Enterprise Knowledge Portal IT–Enabling Framework Content
Enterprise Knowledge Portal Map	• Enterprise Knowledge Portal Map Template ▪ Add Knowledge Management Objectives ▪ Add Enterprise Knowledge Portal IT–Enabling Framework ▪ Prioritize Knowledge Management Objectives ▪ Prioritize Enterprise Knowledge Portal Features

- ❒ Research the enterprise portal market.
- ❒ Document the myCompany knowledge management objectives.
- ❒ Document the myCompany enterprise knowledge portal IT-enabling framework.
- ❒ Document the myCompany enterprise knowledge portal map.

Enterprise Portal Market Overview

The enterprise portal market grew out of the need to mainstream information on the Internet. Users became confused and frustrated trying to navigate through the vast number of Web pages and information available on Internet sites. Companies like Yahoo and AOL became popular search sites that also had the ability to guide users to specific Internet destinations. The next generation of these Internet solutions provided personalization to users by allowing them to configure hyperlinks to their favorite news sites, stock market information, sports teams, weather, and local content sites. Additional functionality like instant messaging, community groups, family picture galleries, and free e-mail have created virtual home pages for users to organize their personal electronic lives.

Your organization is looking to the enterprise portal to deliver the same type of organization and centralization of company resources and information launched from an employee home page. The current enterprise portal software vendors offer a collection of several features and functions that work together to provide the benefits your organization is expecting in the enterprise knowledge portal solution. There are a lot of products and vendors in the business intelligence, enterprise resource planning (ERP), document management, search engine, and other markets that partially fill our definition of an enterprise knowledge portal. A review of the enterprise portal market segment identifies at least nine different types of Web-based applications that have labeled themselves enterprise portal solutions. A collection of these enterprise portal market segments must be combined to match our definition of a complete enterprise knowledge portal solution. Your organization will want to consider an enterprise portal software solution to facilitate the implementation of a scalable enterprise knowledge portal. The relationship of these portal market segments outlined to match our enterprise portal definition is diagrammed in Figure 3-2.

Your organization should look for enterprise portal vendors that provide a framework based on application servers and integration services with the best combination of features, performance, and reliability. The long-term strategy is to establish a common enterprise knowledge portal infrastructure to support your knowledge management business objectives. The relationship between the enterprise portal solution, knowledge management

Figure 3-2. Enterprise portal market segments.

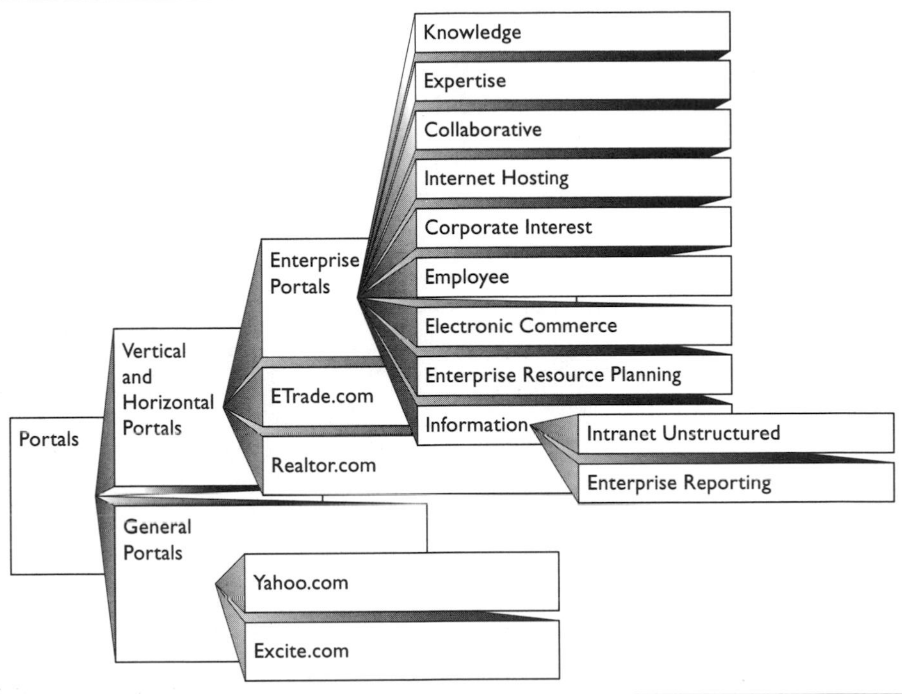

objectives, and the enterprise knowledge portal market are outlined in Figure 3-3. A listing of leading portal vendors and types of portal products they offer is presented in Figure 3-4. There are several vendors that offer products with portal features that provide stand-alone services or as functionality in a larger portal architecture. Several of these vendors and the services they offer are listed in Figure 3-5.

Understanding the overlap of technologies available in the enterprise portal market with technologies in the business intelligence, content management, collaboration, knowledge management, learning, and many other markets is useful. How these vendors and products design, architect, and support all of this functionality is often unique and very different. In most cases you want to minimize or standardize on the number of products that are providing the same functionality to users in your organization. At the same time it is true that business objectives can be unique enough that two or three different software solutions in the same category of technologies can be required. For example, there are personal and workgroup document management requirements as well as sophisticated ISO9000 document management requirements that must be addressed. Using the same document management solution for these very different user requirements might be difficult, complicated, and expensive. A high-functionality

(text continues on page 86)

Figure 3-3. Enterprise portal considerations.

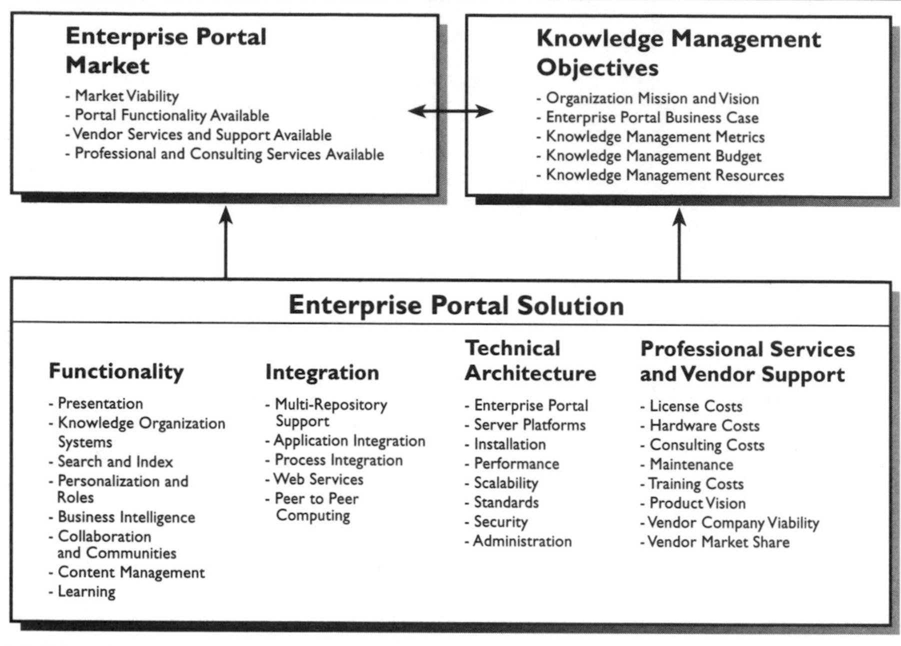

Figure 3-4. Leading portal vendors and their product offerings.

Portal Products—Portal Server–Based Architecture	
Vendor	**Products**
Brio	Brio.Portal
BroadVision	BroadVision One-To-One
Corechange	Coreport
DataChannel	DataChannel Server
Epicentric	Portal Server
Hummingbird	Enterprise Information Portal
Plumtree	Plumtree Corporate Portal
Viador	Viador E-Portal
Vignette	V/5

Figure 3-5. Leading supporting product vendors and their offerings.

Supporting Products—Application Server–Based Architecture	
Vendor	**Supporting Products**
2Bridge	Content Management (categorization, search)
Allaire	Content Management Personalization Multiple Language Runtime
ATG	Personalization
Autonomy	Content Management (categorization)
Aventail	Application Access
BEA	Content Management Integration
Business Objects	Business Intelligence (reporting, data access)
Eureka (CA)	Business Intelligence (reporting, data access)
Citrix NFuse	Application Integration
Corporate Yahoo	Content Syndication
Documentum	Content Management (document life cycle)
Eprise	Content Management (personalization)
IBM	Application and Integration Services
IntraNet Solutions	Content Management (document life cycle)
Iona	Application Access
Microsoft (SharePoint)	Content Management (categorization, search)
MicroStrategy	Business Intelligence (reporting, data access)
Oracle	Presentation
Neon	Application Access
SAP (SAP Portals)	Business Intelligence (reporting, data access) Content Management Integration
Semio	Content Management (categorization)
Sun (iPlanet)	Collaboration Application Integration Solaris Only
Sybase	External Portal
Tibco	Application Access
Verity	Content Management (search)

document management solution will be more expensive to deploy and support, and will require training for features that are not needed by workgroups to meet their document management requirements. In this case, providing two document management solutions in the organization might be the best solution. Your enterprise knowledge portal infrastructure will want to standardize on as few duplicate technologies as necessary to provide the complete range of functionality users will need.

Determining the right vendor and products to get started on your enterprise knowledge portal is complicated. The most effective approach is to consider the enterprise knowledge portal features and functions separate from the vendors and products, map the functionality needed to your knowledge management objectives, and create a request for proposal to enterprise portal vendors. Vendors will be able to demonstrate their proposed enterprise portal design and architecture that will be able to deliver the enterprise knowledge portal functionality you need, taking full advantage of the technologies that currently exist in your organization.

Document Your Knowledge Management Objectives

Take some time to review your organization's mission statement and top initiatives. Review the change management plans associated with your top initiatives to review what differences in culture and behavior you are trying to achieve. This information will help you realize the three or four most important programs that all employees are supposed to think about and support as they do their jobs. Knowledge workers and their work processes, managers and their effort to find resources and optimize work processes, executives and their effort to prioritize current and future work, all need to function together. You will want to create or review your knowledge management objectives to make sure they target all aspects of your organization and tie into your top initiatives. We all need to have a better way to locate, learn, capture, and reuse. Using our knowledge management categories from Chapter 1 to consider the entire organization, the following steps are completed:

1. *Understand your organization's mission and initiatives*. Review your organization's mission statement, top initiatives, and business drivers. Make sure you understand the business strategies and programs created to support these initiatives. As you outline your knowledge management objectives you want to tie them into these business strategies and programs where possible.
2. *Create a knowledge management objectives questionnaire.* Use the categories defined in Chapter 1 or identify four to eight unique knowl-

edge management categories that encompass all aspects of your organization. Compile a document with several questions in each of these categories to address knowledge management objectives across your entire organization. The questions provided here are specific to the knowledge management definition in this book. If necessary, you will want to modify the questions created in the steps below to match your unique categories.

3. *Identify a knowledge expert community.* Identify knowledge workers in your organization with a broad understanding of how work gets done. Work with these knowledge workers to complete the knowledge management objectives questionnaire. Look for ways to discuss the value of adding locate, learn, capture, and reuse activities into improving how work gets done.
4. *Schedule interviews with the knowledge expert community.* Schedule interviews with your knowledge experts and review or complete the questionnaire. This research will allow you to prioritize the knowledge management objectives in each category. Keeping the top knowledge management objectives in each category will give you enough information to know where to focus your efforts as you move forward with an enterprise knowledge portal.
5. *Complete the knowledge management objectives template.* Summarize your interview results into the knowledge management objectives template using the categories that you defined for your organization.

Understand Your Organization's Mission and Initiatives

Purpose: Review your organization's mission statement, top initiatives, and business drivers. Make sure you understand the business strategies and programs created to support these initiatives. As you outline your knowledge management objectives, you want to tie them into these business strategies and programs where possible.

There are several sources of information in your organization to learn about current initiatives. Look at the intranet for information regarding your organization's vision and mission. Review the latest planning, budgeting, and forecasting information to review the business strategies and supporting programs that are being funded as ongoing or new activities in the budget. Talk to the business units that are leading the different programs to learn more about the details and begin to understand the relationships between the individual efforts.

Review the questions outlined in Chapter 1. Consider compiling the questions into a single document as a way to survey the leaders or team members of the initiatives in your organization. You should consider this an optional activity. If you need a greater depth of knowledge about your company, this activity will give you some perspective on the impact of individual corporate initiatives on different aspects of the organization. The research you complete will provide you the background and information needed to infer details about your organization into the remaining steps to outline your knowledge management objectives and map them into a complete enterprise knowledge portal solution.

MYCOMPANY CASE STUDY

As part of myCompany's knowledge management initiative, a small three-person team has been formed to evaluate an enterprise knowledge portal as a program. The enterprise knowledge portal team consists of a business analyst, a systems analyst, and a project manager. To get started the team is reviewing myCompany's mission statement, top initiatives, and business drivers. The team wants to gain a clear understanding of the business strategies and programs created to support these initiatives. The goal is to tie their knowledge management objectives into these business strategies and programs where possible. An organization mission and initiatives questionnaire has been created and will be completed by the enterprise knowledge portal team as they complete their research of myCompany's initiatives and can be referenced in Figure 3-6.

The enterprise knowledge portal team has reviewed the latest planning, budgeting, and forecasting information and several business strategies and supporting programs that are being funded as ongoing or new activities in the budget. Several phone conversations and demonstrations have been conducted with the business units that are leading the different programs to learn more about the details and begin to understand the relationships between the individual efforts. The results of their work are displayed in Figure 3-7 as a completed organization mission and initiatives report.

Create a Knowledge Management Objectives Questionnaire

Purpose: Use the categories defined in Chapter 1 or identify four to eight unique knowledge management categories that encompass all aspects of your organization. Compile a document with several questions in each of these categories to address knowledge management objectives across your entire organization. The questions provided here are specific to the knowledge management definition in this book. If necessary, you will want to modify the questions created in the steps below to match your unique categories.

You are using these leading questions to find out what is the most frus-

(text continues on page 94)

Figure 3-6. Organization mission and initiatives questionnaire.

To: Knowledge Expert Community

From: Enterprise Knowledge Portal Team

Re: Understanding Corporate Mission and Initiatives

How to Use This Questionnaire

Review the questions here to discuss the organization's mission and initiatives with knowledge expert community members to gain a clear understanding of strategic efforts and how they are perceived throughout the organization. This information will be used as a starting point to define what an enterprise knowledge portal will need to deliver. The questions contained here are organized in several sections to review different aspects of the organization and how current initiatives affect different groups of people. Consider reducing the number of questions contained in each section to focus these interviews to the most relevant discussion points of the organization.

Section One: Be Organized Around Work Processes

1. Do knowledge workers and managers follow a consistent work process where common goals are defined? Are major areas of responsibility in terms of expected results outlined?

2. Do business units have defined measures as guides for assessing their overall performance? Do individual knowledge workers have defined measures for their contribution to the business units' metrics?

3. Do knowledge workers and managers understand the results to be accomplished? Do these objectives tie into the organization's mission or purpose?

4. Do the performance metrics of the individual business units support and complement each other?

5. Are success indicators or change measurements for accomplishments understood? Are quantity, quality, time, and cost represented in these measurements?

(continues)

Figure 3-6. (Continued).

6. Are work processes and other defined activities by knowledge workers and managers well defined and understood?

7. Are the resources or other requirements and equipment needed to do work available for knowledge workers and managers when they need them?

8. Are accomplishments or the outcome of the work process efforts by knowledge workers and managers well defined and understood?

Section Two: Maintain Knowledge and Facilitate Communication

1. What were the results of the performance metrics evaluation of your current work processes?

2. What is the analysis process to determine what future work processes and performance metrics should be?

3. Did you accomplish your defined objectives for the organization? For individual knowledge workers and managers?

4. Who was responsible and accountable for the defined objectives? How were these managers and knowledge workers rewarded?

5. How were the defined objectives for the organization met? For individual knowledge workers and managers?

6. How is continuous improvement built into work processes?

7. What changes will be implemented to work processes for managers and knowledge workers?

Section Three: Focus on the Future

1. Does your organization have a plan for identifying future opportunities and incorporating them into the planning and forecasting of work processes?

2. Do you have checkpoints for monitoring work in progress and using that information to plan for future programs, products, and projects?

3. Does your organization have a clear understanding of the work being done by your collective business units?

4. Does your organization grasp the issues involved in making changes in existing work processes?

5. Does your organization meet their assigned performance metrics?

6. Do business units successfully coordinate shared work responsibilities?

7. Do any business units indicate excessive complaints, serious schedule overruns, or other quality and performance issues?

(continues)

Figure 3-6. (Continued).

8. Does your organization have recent unexplainable crises?

9. Do you have resources with the appropriate skills to continue to maintain the business as knowledge workers change positions or leave the organization?

10. Can your organization accurately evaluate their potential and limitations?

Section Four: Support Your Organization's Business Objectives

1. Does your chief executive officer (CEO) and top management have the appropriate commitment to communicating and enforcing your organization's mission and objectives?

2. Does your organization set objectives autocratically or participatively?

3. Do you successfully negotiate on acceptable ranges for performance metrics between managers and knowledge workers?

4. Does management explain to knowledge workers the full responsibility of their assigned performance metrics and necessary resources?

5. Does your organization use performance-based metrics as a management system for decision making and problem solving?

6. Does your organization experience any resistance at different or lower levels of management?

7. Does your organization fear that at different or lower management levels performance-based metrics will jeopardize existing management information systems or at least not be compatible with existing operational data?

8. Does your organization have a plan to introduce performance-based metrics? What is the time frame and effort anticipated?

9. Is a performance-based metrics program supported at all levels of management and with all knowledge workers?

10. Is there an appropriate amount of training opportunities, feedback, reviews, and commensurate compensation in your organization?

Section Five: Promote Innovations

1. Do you encourage managers and knowledge workers to be self-starters?

2. Do your managers and knowledge workers plan for "what if" scenarios?

3. Do knowledge workers give their best efforts every day?

4. Are managers and knowledge workers allowed to determine what is best and then implement the changes?

5. Are managers and knowledge workers empowered to make their own decisions?

(continues)

Figure 3-6. (Continued).

Section Six: Maintain a Knowledge-Creating Organization

1. Does your organization support ideas and negotiate for results?

2. Does your organization plan before doing?

3. Do you have a mentoring organization?

4. Are your managers and knowledge workers self-disciplined?

5. Does your organization have a good balance between building and maintaining?

trating part of getting work done in your organization. It might be different from one business unit to another. Work might be well understood in one business unit but becomes difficult to complete tasks when working on cross-functional teams with individuals from several different business units. Because the enterprise knowledge portal is designed to be a solution for your entire organization, look for consistent problems and issues as your highest priority knowledge management objectives.

Be Organized Around Work Processes Section

Add the knowledge management objectives that focus on the functions of employees and the defined activities they perform throughout all levels of your organizations. Concentrate on objectives for knowledge workers, their individual roles, skills, and knowledge base that will improve work processes for the general knowledge and performance of the organization. Your knowledge management objectives that will be organized around work processes will focus on employees and the work they are responsible for. You might find that breaking down these issues into two groups will

(text continues on page 98)

Figure 3-7. Organization mission and initiatives report.

To: Knowledge Expert Community

From: Enterprise Knowledge Portal Team

Re: Corporate Mission and Initiatives Summary

Executive Summary

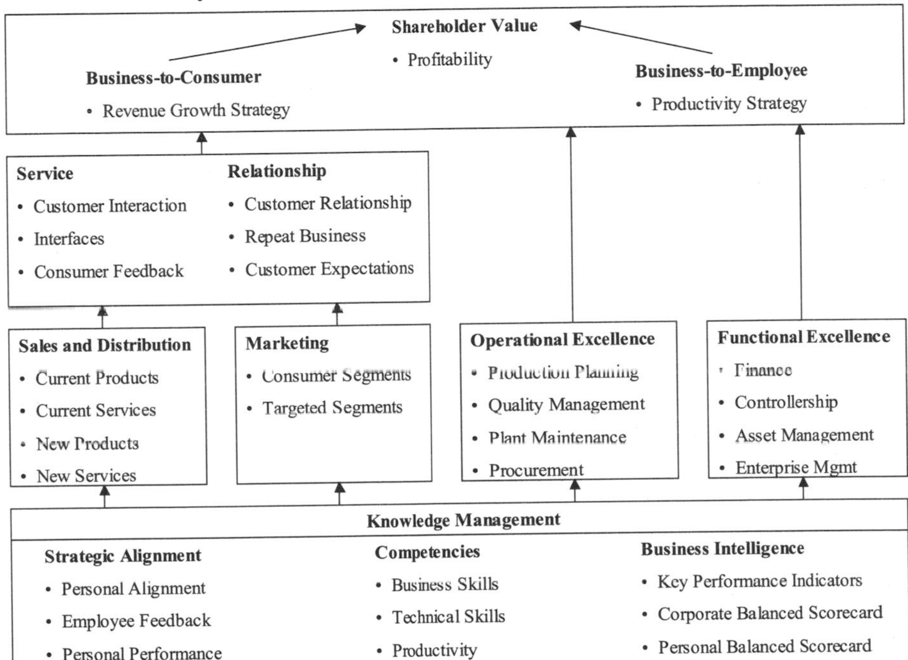

There are several corporate initiatives at myCompany. There are business-to-employee efforts to support strategic alignment, competencies, and business intelligence. Knowledge management activities are used pervasively to enhance how employees relate and interact with myCompany. Initiatives to improve work processes in sales and distribution, marketing, operational excellence, and functional excellence are central to the future success. In addition, work process improvements for customer services and customer relationships are critical to the business strategy. The current initiatives that are central to revenue growth and improving productivity have the highest priority at myCompany. There are three corporate initiatives:

- Work process improvements
- Business-to-employee opportunities
- Business-to-consumer opportunities

(continues)

Figure 3-7. (Continued).

Section One: Be Organized Around Work Processes

The work process initiatives are focused in six categories at myCompany. There are specific subcategories of work processes that have been targeted for continuous improvement in each category. These include:

- Sales and distribution
  - ➢ Current products and services
  - ➢ New products and services
- Marketing
  - ➢ Understanding consumer segments
  - ➢ Improving share of target segments
- Operational excellence
  - ➢ Production planning
  - ➢ Quality management
  - ➢ Plant maintenance
  - ➢ Optimization
  - ➢ Material management
  - ➢ Procurement
- Functional excellence
  - ➢ Finance
  - ➢ Controllership
  - ➢ Asset management
  - ➢ Enterprise management
- Service
  - ➢ Customer interaction
  - ➢ Interfaces
  - ➢ Consumer feedback
- Relationship
  - ➢ Customer relationship management
  - ➢ Repeat business
  - ➢ Customer expectations

Section Two: Maintain Knowledge and Facilitate Communication

For the work process categories and subcategories targeted, management is reviewing how work is done. These work processes are documented, and redundancies, confusion, and other opportunities to optimize work are analyzed. There are three focus areas with specific opportunities for improvement in each work process that are used in the analysis process. These include:

- Capture
  - ➢ Business decisions
  - ➢ Opportunities
  - ➢ Best practices

- Subscribe To
  - ➢ Performance-based metrics
  - ➢ Analysis
  - ➢ Topics of interest
- Collaborate
  - ➢ Locate and reuse work
  - ➢ Document results
  - ➢ Join communities

Section Three: Focus on the Future

The business strategy concentrates on revenue growth and productivity to achieve greater shareholder value and profitability. The strategic efforts to improve work process, maintain knowledge, and facilitate communication are organized into three categories to evaluate which work process effort to concentrate improvements in. These include:

- Shareholder value
  - ➢ Profitability
- Business-to-consumer (revenue growth strategy)
  - ➢ Service
  - ➢ Relationship
  - ➢ Sales and distribution
  - ➢ Marketing
- Business-to-employee (productivity strategy)
  - ➢ Operational excellence
  - ➢ Functional excellence

Section Four: Support Your Organization's Business Objectives

The focus on initiatives to support myCompany's business objectives is aligned with the business-to-employee opportunity. These knowledge management opportunities are to improve strategic alignment of employees to the business strategy. Current efforts are focused on:

- Personal awareness
- Personal alignment
- Employee feedback
- Personal performance

Section Five: Promote Innovations

Another business-to-employee opportunity is the focus on initiatives to promote innovations. The effort is around employee competencies, retention, and career development. The focus is to identify and optimize:

- Business skills
- Technical skills
- Productivity

(continues)

Figure 3-7. (Continued).

Section Six: Maintain a Knowledge-Creating Organization

To maintain a knowledge-creating organization, there is a business intelligence effort tied to business-to-employee opportunities. The goal is to establish measurements that will easily demonstrate progress in the work process improvement initiatives. The focus is to define and promote:

- Key performance indicators
- Corporate balanced scorecard
- Personal balanced scorecard

create additional value in future activities to design the enterprise knowledge portal. If this is the case, then subcategorize objectives in one group for employees and a second group for their work processes. Consider the following questions for the Be Organized Around Work Processes section of the questionnaire:

- ☐ How effective are employees at their jobs? What would you do to make them more effective?
- ☐ What types of decisions do employees make? Are they consistent, accurate, and timely? What would be the value of employees making better decisions faster?
- ☐ How easy is it for employees to find the information they need to do their jobs? Do they know what information they need? What makes it difficult to find?
- ☐ Look at one or two work processes in detail. What is the time it takes to complete one cycle? Where are the inefficiencies? What would be the benefits of completing the process in less time, with fewer resources, and more cost-effectively?
- ☐ In these work processes, where are their deficiencies in locating, learning, capturing, and sharing information? Can they be integrated or included as part of the work processes? How much insight would the individual employees involved in the work processes gain if knowledge management activities were part of the work processes?
- ☐ What would be the improvement in response times if knowledge management activities were integrated into work processes?
- ☐ How can work and ideas captured as part of knowledge management activities integrated into your work processes be reused? Will the information captured in this one work process benefit other business units, teams, or work processes?

Maintain Knowledge and Facilitate Communication Section

Add the knowledge management objectives that define consistency and coordinate work processes throughout your organization. Outline objectives that relate to management standards, guidelines, priorities, best practices, and the audit as well as quality of your management standards. Improving communication throughout your managers in your organization might provide significant value. There are opportunities to improve adherence to standards, create better alignment of business objectives between business units, and create more effective communication channels and relationships between managers. There are two subcategories of objectives included here, one group for management and a second group for auditing the success of individual business units. Consider the following questions for the Maintain Knowledge and Facilitate Communication section of the questionnaire:

- ☐ Are management objectives aligned in the organization? Are management objectives aligned in your business unit? Would more formal communication between managers be beneficial? How do managers collaborate? Do you have any suggestions on how to increase and improve collaboration between managers?
- ☐ Do employees throughout the company know the responsibilities of knowledge experts and managers in the organization? What about your business unit? Are knowledge experts and managers easy to find and get a response from?
- ☐ Are business units accountable for the organization's success? Do managers understand and share budgets, financial information, internal control, quality, and safety standards?
- ☐ How can the span of influence for knowledge experts and managers be expanded?
- ☐ How can improved access to knowledge experts and managers improve operational efficiencies? How can improved communications between managers improve operational efficiencies?

Focus on the Future Section

Add the knowledge management objectives that concentrate on understanding the market, process innovation, recruitment, and planning and forecasting to maintain viability and implement new initiatives. These objectives are designed to create shorter product cycles, manage intellectual capital, and should include how your organization will be differentiated from your competitors. Depending on the complexity of your organization, you might consider two subcategories of questions, one for strategy and vision and a second for planning and forecasting. Consider the following questions for the Focus on the Future section of the questionnaire:

- ☐ How effective are current business strategies that support market knowledge? How can they be improved?

- ☐ How effective are current business strategies that support work process innovation? How can they be improved?
- ☐ How do we continue to support and improve product innovation? How can they be improved?
- ☐ How effective are current business strategies that support recruitment and succession? How can they be improved?
- ☐ How effective are new initiatives at meeting the corporate mission? Are improvements needed in the planning, budgeting, and forecasting work processes? How can they be improved?
- ☐ What is the current e-business strategy? Is it important to provide a browser-based work environment for employees, customers, vendors, and suppliers? How should we continue to emerge the intranet, extranet, and Internet?

Support Your Organization's Business Objectives Section

Add the knowledge management objectives that are designed to modify the culture and behavior of your organization. To meet your organization's mission and vision, focus on setting context and building and maintaining identity coherence in support of your top initiatives and enterprise strategies. Consider the following questions for the Support Your Organization's Business Objectives section of the questionnaire:

- ☐ Do employees and managers have a clear understanding of the organization's business objectives? Is there synergy at all levels of the organization around the organization's business objectives? How can understanding and synergy around the organization's business objectives be improved?
- ☐ How do employees and managers learn about new and existing enterprise strategies? How do we integrate learning and accomplishing enterprise strategies into work processes?
- ☐ In addition to integrating enterprise strategies into work processes, what else can be done to drive business value?

Promote Innovations Section

Add the knowledge management objectives to improve human capital in your organization. Concentrate on where your organization can turn information into knowledge to directly impact career and personal goals, network affiliation, personal relationships, team membership, and civic and occupational affiliations. Positive results and efficiencies can be gained from skill improvement opportunities, career opportunities, work life improvements, and human resource–related improvements. Consider the following questions for the Promote Innovations section of the questionnaire:

- ☐ Do employees and managers feel enriched by their work throughout the organization? What about your business unit?
- ☐ Are the career development opportunities available in the organization effective? What about your business unit?
- ☐ How autonomously are individuals and teams able to function in the organization? How can this be improved?
- ☐ How involved is the organization in community activities? What about individuals? Does community involvement add business value for the organization? Does community involvement improve the work-life benefits of employees?

Maintain a Knowledge-Creating Organization Section

Add the knowledge management objectives that bring continuous learning and improvement into work processes, management best practices, strategy, planning, vision, change management, and human resources activities. These objectives are designed to capture and deliver online information in a variety of formats to meet the needs of managers, employees, clients, customers, and suppliers. Consider the following questions for the Maintain a Knowledge-Creating Organization section of the questionnaire:

- ☐ Do you have a well-understood business strategy to create a Web-based working environment? Do you have a well-understood e-business strategy? What would be the business value?
- ☐ What are the benefits of creating a consistent categorization scheme for content in the organization? What about your business unit?
- ☐ What are the benefits of being able to search across the organization to locate information? What about your business unit?
- ☐ Are there advantages to bringing content, applications, and services throughout your organization into a single user interface? Are there additional benefits by allowing users to personalize the user interface to the way individuals work?
- ☐ Do a wide range of internal and external information sources need to work together, interact with each other, and provide the appropriate context to users?

MYCOMPANY CASE STUDY

The enterprise knowledge portal team has defined six unique knowledge management categories that encompass all aspects of

the organization. Using the six knowledge management categories as a way to group questions, the knowledge management objectives questionnaire has been created. An example of the questionnaire can be seen in Figure 3-8.

Identify a Knowledge Expert Community

Purpose: Identify knowledge workers in your organization with a broad understanding of how work gets done. Work with these knowledge workers to complete the knowledge management objectives questionnaire. Look for ways to discuss the value of adding locate, learn, capture, and reuse activities into improving how work gets done.

Selecting the knowledge expert community as a group of subject matter experts is critical to a successful enterprise knowledge portal. Consider establishing the membership out of the business unit leaders identified from your research in step one. Establish the knowledge expert community as a short-term team to establish and prioritize your knowledge management objectives, identify the enterprise portal features and functions that would add the most business value to their existing business initiatives, and support establishing an enterprise knowledge portal solution for your organization. Once these initial activities are complete and you are moving forward with an enterprise knowledge portal, a long-term knowledge expert community will be established to work on future activities and tasks. The short-term knowledge expert community will work with you to:

- ❒ Complete the knowledge management objectives questionnaire
- ❒ Review the summarized knowledge management objectives
- ❒ Review the technologies summarized in the enterprise knowledge portal IT–enabling framework
- ❒ Review your knowledge management objectives and available enterprise portal technologies combined in the enterprise knowledge portal map
- ❒ Make the decision on whether or not to continue to move forward with the enterprise knowledge portal solution

MYCOMPANY CASE STUDY

The enterprise knowledge portal team has recruited the short-term knowledge expert community in one-on-one conversations with corporate initiative leaders. The knowledge enterprise portal concepts and possible opportunities were discussed briefly. Each cor-

(text continues on page 107)

Figure 3-8. Knowledge management objectives questionnaire.

To: Knowledge Expert Community

From: Enterprise Knowledge Portal Team

Re: Understanding Knowledge Management Objectives

How to Use This Questionnaire

Review the questions here to discuss the organization's knowledge management objectives with knowledge expert community members to gain a clear understanding of the current efforts to locate, learn, capture, and reuse. This information will be used as a starting point to define what an enterprise knowledge portal will need to achieve. The questions contained here are organized in several sections to review different aspects of the organization and how current knowledge management efforts affect different groups of people. Consider reducing the number of questions contained in each section to focus these interviews to the most relevant discussion points of the organization.

Section One: Be Organized Around Work Processes

1. How effective are employees at their jobs? What would you do to make them more effective?

2. What types of decisions do employees make? Are they consistent, accurate, and timely? What would be the value of employees making better decisions faster?

3. How easy is it for employees to find the information they need to do their jobs? Do they know what information they need? What makes it difficult to find?

4. Look at one or two work processes in detail. What is the time it takes to complete one cycle? Where are the inefficiencies? What would be the benefits of completing the process in less time, with fewer resources, and more cost-effectively?

(continues)

Figure 3-8. (Continued).

5. In these work processes, where are their deficiencies in locating, learning, capturing, and sharing information? Can they be integrated or included as part of the work processes? How much insight would the individual employees involved in the work processes gain if knowledge management activities were part of the work processes?

6. What would be the improvement in response times if knowledge management activities were integrated into work processes?

7. How can work and ideas captured as part of knowledge management activities integrated into your work processes be reused? Will the information captured in this one work process benefit other business units, teams, or work processes?

Section Two: Maintain Knowledge and Facilitate Communication

1. Are management objectives aligned in the organization? Are management objectives aligned in your business unit? Would more formal communication between managers be beneficial? How do managers collaborate? Do you have any suggestions on how to increase and improve collaboration between managers?

2. Do employees throughout the company know the responsibilities of knowledge experts and managers in the organization? What about your business unit? Are knowledge experts and managers easy to find and get a response from?

3. Are business units accountable for the organization's success? Do managers understand and share budgets, financial information, internal control, quality, and safety standards?

4. How can the span of influence for knowledge experts and managers be expanded?

5. How can improved access to knowledge experts and managers improve operational efficiencies? How can improved communications between managers improve operational efficiencies?

Section Three: Focus on the Future

1. How effective are current business strategies that support market knowledge? How can they be improved?

2. How effective are current business strategies that support work process innovation? How can they be improved?

3. How do we continue to support and improve product innovation? How can they be improved?

4. How effective are current business strategies that support recruitment and succession? How can they be improved?

5. How effective are new initiatives at meeting the corporate mission? Are improvements needed in the planning, budgeting, and forecasting work processes? How can they be improved?

6. What is the current e-business strategy? Is it important to provide a browser-based work environment for employees, customers, vendors, and suppliers? How should we continue to emerge the intranet, extranet, and Internet?

(continues)

Figure 3-8. (Continued).

Section Four: Support Your Organization's Business Objectives

1. Do employees and managers have a clear understanding of the organization's business objectives? Is there synergy at all levels of the organization around the organization's business objectives? How can understanding and synergy around the organization's business objectives be improved?

2. How do employees and managers learn about new and existing enterprise strategies? How do we integrate learning and accomplishing enterprise strategies into work processes?

3. In addition to integrating enterprise strategies into work processes, what else can be done to drive business value?

Section Five: Promote Innovations

1. Do employees and managers feel enriched by their work throughout the organization? What about your business unit?

2. Are the career development opportunities available in the organization effective? What about your business unit?

3. How autonomously are individuals and teams able to function in the organization? How can this be improved?

4. How involved is the organization in community activities? What about individuals? Does community involvement add business value for the organization? Does community involvement improve the work-life benefits of employees?

Section Six: Maintain a Knowledge-Creating Organization

1. Do you have a well-understood business strategy to create a Web-based working environment? Do you have a well-understood e-business strategy? What would be the business value?

2. What are the benefits of creating a consistent categorization scheme for content in the organization? What about your business unit?

3. What are the benefits of being able to search across the organization to locate information? What about your business unit?

4. Are there advantages to bringing content, applications, and services throughout your organization into a single user interface? Are there additional benefits to allowing users to personalize the user interface to the way individuals work?

5. Do a wide range of internal and external information sources need to work together, interact with each other, and provide the appropriate context to users?

---

porate initiative leader selected a member of their team to serve on the knowledge expert community for a total of sixteen to twenty-four hours over a three- to four-week time period. The result of their time will be a clear understanding of how the enterprise knowledge portal will be able to help the organization and their individual business initiatives. Once the knowledge expert community was formed, a welcome letter was sent to the members and their sponsors. A sample welcome letter is available for you to review in Figure 3-9.

Schedule Interviews with the Knowledge Expert Community

Purpose: Schedule interviews with your knowledge experts and review or complete the questionnaire. This research will allow you to prioritize the

Figure 3-9. Knowledge expert community welcome letter.

Re: Welcome Aboard

Welcome Knowledge Expert Community,

I would like to take the time to introduce the **Enterprise Knowledge Portal Map** project to everyone. Your names were collected as the experts throughout myCompany on the topic of knowledge management, strategic thinking, and business strategy. This project is our start or beginning to briefly outline our knowledge management objectives and available enterprise portal technologies. Understanding the needs of all of us is important to create an enterprise knowledge portal recommendation for myCompany, and I know we can grow this solution to meet enterprise needs as we continue to achieve our corporate mission and initiatives. Additionally this effort will give us a chance to discontinue evaluation or prepare to create a long-term enterprise knowledge portal strategy moving forward.

Our goal over the next three to four weeks will be to:

- Complete the knowledge management objectives questionnaire
- Review the summarized knowledge management objectives
- Review the technologies summarized in the enterprise knowledge portal IT–enabling framework
- Review knowledge management objectives and available enterprise portal technologies combined in the enterprise knowledge portal map
- Make the decision on whether or not to continue to move forward with the enterprise knowledge portal solution at myCompany

We will need approximately twenty-four hours of your time over the next few weeks to collect information about your knowledge management objectives, work process improvement, and the functionality or technology you need to use to be successful. You should expect to see a kick-off meeting on your calendars for next week to discuss the project in more detail and get started on our deliverables. Please contact Heidi Collins, Michael Douglas, or David Kennedy if you have questions now or would like to talk about any specific aspects of this current project.

We are excited about learning more about you and your knowledge management needs.

The Enterprise Knowledge Portal Team

---

knowledge management objectives in each category. Keeping the top knowledge management objectives in each category will give you enough information to know where to focus your efforts as you move forward with an enterprise knowledge portal.

Every member of the knowledge expert community will have both a similar and a different perspective on knowledge management objectives for the organization. Your goal is to understand these similarities and differences. To be effective, you need to listen and learn from the knowledge expert community about the organization and their specific initiatives. There are several group and individual activities to complete with your newly formed knowledge expert community. Here are some suggested activities:

❒ Hold a kick-off meeting to introduce the knowledge expert community members to each other and their initiatives, review the technologies that will be used to communicate and share information, discuss the knowledge management objectives questionnaire, and schedule interview times with each of the knowledge expert community members.

❒ Host an enterprise portal overview webcast for the knowledge expert community members and their sponsors. You might work with an enterprise portal vendor to either make the presentation or to copresent with you. This will give you an excellent opportunity to discuss the enterprise knowledge portal and look more closely at a smaller number of vendors that impressed you during your research of the enterprise portal market.

❒ Hold individual interview sessions to complete the knowledge management objectives questionnaire, document the discussions, and post the results for the entire knowledge expert community members to read.

❒ Create a communication to share the highlights of the individual interviews and encourage knowledge expert community members to review details.

MYCOMPANY CASE STUDY

The enterprise knowledge portal team has scheduled interviews with each member of the knowledge expert community to review or complete the questionnaire. The interviews allow the enterprise knowledge portal team to discuss enterprise and business unit knowledge management objectives. Keeping the top knowledge management objectives in each category will give the enterprise knowledge portal team an overview of myCompany that includes enough information to design an enterprise knowledge portal that will impact all aspects of the organization. The activities and tasks completed by the enterprise knowledge portal team included:

❒ A kick-off meeting to introduce the knowledge expert community members and their initiatives to each other, review the technologies that will be used to communicate and share information over the next three to four weeks, discuss the knowledge management objectives questionnaire, and schedule interview times with each of the knowledge expert community members. An example of a meeting invitation and a proposed agenda are presented in Figure 3-10.

- A webcast held for the knowledge expert community members and sponsors to learn, visualize, and ask questions about the enterprise portal. The demonstration was tailored around locating, learning, capturing, and reusing information and human expertise. Highlights from the demonstration are presented in Figure 3-11.
- Individual interview sessions to complete the knowledge management objectives questionnaire, document the discussions, and post the results for the entire knowledge expert community members to read.
- Distributing a communication (shown in Figure 3-12) to members of the knowledge expert community to share the highlights of the individual interviews and encourage individual members to review details.

Complete the Knowledge Management Objectives Template

Purpose: Summarize your interview results into the knowledge management objectives template using the categories that you defined for your organization.

Once all the knowledge expert community interviews are completed,

Figure 3-10. A sample meeting invitation and proposed agenda to the enterprise knowledge portal map kick-off.

Agenda	Enterprise Knowledge Portal Map Kick-Off Conference Room One	
Type of meeting:	Kick-Off Meeting	
Facilitator:	Heidi Collins	
Note taker:	David Kennedy	
Attendees:	Knowledge Expert Community Members	
	Agenda Topics	
15 Minutes	Knowledge Expert Community Members Introduction	Heidi Collins
15 Minutes	Review Project Logistics and Tools	Heidi Collins
20 Minutes	Knowledge Management Objectives Questionnaire Review	Heidi Collins
10 Minutes	Schedule Knowledge Management Objectives Interviews	Heidi Collins

Figure 3-11. Business-to-business enterprise portal demonstration: track order status activity.

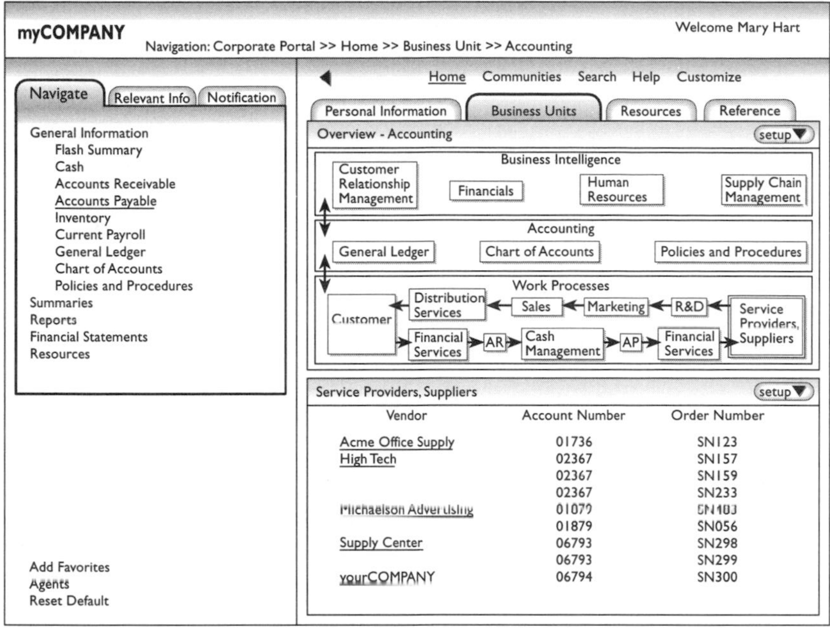

From the overview-accounting content window select service providers, suppliers to review vendors.

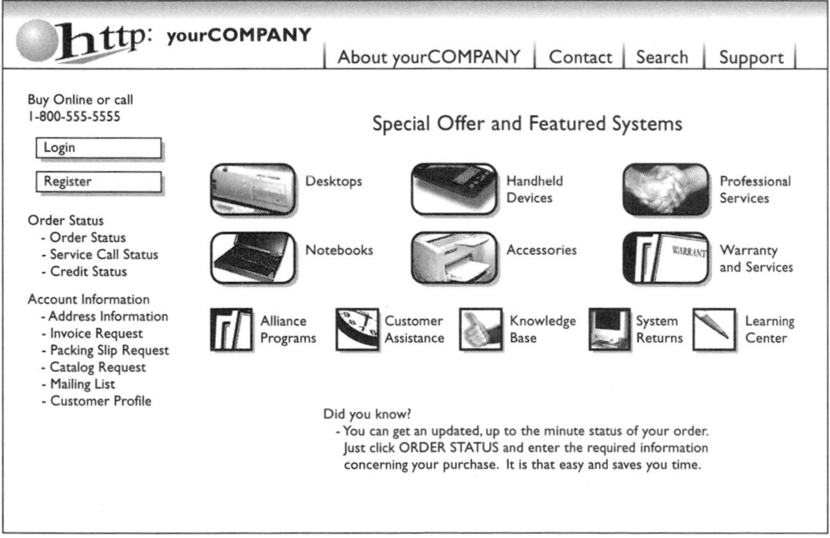

Review myCompany's order with yourCompany in a single click.

Figure 3-12. Knowledge expert community—communication one.

Re: Knowledge Expert Community Interviews Available

Hello Knowledge Expert Community,

We would like to take the time to share the **Knowledge Management Objectives** interview results with you. The **Enterprise Knowledge Portal Team** has started the project and established the deliverables. They continue to monitor that the goals and objectives of the **Enterprise Knowledge Portal Map** project are effectively being delivered on time and in budget. To review any project documents, research material, completed interviews, or other information please visit:
www.myCompany.com/EKP/enterprise_knowledge_portal_map/material

The enterprise knowledge portal team members have completed several individual interviews with the knowledge expert community. This was the most effective approach to collect and understand myCompany's knowledge management objectives. The information collected represents an enterprise sampling of knowledge management objectives across myCompany to plan for the future. Please take the time to review the interviews in detail.

Once the knowledge management objectives interviews are completed, a meeting will be scheduled to review the material followed by a discussion session to answer any questions and provide additional detail. Please attend or send a representative to the knowledge management objectives review meeting. There will be AT&T conference call numbers and a videoconference set up for these sessions for anyone that cannot attend in person.

Please contact Heidi Collins or Michael Douglas if you have questions or need additional information.

---

you will want to summarize the results. The knowledge management objectives template will provide a spreadsheet to document the results of the interviews. To make certain you have a complete set of knowledge management objectives guaranteed to encompass all aspects of your organization, maintain the same categories used in the knowledge management objectives questionnaire. The knowledge management objectives template can be seen in Figure 3-13. The knowledge management categories make up the rows in the spreadsheet. Using the categories outlined in step two, possible knowledge management objectives are included in the spreadsheet. You will want to add, edit, or delete the listed knowledge management objectives based on your interview results. The individual initiatives or business units represented by the knowledge expert community members make up the columns in the spreadsheet. You will want to add, edit, or delete the initiatives or business units to match your knowledge expert community.

The knowledge management objectives report is the result of the completed knowledge management objectives template. You will want to share

Figure 3-13. Knowledge management objectives template.

	Work Process Improvements	Business-to-Employee Opportunities	Business-to-Consumer Opportunities
Be Organized Around Work Processes			
Improve employee effectiveness			
Make better decisions faster			
Improve information availability and access			
Improve cycle times			
Embed knowledge management activities			
Improve response times			
Improve information reuse			
Maintain Knowledge and Facilitate Communication			
Improve communication between managers			
Improve alignment of management objectives			
Improve awareness of roles and responsibilities			
Improve strategic alignment			
Improve span of influence of human expertise			
Improve operational efficiencies through information reuse			
Focus on the Future			
Improve market knowledge business strategy effectiveness			
Improve work process innovation			
Improve product innovation			
Improve recruitment and succession			
Improve planning, budgeting, and forecasting processes			
Improve e-business opportunities and strategies			
Support Your Organization's Business Objectives			
Improve personal alignment to your business strategy			
Embed learning into doing			
Drive business value			
Promote Innovations			
Enrich employee work-life experience			
Improve career development opportunities			
Improve employee autonomy			
Improve community involvement			
Maintain a Knowledge-Creating Organization			
Improve Web-centric business strategy			
Improve content management			
Improve enterprise search			
Improve user interface and usability consistency			
Improve cross-functional work processes			

and review the results with the knowledge expert community. During this review you will be teaching as much as sharing information as you walk through the knowledge management objectives report. To teach and share the results effectively, you should consider bringing the knowledge expert community together in a meeting format. Create a supporting presentation to accompany the knowledge management objectives report. You will want to have an open discussion of the summarized knowledge management objectives and make any adjustments agreed on by the knowledge expert community to create the final version of the knowledge management objectives report.

MYCOMPANY CASE STUDY

The knowledge management objectives report has been created using the six categories outlined in the knowledge management objectives questionnaire. The final activities completed by the enterprise knowledge portal team to define the knowledge management objectives for myCompany included:

- ❒ Summarizing the interview results from the enterprise knowledge experts into the knowledge management objectives template creating the knowledge management objectives report. This first release of the knowledge management objectives report is shown in Figure 3-14.
- ❒ Creating a supporting presentation to accompany and explain the summarized results. The knowledge management objectives report review presentation can be reviewed in Figure 3-15.
- ❒ Holding a review meeting to discuss and clarify the results of knowledge management objectives report. An example meeting invitation and a proposed agenda are presented in Figure 3-16.
- ❒ Completing the final version of the knowledge management objectives report as a result of the review meeting. It can be seen in Figure 3-17.
- ❒ Distributing a communication (shown in Figure 3-18) to members of the knowledge expert community to share the final version of the knowledge management objectives report and encourage individual members to review details with their business units.

Enterprise Knowledge Portal IT–Enabling Framework

With the definition of the enterprise portal from Chapter 2 and an overview of the enterprise portal market, you can begin to outline the enterprise

Figure 3-14. Knowledge management objectives report (first release).

	Work Process Improvements	Business-to-Employee Opportunities	Business-to-Consumer Opportunities
Be Organized Around Work Processes			
Improve employee effectiveness	x	x	
Make better decisions faster	x	x	x
Improve information availability and access	x	x	x
Improve cycle times	x		
Embed knowledge management activities	x	x	x
Improve response times	x	x	x
Improve information reuse	x	x	
Maintain Knowledge and Facilitate Communication			
Improve communication between managers	x	x	
Improve alignment of management objectives	x	x	
Improve awareness of roles and responsibilities	x	x	x
Improve strategic alignment	x	x	x
Improve span of influence of human expertise		x	x
Improve operational efficiencies through information reuse	x	x	
Focus on the Future			
Improve market knowledge business strategy effectiveness	x		x
Improve work process innovation	x	x	x
Improve product innovation	x		x
Improve recruitment and succession		x	
Improve planning, budgeting, and forecasting processes	x		
Improve e-business opportunities and strategies			x
Support Your Organization's Business Objectives			
Improve personal alignment to your business strategy	x	x	x
Embed learning into doing	x	x	x
Drive business value	x	x	x
Promote Innovations			
Enrich employee work-life experience		x	
Improve career development opportunities		x	
Improve employee autonomy		x	
Improve community involvement		x	
Maintain a Knowledge-Creating Organization			
Improve Web-centric business strategy	x	x	x
Improve content management	x	x	x
Improve enterprise search	x	x	x
Improve user interface and usability consistency		x	x
Improve cross-functional work processes	x	x	x

Figure 3-15. Knowledge management objectives report review.

- The knowledge management objectives questionnaire was completed with selected knowledge expert community members
- The interview details are available and can be reviewed:
  knowledge management objectives interviews (Word documents)
- The knowledge management objectives were analyzed from the interviews and broken into rows on the spreadsheet:
  —Be organized around work processes
  —Maintain knowledge and facilitate communication
  —Focus on the future
  —Support your organization's business objectives
  —Promote innovations
  —Maintain a knowledge-creating organization
- The corporate initiatives were outlined from the interviews and broken into columns on the spreadsheet:
  —Work process improvement
  —Business-to-employee opportunities
  —Business-to-consumer opportunities
- The knowledge management objectives report has summarized the knowledge management objectives and corporate initiatives in the following spreadsheet:
  knowledge management objectives report (Excel spreadsheet)
- Open discussion of the knowledge management objectives report
- Updates to the knowledge management objectives report

- Note: Rows and columns can be added, updated, and removed from the knowledge management objectives report to reflect the appropriate level of detail

knowledge portal information technology–enabling framework. The purpose of this template is to outline the enterprise knowledge portal features that either exist or will need to exist in your information technology infrastructure to meet your knowledge management objectives. The enterprise knowledge portal IT–enabling framework is an overview of the technologies and associated software features that have been identified to include in the enterprise knowledge portal solution. The software solutions and applications that are currently available in your IT infrastructure are included in the documentation. This information will be used to create the enterprise knowledge portal map that ties your knowledge management objectives directly to the enterprise knowledge portal IT–enabling framework. The enterprise knowledge portal IT–enabling framework has three steps. These include:

1. *Identify primary enterprise knowledge portal technologies.* Establish a hierarchy of enterprise portal technologies in your organization. Focus on creating five to eight categories that will represent your information technology–enabling framework for capturing and delivering your knowledge management objectives.

Figure 3-16. A sample meeting invitation and agenda to knowledge management objectives report review.

Agenda	Knowledge Management Objectives Report Review Conference Room One	
Type of meeting:	Knowledge Management Objectives Report Review Meeting	
Facilitator:	Heidi Collins	
Note taker:	David Kennedy	
Attendees:	Knowledge Expert Community Members	
	Agenda Topics	
30 Minutes	Knowledge Management Objectives identified from Knowledge Expert Community interviews are reviewed (rows in the template)	Heidi Collins
30 Minutes	Corporate Initiatives identified from myCompany are reviewed (columns in the template)	Heidi Collins
10 Minutes	Break	
30 Minutes	Summarize and prioritize the relationships between knowledge management objectives and corporate initiatives	Heidi Collins
10 Minutes	Review action items	Heidi Collins
10 Minutes	Review Enterprise Knowledge Portal Map progress and discuss our next steps and activities	Heidi Collins

2. *Add features to the enterprise knowledge portal technologies.* Continue to expand the features associated with each technology category created in step one. Compose a hierarchy of enterprise knowledge portal features below each technology category. Add additional levels below each feature when additional detail is needed to add clarity.
3. *Document existing applications, systems, or services.* Add the existing applications, systems, or services that provide some or all of the functionality needed to support the enterprise knowledge portal features. Include this information in each node of the enterprise knowledge portal IT–enabling framework.

The challenge is to create a logical categorization of enterprise knowledge portal features and functions that can be mapped to your knowledge management objectives. The enterprise knowledge portal IT–enabling framework diagram should be covered in enough detail to represent 70 percent to 80 percent of the unique features and functions that need to be supported in your IT infrastructure in the next twelve to twenty-four months to successfully deploy the enterprise knowledge portal. You are compiling

Figure 3-17. Knowledge management objectives report (final release).

	Work Process Improvements	Business-to-Employee Opportunities	Business-to-Consumer Opportunities
Be Organized Around Work Processes			
Improve employee effectiveness	Medium	High	
Make better decisions faster	High	High	Medium
Improve information availability and access	High	High	High
Improve cycle times	High		
Embed knowledge management activities	Medium	High	High
Improve response times	High	High	Medium
Improve information reuse	Medium	Medium	
Maintain Knowledge and Facilitate Communication			
Improve communication between managers	High	Medium	
Improve alignment of management objectives	High	High	
Improve awareness of roles and responsibilities	High	High	High
Improve strategic alignment	High	High	Medium
Improve span of influence of human expertise		Medium	Low
Improve operational efficiencies through information reuse	High	Medium	
Focus on the Future			
Improve market knowledge business strategy effectiveness	Medium		High
Improve work process innovation	High	Medium	Low
Improve product innovation	High		Medium
Improve recruitment and succession		High	
Improve planning, budgeting, and forecasting processes	High		
Improve e-business opportunities and strategies			High
Support Your Organization's Business Objectives			
Improve personal alignment to your business strategy	Medium	Medium	Medium
Embed learning into doing	Medium	Medium	Medium
Drive business value	Low	Low	Medium
Promote Innovations			
Enrich employee work-life experience		Medium	
Improve career development opportunities		Medium	
Improve employee autonomy		High	
Improve community involvement		Low	
Maintain a Knowledge-Creating Organization			
Improve Web-centric business strategy	Medium	High	High
Improve content management	High	High	High
Improve enterprise search	High	High	High
Improve user interface and usability consistency		Medium	High
Improve cross-functional work processes	High	High	Low

Figure 3-18. Knowledge expert community—communication two.

Re: Knowledge Management Objectives Report

Hello Knowledge Expert Community,

The final version of the **Knowledge Management Objectives** report is available. The **Enterprise Knowledge Portal Team** would like to thank each of you for your contribution in completing this effort. To review the final report please visit:
Knowledge Management Objectives Report (Excel Spreadsheet)

We are asking the **Knowledge Expert Community** members to share this information with other managers and teams in your business units. Review the **Knowledge Management Objectives Report** at team meetings or other events to begin to create awareness of myCompany's knowledge management objectives and corporate initiatives, and of how knowledge management can support and improve our corporate initiatives. If you need additional presentation information or material, please let Heidi Collins, Michael Douglas, or David Kennedy know and we will post it for everyone to use and access.

these details as one input for the enterprise knowledge portal map and an enterprise knowledge portal request for proposal.

Identify Primary Enterprise Knowledge Portal Technologies

Purpose: Establish a hierarchy of enterprise portal technologies in your organization. Focus on creating five to eight categories that will represent your information technology–enabling framework for capturing and delivering your knowledge management objectives.

Once you have a definition of the enterprise portal and an overview of the enterprise portal market, you are ready to get started. First, you should pick five to eight categories that provide the basis for organizing features and functions to make available in the enterprise knowledge portal. Think of these technologies or categories as a way to group the features and functions required to support knowledge management in your organization. Many features will be common in two or more of the technologies, and you will be required to establish a logical break to map each feature into a discrete technology. The logical map of enterprise knowledge portal features will give nontechnical knowledge workers a description of the technologies available to support their knowledge management objectives.

Due to the complexity of the infrastructure required to support the enterprise knowledge portal, this collection of primary technologies can be useful as a starting point to introduce several different technologies. As the enterprise knowledge portal grows and new features need to be added or existing features need to be drilled into, the enterprise knowledge portal

IT–enabling framework can continue to grow. This effort produces a complete range of enterprise knowledge portal documented features. You should consider adding a definition or description to each object added into the enterprise knowledge portal IT–enabling framework document.

As the enterprise knowledge portal IT–enabling framework document grows, you might realize that the original five to eight categories selected need to be reevaluated, updated, and the features realigned to the new categories. Consider your first attempt at creating the enterprise knowledge portal IT–enabling framework a learning experience. When the enterprise knowledge portal features no longer logically fit into the existing categories, take the experience and lessons learned from the enterprise knowledge portal team as well as the knowledge expert community and outline a new logical map of technology categories.

MYCOMPANY CASE STUDY

Once the knowledge management objectives that need to be integrated into the enterprise knowledge portal have been identified, it is important to understand the information technology features available to support these objectives. Five types of information technology categories have been selected to organize the enterprise knowledge portal features. The technologies and a brief description of each that will be used to organize myCompany's knowledge management objectives are shown in Figure 3-19 and include:

- *The Enterprise Portal.* This is a knowledge desktop to facilitate a comprehensive range of functionality including single point of access to relevant structured and unstructured information.
- *Business Intelligence.* Business intelligence technology is designed for specific business objectives for data warehousing, routine data analysis, standard report writing, ad hoc querying, online analytic processing (OLAP), and data mining. New systems are being deployed to deliver on customer relationship management (CRM) and other more complex activities.
- *Collaboration and Communities.* These technologies facilitate workplace discussion and the creation of communities of interest and best practices. They also enable virtual workspaces and workrooms enabling collaborative e-commerce.
- *Content Management.* This technology provides the ability to maintain, organize, and search across all organization structured

Figure 3-19. Enterprise knowledge portal IT–enabling framework.

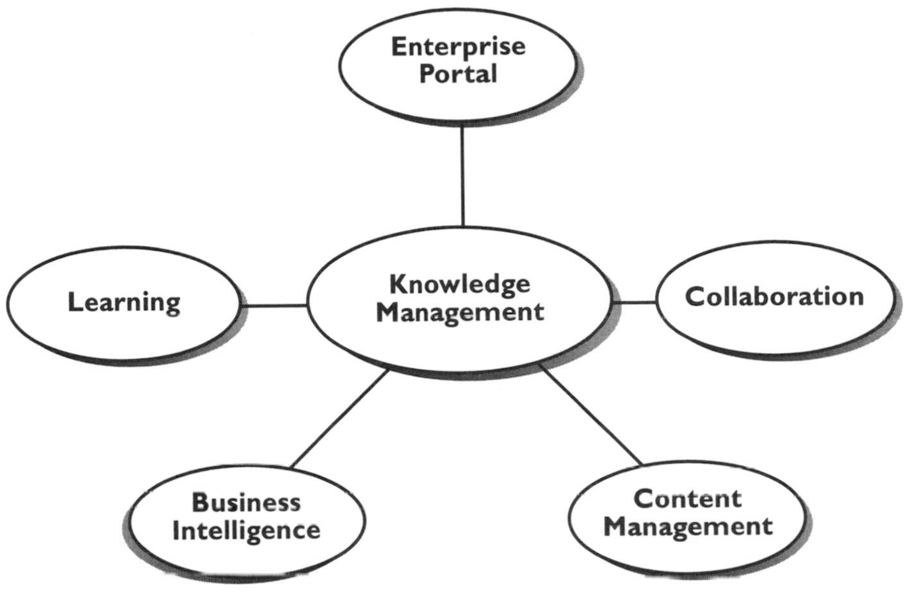

(databases) and unstructured (documents, records, e-mails, video and audio files, other) information sources.

- *Learning.* Learning technology has the ability to integrate learning into doing as electronic learning, training, and mentoring through simulations, built-in wizards, online job aids, integrated help, on-demand video and audio presentations through the Web, and wearable computers.

These categories are the first nodes in the tree and represent the technologies used to support knowledge management at myCompany. These few categories provide the basis for future information technology architecture and infrastructure activities to support the enterprise knowledge portal. Because of the broad scope of technologies that will be integrated into the enterprise knowledge portal, plans to implement new technologies into our existing architecture and infrastructure are more easily managed as strategies and implementation plans within each of these first node categories.

Add Features to the Enterprise Knowledge Portal Technologies

Purpose: Continue to expand the features associated with each technology category created in step one. Compose a hierarchy of enterprise knowledge portal features below each technology category. Add additional levels below each feature when additional detail is needed to add clarity.

Once the enterprise knowledge portal categories and first subcategories of features are outlined, continue to add hierarchies of features. These subsets of information represent clarification, details, and depth to describe the features included in the enterprise knowledge portal IT–enabling framework. One way to begin is to think about applications, services, and systems in your organization and break them down into the features they provide. Focus on the features and not the applications, systems, and services. For example, Microsoft Outlook provides electronic messaging, personal task management, calendar management, and notification features that will be needed to successfully meet your knowledge management objectives. Review the enterprise knowledge portal categories and hierarchies and add the electronic messaging, personal task management, calendar management, and notification features into the tree diagram where they logically fit. The logical representation of enterprise knowledge portal features will provide a nontechnical representation of your information technology environment. The point is to make your information technology environment look like the features available in your organization that are needed to support your knowledge management objectives.

MYCOMPANY CASE STUDY

The knowledge management objectives have been reviewed and the software features to best support them are added as the second and additional layer of nodes in the enterprise knowledge portal IT–enabling framework. These software features will need to map into one of these discrete technologies. The logical representation of enterprise knowledge portal features is created as individual diagrams for each technology category. These include:

- ❐ The enterprise portal
- ❐ Business intelligence
- ❐ Collaboration and communities
- ❐ Content management
- ❐ Learning

Enterprise Knowledge Portal IT–Enabling Framework—The Enterprise Portal

Additional sources of enterprise portal information can be found in Appendix C: Recommended Reading. The enterprise portal software features that will be used to support our knowledge management objectives are shown in Figure 3-20 and include:

- Search
  1. Federated search
- The knowledge organization system
  1. Term lists
  2. Relationship lists
  3. Taxonomies
  4. Semantic representatives
  5. Ontologies
- Presentation
  1. Abstraction layer
  2. Federated portals
  3. Caching
- Plug and play features
  1. Process and action
  2. Intelligent agents
  3. Component libraries

Figure 3-20. Enterprise knowledge portal IT–enabling framework: enterprise portal.

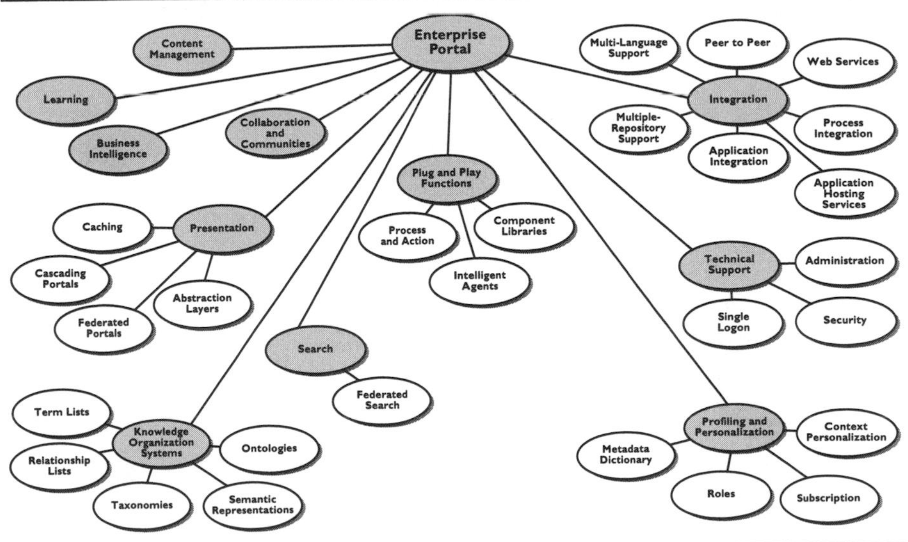

- Profiling and personalization
  1. Context personalization
  2. Roles
  3. Metadata dictionary
  4. Subscription
- Access and integration
  1. Multiple repository support
  2. Application integration
  3. Multilanguage support
  4. Peer-to-peer
  5. Web services
  6. Process integration
  7. Application hosting services
- Technical support
  1. Administration
  2. Single sign-on
  3. Security

Enterprise Knowledge Portal IT–Enabling Framework—Business Intelligence

Additional sources of business intelligence information can be found in Appendix C: Recommended Reading. The business intelligence software features that will be used to support our knowledge management objectives are shown in Figure 3-21 and include:

- Decision support
  1. Executive information system
  2. Online analytical processing (OLAP)
  3. Relational database management systems
  4. Query tools
- Performance-based metrics
  1. Business models
  2. Business structures
  3. Quality control
  4. Forecasting
  5. Process management

Figure 3-21. Enterprise knowledge portal IT–enabling framework: business intelligence.

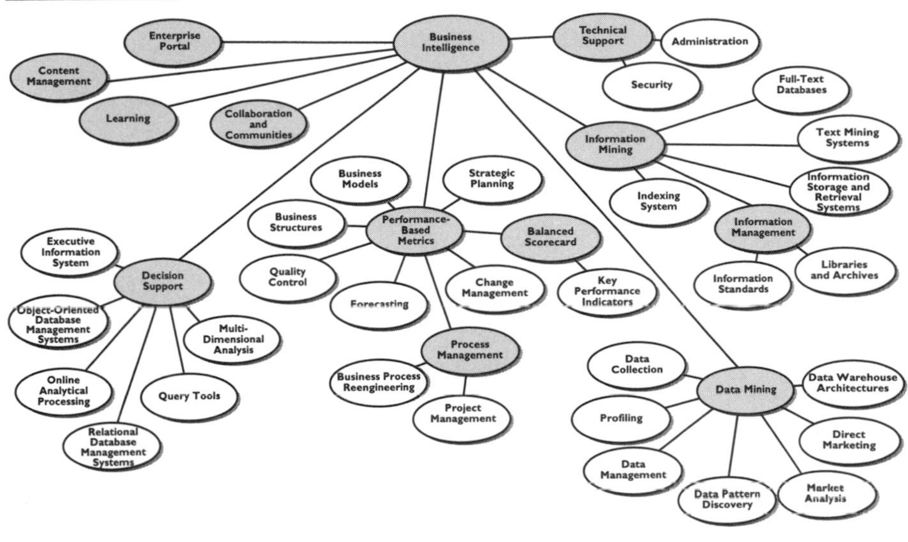

6. Change management
7. Balanced scorecard
8. Strategic planning

- Data mining
  1. Data collection
  2. Profiling
  3. Data management
  4. Data pattern discovery
  5. Market analysis
  6. Direct marketing
  7. Data warehouse architectures
- Information mining
  1. Indexing system
  2. Information management
  3. Information storage and retrieval systems
  4. Text mining systems
  5. Full-text databases
- Technical support
  1. Administration
  2. Security

Enterprise Knowledge Portal IT–Enabling Framework—Collaboration and Communities

Additional sources of collaboration and community information can be found in Appendix C: Recommended Reading. The collaboration and community software features that will be used to support our knowledge management objectives are shown in Figure 3-22 and include:

- ❒ Electronic messaging management
  1. E-mail
  2. Extranets
  3. Intranets
  4. Wireless communications systems
- ❒ Real-time collaboration
  1. Video- and audioconferencing
  2. Internet chat
  3. Instant messaging
  4. Electronic whiteboards
  5. Data conferencing
- ❒ Team-based collaboration
  1. Calendaring and scheduling

Figure 3-22. Enterprise knowledge portal IT–enabling framework: collaboration and communitites.

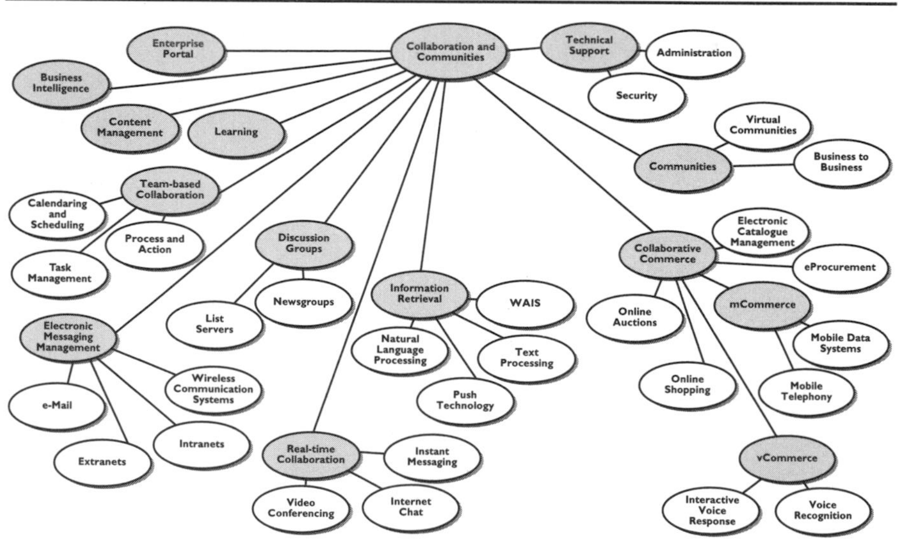

2. Task management
3. Process and action

- ❒ Discussion groups
  1. List servers
  2. Newsgroups
- ❒ Information retrieval
  1. Natural language processing
  2. Push technology
  3. Text processing
- ❒ Collaborative commerce
  1. Online auctions
  2. Online shopping
  3. Interactive voice response
  4. Voice recognition
  5. Mobile telephony
  6. Mobile data systems
  7. Electronic procurement
  8. Electronic catalog management
- ❒ Communities
  1. Virtual communities
  2. Business-to-business
- ❒ Technical support
  1. Administration
  2. Security

Enterprise Knowledge Portal IT–Enabling Framework—Content Management

Additional sources of content management information can be found in Appendix C: Recommended Reading. The content management software features that will be used to support our knowledge management objectives are shown in Figure 3-23 and include:

- ❒ Document management and Web content management
  1. Repositories
  2. Caching
  3. Search

Figure 3-23. Enterprise knowledge portal IT–enabling framework: content management.

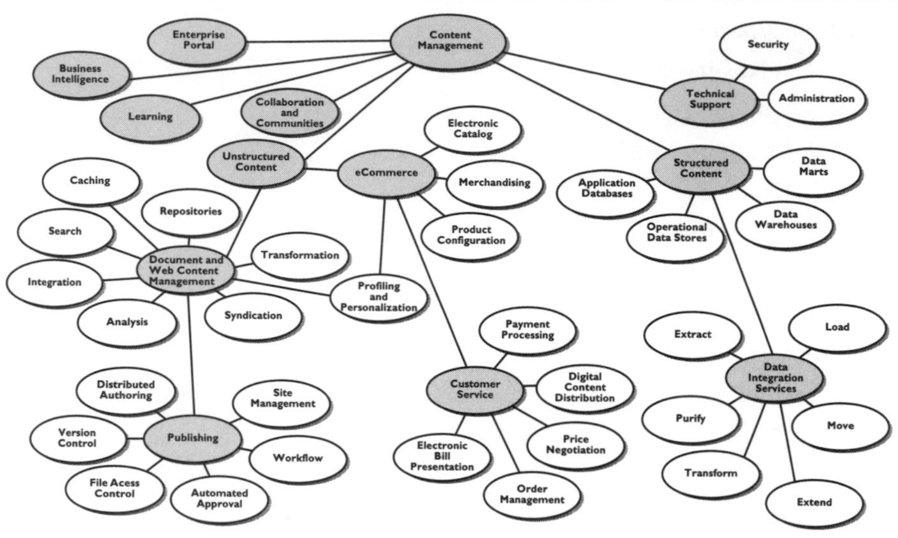

4. Integration
5. Analysis
6. Syndication
7. Publishing
8. Transformation
9. Profiling and personalization

- Electronic commerce
  1. Electronic catalog
  2. Merchandising
  3. Product configuration
  4. Customer service
  5. Profiling and personalization
- Relational database management system
  1. Application databases
  2. Operational data stores
  3. Data warehouses
  4. Data marts
  5. Data integration services

- Technical support
  1. Administration
  2. Security

Enterprise Knowledge Portal IT–Enabling Framework—Learning

Additional sources of learning information can be found in Appendix C: Recommended Reading. The learning software features that will be used to support our knowledge management objectives are shown in Figure 3-24 and include:

- Electronic performance support systems
  1. Reference information
  2. Expert systems
  3. Online job aids
  4. Application help
  5. Online analytical processing
  6. Integrated tracking and reporting
  7. Task performance tools
- Video- and audioconferencing
  1. Webcasts
  2. Simulation models

Figure 3-24. Enterprise knowledge portal IT–enabling framework: learning.

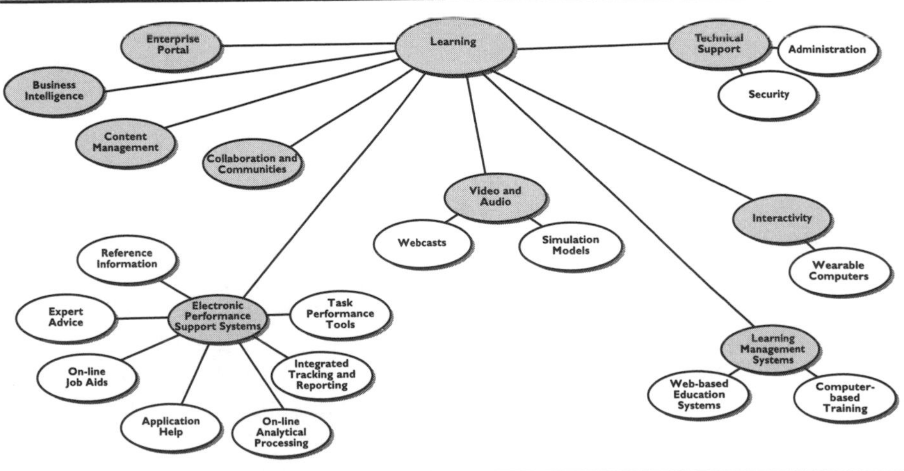

- ❐ Learning management systems
    1. Web-based education systems
    2. Computer-based training
- ❐ Technical support
    1. Administration
    2. Security

Document Existing Applications, Systems, or Services

Purpose: Add the existing applications, systems, or services that provide some or all of the functionality needed to support the enterprise knowledge portal features. Include this information in each node of the enterprise knowledge portal IT–enabling framework.

Once the enterprise knowledge portal features have been documented and defined into the desired level of detail needed to support your knowledge management portal objectives, you will want to review the applications, solutions, and services currently available in your organization that provide these features. The result will be a listing of the applications, solutions, and services in your organization that need to be integrated or linked into the enterprise knowledge portal. In some cases there might be a feature that has no supporting applications, solutions, or services. In several cases you might identify duplicate applications and solutions providing the same feature or very similar features in your organization. The information added to the enterprise knowledge portal IT–enabling framework will be used to document your current IT landscape to be incorporated into the enterprise knowledge portal. If it makes sense, you will want to evaluate when or why you would use the features from one application over another or whether to standardize on a single application to provide the features needed by the enterprise knowledge portal.

As you evaluate your IT landscape, and it does make sense to provide the same features to users through multiple applications, the enterprise knowledge portal can seamlessly make only the screens from the applications required to provide the features needed into the user interface. Imagine that you support several applications to manage discussions in your organization. You could have Lotus Notes discussion databases, Microsoft SharePoint Portal Server discussions, and others. Human resources uses SharePoint Portal Server discussions to manage their interactions, suggestions, and feedback with employees, and Lotus Notes discussion databases are used throughout the rest of the organization. When the enterprise knowledge portal user has a suggestion to improve the benefits renewal work process, the process is to click on "feedback" to complete the suggestion, and then click on "submit" to send. The screens that appear in the enterprise knowledge portal desktop are directly linked or presented from

SharePoint Portal Server. For any other interactions, suggestions, and feedback activities selected by enterprise knowledge portal users, the screens would be linked or presented from a Lotus Notes database. The employee does not have to sign in to the discussion application, navigate somewhere in the application to get started, or have a thorough understanding of the differences between Lotus Notes discussion databases and Microsoft SharePoint Portal Server discussions to work effectively.

You might find it useful to reformat the information in the enterprise knowledge portal IT–enabling framework document into a spreadsheet. The enterprise knowledge portal features, definitions, current product offerings available, and when to use the current product offerings might be a useful reference document for the enterprise knowledge portal team and knowledge experts community. The enterprise knowledge portal IT–enabling framework document and spreadsheet will continue to be updated with information about new and existing features as part of each enterprise knowledge portal project to keep the information current and reusable.

MYCOMPANY CASE STUDY

After the enterprise knowledge portal software features have been documented in the second and additional layer of nodes of the enterprise knowledge portal IT–enabling framework, continue to add details about the applications, solutions, and services in the organization that currently support these software features. This detail will provide information that describes myCompany's existing information technology environment. Each technology category was evaluated individually and documented. The technology categories include:

- The enterprise portal
- Business intelligence
- Collaboration and communities
- Content management
- Learning

Enterprise Portal Applications

The applications, solutions, and services available found throughout myCompany to support enterprise portal software features are documented into the individual nodes of the enterprise knowledge portal IT–enabling framework. There are several questions to consider in your research of applications, solutions, and services. Some of these include:

- ☐ What applications or solutions are available in your organization to support your knowledge management initiatives for knowledge workers and other networks of users? Do they provide a personalized interface to online resources that integrate and organize applications and data? Do these solutions support caching content, portals, or abstraction layers that present only the information individuals need to do their jobs?
- ☐ What applications or solutions are available in your organization for mapping or tagging attributes to content? Do you have well defined term lists, relationships of these terms, the history of how these terms have changed over time, taxonomies, and ontologies or rules and agents that tie terms and taxonomies together?
- ☐ What applications or solutions are available in your organization for search and index features?
- ☐ What applications and solutions provide work flow, user-defined or intelligent agents, and libraries of reusable objects that have been developed or purchased?
- ☐ What applications and solutions provide profiling and personalization? Is there a metadata dictionary to maintain? Are user roles defined? Can users subscribe to content in your organization and have it delivered to them electronically? Can the user add, delete, and move content to customize the way they work?
- ☐ What applications and solutions provide integration services? Do these services include multilanguage support, peer-to-peer services, Web services, process integration, application hosting services, application integration, and multiple repository support?

The updated enterprise knowledge portal IT–enabling framework—enterprise portal document is updated with information about applications, solutions, and services available at myCompany in Figure 3-25. The spreadsheet version of this information is available for review in Figure 3-26.

Business Intelligence Applications

The applications, solutions, and services available found throughout myCompany to support business intelligence software features are documented into the individual nodes of the enterprise knowledge portal IT–enabling framework. There are several questions to consider in your research of applications, solutions, and services. Some of these include:

Figure 3-25. Enterprise knowledge portal IT–enabling framework: enterprise portal.

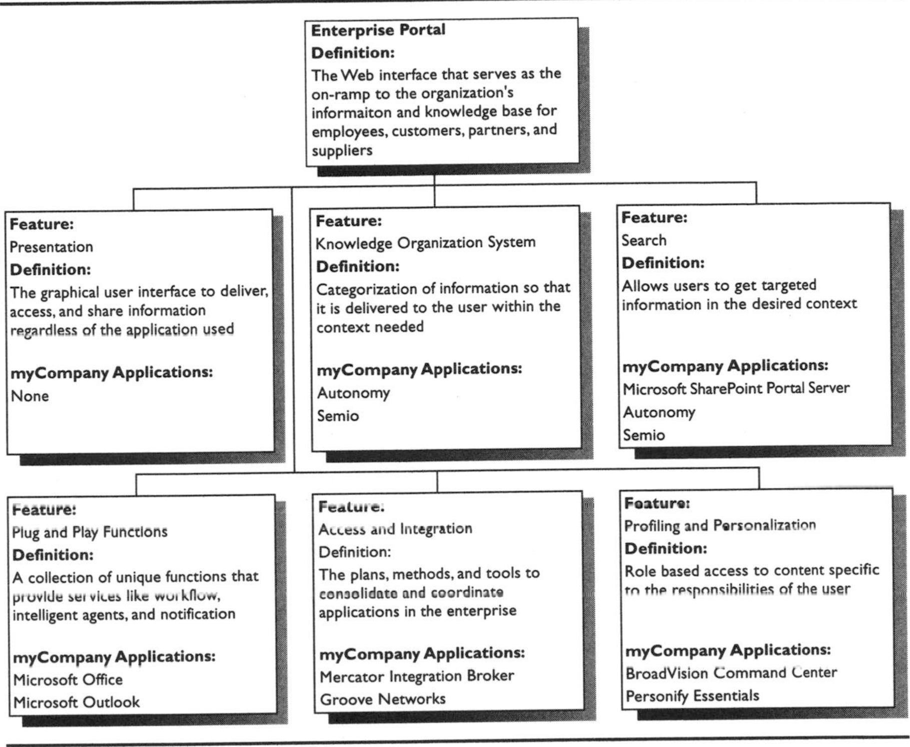

- ☐ What applications or solutions are available in your organization for decision support services? Are additional applications and solutions available for an executive information system, object-oriented database management systems, relational database management systems, online analytical processing, query tools, or multidimensional analysis?
- ☐ What applications or solutions are available in your organization for performance-based metrics and process management? Have you already deployed a set of balanced scorecards?
- ☐ What applications or solutions are available in your organization for data mining? Are these solutions used for direct marketing, market analysis, and data pattern discovery? What data warehouse architecture, data management, and data collection features are available and supported?
- ☐ What applications or solutions are available in your organization for information mining and information management? What additional features are available and supported?

Figure 3-26. Enterprise knowledge portal IT–enabling framework: enterprise portal (spreadsheet version).

Enterprise Portal	Functionality	myCompany Applications	Vendor
Presentation	Caching	None	None
	Cascading Portals		
	Federated Portals		
	Abstraction Layers		
	Abstraction Layers		
Knowledge Organization System	Term Lists	Autonomy	www.autonomy.com
	Relationship Lists	Semio	www.semio.com
	Taxonomies		
	Semantic Representations		
	Ontologies		
Search	Federated Search	Microsoft SharePoint Portal Server	www.microsoft.com
		Autonomy	www.autonomy.com
		Semio	www.semio.com
Plug and Play Functions	Process and Action	Microsoft Office	www.microsoft.com
	Intelligent Agents	Microsoft Outlook	www.microsoft.com
	Component Libraries		
Access and Integration	Multiple-Repository Support	Mercator Integration Broker	www.mercator.com
	Application Integration	Groove Networks	www.groove.net
	Application Hosting Services		
	Process Integration		
	Web Services		
	Peer to Peer		
	Multi-Language Support		
Profiling and Personalization	Metadata Dictionary	BroadVision Command Center	www.broadvision.com
	Roles	Personify Essentials	www.personify.com
	Subscription		
	Context Personalization		

The updated enterprise knowledge portal IT–enabling framework—business intelligence document is updated with information about applications, solutions, and services available at myCompany in Figure 3-27. The spreadsheet version of this information is available for review in Figure 3-28.

Collaboration and Communities Applications

The applications, solutions, and services available found throughout myCompany to support collaboration and community software features are documented into the individual nodes of the enterprise knowledge portal IT–enabling framework. There are several questions to consider in your research of applications, solutions, and services. Some of these include:

- ☐ What applications and solutions are available in your organization for electronic messaging management?
- ☐ What applications and solutions are available in your organization for team-based collaboration?
- ☐ What applications and solutions are available in your organization for discussion groups?
- ☐ What applications and solutions are available in your organization for real-time collaboration?

Figure 3-27. Enterprise knowledge portal IT–enabling framework: business intelligence organization chart.

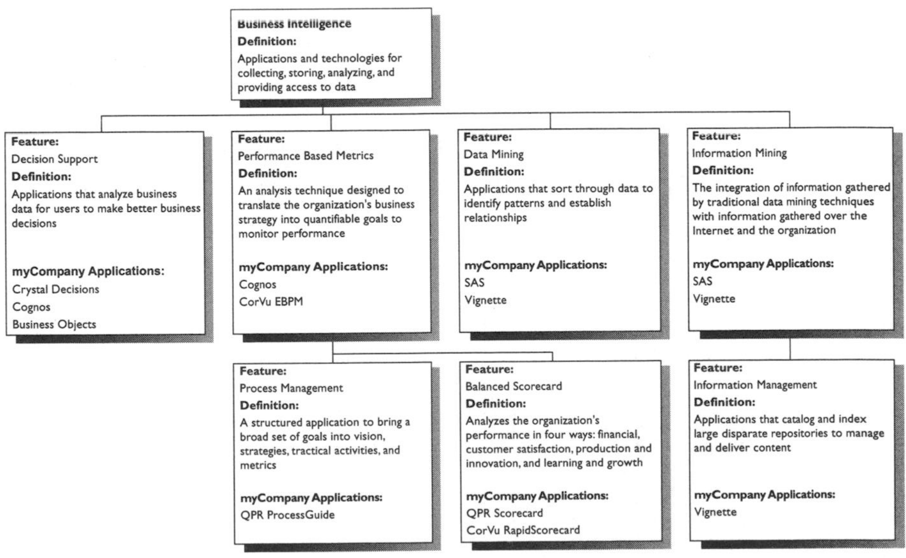

Figure 3-28. Enterprise knowledge portal IT–enabling framework: business intelligence (spreadsheet version).

Business Intelligence	Functionality	myCompany Applications	Vendor
Decision Support	Executive Information System	Crystal Decisions	www.crystaldecisions.com
	Object-Oriented Database Management System	Cognos	www.cognos.com
	Relational Database Management System	Business Objects	www.businessobjects.com
	Online Analytical Processing		
	Multi-Dimensional Analysis		
	Query Tools		
Performance-Based Metrics	Business Models	Cognos	www.cognos.com
	Business Structures	CorVu Electronic Business Process Management	www.corvu.com
	Quality Control		
	Forecasting		
	Change Management		
	Strategic Planning		
Process Management	Business Process Reengineering	QPR ProcessGuide	www.qpr.com
	Project Management		
Balanced Scorecard	Key Performance Indicators	QPR Scorecard	www.qpr.com
		CorVu RapidScorecard	www.corvu.com
Data Mining	Data Collection	SAS	www.sas.com
	Profiling	Vignette	www.vignette.com
	Data Management		
	Data Pattern Discovery		
	Market Analysis		
	Direct Marketing		
	Data Warehouse Architecture		
Information Mining	Indexing System	SAS	www.sas.com
	Full-Text Databases	Vignette	www.vignette.com
	Text Mining Systems		
	Information Storage and Retrieval System		
Information Management	Information Standards	Vignette	www.vignette.com
	Libraries and Archives		

- ☐ What applications and solutions are available in your organization for information retrieval?
- ☐ What applications and solutions are available in your organization for process and action or work flow?
- ☐ What applications and solutions are available in your organization for collaborative commerce, mobile commerce, and voice commerce?
- ☐ What applications and solutions are available in your organization for communities and their collaboration and content-sharing requirements?

The updated enterprise knowledge portal IT–enabling framework—collaboration and communities document is updated with information about applications, solutions, and services available at myCompany in Figure 3-29. The spreadsheet version of this information is available for review in Figure 3-30.

Content Management Applications

The applications, solutions, and services available found throughout myCompany to support content management software features are docu-

Figure 3-29. Enterprise knowledge portal IT–enabling framework: collaboration and communities organization chart.

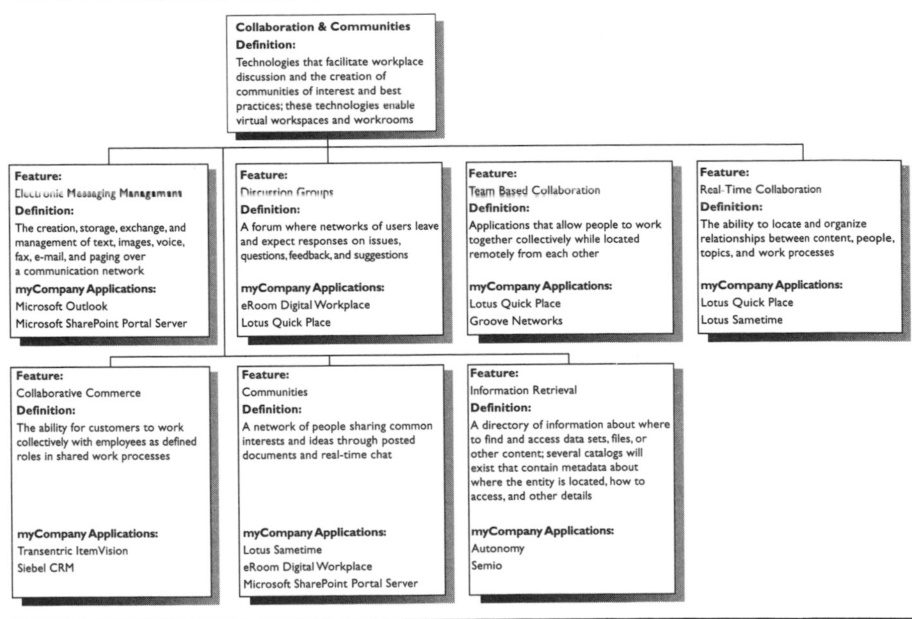

Figure 3-30. Enterprise knowledge portal IT–enabling framework: collaboration and communities (spreadsheet version).

Collaboration & Communities	Functionality	myCompany Applications	Vendor
Electronic Messaging Management	e-Mail	Microsoft Outlook	www.microsoft.com
	Extranets	Microsoft SharePoint Portal Server	www.microsoft.com
	Intranets		
	Wireless Communication Systems		
Discussion Groups	List Servers	eRoom Digital Workplace	www.eroom.com
	Newsgroups	Lotus Quick Place	www.lotus.com
Team-Based Collaboration	Process and Action	Lotus Quick Place	www.lotus.com
	Calendaring and Scheduling	Groove Networks	www.groove.net
	Task Management		
Real-Time Collaboration	Video Conferencing	Lotus Quick Place	www.lotus.com
	Internet Chat	Lotus Sametime	www.lotus.com
	Instant Messaging		
Collaborative Commerce	Online Auctions	Transcentric ItemVision	www.transcentric.com
	Online Shopping	Siebel CRM	www.siebel.com
	Electronic Catalog Management		
	eProcurement		
Communities	Virtual Communities	Lotus Sametime	www.lotus.com
	Business-to-Business	eRoom Digital Workplace	www.eroom.com
		Microsoft SharePoint Portal Server	www.microsoft.com
Information Retrieval	Natural Language Processing	Autonomy	www.autonomy.com
	Push Technology	Semio	www.semio.com
	Text Processing		
	WAIS		

mented into the individual nodes of the enterprise knowledge portal IT–enabling framework. There are several questions to consider in your research of applications, solutions, and services. Some of these include:

- ☐ What applications and solutions are available in your organization for document management and Web-content management? What features are provided for publishing requirements?
- ☐ What applications and solutions are available in your organization for e-commerce and customer service?
- ☐ What applications and solutions are available in your organization for structured content including application databases, operational data stores, data warehouses, and data marts? What features are provided for data integration services?

The updated enterprise knowledge portal IT–enabling framework—content management document is updated with information about applications, solutions, and services available at myCompany in Figure 3-31. The spreadsheet version of this information is available for review in Figure 3-32.

Learning Applications

The applications and solutions available at myCompany for providing help and learning features are exploded and added into the IT–enabling framework. Some of the questions to consider include:

- ☐ What applications and solutions are available in your organization for electronic performance support systems that include reference information, expert advice, online job aids, application help, online analytical processing, integrated tracking and reporting, and task performance tools?
- ☐ What applications and solutions are available in your organization for video and audio services? Do you provide webcasts and simulation models as learning tools?
- ☐ What applications and solutions are available in your organization for learning management systems?
- ☐ What applications and solutions are available in your organization that interacts directly with the knowledge worker (i.e., wearable computers)?

The updated enterprise knowledge portal IT–enabling framework—learning document is updated with information about applications, solutions, and services available at myCompany in Figure 3-33. The spreadsheet version of this information is available for review in Figure 3-34.

Figure 3-31. Enterprise knowledge portal IT–enabling framework: content management organization chart.

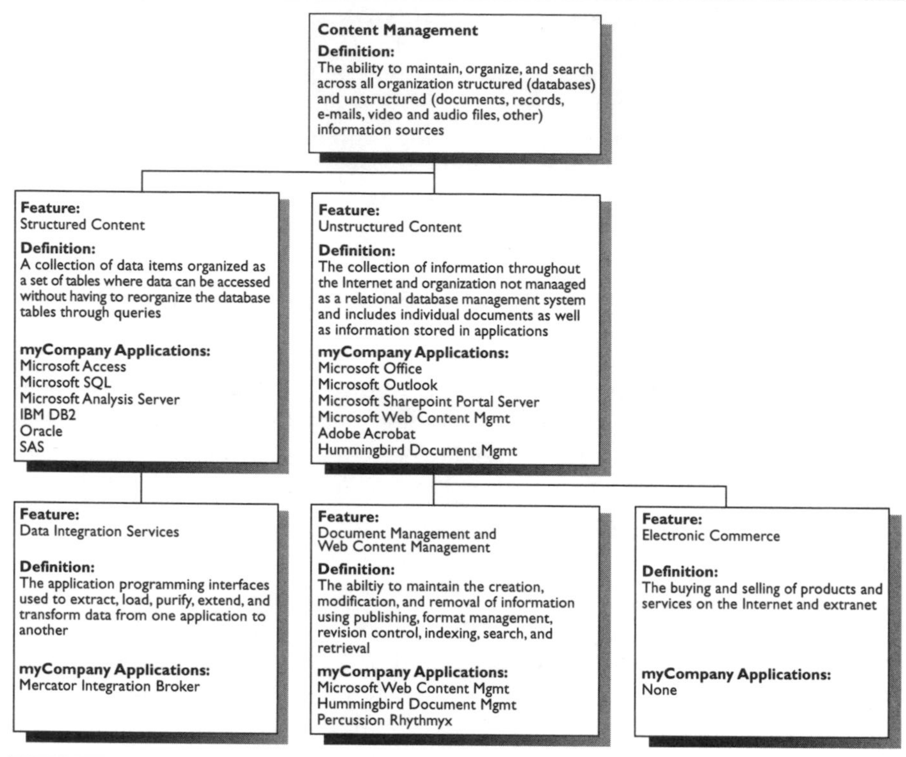

Enterprise Knowledge Portal Map

The final effort is to combine the information from the enterprise knowledge portal objectives report and the enterprise knowledge portal IT–enabling framework report into the enterprise knowledge portal map template. The enterprise knowledge portal map provides an avenue to prioritize and plan what knowledge management objectives and enterprise portal features your organization could focus on moving forward within an enterprise knowledge portal initiative. The ultimate purpose of this template is to combine your knowledge management objectives and the enterprise knowledge portal features to determine whether or not to implement an enterprise knowledge portal for your organization. If the knowledge expert community and enterprise portal team agree to continue to promote the enterprise knowledge portal, this information will be used to develop the enterprise knowledge portal program discussed in Part II of the book.

Figure 3-32. Enterprise knowledge portal IT–enabling framework: content management (spreadsheet version).

Content Management	Functionality	myCompany Applications	Vendor
Structured Content	Application Databases	Microsoft Access	www.microsoft.com
	Operational Data Stores	Microsoft SQL	www.microsoft.com
	Data Warehouses	Microsoft Analysis Server	www.microsoft.com
	Data Marts	IBM DB2	www.ibm.com
		Oracle	www.oracle.com
		SAS	www.sas.com
Data Integration Services	Extract	Mercator Integration Broker	www.mercator.com
	Purify		
	Transform		
	Extend		
	Move		
	Load		
Unstructured Content	Content Management Application	Microsoft Office	www.microsoft.com
	Content Delivery Application	Microsoft Outlook	www.microsoft.com
		Microsoft SharePoint Portal Server	www.microsoft.com
		Microsoft Web Content Management	www.microsoft.com
		Adobe Acrobat	www.adobe.com
		Hummingbird Document Management	www.hummingbird.com
Document Management	Repositories	Microsoft Web Content Management	www.microsoft.com
Web Content Management	Caching	Hummingbird Document Management	www.hummingbird.com
	Search	Percussion Rhythmyx	www.percussion.com
	Integration		
	Analysis		
	Publishing		
	Syndication		
	Transformation		
	Profiling and Personalization		
Electronic Commerce	Electronic Catalog	None	None
	Merchandising		
	Product Configuration		
	Customer Service		
	Profiling and Personalization		

Figure 3-33. Enterprise knowledge portal IT–enabling framework: learning organization chart.

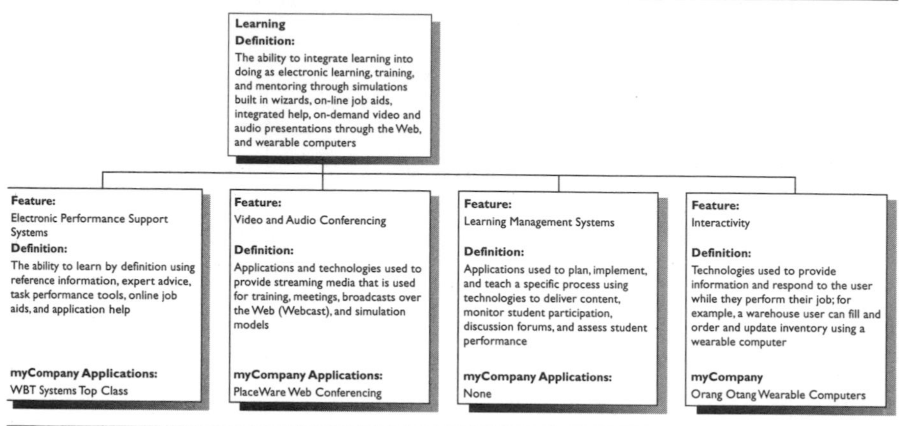

The enterprise knowledge portal map is outlined in four steps. The steps involved include:

1. *Add knowledge management objectives.* Add the knowledge management objectives report details into the enterprise knowledge portal map template.
2. *Add enterprise knowledge portal IT–enabling framework.* Add the enterprise knowledge portal IT–enabling framework report details into the enterprise knowledge portal map template.
3. *Prioritize knowledge management objectives.* On the basis of the research and information available, prioritize the knowledge management objectives that will be targeted for implementation in the initial releases of the enterprise knowledge portal.
4. *Prioritize enterprise knowledge portal features.* On the basis of the research and information available, prioritize the enterprise knowledge portal features that will be targeted to include in the initial releases of the enterprise knowledge portal.

Add Knowledge Management Objectives

Purpose: Add the knowledge management objectives report details into the enterprise knowledge portal map template.

The enterprise knowledge portal map template will provide a spreadsheet to post the information from the knowledge management objectives report. The enterprise knowledge portal map template can be seen in Figure 3-35. The knowledge management objectives are documented in the rows of the spreadsheet. Continue to maintain the categories used in the knowledge management objectives report. The enterprise knowledge portal map template includes the default categories from the knowledge man-

Figure 3-34. Enterprise knowledge portal IT–enabling framework: learning (spreadsheet version).

Learning	Functionality	myCompany Applications	Vendor
Electronic Performance Support Systems	Reference Information	WBT Systems Top Class	www.wbtsystems.com
	Expert Advice		
	Online Job Aids		
	Application Help		
	Online Analytical Processing		
	Integration Tracking and Reporting		
	Task Performance Tools		
Video and Audio Conferencing	Webcasts	PlaceWare Web Conferencing	www.placeware.com
	Simulation Models		
Learning Management Systems	Web-Based Education Systems	None	None
	Computer-Based Training		
Interactivity	Wearable Computers	Orang Otang	www.orang-otang.com

Figure 3-35. Enterprise knowledge portal map template.

	Enterprise Portal	[Add IT–Enabling Framework Features]	Business Intelligence	[Add IT–Enabling Framework Features]	Collaboration & Communities	[Add IT–Enabling Framework Features]	Content Management	[Add IT–Enabling Framework Features]	Learning	[Add IT–Enabling Framework Features]
Be Organized Around Work Processes										
[Add Individual Knowledge Management Objectives]										
Maintain Knowledge and Facilitate Communication										
[Add Individual Knowledge Management Objectives]										
Focus on the Future										
[Add Individual Knowledge Management Objectives]										
Support Your Organization's Business Objectives										
[Add Individual Knowledge Management Objectives]										
Promote Innovations										
[Add Individual Knowledge Management Objectives]										
Maintain a Knowledge-Creating Organization										
[Add Individual Knowledge Management Objectives]										

agement objectives template. You will want to modify the rows to match the categories you established in your version of the knowledge management objectives report.

MYCOMPANY CASE STUDY

The knowledge management objectives report information has been added to the enterprise knowledge portal map template. The results are posted in the enterprise knowledge portal map shown in Figure 3-36. The knowledge management categories used in the rows for myCompany include:

- ❒ Be organized around work processes
- ❒ Maintain knowledge and facilitate communication
- ❒ Focus on the future
- ❒ Support your organization's business objectives
- ❒ Promote innovations
- ❒ Maintain a knowledge-creating organization

Add Enterprise Knowledge Portal IT–Enabling Framework

Purpose: Add the enterprise knowledge portal IT–enabling framework report details into the enterprise knowledge portal map template.

After completing step one, you will use the enterprise knowledge portal

Figure 3-36. Enterprise knowledge portal map with knowledge management objectives.

	Enterprise Portal	[Add IT–Enabling Framework Features]	**Business Intelligence**	[Add IT–Enabling Framework Features]	**Collaboration & Communities**	[Add IT–Enabling Framework Features]	**Content Management**	[Add IT–Enabling Framework Features]	**Learning**	[Add IT–Enabling Framework Features]
Be Organized Around Work Processes										
Improve employee effectiveness										
Make better decisions faster										
Improve information availability and access										
Improve cycle times										
Embed knowledge management activities										
Improve response times										
Improve information reuse										
Maintain Knowledge and Facilitate Communication										
Improve communication between managers										
Improve alignment of management objectives										
Improve awareness of roles and responsibilities										
Improve strategic alignment										
Improve span of influence of human expertise										
Improve operational efficiencies through information reuse										
Focus on the Future										
Improve market knowledge business strategy effectiveness										
Improve work process innovation										
Improve product innovation										
Improve recruitment and succession										
Improve planning, budgeting, and forecasting processes										
Improve e-business opportunities and strategies										
Support Your Organization's Business Objectives										
Improve personal alignment to your business strategy										
Embed learning into doing										
Drive business value										
Promote Innovations										
Enrich employee work-life experience										
Improve career development opportunities										
Improve employee autonomy										
Improve community involvement										
Maintain a Knowledge-Creating Organization										
Improve Web-centric business strategy										
Improve content management										
Improve enterprise search										
Improve user interface and usability consistency										
Improve cross-functional work processes										

map template to add the details of the enterprise knowledge portal IT–enabling framework report. The enterprise knowledge portal features are documented in the columns of the spreadsheet. Continue to maintain the technology categories used in the enterprise knowledge portal IT–enabling framework report. The enterprise knowledge portal map template includes the default technology categories from the enterprise knowledge portal IT–enabling framework report. You will want to modify the columns to match the categories you established in your version of the enterprise knowledge portal IT–enabling framework report.

MYCOMPANY CASE STUDY

The enterprise knowledge portal IT–enabling framework report information has been added to the enterprise knowledge portal map template. The results are posted in the enterprise knowledge portal map shown in Figure 3-37. The enterprise knowledge portal technology categories used in the columns for myCompany include:

- The enterprise portal
- Business intelligence
- Collaboration and communities
- Content management
- Learning

Prioritize Knowledge Management Objectives

Purpose: With the research and information available, prioritize the knowledge management objectives that will be targeted for implementation in the initial releases of the enterprise knowledge portal.

Within each knowledge management category you will want to prioritize your knowledge management objectives. Rate each objective from one—not critical to five—critical. The goal is to make a first-pass prioritization of your knowledge management objectives. You want to establish critical knowledge management objectives within each category to make certain that you are targeting all aspects of your organization as part of your enterprise knowledge portal effort.

MYCOMPANY CASE STUDY

The knowledge management objectives within each category have been prioritized in the enterprise knowledge portal map template

(text continues on page 151)

Figure 3-37. Enterprise knowledge portal map with enterprise knowledge portal IT–enabling framework.

	Enterprise Portal	Presentation	Knowledge Organization System	Search	Plug and Play Functions	Access and Integration	Profiling and Personalization	**Business Intelligence**	Decision Support	Performance-Based Metrics	Process Management	Balanced Scorecard	Data Mining	Information Mining	Information Management	**Collaboration & Communities**	Electronic Messaging Managemen	Discussion Groups	Team-Based Collaboration	Real-Time Collaboration	Collaborative Commerce
Be Organized Around Work Processes																					
Improve employee effectiveness																					
Make better decisions faster																					
Improve information availability and access																					
Improve cycle times																					
Embed knowledge management activities																					
Improve response times																					
Improve information reuse																					
Maintain Knowledge and Facilitate Communication																					
Improve communication between managers																					
Improve alignment of management objectives																					
Improve awareness of roles and responsibilities																					
Improve strategic alignment																					
Improve span of influence of human expertise																					
Improve operational efficiencies through information reuse																					
Focus on the Future																					
Improve market knowledge business strategy effectiveness																					
Improve work process innovation																					
Improve product innovation																					
Improve recruitment and succession																					
Improve planning, budgeting, and forecasting processes																					
Improve e-business opportunities and strategies																					

(continues)

Figure 3-37. (Continued).

	Enterprise Portal	Presentation	Knowledge Organization System	Search	Plug and Play Functions	Access and Integration	Profiling and Personalization	**Business Intelligence**	Decision Support	Performance-Based Metrics	Process Management	Balanced Scorecard	Data Mining	Information Mining	Information Management	**Collaboration & Communities**	Electronic Messaging Managemen	Discussion Groups	Team-Based Collaboration	Real-Time Collaboration	Collaborative Commerce
Support Your Organization's Business Objectives																					
Improve personal alignment to your business strategy																					
Embed learning into doing																					
Drive business value																					
Promote Innovations																					
Enrich employee work-life experience																					
Improve career development opportunities																					
Improve employee autonomy																					
Improve community involvement																					
Maintain a Knowledge-Creating Organization																					
Improve Web-centric business strategy																					
Improve content management																					
Improve enterprise search																					
Improve user interface and usability consistency																					
Improve cross-functional work processes																					

	Communities	Information Retrieval	**Content Management**	Structured Content	Data Integration Services	Unstructured Content	Document Management	Web Content Management	Electronic Commerce	**Learning**	EPSS	Video and Audio Conferencing	Learning Management System	Interactivity
Be Organized Around Work Processes														
Improve employee effectiveness														
Make better decisions faster														
Improve information availability and access														
Improve cycle times														
Embed knowledge management activities														
Improve response times														
Improve information reuse														
Maintain Knowledge and Facilitate Communication														
Improve communication between managers														
Improve alignment of management objectives														
Improve awareness of roles and responsibilities														
Improve strategic alignment														
Improve span of influence of human expertise														
Improve operational efficiencies through information reuse														
Focus on the Future														
Improve market knowledge business strategy effectiveness														
Improve work process innovation														
Improve product innovation														
Improve recruitment and succession														
Improve planning, budgeting, and forecasting processes														
Improve e-business opportunities and strategies														

(continues)

Figure 3-37. (Continued).

	Communities	Information Retrieval	**Content Management**	Structured Content	Data Integration Services	Unstructured Content	Document Management	Web Content Management	Electronic Commerce	**Learning**	EPSS	Video and Audio Conferencing	Learning Management System	Interactivity
Support Your Organization's Business Objectives														
Improve personal alignment to your business strategy														
Embed learning into doing														
Drive business value														
Promote Innovations														
Enrich employee work-life experience														
Improve career development opportunities														
Improve employee autonomy														
Improve community involvement														
Maintain a Knowledge-Creating Organization														
Improve Web-centric business strategy														
Improve content management														
Improve enterprise search														
Improve user interface and usability consistency														
Improve cross-functional work processes														

by the enterprise portal team. The results are posted in the enterprise knowledge portal map shown in Figure 3-38. The knowledge management prioritization scheme used for myCompany includes:

- ❐ Five—critical
- ❐ Four—must have
- ❐ Three—important
- ❐ Two—nice to have
- ❐ One—not critical

Prioritize Enterprise Knowledge Portal Features

Purpose: Based on the research and information available, prioritize the enterprise knowledge portal features that will be targeted to include in the initial releases of the enterprise knowledge portal.

Within each technology category you will want to prioritize your enterprise knowledge portal features. Rate each feature from one—not critical to five—critical. The goal is to make a first-pass prioritization of your enterprise knowledge portal features. You want to establish critical enterprise knowledge portal features within each technology category to make certain that you capitalize on the applications, solutions, and services within your information technology environment as part of your enterprise knowledge portal effort.

MYCOMPANY CASE STUDY

The enterprise knowledge portal features within each technology category have been prioritized in the enterprise knowledge portal map template by the enterprise portal team. The results are posted in the enterprise knowledge portal map shown in Figure 3-39. The knowledge management prioritization scheme used for myCompany includes:

- ❐ Five—critical
- ❐ Four—must have
- ❐ Three—important
- ❐ Two—nice to have
- ❐ One—not critical

The enterprise knowledge portal map report is the result of the completed enterprise knowledge portal map template. You will

(text continues on page 160)

Figure 3-38. Enterprise knowledge portal map with prioritized knowledge management objectives.

	Enterprise Portal	Presentation	Knowledge Organization System	Search	Plug and Play Functions	Access and Integration	Profiling and Personalization	**Business Intelligence**	Decision Support	Performance-Based Metrics	Process Management	Balanced Scorecard	Data Mining	Information Mining	Information Management	**Collaboration & Communities**	Electronic Messaging Managemen	Discussion Groups	Team-Based Collaboration	Real-Time Collaboration	Collaborative Commerce
Be Organized Around Work Processes																					
Improve employee effectiveness		5	4	5	4	5	5		4	4	3	3	2	3	4		5	5	5	5	1
Make better decisions faster		5	5	5	3	5	4		5	4	5	3	1	5	5		3	4	5	5	1
Improve information availability and access		5	5	5	2	5	5		5	3	3	3	1	4	5		4	4	4	4	1
Improve cycle times		3	4	5	2	4	4		4	5	5	5	1	2	4		3	4	5	5	1
Embed knowledge management activities		4	5	5	2	4	5		3	3	3	3	3	4	4		4	5	5	5	3
Improve response times		4	4	5	2	3	3		4	5	5	5	1	2	3		3	4	5	5	1
Improve information reuse		5	5	5	3	4	5		4	4	4	4	4	4	4		2	5	5	5	3
Maintain Knowledge and Facilitate Communication																					
Improve communication between managers		4	5	5	2	4	5		3	3	3	3	3	4	4		4	5	5	5	3
Improve alignment of management objectives		5	4	5	4	5	5		4	4	3	3	2	3	4		5	5	5	5	1
Improve awareness of roles and responsibilities		5	5	5	3	5	4		5	4	5	3	1	5	5		3	4	5	5	1
Improve strategic alignment		5	4	5	4	5	5		4	4	3	3	2	3	4		5	5	5	5	1
Improve span of influence of human expertise		4	5	5	2	4	5		3	3	3	3	3	4	4		4	5	5	5	3
Improve operational efficiencies through information reuse		5	5	5	2	5	5		5	3	3	3	1	4	5		4	4	4	4	1
Focus on the Future																					
Improve market knowledge business strategy effectiveness																					
Improve work process innovation		4	5	5	2	4	5		4	4	4	4	4	5	5		4	5	5	5	4
Improve product innovation		3	4	5	2	4	4		4	5	5	5	1	2	4		3	4	5	5	1
Improve recruitment and succession		5	5	5	3	5	5		5	3	3	3	1	4	5		4	4	5	5	1
Improve planning, budgeting, and forecasting processes		5	5	5	2	5	5		5	3	3	3	1	4	5		4	4	4	4	1
Improve e-business opportunities and strategies		5	5	5	3	5	5		5	3	3	3	1	4	5		4	4	5	5	4

	Enterprise Portal	Presentation	Knowledge Organization System	Search	Plug and Play Functions	Access and Integration	Profiling and Personalization	Business Intelligence	Decision Support	Performance-Based Metrics	Process Management	Balanced Scorecard	Data Mining	Information Mining	Information Management	Collaboration & Communities	Electronic Messaging Managemen	Discussion Groups	Team-Based Collaboration	Real-Time Collaboration	Collaborative Commerce
Support Your Organization's Business Objectives																					
Improve personal alignment to your business strategy		4	5	5	2	4	5		4	4	4	4	4	5	5		4	5	5	5	4
Embed learning into doing		4	5	5	2	4	5		4	4	4	4	4	5	5		4	5	5	5	4
Drive business value		5	5	5	2	5	5		5	3	3	3	1	4	5		4	4	4	4	1
Promote Innovations																					
Enrich employee work-life experience		5	5	5	3	5	5		5	3	3	3	1	4	5		4	4	5	5	1
Improve career development opportunities		5	5	5	3	5	5		5	4	4	4	2	3	4		4	5	5	5	1
Improve employee autonomy		4	5	5	2	4	5		4	4	4	4	4	5	5		4	5	5	5	4
Improve community involvement		3	5	5	2	3	5		3	3	3	3	3	3	3		4	3	3	3	1
Maintain a Knowledge-Creating Organization																					
Improve Web-centric business strategy		5	5	5	2	5	5		5	3	3	3	1	4	5		4	4	4	4	1
Improve content management		5	5	5	3	4	5		4	4	4	4	4	4	4		2	5	5	5	3
Improve enterprise search		5	5	5	2	5	5		5	3	3	3	1	4	5		4	4	4	4	1
Improve user interface and usability consistency		5	4	5	4	5	5		4	4	3	3	2	3	4		5	5	5	5	1
Improve cross-functional work processes		3	4	5	2	4	4		4	5	5	5	1	2	4		3	4	5	5	1

(continues)

Figure 3-38. (Continued).

	Communities	Information Retrieval	**Content Management**	Structured Content	Data Integration Services	Unstructured Content	Document Management	Web Content Management	Electronic Commerce	**Learning**	EPSS	Video and Audio Conferencing	Learning Management System	Interactivity
Be Organized Around Work Processes														
Improve employee effectiveness	4	5		4	5	5	5	5			5	5	2	
Make better decisions faster	3	5		5	5	5	5	5			5	5	2	
Improve information availability and access	2	5		5	5	5	5	5			5	5	1	2
Improve cycle times	3	5		4	4	4	4	4			4	4		
Embed knowledge management activities	5	5		3	3	3	3	3	2		5	5	1	2
Improve response times	3	5		4	4	4	4	4			4	4		
Improve information reuse	5	5		3	3	3	3	3	2		5	5	1	
Maintain Knowledge and Facilitate Communication														
Improve communication between managers	5	5		3	3	3	3	3	2		5	5	1	2
Improve alignment of management objectives	4	5		4	5	5	5	5			5	5	2	
Improve awareness of roles and responsibilities	3	5		5	5	5	5	5			5	5	2	
Improve strategic alignment	4	5		4	5	5	5	5			5	5	2	
Improve span of influence of human expertise	5	5		3	3	3	3	3	2		5	5	1	
Improve operational efficiencies through information reuse	2	5		5	5	5	5	5			5	5	1	2
Focus on the Future														
Improve market knowledge business strategy effectiveness														
Improve work process innovation	5	5		4	4	4	4	4	1		5	5	4	2
Improve product innovation	3	5		4	4	4	4	4			4	4		
Improve recruitment and succession	3	5		5	5	5	5	5	4		5	5	3	
Improve planning, budgeting, and forecasting processes	2	5		5	5	5	5	5			5	5	1	2
Improve e-business opportunities and strategies	3	5		5	5	5	5	5	4		5	5	3	

	Communities	Information Retrieval	**Content Management**	Structured Content	Data Integration Services	Unstructured Content	Document Management	Web Content Management	Electronic Commerce	**Learning**	EPSS	Video and Audio Conferencing	Learning Management System	Interactivity
Support Your Organization's Business Objectives														
Improve personal alignment to your business strategy	5	5		4	4	4	4	4	1		5	5	4	
Embed learning into doing	5	5		4	4	4	4	4	1		5	5	4	2
Drive business value	2	5		5	5	5	5	5			5	5	1	2
Promote Innovations														
Enrich employee work-life experience	3	5		5	5	5	5	5	4		5	5	3	
Improve career development opportunities	4	5		4	4	4	4	4	1		5	4	4	2
Improve employee autonomy	5	5		4	4	4	4	4	1		5	5	4	
Improve community involvement	4	5		3	3	3	3	3	1		3	4	2	
Maintain a Knowledge-Creating Organization														
Improve Web-centric business strategy	2	5		5	5	5	5	5			5	5	1	2
Improve content management	5	5		3	3	3	3	3	2		5	5	1	
Improve enterprise search	2	5		5	5	5	5	5			5	5	1	2
Improve user interface and usability consistency	4	5		4	5	5	5	5			5	5	2	
Improve cross-functional work processes	3	5		4	4	4	4	4			4	4		

Figure 3-39. Enterprise knowledge portal map report (first release).

	Enterprise Portal	Presentation	Knowledge Organization System	Search	Plug and Play Functions	Access and Integration	Profiling and Personalization	**Business Intelligence**	Decision Support	Performance-Based Metrics	Process Management	Balanced Scorecard	Data Mining	Information Mining	Information Management	**Collaboration & Communities**	Electronic Messaging Management	Discussion Groups	Team-Based Collaboration	Real-Time Collaboration	Collaborative Commerce
Be Organized Around Work Processes																					
Improve employee effectiveness		5-2	4-5	5-5	4-3	5-5	5-5		4-5	4-4	3-4	3-4	2-2	3-4	4-5		5-3	5-4	5-5	5-5	1-2
Make better decisions faster		5-2	5-5	5-5	3-3	5-5	4-5		5-5	4-4	5-4	3-4	1-2	5-4	5-5		3-3	4-4	5-5	5-5	1-2
Improve information availability and access		5-2	5-5	5-5	2-3	5-5	5-5		5-5	3-4	3-4	3-4	1-2	4-4	5-5		4-3	4-4	4-5	4-5	1-2
Improve cycle times		3-2	4-5	5-5	2-3	4-5	4-5		4-5	5-4	5-4	5-4	1-2	2-4	4-5		3-3	4-4	5-5	5-5	1-2
Embed knowledge management activities		4-2	5-5	5-5	2-3	4-5	5-5		3-5	3-4	3-4	3-4	3-2	4-4	4-5		4-3	5-4	5-5	5-5	3-2
Improve response times		4-2	4-5	5-5	2-3	3-5	3-5		4-5	5-4	5-4	5-4	1-2	2-4	3-5		3-3	4-4	5-5	5-5	1-2
Improve information reuse		5-2	5-5	5-5	3-3	4-5	5-5		4-5	4-4	4-4	4-4	4-2	4-4	4-5		2-3	5-4	5-5	5-5	3-2
Maintain Knowledge and Facilitate Communication																					
Improve communication between managers		4-2	5-5	5-5	2-3	4-5	5-5		3-5	3-4	3-4	3-4	3-2	4-4	4-5		4-3	5-4	5-5	5-5	3-2
Improve alignment of management objectives		5-2	4-5	5-5	4-3	5-5	5-5		4-5	4-4	3-4	3-4	2-2	3-4	4-5		5-3	5-4	5-5	5-5	1-2
Improve awareness of roles and responsibilities		5-2	5-5	5-5	3-3	5-5	4-5		5-5	4-4	5-4	3-4	1-2	5-4	5-5		3-3	4-4	5-5	5-5	1-2
Improve strategic alignment		5-2	4-5	5-5	4-3	5-5	5-5		4-5	4-4	3-4	3-4	2-2	3-4	4-5		5-3	5-4	5-5	5-5	1-2
Improve span of influence of human expertise		4-2	5-5	5-5	2-3	4-5	5-5		3-5	3-4	3-4	3-4	3-2	4-4	4-5		4-3	5-4	5-5	5-5	3-2
Improve operational efficiencies through information reuse		5-2	5-5	5-5	2-3	5-5	5-5		5-5	3-4	3-4	3-4	1-2	4-4	5-5		4-3	4-4	4-5	4-5	1-2
Focus on the Future																					
Improve market knowledge business strategy effectiveness		5-2	5-5	5-5	2-3	5-5	5-5		5-5	3-4	3-4	3-4	1-2	4-4	5-5		4-3	4-4	4-5	4-5	1-2
Improve work process innovation		4-2	5-5	5-5	2-3	4-5	5-5		4-5	4-4	4-4	4-4	4-2	5-4	5-5		4-3	5-4	5-5	5-5	4-2
Improve product innovation		3-2	4-5	5-5	2-3	4-5	4-5		4-5	5-4	5-4	5-4	1-2	2-4	4-5		3-3	4-4	5-5	5-5	1-2
Improve recruitment and succession		5-2	5-5	5-5	3-3	5-5	5-5		5-5	3-4	3-4	3-4	1-2	4-4	5-5		4-3	4-4	5-5	5-5	1-2
Improve planning, budgeting, and forecasting processes		5-2	5-5	5-5	2-3	5-5	5-5		5-5	3-4	3-4	3-4	1-2	4-4	5-5		4-3	4-4	4-5	4-5	1-2
Improve e-business opportunities and strategies		5-2	5-5	5-5	3-3	5-5	5-5		5-5	3-4	3-4	3-4	1-2	4-4	5-5		4-3	4-4	5-5	5-5	4-2

	Enterprise Portal	Presentation	Knowledge Organization System	Search	Plug and Play Functions	Access and Integration	Profiling and Personalization	**Business Intelligence**	Decision Support	Performance-Based Metrics	Process Management	Balanced Scorecard	Data Mining	Information Mining	Information Management	**Collaboration & Communities**	Electronic Messaging Managemen	Discussion Groups	Team-Based Collaboration	Real-Time Collaboration	Collaborative Commerce
Support Your Organization's Business Objectives																					
Improve personal alignment to your business strategy		4-2	5-5	5-5	2-3	4-5	5-5		4-5	4-4	4-4	4-4	4-2	5-4	5-5		4-3	5-4	5-5	5-5	4-2
Embed learning into doing		4-2	5-5	5-5	2-3	4-5	5-5		4-5	4-4	4-4	4-4	4-2	5-4	5-5		4-3	5-4	5-5	5-5	4-2
Drive business value		5-2	5-5	5-5	2-3	5-5	5-5		5-5	3-4	3-4	3-4	1-2	4-4	5-5		4-3	4-4	4-5	4-5	1-2
Promote Innovations																					
Enrich employee work-life experience		5-2	5-5	5-5	3-3	5-5	5-5		5-5	3-4	3-4	3-4	1-2	4-4	5-5		4-3	4-4	5-5	5-5	1-2
Improve career development opportunities		5-2	5-5	5-5	3-3	5-5	5-5		5-5	4-4	4-4	4-4	2-2	3-4	4-5		4-3	5-4	5-5	5-5	1-2
Improve employee autonomy		4-2	5-5	5-5	2-3	4-5	5-5		4-5	4-4	4-4	4-4	4-2	5-4	5-5		4-3	5-4	5-5	5-5	4-2
Improve community involvement		3-2	5-5	5-5	2-3	3-5	5-5		3-5	3-4	3-4	3-4	3-2	3-4	3-5		4-3	3-4	3-5	3-5	1-2
Maintain a Knowledge-Creating Organization																					
Improve Web-centric business strategy		5-2	5-5	5-5	2-3	5-5	5-5		5-5	3-4	3-4	3-4	1-2	4-4	5-5		4-3	4-4	4-5	4-5	1-2
Improve content management		5-2	5-5	5-5	3-3	4-5	5-5		4-5	4-4	4-4	4-4	4-2	4-4	4-5		2-3	5-4	5-5	5-5	3-2
Improve enterprise search		5-2	5-5	5-5	2-3	5-5	5-5		5-5	3-4	3-4	3-4	1-2	4-4	5-5		4-3	4-4	4-5	4-5	1-2
Improve user interface and usability consistency		5-2	4-5	5-5	4-3	5-5	5-5		4-5	4-4	3-4	3-4	2-2	3-4	4-5		5-3	5-4	5-5	5-5	1-2
Improve cross-functional work processes		3-2	4-5	5-5	2-3	4-5	4-5		4-5	5-4	5-4	5-4	1-2	2-4	4-5		3-3	4-4	5-5	5-5	1-2

(continues)

Figure 3-39. (Continued).

	Communities	Information Retrieval	**Content Management**	Structured Content	Data Integration Services	Unstructured Content	Document Management	Web Content Management	Electronic Commerce	**Learning**	EPSS	Video and Audio Conferencing	Learning Management System	Interactivity
Be Organized Around Work Processes														
Improve employee effectiveness	4-4	5-5		4-4	5-4	5-3	5-3	5-3	0-2		5-4	5-5	2-2	0-1
Make better decisions faster	3-4	5-5		5-4	5-4	5-3	5-3	5-3	0-2		5-4	5-5	2-2	0-1
Improve information availability and access	2-4	5-5		5-4	5-4	5-3	5-3	5-3	0-2		5-4	5-5	1-2	2-1
Improve cycle times	3-4	5-5		4-4	4-4	4-3	4-3	4-3	0-2		4-4	4-5	0-2	0-1
Embed knowledge management activities	5-4	5-5		3-4	3-4	3-3	3-3	3-3	2-2		5-4	5-5	1-2	2-1
Improve response times	3-4	5-5		4-4	4-4	4-3	4-3	4-3	0-2		4-4	4-5	0-2	0-1
Improve information reuse	5-4	5-5		3-4	3-4	3-3	3-3	3-3	2-2		5-4	5-5	1-2	0-1
Maintain Knowledge and Facilitate Communication														
Improve communication between managers	5-4	5-5		3-4	3-4	3-3	3-3	3-3	2-2		5-4	5-5	1-2	2-1
Improve alignment of management objectives	4-4	5-5		4-4	5-4	5-3	5-3	5-3	0-2		5-4	5-5	2-2	0-1
Improve awareness of roles and responsibilities	3-4	5-5		5-4	5-4	5-3	5-3	5-3	0-2		5-4	5-5	2-2	0-1
Improve strategic alignment	4-4	5-5		4-4	5-4	5-3	5-3	5-3	0-2		5-4	5-5	2-2	0-1
Improve span of influence of human expertise	5-4	5-5		3-4	3-4	3-3	3-3	3-3	2-2		5-4	5-5	1-2	0-1
Improve operational efficiencies through information reuse	2-4	5-5		5-4	5-4	5-3	5-3	5-3	0-2		5-4	5-5	1-2	2-1
Focus on the Future														
Improve market knowledge business strategy effectiveness	2-4	5-5		5-4	5-4	5-3	5-3	5-3	0-2		5-4	5-5	1-2	2-1
Improve work process innovation	5-4	5-5		4-4	4-4	4-3	4-3	4-3	1-2		5-4	5-5	4-2	2-1
Improve product innovation	3-4	5-5		4-4	4-4	4-3	4-3	4-3	0-2		4-4	4-5	0-2	0-1
Improve recruitment and succession	3-4	5-5		5-4	5-4	5-3	5-3	5-3	4-2		5-4	5-5	3-2	0-1
Improve planning, budgeting, and forecasting processes	2-4	5-5		5-4	5-4	5-3	5-3	5-3	0-2		5-4	5-5	1-2	2-1
Improve e-business opportunities and strategies	3-4	5-5		5-4	5-4	5-3	5-3	5-3	4-2		5-4	5-5	3-2	0-1

	Communities	Information Retrieval	**Content Management**	Structured Content	Data Integration Services	Unstructured Content	Document Management	Web Content Management	Electronic Commerce	**Learning**	EPSS	Video and Audio Conferencing	Learning Management System	Interactivity
Support Your Organization's Business Objectives														
Improve personal alignment to your business strategy	5-4	5-5		4-4	4-4	4-3	4-3	4-3	1-2		5-4	5-5	4-2	0-1
Embed learning into doing	5-4	5-5		4-4	4-4	4-3	4-3	4-3	1-2		5-4	5-5	4-2	2-1
Drive business value	2-4	5-5		5-4	5-4	5-3	5-3	5-3	0-2		5-4	5-5	1-2	2-1
Promote Innovations														
Enrich employee work-life experience	3-4	5-5		5-4	5-4	5-3	5-3	5-3	4-2		5-4	5-5	3-2	0-1
Improve career development opportunities	4-4	5-5		4-4	4-4	4-3	4-3	4-3	1-2		5-4	4-5	4-2	2-1
Improve employee autonomy	5-4	5-5		4-4	4-4	4-3	4-3	4-3	1-2		5-4	5-5	4-2	0-1
Improve community involvement	4-4	5-5		3-4	3-4	3-3	3-3	3-3	1-2		3-4	4-5	2-2	0-1
Maintain a Knowledge-Creating Organization														
Improve Web-centric business strategy	2-4	5-5		5-4	5-4	5-3	5-3	5-3	0-2		5-4	5-5	1-2	2-1
Improve content management	5-4	5-5		3-4	3-4	3-3	3-3	3-3	2-2		5-4	5-5	1-2	0-1
Improve enterprise search	2-4	5-5		5-4	5-4	5-3	5-3	5-3	0-2		5-4	5-5	1-2	2-1
Improve user interface and usability consistency	4-4	5-5		4-4	5-4	5-3	5-3	5-3	0-2		5-4	5-5	2-2	0-1
Improve cross-functional work processes	3-4	5-5		4-4	4-4	4-3	4-3	4-3	0-2		4-4	4-5	0-2	0-1

want to share and review the results with the knowledge expert community. During this review you will be making decisions as much as sharing information as you walk through the enterprise knowledge portal map report. To review the results effectively, you should consider bringing the knowledge expert community together in a meeting format. Create a supporting presentation to accompany the enterprise knowledge portal map report. You will want to have an open discussion of the prioritized knowledge management objectives and enterprise knowledge portal features. You will make any adjustments agreed on by the knowledge expert community to create the final version of the enterprise knowledge portal map report. The final activities completed by the enterprise knowledge portal team to outline the value of an enterprise knowledge portal for myCompany include:

- ❒ Completing the first release of the enterprise knowledge portal map report.
- ❒ Creating a supporting presentation to accompany and explain the proposed path forward for an enterprise knowledge portal at myCompany. (The enterprise knowledge portal map report review presentation can be reviewed in Figure 3-40.)
- ❒ Holding a review meeting to discuss and clarify the results of the enterprise knowledge portal map report. (An example meeting invitation and proposed agenda are presented in Figure 3-41.)
- ❒ Deciding to continue to move forward with an enterprise knowledge portal and completing the final version of the enterprise knowledge portal map report as a result of the review meeting. (The report can be seen in Figure 3-42.)
- ❒ Adding an executive sponsor to the enterprise knowledge portal effort as it moves forward. (Executives with existing corporate initiatives that were closely related or would benefit the most from the enterprise knowledge portal were considered the best candidates. The list of executive sponsors considered included the executives responsible for e-business, the intranet, customer relationship management, and supply chain management.)
- ❒ Distributing a communication (shown in Figure 3-43) to members of the knowledge expert community to share the new enterprise knowledge portal initiative, introduce the executive sponsor, present the final version of the enterprise knowledge portal map report, and encourage individual members to review details with their business units.

Figure 3-40. Enterprise knowledge portal map report review.

- The enterprise knowledge portal map was completed by the enterprise knowledge portal team with selected input from knowledge expert community members
- The knowledge management objectives were pulled from the knowledge management objectives report and broken into rows on the spreadsheet:
  —Be organized around work processes
  —Maintain knowledge and facilitate communication
  —Focus on the future
  —Support your organization's business objectives
  —Promote innovations
  —Maintain a knowledge-creating organization
- The applications and services were pulled from the enterprise knowledge portal IT–enabling framework and broken into columns on the spreadsheet:
  —Enterprise portal
  —Business intelligence
  —Collaboration and communities
  —Content management
  —Learning
- Each knowledge management objective was ranked against each enterprise knowledge portal IT–enabling framework feature to assign a value of importance the feature brings to accomplishing the objective. Values between 0 and 5 were assigned. The higher the value, the more critical the feature is to meet the objective.
- Each enterprise knowledge portal IT–enabling framework feature was assigned a value based on the available feature in the current IT environment to meet the intent of the knowledge management objective. Values between 0 and 5 were assigned. The higher the value, the more likely the current IT environment can meet the intent of the objective.
- The enterprise knowledge portal map report is available for review in the following spreadsheet:
  Enterprise Knowledge Portal Map Report (Excel Spreadsheet)
- Open discussion of the enterprise knowledge portal map report
- Updates to the enterprise knowledge portal map report
- Note: Rows and columns can be added, updated, and removed from the enterprise knowledge portal map report to reflect the appropriate level of detail

Key Points

Your enterprise knowledge portal is a custom-designed solution that maps your knowledge management objectives to enterprise portal features and functions. The resulting enterprise knowledge portal is a central location for finding content, working with selected screens from applications, seamlessly interacting with a multitude of applications and systems in the same portal page, identifying where human expertise can be found and utilized in your organization, and working effectively within work processes. A collection of templates has been created to document your knowledge management objectives and enterprise knowledge portal required features and

Figure 3-41. A sample invitation and agenda to the enterprise knowledge portal map report review.

Agenda	Enterprise Knowledge Portal Map Report Review Conference Room One	
Type of meeting:	Enterprise Knowledge Portal Map Report Review Meeting	
Facilitator:	Heidi Collins	
Note taker:	David Kennedy	
Attendees:	Knowledge Expert Community Members	
	Agenda Topics	
50 Minutes	Review each knowledge management objective (rows in the template) and the assigned value of importance (0 to 5) each IT Enabling Framework feature brings to accomplishing the objective	Heidi Collins
10 Minutes	Break	
50 Minutes	Review each IT-Enabling Framework feature (columns in the template) and the assigned value (0 to 5) based on the availability of the feature in the current IT environment to meet the intent of the knowledge management objective	Heidi Collins
10 Minutes	Break	
30 Minutes	Review the Knowledge Management Objectives Report for high priority objectives and compare to the Enterprise Knowledge Portal Map Report	Heidi Collins
15 Minutes	Review action items	Heidi Collins
15 Minutes	Review Enterprise Knowledge Portal Map progress and discuss our next steps and activities	Heidi Collins

functions, and map the two together. The enterprise knowledge portal templates include:

- ❒ Document your knowledge management objectives
  1. Organization mission and initiatives questionnaire
  2. Knowledge management objectives questionnaire
  3. Knowledge management objectives template
- ❒ Enterprise knowledge portal IT–enabling framework
  1. Enterprise knowledge portal IT–enabling framework template
  2. Enterprise knowledge portal IT–enabling spreadsheet
- ❒ Enterprise knowledge portal map
  1. Enterprise knowledge portal map template

(text continues on page 167)

Figure 3-42. Enterprise knowledge portal map report (final release).

	Enterprise Portal	Presentation	Knowledge Organization System	Search	Plug and Play Functions	Access and Integration	Profiling and Personalization	**Business Intelligence**	Decision Support	Performance-Based Metrics	Process Management	Balanced Scorecard	Data Mining	Information Mining	Information Management	**Collaboration & Communities**	Electronic Messaging Management	Discussion Groups	Team-Based Collaboration	Real-Time Collaboration	Collaborative Commerce
Be Organized Around Work Processes																					
Improve employee effectiveness		5-2	4-3	5-3	4-3	5-4	5-3		4-4	4-4	3-4	3-4	2-2	3-4	4-3		5-3	5-4	5-4	5-3	1-2
Make better decisions faster		5-2	5-3	5-3	3-3	5-4	4-3		5-4	4-4	5-4	3-4	1-2	5-4	5-3		3-3	4-4	5-4	5-3	1-2
Improve information availability and access		5-2	5-3	5-3	2-3	5-4	5-3		5-4	3-4	3-4	3-4	1-2	4-4	5-3		4-3	4-4	4-4	4-3	1-2
Improve cycle times		3-2	4-3	5-3	2-3	4-4	4-3		4-4	5-4	5-4	5-4	1-2	2-4	4-3		3-3	4-4	5-4	5-3	1-2
Embed knowledge management activities		4-2	5-3	5-3	2-3	4-4	5-3		3-4	3-4	3-4	3-4	3-2	4-4	4-3		4-3	5-4	5-4	5-3	3-2
Improve response times		4-2	4-3	5-3	2-3	3-4	3-3		4-4	5-4	5-4	5-4	1-2	2-4	3-3		3-3	4-4	5-4	5-3	1-2
Improve information reuse		5-2	5-3	5-3	3-3	4-4	5-3		4-4	4-4	4-4	4-4	4-2	4-4	4-3		2-3	5-4	5-4	5-3	3-2
Maintain Knowledge and Facilitate Communication																					
Improve communication between managers		4-2	5-3	5-3	2-3	4-4	5-3		3-4	3-4	3-4	3-4	3-2	4-4	4-3		4-3	5-4	5-4	5-3	3-2
Improve alignment of management objectives		5-2	4-3	5-3	4-3	5-4	5-3		4-4	4-4	3-4	3-4	2-2	3-4	4-3		5-3	5-4	5-4	5-3	1-2
Improve awareness of roles and responsibilities		5-2	5-3	5-3	3-3	5-4	4-3		5-4	4-4	5-4	3-4	1-2	5-4	5-3		3-3	4-4	5-4	5-3	1-2
Improve strategic alignment		5-2	4-3	5-3	4-3	5-4	5-3		4-4	4-4	3-4	3-4	2-2	3-4	4-3		5-3	5-4	5-4	5-3	1-2
Improve span of influence of human expertise		4-2	5-3	5-3	2-3	4-4	5-3		3-4	3-4	3-4	3-4	3-2	4-4	4-3		4-3	5-4	5-4	5-3	3-2
Improve operational efficiencies through information reuse		5-2	5-3	5-3	2-3	5-4	5-3		5-4	3-4	3-4	3-4	1-2	4-4	5-3		4-3	4-4	4-4	4-3	1-2
Focus on the Future																					
Improve market knowledge business strategy effectiveness		5-2	5-3	5-3	2-3	5-4	5-3		5-4	3-4	3-4	3-4	1-2	4-4	5-3		4-3	4-4	4-4	4-3	1-2
Improve work process innovation		4-2	5-3	5-3	2-3	4-4	5-3		4-4	4-4	4-4	4-4	4-2	5-4	5-3		4-3	5-4	5-4	5-3	4-2
Improve product innovation		3-2	4-3	5-3	2-3	4-4	4-3		4-4	5-4	5-4	5-4	1-2	2-4	4-3		3-3	4-4	5-4	5-3	1-2
Improve recruitment and succession		5-2	5-3	5-3	3-3	5-4	5-3		5-4	3-4	3-4	3-4	1-2	4-4	5-3		4-3	4-4	5-4	5-3	1-2
Improve planning, budgeting, and forecasting processes		5-2	5-3	5-3	2-3	5-4	5-3		5-4	3-4	3-4	3-4	1-2	4-4	5-3		4-3	4-4	4-4	4-3	1-2
Improve e-business opportunities and strategies		5-2	5-3	5-3	3-3	5-4	5-3		5-4	3-4	3-4	3-4	1-2	4-4	5-3		4-3	4-4	5-4	5-3	4-2

(continues)

Figure 3-42. (Continued).

	Enterprise Portal	Presentation	Knowledge Organization System	Search	Plug and Play Functions	Access and Integration	Profiling and Personalization	**Business Intelligence**	Decision Support	Performance-Based Metrics	Process Management	Balanced Scorecard	Data Mining	Information Mining	Information Management	**Collaboration & Communities**	Electronic Messaging Managemen	Discussion Groups	Team-Based Collaboration	Real-Time Collaboration	Collaborative Commerce
Support Your Organization's Business Objectives																					
Improve personal alignment to your business strategy		4-2	5-3	5-3	2-3	4-4	5-3		4-4	4-4	4-4	4-4	4-2	5-4	5-3		4-3	5-4	5-4	5-3	4-2
Embed learning into doing		4-2	5-3	5-3	2-3	4-4	5-3		4-4	4-4	4-4	4-4	4-2	5-4	5-3		4-3	5-4	5-4	5-3	4-2
Drive business value		5-2	5-3	5-3	2-3	5-4	5-3		5-4	3-4	3-4	3-4	1-2	4-4	5-3		4-3	4-4	4-4	4-3	1-2
Promote Innovations																					
Enrich employee work-life experience		5-2	5-3	5-3	3-3	5-4	5-3		5-4	3-4	3-4	3-4	1-2	4-4	5-3		4-3	4-4	5-4	5-3	1-2
Improve career development opportunities		5-2	5-3	5-3	3-3	5-4	5-3		5-4	4-4	4-4	4-4	2-2	3-4	4-3		4-3	5-4	5-4	5-3	1-2
Improve employee autonomy		4-2	5-3	5-3	2-3	4-4	5-3		4-4	4-4	4-4	4-4	4-2	5-4	5-3		4-3	5-4	5-4	5-3	4-2
Improve community involvement		3-2	5-3	5-3	2-3	3-4	5-3		3-4	3-4	3-4	3-4	3-2	3-4	3-3		4-3	3-4	3-4	3-3	1-2
Maintain a Knowledge-Creating Organization																					
Improve Web-centric business strategy		5-2	5-3	5-3	2-3	5-4	5-3		5-4	3-4	3-4	3-4	1-2	4-4	5-3		4-3	4-4	4-4	4-3	1-2
Improve content management		5-2	5-3	5-3	3-3	4-4	5-3		4-4	4-4	4-4	4-4	4-2	4-4	4-3		2-3	5-4	5-4	5-3	3-2
Improve enterprise search		5-2	5-3	5-3	2-3	5-4	5-3		5-4	3-4	3-4	3-4	1-2	4-4	5-3		4-3	4-4	4-4	4-3	1-2
Improve user interface and usability consistency		5-2	4-3	5-3	4-3	5-4	5-3		4-4	4-4	3-4	3-4	2-2	3-4	4-3		5-3	5-4	5-4	5-3	1-2
Improve cross-functional work processes		3-2	4-3	5-3	2-3	4-4	4-3		4-4	5-4	5-4	5-4	1-2	2-4	4-3		3-3	4-4	5-4	5-3	1-2

	Communities	Information Retrieval	**Content Management**	Structured Content	Data Integration Services	Unstructured Content	Document Management	Web Content Management	Electronic Commerce	**Learning**	EPSS	Video and Audio Conferencing	Learning Management System	Interactivity
Be Organized Around Work Processes														
Improve employee effectiveness	4-3	5-3		4-4	5-4	5-3	5-3	5-3	0-1		5-3	5-4	2-1	0-0
Make better decisions faster	3-3	5-3		5-4	5-4	5-3	5-3	5-3	0-1		5-3	5-4	2-1	0-0
Improve information availability and access	2-3	5-3		5-4	5-4	5-3	5-3	5-3	0-1		5-3	5-4	1-1	2-0
Improve cycle times	3-3	5-3		4-4	4-4	4-3	4-3	4-3	0-1		4-3	4-4	0-1	0-0
Embed knowledge management activities	5-3	5-3		3-4	3-4	3-3	3-3	3-3	2-1		5-3	5-4	1-1	2-0
Improve response times	3-3	5-3		4-4	4-4	4-3	4-3	4-3	0-1		4-3	4-4	0-1	0-0
Improve information reuse	5-3	5-3		3-4	3-4	3-3	3-3	3-3	2-1		5-3	5-4	1-1	0-0
Maintain Knowledge and Facilitate Communication														
Improve communication between managers	5-3	5-3		3-4	3-4	3-3	3-3	3-3	2-1		5-3	5-4	1-1	2-0
Improve alignment of management objectives	4-3	5-3		4-4	5-4	5-3	5-3	5-3	0-1		5-3	5-4	2-1	0-0
Improve awareness of roles and responsibilities	3-3	5-3		5-4	5-4	5-3	5-3	5-3	0-1		5-3	5-4	2-1	0-0
Improve strategic alignment	4-3	5-3		4-4	5-4	5-3	5-3	5-3	0-1		5-3	5-4	2-1	0-0
Improve span of influence of human expertise	5-3	5-3		3-4	3-4	3-3	3-3	3-3	2-1		5-3	5-4	1-1	0-0
Improve operational efficiencies through information reuse	2-3	5-3		5-4	5-4	5-3	5-3	5-3	0-1		5-3	5-4	1-1	2-0
Focus on the Future														
Improve market knowledge business strategy effectiveness	2-3	5-3		5-4	5-4	5-3	5-3	5-3	0-1		5-3	5-4	1-1	2-0
Improve work process innovation	5-3	5-3		4-4	4-4	4-3	4-3	4-3	1-1		5-3	5-4	4-1	2-0
Improve product innovation	3-3	5-3		4-4	4-4	4-3	4-3	4-3	0-1		4-3	4-4	0-1	0-0
Improve recruitment and succession	3-3	5-3		5-4	5-4	5-3	5-3	5-3	4-1		5-3	5-4	3-1	0-0
Improve planning, budgeting, and forecasting processes	2-3	5-3		5-4	5-4	5-3	5-3	5-3	0-1		5-3	5-4	1-1	2-0
Improve e-business opportunities and strategies	3-3	5-3		5-4	5-4	5-3	5-3	5-3	4-1		5-3	5-4	3-1	0-0

(continues)

Figure 3-42. (Continued).

	Communities	Information Retrieval	**Content Management**	Structured Content	Data Integration Services	Unstructured Content	Document Management	Web Content Management	Electronic Commerce	**Learning**	EPSS	Video and Audio Conferencing	Learning Management System	Interactivity
Support Your Organization's Business Objectives														
Improve personal alignment to your business strategy	5-3	5-3		4-4	4-4	4-3	4-3	4-3	1-1		5-3	5-4	4-1	0-0
Embed learning into doing	5-3	5-3		4-4	4-4	4-3	4-3	4-3	1-1		5-3	5-4	4-1	2-0
Drive business value	2-3	5-3		5-4	5-4	5-3	5-3	5-3	0-1		5-3	5-4	1-1	2-0
Promote Innovations														
Enrich employee work-life experience	3-3	5-3		5-4	5-4	5-3	5-3	5-3	4-1		5-3	5-4	3-1	0-0
Improve career development opportunities	4-3	5-3		4-4	4-4	4-3	4-3	4-3	1-1		5-3	4-4	4-1	2-0
Improve employee autonomy	5-3	5-3		4-4	4-4	4-3	4-3	4-3	1-1		5-3	5-4	4-1	0-0
Improve community involvement	4-3	5-3		3-4	3-4	3-3	3-3	3-3	1-1		3-3	4-4	2-1	0-0
Maintain a Knowledge-Creating Organization														
Improve Web-centric business strategy	2-3	5-3		5-4	5-4	5-3	5-3	5-3	0-1		5-3	5-4	1-1	2-0
Improve content management	5-3	5-3		3-4	3-4	3-3	3-3	3-3	2-1		5-3	5-4	1-1	0-0
Improve enterprise search	2-3	5-3		5-4	5-4	5-3	5-3	5-3	0-1		5-3	5-4	1-1	2-0
Improve user interface and usability consistency	4-3	5-3		4-4	5-4	5-3	5-3	5-3	0-1		5-3	5-4	2-1	0-0
Improve cross-functional work processes	3-3	5-3		4-4	4-4	4-3	4-3	4-3	0-1		4-3	4-4	0-1	0-0

Figure 3-43. Knowledge expert community—communication three.

Re: Enterprise Knowledge Portal Map Report

Hello Knowledge Expert Community,

The final version of the **Enterprise Knowledge Portal Map** report is available. The **Enterprise Knowledge Portal Team** would like to thank each of you for your contribution in completing this effort. To review the final report please visit:
Enterprise Knowledge Portal Map Report (Excel Spreadsheet)

We are asking the **Knowledge Expert Community** members to share this information with other managers and teams in your business units. Review the **Enterprise Knowledge Portal Map Report** at team meetings or other events to begin to create awareness of myCompany's knowledge management objectives, corporate initiatives, and how knowledge management can support and improve our corporate initiatives. If you need additional presentation information or material, please let Heidi Collins, Michael Douglas, or David Kennedy know and we will post it for everyone to use and access.

Using the basic knowledge you have collected around knowledge management in your organization and enterprise portal software solutions, take some time to learn more about the enterprise portal market. There are several differences among enterprise portal vendors and products, and trying to compare them with each other can be impossible. The most effective approach is to consider the enterprise knowledge portal features and functions separate from the vendors and products. Weave the features and functionality needed to your knowledge management objectives. Create a request for proposal to the enterprise portal vendors that will closely match your requirements. You will want each vendor to demonstrate his proposed enterprise portal design and architecture that will be able to deliver the enterprise knowledge portal functionality you need taking full advantage of the technologies that currently exist in your organization. The first set of activities will be to create an overview of your organization by mapping your knowledge management objectives into an enterprise portal. You will want to complete the following activities:

- ❒ Research the enterprise knowledge portal market
- ❒ Document your knowledge management objectives
  1. Understand your organization's mission and initiatives
  2. Create a knowledge management objectives questionnaire
  3. Identify a knowledge expert community
  4. Schedule interviews with the knowledge expert community
  5. Complete the knowledge management objectives template

❒ Document your enterprise knowledge portal IT–enabling framework
  1. Identify primary enterprise knowledge portal technologies
  2. Add features to the enterprise knowledge portal technologies
  3. Document existing applications, systems, or services

❒ Document your enterprise knowledge portal map
  1. Add knowledge management objectives
  2. Add enterprise knowledge portal IT–enabling framework
  3. Prioritize knowledge management objectives
  4. Prioritize enterprise knowledge portal features

Once your initial research is complete and several key knowledge experts in your organization have approved moving forward to define an enterprise knowledge portal, the next phase of the enterprise knowledge portal is to create a program. A program outlines what, who, how, and when for the enterprise knowledge portal. The enterprise knowledge portal program is what bridges your enterprise knowledge portal map created in Part I to your organizational structure to manage, the resources to build, and the methodology to deploy and maintain the enterprise knowledge portal.

You are going to need an enterprise knowledge portal program that provides a well-understood path forward for your organization to be able to deliver a cohesive and comprehensive enterprise knowledge portal. Chapter 4 identifies a series of activities and tasks as well as templates you can use or modify to create your enterprise knowledge portal program.

II

The Enterprise Knowledge Portal Program

4

Outline the Enterprise Knowledge Portal Program

"The most important invention that will come out of the corporate research lab in the future will be the corporation itself. As companies try to keep pace with rapid changes in technology and cope with unstable business environments, the research department has to do more than simply innovate new products. It must design the new technological and organizational 'architectures' that make a continuously innovating company possible."

JOHN SEELY BROWN, *RESEARCH THAT REINVENTS THE CORPORATION*

With your enterprise knowledge portal map report complete, and an agreement from knowledge experts throughout the company that an enterprise knowledge portal will add business value, you are ready to outline the enterprise knowledge portal program. In simple terms, the enterprise portal program is a series of future events. You are trying to create a logical set of steps to clarify the scope of the enterprise knowledge portal and the roles and responsibilities within the organization to create and maintain the enterprise knowledge portal, outline a methodology and collection of supporting work processes to keep it running, and create a timeline describing the enterprise knowledge portal deployment schedule. The result will be a clear definition of an enterprise knowledge portal that provides a better way to locate, learn, capture, and reuse information and human expertise throughout your organization. The enterprise knowledge portal program will take your vision from the enterprise knowledge portal map and outline a one, three, or five-year picture and plan to implement your enterprise knowledge portal.

You can get started creating the enterprise knowledge portal program as a small cross-functional team. The extended team members will be a community of knowledge experts with a broad and deep understanding of your work processes. This knowledge expert community has more specific knowledge about how work gets done in your organization than the community working on the enterprise knowledge portal map. The enterprise knowledge portal team and the revised knowledge expert community will work together to complete several templates designed to define the enterprise knowledge portal program. The template collection presented here is used to provide the details needed to describe how the enterprise knowledge portal ties into your existing business strategy, what the scope will be, and when you expect to complete several identified activities. The enterprise knowledge portal program will provide the details needed to deploy a cohesive and consistent enterprise knowledge portal through a cross-functional organizational structure that will manage the work processes and governance to remain successful. The execution of the enterprise knowledge portal program will be through the successful implementation of several enterprise knowledge portal development and infrastructure projects. Details around the design methodology to implement a work process–focused enterprise knowledge portal as a series of projects are included in Part III of the book. The enterprise activities and deliverables to complete the enterprise knowledge portal program are presented in Figure 4-1 and covered in detail throughout the remaining sections.

Enterprise Knowledge Portal Value Proposition

Your organization is going to want to understand the value of the enterprise knowledge portal. According to the prioritization of your enterprise knowledge portal features and your knowledge management objectives, you will have some perspective of whether your focus is on business-to-employee opportunities, e-business opportunities, customer relationship management (CRM), or supply chain management (SCM). The enterprise knowledge portal will provide value in many areas. The value proposition for your organization will be unique based on your enterprise knowledge portal priorities. Several value propositions include:

- *Competitive Advantage.* Your organization has to continuously identify and execute new products and opportunities. If your organization has the competency to make these changes rapidly you will have an advantage. You can use the enterprise knowledge portal to focus on e-business

Figure 4-1. Enterprise knowledge portal program activities and deliverables.

Activities	Deliverables
Enterprise Knowledge Portal Program Charter	• Enterprise Knowledge Portal Program Charter Template ▪ Add Section One: Scope and Objectives ▪ Add Section Two: Team Members and Stakeholders ▪ Add Section Three: Strategic Relationships and Other Corporate Initiatives ▪ Add Section Four: Benefits ▪ Add Section Five: Risks ▪ Add Section Six: Budgets and Funding ▪ Add Section Seven: Communication Plan ▪ Add Section Eight: Change Management Plan • Enterprise Knowledge Portal Risks Template ▪ Format to create a formal Enterprise Knowledge Portal Risks Assessment • Enterprise Knowledge Portal Communication Plan Template ▪ Format to create a formal Enterprise Knowledge Portal Communication Plan • Enterprise Knowledge Portal Change Management Plan Template ▪ Format to create a formal Enterprise Knowledge Portal Change Management Plan
Enterprise Knowledge Portal Requirements Template	• Enterprise Knowledge Portal Requirements Template ▪ Add Enterprise Knowledge Portal IT–Enabling Framework ▪ Add Work Processes and other Job-Related Activities ▪ Determine the Enterprise Knowledge Portal IT–Enabling Framework features that are critical to meet the work process requirements
Enterprise Knowledge Portal Strategy Template	• Enterprise Knowledge Portal Strategy Template ▪ Add Knowledge Management Objectives ▪ Add Enterprise Knowledge Portal Projects ▪ Determine the order and proposed timeline the Enterprise Knowledge Portal Projects will be completed

(continues)

Figure 4-1. (Continued).

Enterprise Knowledge Portal Architecture and Infrastructure Template	• Enterprise Knowledge Portal Architecture and Infrastructure Template ▪ Add Enterprise Knowledge Portal IT–Enabling Framework ▪ Add Enterprise Knowledge Portal Projects ▪ Determine the order and proposed timeline that the Enterprise Knowledge Portal IT–Enabling Framework features will need to be available in the IT environment
Enterprise Knowledge Portal Program Plan	• Enterprise Knowledge Portal Program Plan Template ▪ Identify Activities and Tasks ▪ Outline the Task List ▪ Assign Resources, Roles, and Team Members to Activities and Tasks ▪ Determine the Relationships Between Activities and Tasks

and e-commerce initiatives for critical work processes that require constant and continuous improvement.

- *Change Management.* You will need to review and introduce new technologies and new releases of products, services, corporate initiatives, and other elements that change the landscape of your organization. The products, work processes, corporate strategies, and other value chain components that need to be continuously explained and updated to knowledge workers and customers can be dynamically incorporated into your enterprise knowledge portal.
- *Knowledge Management Deliverables.* The value proposition you offer must be compelling to everyone that comes in contact with your organization. You must be able to transform critical business work processes with the help of technology. Web-based technologies and applications are, for the most part, easier to develop, and easier to use. The enterprise knowledge portal can deliver every locate, learn, capture, and reuse requirement you will need to complete your knowledge management objectives.
- *Intellectual Growth.* The enterprise knowledge portal provides a way to shift from hierarchical or linear thinking to a multidisciplinary and dynamic planning approach. You will be able to work in a proactive rather than a reactive business model. Your enterprise knowledge portal solution will provide you with the ability to permit dynamic shifts in work process execution and resource allocation.
- *Partnership Development.* You need to be able to quickly create virtual teams, allow networks of people to be productive, and just as rapidly

dissolve those partnerships to be successful in your industry. The enterprise knowledge portal can provide the environment you need to develop and manage partnerships.

- *Early Adopter Advantages.* Your organization can deploy and accrue the benefits of being the first to deliver new products, services, and business models through the management of your intellectual capital. The enterprise knowledge portal will create a dynamic environment that can quickly integrate every element of your organization to reduce cycle times in targeted work processes.

The enterprise knowledge portal should be implemented from the beginning as a major component of your business strategy. The complexity of planning an enterprise effort requires the appropriate knowledge and understanding of the objectives and benefits of the enterprise knowledge portal. If people can understand how the enterprise knowledge portal fits into your organization's business strategy from the beginning, the easier they will be able to understand the value and want to be involved in the enterprise knowledge portal initiative. In this regard, to be successful, you need to know how to establish standards, guidelines, and best practices for the technologies, people, and enterprise knowledge portal to fulfill your value propositions.

Enterprise Knowledge Portal Program Charter

The enterprise knowledge portal program charter is the document that defines the enterprise knowledge portal for your organization. It describes the enterprise knowledge portal in terms specific to you and your organization. The previous work you have done is critical to evaluating the value an enterprise knowledge portal has for your organization. The program charter allows you to define the enterprise knowledge portal initiative in terms that allow you to map the value proposition directly into your organization. The enterprise knowledge portal program charter covers:

- The scope and objectives of the enterprise knowledge portal to meet your specific requirements
- The team members and stakeholders who will create the enterprise knowledge portal program as well as the team members and stakeholders who will implement the enterprise knowledge portal solution
- The relationship of the enterprise knowledge portal initiative to your other corporate initiatives

- ❒ The enterprise knowledge portal benefits you will focus on to meet your identified scope and objectives
- ❒ The enterprise knowledge portal risks you might encounter and how you plan to minimize or eliminate them
- ❒ The enterprise knowledge portal costs you will need to estimate and the appropriate budgets allocated to cover the identified costs
- ❒ A communication plan to share and teach people about the enterprise knowledge portal
- ❒ The change management effort and associated plan to address the culture and behavior adjustments people will need to make as the enterprise knowledge portal is integrated into your organization

Using the enterprise knowledge portal map report and information gathered from the change management plans associated with existing corporate initiatives and business strategies, look for common threads or consistent messages that exist throughout these documents and Web pages. This information will help you define the relationship between the enterprise knowledge portal and other activities and priorities in your organization. The enterprise knowledge portal creates a user interface with several unique opportunities to change the way knowledge workers interact within work processes and share human expertise. There should be several initiatives that will incur significant benefits from the enterprise knowledge portal. If this is the case, adding the enterprise knowledge portal into your business strategy as a way to deliver and integrate information, applications, and services from a single Web-based user interface should be considered. You need to complete several research activities and document them in an enterprise knowledge portal program charter. The enterprise knowledge portal program charter is outlined in eight steps. The steps involved include:

1. *Document Scope and Objectives.* Define the content and context of the enterprise knowledge portal in terms of what is included and what is not included. Describe several clearly defined goals associated with the enterprise knowledge portal. Outline the relationship of the enterprise knowledge portal initiative to your existing business strategy.
2. *Identify Team Members and Stakeholders.* Identify the enterprise portal team and individuals who are accountable for the enterprise knowledge portal in your organization. Make certain the executive sponsor is included in the initial teams formed for the enterprise knowledge portal. Document stakeholders included in the communication and decision-making processes associated with the enterprise knowledge portal.

3. *Define Strategic Relationships to Other Corporate Initiatives.* Identify the relationship between the enterprise knowledge portal and other strategic initiatives or business strategies. Consider predecessor and successor events; common tasks, milestones, and deliverables; common schedule requirements; and common resource requirements.
4. *Add Benefits.* Add the quantitative (associated with cost and financial benefits) and qualitative (associated with the value proposition) benefits of the enterprise knowledge portal.
5. *Add Risks.* Add the quantitative and qualitative risks associated with the enterprise knowledge portal. Include any plans to address and mitigate identified risks.
6. *Document Budgets and Funding.* Document the estimated program costs and the methods and budgets used to cover the identified costs.
7. *Document the Communication Plan.* Define the technologies and work processes used to share information within the enterprise portal team, the extended team, the knowledge expert community, and the rest of the organization.
8. *Document the Change Management Plan.* Define how adjustments and changes to work processes, existing solutions, organizational structure, behavior, and culture will be addressed and managed.

The enterprise knowledge portal program charter template is a word processing document used to summarize the enterprise knowledge portal program. The enterprise knowledge portal program charter template can be seen in Figure 4-2. Your organization might have a defined project management system or methodology. You should substitute the enterprise knowledge portal program charter template presented here with the template that best fits your project management system.

Document Scope and Objectives

Purpose: Define the content and context of the enterprise knowledge portal in terms of what is included and what is not included. Describe several clearly defined goals associated with the enterprise knowledge portal. Outline the relationship of the enterprise knowledge portal initiative to your existing business strategy.

The first section of the enterprise knowledge portal program charter defines the scope and objectives. You will want to document what the enterprise knowledge portal program will deliver to your organization and how it maps into your business strategy. If there are specific system boundaries being set for the enterprise knowledge portal, you will want to include this information as well. Make certain that the specific knowledge management objectives that you are focusing on are documented and clearly out-

Figure 4-2. Enterprise knowledge portal program charter template.

To: Executive Sponsor

From: Enterprise Knowledge Portal Team

Re: Enterprise Knowledge Portal Program Charter

Section One: Scope and Objectives

Section Two: Team Members and Stakeholders

Section Three: Strategic Relationships and Other Corporate Initiatives

Section Four: Benefits

Section Five: Risks

Section Six: Budgets and Funding

Section Seven: Communication Plan

Section Eight: Change Management Plan

lined. This detail will demonstrate the prioritization of knowledge management objectives being addressed through the enterprise knowledge portal in the short term and the long term.

MYCOMPANY CASE STUDY

The enterprise knowledge portal team has researched current corporate initiatives and business strategy. Combining this information with the enterprise knowledge portal map report, several value propositions were found to be consistent across myCompany's corporate initiatives. These shared value propositions were used to define the scope and objectives for the enterprise knowledge portal program. Links and copies of the research material were documented by the enterprise knowledge portal team and saved for discussion and review. The summarized enterprise knowledge portal scope and objectives are included in Section One: Scope and Objectives of the enterprise knowledge portal program charter and can be seen in Figure 4-3. The details have been outlined and are available as a supporting appendix to the enterprise knowledge portal program charter.

Identify Team Members and Stakeholders

Purpose: Identify the enterprise portal team and individuals who are accountable for the enterprise knowledge portal in your organization. Make certain the executive sponsor is included in the initial teams formed for the enterprise knowledge portal. Document stakeholders included in the communication and decision-making processes associated with the enterprise knowledge portal.

The second section of the enterprise knowledge portal program charter identifies the team members and stakeholders to be accountable and responsible for the enterprise knowledge portal in your organization. There are two efforts that need to be documented for staffing. The first are the resources needed to establish the enterprise knowledge portal initiative into your organization. The second are the resources that will own the ongoing enterprise knowledge portal solution once the program is established; these are discussed in detail in Chapter 5. There are four roles to consider as you work to establish the enterprise portal initiative. These include:

- The enterprise portal team
- The executive sponsor

Figure 4-3. Enterprise knowledge portal program charter—Section One: Scope and Objectives.

To:	Executive Sponsor Steering Committee
From:	Enterprise Knowledge Portal Team
Re:	Enterprise Knowledge Portal Program Executive Summary

Section One: Scope and Objectives

The enterprise knowledge portal is aligned to enhance and support several corporate initiatives at myCompany. The objective will be to bring business intelligence, managed content, collaboration, and learning to support our three corporate initiatives in an enterprise knowledge portal interface. The corporate initiatives that the enterprise knowledge portal will focus on include:

- Work process improvements
- Business-to-employee opportunities
- Business-to-consumer opportunities

Work processes at myCompany will be reviewed for inefficiencies where specific transitions between roles, business units, and cross-functional teams are confusing. These transitions require personalized content used by each user role and content in several formats from several data sources to meet the purpose and intent of each work process. The enterprise knowledge portal will provide the user environment to achieve the productivity enhancements and revenue growth outlined in our corporate business strategy by improving work processes throughout myCompany.

- ❐ The knowledge expert community
- ❐ The stakeholders

The Enterprise Portal Team

The enterprise knowledge portal team continues to consist of a business analyst, a systems analyst, and a project manager to establish the enterprise knowledge portal initiative. For consistency and familiarity at least one of the enterprise knowledge portal team members should transition from defining the enterprise knowledge portal map to establishing the enterprise knowledge portal initiative. The enterprise knowledge portal team members will need to work full-time on the enterprise knowledge portal initiative. You should expect the enterprise knowledge portal team to lead the effort to complete the enterprise knowledge portal initiative work in six to eight weeks.

The Executive Sponsor

The executive sponsor should be working with the enterprise knowledge portal team in their effort to get started establishing the enterprise knowledge portal initiative. The executive sponsor and the enterprise knowledge portal team need to validate the vision of the enterprise knowledge portal and review the activities, tasks, and deliverables to be successful in establishing an enterprise knowledge portal program. The executive sponsor will be instrumental in promoting and communicating the enterprise knowledge portal program and helping to finalize funding and resources. The executive sponsor will be a role that continues to lead the enterprise knowledge portal solution for your organization.

The Expert Knowledge Community

The enterprise knowledge portal team will need to recruit a revised knowledge expert community. Knowledge about work processes, strategy, and infrastructure will be needed to provide the details for the enterprise knowledge portal initiative. You might need to add or adjust members of the knowledge expert community for this additional experience. The knowledge expert community members should be expected to serve a total of forty to sixty hours over a six- to eight-week time period. They will be working on three different deliverables. The result of their time will be a clear understanding of the enterprise knowledge portal requirements for the work processes and business units and the supporting infrastructure targeted for the first deployment of the enterprise knowledge portal solution. Once the revised knowledge expert community is formed, a welcome letter should be sent to the members and their sponsors. A sample welcome letter is available for you to review in Figure 4-4.

The Stakeholders

There will be several individuals and business units throughout your organization that need to be aware of the enterprise knowledge portal initiative. The executive sponsor, the enterprise portal team, and the expert knowledge community should outline the stakeholders and their concerns. Several activities, tasks, communication, and change management efforts should be outlined to address the individual concerns of the stakeholders as you work through the effort to define the enterprise knowledge portal initiative. Once the stakeholders have been identified, a letter to introduce the enterprise knowledge portal initiative should be sent. A sample stakeholder letter is available in Figure 4-5.

Figure 4-4. Knowledge expert community welcome letter.

Re: Welcome Aboard

Welcome Knowledge Expert Community,

The **Enterprise Knowledge Portal Map** project has been successfully completed with the approval to create a long-term enterprise knowledge portal initiative at myCompany. I would like to take the time to introduce the **Enterprise Knowledge Portal Program** effort to everyone. Your names were collected as the experts throughout myCompany on the topic of knowledge management, strategic thinking, and business strategy. This effort is to provide a well-defined path forward to deliver a cohesive and comprehensive enterprise knowledge portal that will meet the knowledge management objectives we outlined in the **Enterprise Knowledge Portal Map** report.

Using the information from the **Enterprise Knowledge Portal Map** report, the **Enterprise Knowledge Portal** team will complete the following activities:

- Complete the enterprise knowledge portal program charter

The **Knowledge Expert Community** will be divided into three unique teams. The **Enterprise Knowledge Portal Requirements** team will complete the following activities:

- Review the enterprise knowledge portal program charter
- Document the enterprise knowledge portal requirements
- Review the work processes requirements identified in the enterprise knowledge portal requirements report

The **Enterprise Knowledge Portal Strategy** team will complete the following activities:

- Review the enterprise knowledge portal program charter
- Document the enterprise knowledge portal strategy
- Review the order and proposed timeline in which enterprise knowledge portal projects will be completed in the enterprise knowledge portal strategy report

The **Enterprise Knowledge Portal Architecture and Infrastructure** team will complete the following activities:

- Review the enterprise knowledge portal program charter
- Document the Enterprise Knowledge Portal Architecture and Infrastructure
- Review the order and proposed timeline in which the Enterprise Knowledge Portal IT–Enabling Framework features will need to be available in the IT environment

Using the information compiled from the three **Knowledge Expert Community** teams, the **Enterprise Knowledge Portal** team will:

- Document the enterprise knowledge portal program plan

The **Executive Sponsor** will complete the following activities:

- Review the complete enterprise knowledge portal program
- Provide executive approval to move forward with the proposed enterprise knowledge portal

We will need approximately forty hours of your time over the next several weeks to collect information about your knowledge management requirements, the enterprise knowledge portal strategy to meet the defined requirements, and the functionality or technology you need to implement the strategy. You should expect to see a kick-off meeting on your calendars for next week to discuss the **Enterprise Knowledge Portal Program** effort in more detail and get started on our deliverables. Please contact Heidi Collins, Michael Douglas, or David Kennedy if you have questions now or would like to talk about any specific aspects of this current project.

We look forward to building the myCompany Enterprise Knowledge Portal together.

The Enterprise Knowledge Portal Team

MYCOMPANY CASE STUDY

Section Two: Team members and stakeholders of the enterprise knowledge portal program charter will outline several roles and responsibilities. The team members and stakeholders will be broken into two subsections in the enterprise knowledge portal program charter. The enterprise knowledge portal initiative section will name specific team members and their roles and responsibilities to establish the enterprise knowledge portal initiative. The enterprise knowledge portal organization section will provide a proposed long-term organization to design, develop, deploy, and maintain the enterprise knowledge portal for myCompany. The individual roles and team members identified for myCompany include:

Enterprise Knowledge Portal Initiative

- ❒ The executive sponsor
- ❒ The expert knowledge community
- ❒ The stakeholders
- ❒ The enterprise knowledge portal team

Enterprise Knowledge Portal Organization

- ❒ The executive sponsor
- ❒ The steering committee
- ❒ The stakeholders
- ❒ The knowledge expert community
- ❒ The enterprise knowledge portal program management
- ❒ The enterprise knowledge portal support and competency center

Figure 4-5. Stakeholders welcome letter.

Re: Welcome Aboard

Welcome Stakeholders,

We would like to thank each of you for your support of the enterprise knowledge portal initiative at myCompany. The knowledge expert community has been established with the team members you selected. This message is to formally introduce the **Enterprise Knowledge Portal Program** effort to each of you. This effort is to provide a well-defined path forward to deliver a cohesive and comprehensive enterprise knowledge portal that will meet the knowledge management objectives we outlined in the **Enterprise Knowledge Portal Map** report.

Using the information from the **Enterprise Knowledge Portal Map** report, the **Enterprise Knowledge Portal** team and **Knowledge Expert Community** will complete the following activities:

- Complete the enterprise knowledge portal program charter
- Document the enterprise knowledge portal requirements
- Review the work processes requirements identified in the enterprise knowledge portal requirements report
- Document the enterprise knowledge portal strategy
- Review the order and proposed timeline in which enterprise knowledge portal projects will be completed in the enterprise knowledge portal strategy report
- Document the enterprise knowledge portal architecture and infrastructure
- Review the order and proposed timeline in which the enterprise knowledge portal IT–enabling framework features will need to be available in the IT environment
- Document the enterprise knowledge portal program plan

These deliverables will be shared with you throughout the **Enterprise Knowledge Portal Program** effort as a series of communications. Your review and feedback on the deliverables will allow the **Knowledge Expert Community** to focus on your specific business requirements and expectations for the enterprise knowledge portal at myCompany. Please schedule regular one-on-one sessions with your **Knowledge Expert Community** team members to remain informed on the details of the **Enterprise Knowledge Portal Program**.

The **Executive Sponsor** will complete the following activities:

- Review the complete enterprise knowledge portal program
- Provide executive approval to move forward with the proposed enterprise knowledge portal

We will need approximately eight to ten hours of your time over the next several weeks to review the Enterprise Knowledge Portal Program and provide feedback to the **Enterprise Knowledge Portal Team** and the **Knowledge Expert Community** throughout the process. Please contact Heidi Collins, Michael Douglas, or David Kennedy if you have questions now or would like to talk about any specific aspects of this current project.

We look forward to building the myCompany enterprise knowledge portal together.

The Enterprise Knowledge Portal Team

- ❐ The enterprise knowledge portal application development
- ❐ The enterprise knowledge portal architecture and infrastructure
- ❐ The information library services
- ❐ The subject matter experts

The summarized results of Section Two: Team Members and Stakeholders for the enterprise knowledge portal program charter can be reviewed in Figure 4-6. Links, copies of the research material, meeting minutes, and discussions were documented by the enterprise knowledge portal team and saved as research information. The details have been outlined and are available as a supporting appendix to the enterprise knowledge portal program charter.

Define Strategic Relationships to Other Corporate Initiatives

Purpose: Identify the relationship between the enterprise knowledge portal and other strategic initiatives or business strategies. Consider predecessor and successor events; common tasks, milestones, and deliverables; common schedule requirements; and common resource requirements.

The third section of the enterprise knowledge portal program charter defines the strategic relationship between the enterprise knowledge portal and other corporate initiatives. You will want to include a definition of the enterprise knowledge portal and give an overview of the value proposition as it applies to initiatives throughout your organization. If there are details in your organization around existing initiatives, you will want to research this information. Forming strong relationships between corporate initiatives will provide significant benefits for your organization as a whole and will only improve the position for the enterprise knowledge portal initiative moving forward. For example, if you have a corporate e-business initiative, review the planning, budgeting, and forecasting information along with conversations to members of the e-business effort to determine the projects, deliverables, schedule of activities and events, and resources to understand your e-business program. Make certain that you have an e-business member on the knowledge expert community to work with the enterprise knowledge portal team. Using the enterprise knowledge portal map report, look for opportunities to share events, combine projects, marry schedules, and combine resources.

MYCOMPANY CASE STUDY

The enterprise knowledge portal team has researched planning, budgeting, and forecasting information on current corporate initia-

Figure 4-6. Enterprise knowledge portal program chart—Section Two: Team Members and Stakeholders.

Re: Enterprise Knowledge Portal Program Executive Summary

Section Two: Team Members and Stakeholders

The individual roles and team members identified for myCompany are the team members to establish the enterprise knowledge portal program and the organization that will be required to build, maintain, and support the enterprise knowledge portal initiative moving forward. The team members for these efforts include:

Enterprise Knowledge Portal Initiative

- Executive Sponsor—The executive sponsor is the most senior decision maker for the day-to-day enterprise knowledge portal activities and tasks to establish the enterprise knowledge portal program
- Stakeholders—Stakeholders represent all the functional areas of myCompany and provide usability, functionality, and feedback necessary to develop an enterprise knowledge portal program that the full user community will accept
- Expert Knowledge Community—The knowledge expert community is composed of people from Information Technology and each of the business units involved in the development of the Enterprise Knowledge Portal Program
- Enterprise Knowledge Portal Team—The enterprise knowledge portal team will lead and drive to conclusion the work effort to establish the enterprise knowledge portal initiative and supporting program at myCompany

Enterprise Knowledge Portal Organization

- Executive sponsor
- Steering committee
- Stakeholders
- Knowledge expert community
- Enterprise knowledge portal program management
- Enterprise knowledge portal support and competency center
- Enterprise knowledge portal application development
- Enterprise knowledge portal architecture and infrastructure
- Information library services
- Subject matter experts

tives that were closely associated with the highest-value knowledge management objectives defined in the enterprise knowledge portal map report. The myCompany e-business, intranet, business intelligence, content management, and learning initiatives and programs had several shared value propositions. Links and copies of the research material collected were documented by the enterprise knowledge portal team and saved for discussion and review. The summarized enterprise knowledge portal relationship to other

corporate initiatives is included in Section Three of the enterprise knowledge portal program charter and can be seen in Figure 4-7. The details are available to be included as a supporting appendix to the enterprise knowledge portal program charter if necessary.

Add Benefits

Purpose: Add the quantitative (associated with cost and financial benefits) and qualitative (associated with the value proposition) benefits of the enterprise knowledge portal.

The fourth section of the enterprise knowledge portal program charter is to document the benefits of the enterprise knowledge portal. You will

Figure 4-7. Enterprise knowledge portal program chart—Section Three: Strategic Relationships and Other Corporate Initiatives.

Re: Enterprise Knowledge Portal Program Executive Summary

Section Three: Strategic Relationships and Other Corporate Initiatives

The e-business, intranet, knowledge management, business intelligence, content management, and learning initiatives at myCompany all contain the following value propositions. These include:

- Change Management—The work processes, corporate strategies, and other components of myCompany that need to be continuously explained and updated to knowledge workers and customers will be dynamically incorporated into the enterprise knowledge portal.
- Knowledge Management Deliverables—The enterprise knowledge portal will provide technology to deliver locating, learning, capturing, and reusing requirements to integrate knowledge management objectives into myCompany work processes.
- Intellectual Growth—The enterprise knowledge portal will shift myCompany from hierarchical or linear thinking to a multidisciplinary and dynamic planning approach. We will use the enterprise knowledge portal to work in a proactive rather than a reactive business model. The intent is to use the enterprise knowledge portal to permit dynamic shifts in work process execution and resource allocation.
- Partnership Development—We will be able to quickly create virtual teams, allow networks of people to be productive, and just as rapidly dissolve those partnerships to work more effectively. The enterprise knowledge portal will provide the ability and the same technology to virtual teams to develop and manage partnerships.

The enterprise knowledge portal will be incorporated into each of these initiatives to deliver and measure the desired results for these value propositions. MyCompany will create a central enterprise knowledge portal architecture and infrastructure to support a decentralized network of people, work processes, and content. This structure will allow each corporate initiative to work independently while taking advantage of shared enterprise knowledge portal features like search, taxonomies, and navigation schemes.

want to include details about the return on investment (ROI) and the return on value your organization can expect from the enterprise knowledge portal. An enterprise knowledge portal return on investment spreadsheet is discussed in detail in Chapter 7. The summarized benefits included in the program charter reflect the credibility and effectiveness regarding the enterprise knowledge portal recommendation and conclusions. Decision makers and executives want to know whether the enterprise portal solution can accomplish the proposed benefits. The information presented in the enterprise knowledge portal program charter will include the specific measurements that the enterprise knowledge portal initiative is based on. You should include details on how the financial measurements are going to be used. The types of measurements that you may want to consider include:

- ❒ Net cash flow
- ❒ Discounted cash flow (DCF)
- ❒ Internal rate of return (IRR)
- ❒ Payback period
- ❒ Total cost of ownership (TCO)
- ❒ Return on investment (ROI)
- ❒ Cost and benefit analysis

MYCOMPANY CASE STUDY

The enterprise knowledge portal initiative and supporting program being proposed for myCompany needs to be analyzed for direct increases in revenue, direct reduction in expenses, and increased satisfaction of users. The first knowledge management benefit to be realized is increased access to information and human expertise allowing questions, issues, and answers to be resolved 25 percent to 50 percent faster and more accurately. This results in the ability to increase revenue by completing additional IT services and customer engagements each month or quarter using the current number of employees. The reduction in expenses is possible by providing application screens, documents, and reports online, giving users the ability to interact with work processes and submit additional queries and searches from the enterprise knowledge portal user interface. The intuitive user environment will improve job satisfaction for users trying to locate, learn, capture, and reuse information. The summarized enterprise knowledge portal benefits are included in Section Four: Benefits of the enterprise knowledge

portal program charter and can be seen in Figure 4-8. The details are available to be included as a supporting appendix to the enterprise knowledge portal program charter if necessary.

Add Risks

Purpose: Add the quantitative and qualitative risks associated with the enterprise knowledge portal. Include any plans to address and mitigate identified risks.

The fifth section of the enterprise knowledge portal program charter is to document the associated risks of the enterprise knowledge portal. You

Figure 4-8. Enterprise knowledge portal program chart—Section Four: Benefits.

Re: Enterprise Knowledge Portal Program Executive Summary

Section Four: Benefits

MyCompany will deploy the enterprise knowledge portal to incorporate several strategic advantages into existing corporate initiatives. The benefits have been defined as follows:

- *Capitalize on intellectual capital*—Information will be categorized and distributed across networks of users throughout myCompany. The enterprise knowledge portal user interface is used to help capture, store, protect, retrieve, and distribute information needed to complete their assigned responsibilities.
- *Resolve your growing knowledge needs*—The work environment continues to become more complex. There are faster product cycles and releases, increased customer demands for information, limited qualified and experienced knowledge workers, increasing productivity and profitability requirements, and growing technical complexity. The enterprise knowledge portal will create an intuitive work environment for users to access the specific application screens, reports, and other targeted information to reduce the complexity and increase user effectiveness.
- *Incorporate economic benefits*—The learning curve is accelerated for users to expand their ability to understand new information in a short period of time by incorporating learning into doing for work processes presented in the enterprise knowledge portal. Watching expenses and maintaining productivity measurements can be integrated into the enterprise knowledge portal to handle growing workloads, increase productivity, and improve profitability with the same number of existing resources.
- *Provide competitive advantages*—The ability to become more effective, efficient, and innovative is captured by this benefit. One example is to use the enterprise knowledge portal to increase service levels and reduce support costs by incorporating customer service and support center work processes into the user interface.
- *Include a self-service environment*—Allow employees, managers, customers, suppliers, and other networks of users to access information or perform activities through the enterprise knowledge portal. For example, employees can change their medical benefits online and customers can check the status of an order online.

will want to include details about the risks you are aware of, the probability that the risk will happen, the impact the risk will have on the enterprise knowledge portal initiative and solution if it does occur, and any mitigation plans you can implement to avoid the risk or minimize the impact. You can use the enterprise knowledge portal risks spreadsheet shown in Figure 4-9 to summarize your enterprise knowledge portal risks. The risks you define make up the rows in the spreadsheet. Possible enterprise knowledge portal risks are included in the spreadsheet. You will want to add, edit, or delete the listed risks based on your organization's enterprise knowledge portal. Probability, impact, and possible mitigation plans make up the columns in the spreadsheet.

MYCOMPANY CASE STUDY

The risks associated with the enterprise knowledge portal are added next. MyCompany has established two categories of risk for the enterprise knowledge portal effort. The first are the risks associated with establishing the enterprise knowledge portal initiative. The second are the risks to be associated with the ongoing enterprise knowledge portal solution. For each effort there are four categories of risks. These include:

- Content and context
- Culture and behavior
- Process and governance
- Infrastructure and environment

The summarized enterprise knowledge portal risks are included in Section Five: Risks of the enterprise knowledge portal program charter and can be seen in Figure 4-10. The details are available to be included as a supporting appendix to the enterprise knowledge portal program charter if necessary.

Document Budgets and Funding

Purpose: Document the estimated program costs and the methods and budgets used to cover the identified costs.

The sixth section of the enterprise knowledge portal program charter is to define the budgets and funding for the enterprise knowledge portal. You will want to document the estimated costs necessary to carry out the enterprise knowledge portal initiative including the methods by which the costs will be collected and charged. In addition you will want to project the

(text continues on page 194)

Figure 4-9. Enterprise knowledge portal risks template.

	Risk Impact (High, Medium, Low)	Risk Probability (%)	Risk Avoidance Plan	Risk Mitigation Plan
Be Organized Around Work Processes				
[Add individual possible risks you have identified]				
Maintain Knowledge and Facilitate Communication				
[Add individual possible risks you have identified]				
Focus on the Future				
[Add individual possible risks you have identified]				
Support Your Organization's Business Objectives				
[Add individual possible risks you have identified]				
Promote Innovations				
[Add individual possible risks you have identified]				
Maintain a Knowledge-Creating Organization				
[Add individual possible risks you have identified]				

Figure 4-10. Enterprise knowledge portal program charter—Section Five: Risks.

	Risk Impact (High, Medium, Low)	Risk Probability (%)	Risk Avoidance Plan	Risk Mitigation Plan
Be Organized Around Work Processes				
Become a work process–focused organization	H	50	Create the enterprise knowledge portal methodology to focus on designing the user interface around work processes	Establish executive support for a work process–centric approach to the enterprise knowledge portal
Integrate work processes into the enterprise knowledge portal	H	50	Create a knowledge map of how people, work processes, and content are related as part of the documentation created to deploy the enterprise knowledge portal	Establish the enterprise knowledge portal program and project management best practices, standards, and guidelines to implement and grow the enterprise knowledge portal
Maintain Knowledge and Facilitate Communication				
Embed locate, learn, capture, and reuse into the solution	H	25	Build knowledge management activities into work processes that are incorporated into the enterprise knowledge portal	Establish a knowledge management initiative that educates and integrates knowledge management activities and functionality into the enterprise knowledge portal
Create an effective communicaiton plan	H	50	Create a communication plan that includes how to encourage, inform, explain, and learn the details about the enterprise knowledge portal	Create and implement a well-defined and understood enterprise konwledge portal communication plan
Focus on the Future				
Improve work process innovation	H	25	Build process improvement and enhancements into the business to manage the effectiveness of work processes and the support center to deploy additional enterprise knowledge portal functionality on a scheduled basis	Establish work process owners to define and manage work process improvement measurements and actitivies for the enterprise knowledge portal
Improve e-business opportunities and strategies	H	75	Target e-business work processes to be integrated into the enterprise knowledge portal	Establish executive sponsorship, involvement by appropriate stakeholders, and integration with existing corporate initiatives

	Risk Impact (High, Medium, Low)	Risk Probability (%)	Risk Avoidance Plan	Risk Mitigation Plan
Support Your Organization's Business Objectives				
Improve personal alignment to your business strategy	**H**	**40**	Establish corporate communication content windows to keep employees and managers informed on corporate initatives	Establish business owners, corporate communications, and information storage and retrieval to maintain details on myCompany's business strategy
Embed learning into doing	**M**	**60**	Design electronic learning features and functions that are available from the enterprise knowledge portal to integrate learning into work processes	Include electronic learning features and functions in the enterprise knowledge portal to meet user learning requirements
Promote Innovations				
Improve career development opportunities	**H**	**80**	Target employee performance improvement and appraisal work processes to be integrated into the enterprise knowledge portal	Establish executive sponsorship, involvement by appropriate stakeholders, and integration with existing Human Resources initiatives
Maintain a Knowledge-Creating Organization				
Improve Web-centric business strategy	**H**	**75**	Deliver the functionality users require into the enterprise knowledge portal to access work processes through the Web	Establish critical work processes into the enterprise knowledge portal to generate the most value for the organization
Improve content management	**H**	**75**	Define a content management initiative to support the enterprise knowledge portal structured and unstructured content requirements	Establish a content management strategy and program as part of or to support the enterprise knowledge portal program
Improve cross-functional work processes	**H**	**75**	Target work processes that are shared by several users and business units to improve productivity, cycle times, and awareness of how work gets done	Establish executive support for a work process–centric approach to the enterprise knowledge portal

budgets, capital expenditures, authorizations, cost centers, and approvals for the enterprise knowledge portal solution moving forward. Review the budgeting process for your organization and document this section of the enterprise knowledge portal program charter to match.

MYCOMPANY CASE STUDY

The executive sponsor and the enterprise knowledge portal team have identified the budgets and funding for the enterprise knowledge portal. Combining this information with the enterprise knowledge portal scope and objectives, a forecast of budget and capital expenditures has been documented. Links and copies of the budgeting process and research material were documented by the enterprise knowledge portal team and saved for discussion and review. The summarized enterprise knowledge portal budgets and funding are included in Section Six of the enterprise knowledge portal program charter and can be seen in Figure 4-11. The details have been outlined and will be made available as a supporting appendix to the enterprise knowledge portal program charter if requested.

Document the Communication Plan

Purpose: Define the technologies and work processes used to share information within the enterprise portal team, the extended team, the knowledge expert community, and the rest of the organization.

The enterprise knowledge portal communication plan contains several important elements. A thorough communication plan will be a separate document created by the enterprise knowledge portal team. There are several aspects of the enterprise knowledge portal that you will want to concentrate on as part of the communication plan. It is important to establish an image for your enterprise knowledge portal and share this image with the organization. The communication plan you create will be designed to share and teach information in reasonable intervals and content for a variety of audiences throughout the implementation of the enterprise knowledge portal program.

Your communication plan will document for each phase of the enterprise knowledge portal initiative who is responsible for creating the communications, what audiences are being targeted, what is the purpose of the messages being created, and how you will measure the success of the communications. An enterprise knowledge portal communication plan template to use to document the communication plan is available in

Figure 4-11. Enterprise knowledge portal program charter—Section Six: Budgets and Funding.

Results

Return On Investment Year 1	140%
Return On Investment 3 Years	274%

Breakeven Analysis (Years)	0.713
Breakeven Date	09/18/02

Investment

Initial Project Investment	$375,000
Recurring Investment Year 2	$100,000
Recurring Investment Year 3	$100,000
Total Investment Over 3-Year Period	$575,000

Benefits — Estimates in Present Dollar Terms

Year 1

Reduced Labor Costs	$216,000
Reduced Expenses	$310,000
Increased Revenue from New Sources	$0
Increased Revenue from Existing Sources	$0

Year 2

Reduced Labor Costs	$216,000
Reduced Expenses	$310,000
Increased Revenue from New Sources	$0
Increased Revenue from Existing Sources	$0

Year 3

Reduced Labor Costs	$216,000
Reduced Expenses	$310,000
Increased Revenue from New Sources	$0
Increased Revenue from Existing Sources	$0
Total Benefits Over 3-Year Period	$1,578,000

Financial Assumptions

Cost of Capital (assumed interest rate)	10%
Reinvestment Interest Rate	8%
Inflation Rate	3%

Cash Flow

	Year 1	Year 2	Year 3
Cumulative Benefits	$526,000	$1,052,000	$1,578,000
Cumulative Investment	$375,000	$475,000	$575,000
Cumulative Cash Flow	$151,000	$577,000	$1,003,000
Annual Benefits	$526,000	$526,000	$526,000
Annual Investment	($375,000)	($100,000)	($100,000)
Annual Cash Flow	$151,000	$426,000	$426,000

Figure 4-12. You will want to prepare the complete enterprise knowledge portal communication plan document as an appendix to the enterprise knowledge portal program charter. An executive summary of the communication plan will be included in Section Seven of the program charter. Consider the following questions as you complete the enterprise knowledge portal communication plan:

- ☐ What needs to be communicated about the enterprise knowledge portal? How does this change throughout the enterprise knowledge portal program?
- ☐ What is the purpose of the communication?
- ☐ What information needs to be included in the communication? When does the information need to be communicated?
- ☐ Who is responsible for authoring the communication?
- ☐ Who is the audience?
- ☐ What is the right media to deliver the message? What are the constraints?
- ☐ How can you measure the effectiveness of the communication?

MYCOMPANY CASE STUDY

A detailed enterprise knowledge portal communication plan has been researched and completed by the enterprise knowledge portal team. Links and copies of the interviews and conversations were documented by the enterprise knowledge portal team and saved for discussion and review. The summarized enterprise knowledge portal communication plan is included in Section Seven of the enterprise knowledge portal program charter and can be seen in Figure 4-13. The details have been outlined and will be included as a supporting appendix to the enterprise knowledge portal program charter.

Document the Change Management Plan

Purpose: Define how adjustments and changes to work processes, existing solutions, organizational structure, behavior, and culture will be addressed and managed.

The successful implementation of the enterprise knowledge portal change management plan can be considered the second most important deliverable of the enterprise knowledge portal initiative. Second only to delivering a working enterprise knowledge portal, how you address the human elements and concerns intricate to your organization's culture and

Figure 4-12. Enterprise knowledge portal communication plan template.

Re: Enterprise Knowledge Portal Communication Plan Template

How to Use This Template

Review the questions presented here for each enterprise knowledge portal stakeholder in your organization. The compilation of the completed templates will be used to determine the complete communication plan required to successfully implement the enterprise knowledge portal. Consider changing or reducing the number of questions contained here to focus your communication plan on the most relevant communication efforts of the organization.

Section One: What do we need to communicate?

Section Two: What is the purpose of the communication?

Section Three: When do we need to communicate the information?

Section Four: Who is the primary communicator?

Section Five: Who is the audience?

Section Six: What is the strategy for ensuring that the right message is delivered in the most appropriate format and media?

Section Seven: What are the constraints?

Figure 4-13. Enterprise knowledge portal program charter—Section Seven: Communication Plan.

	Phase of Communication	Primary Communicator	Audience	Purpose of Communication	Direction of Communication
Executive Sponsor					
	Improvements, Benchmarking	Enterprise Knowledge Portal Team	Executive Levels	Encourage	One-Way
	Need for Change	Enterprise Knowledge Portal Team	Executive Levels	Inform	Two-Way
	Outline What and Why	Enterprise Knowledge Portal Team	Executive Levels	Explain	Two-Way
	Describing Progress and Status	Enterprise Knowledge Portal Team	Executive Levels	Learn	Two-Way
	Documenting Policy and Practice	Enterprise Knowledge Portal Team	Executive Levels	Recognize	One-Way
Knowledge Expert Community					
	Improvements, Benchmarking	Executive Sponsor	Management, Employees	Encourage	One-Way
	Need for Change	Enterprise Knowledge Portal Team	Management, Employees	Inform	Two-Way
	Outline What and Why	Enterprise Knowledge Portal Team	Management, Employees	Explain	Two-Way
	Describing Progress and Status	Enterprise Knowledge Portal Team	Management, Employees	Learn	Two-Way
	Documenting Policy and Practice	Executive Sponsor	Management, Employees	Recognize	One-Way
Stakeholders					
	Improvements, Benchmarking	Executive Sponsor	Executive Levels, Management	Encourage	One-Way
	Need for Change	Enterprise Knowledge Portal Team	Executive Levels, Management	Inform	Two-Way
	Outline What and Why	Enterprise Knowledge Portal Team	Executive Levels, Management	Explain	Two-Way
	Describing Progress and Status	Enterprise Knowledge Portal Team	Executive Levels, Management	Learn	Two-Way
	Documenting Policy and Practice	Executive Sponsor	Executive Levels, Management	Recognize	One-Way

behavior is critical. You will want to review your value proposition and imagine how the enterprise knowledge portal will affect how people will perform their jobs in the future. There are several elements to include in the enterprise knowledge portal change management plan. These include:

- ❐ *Roles and Responsibilities.* This element identifies the individuals and teams in your organization that will continue to provide the vision, leadership, direction, decisions, and deliverables for the enterprise knowledge portal.
- ❐ *Desired Culture and Behavior.* This element outlines a futuristic picture of the values, competencies, and behavior of the organization doing work through the enterprise knowledge portal.
- ❐ *Current Culture and Behavior.* This element explains the current values, competencies, and behavior of the organization.
- ❐ *Culture and Behavior Analysis.* This is a detailed review of the current and desired culture and behavior of your organization. Consider including the risks and how you might mitigate your change management risks.
- ❐ *Programs and Strategies.* This element identifies the categories of change and drills into the specific methods and activities or projects to create the desired culture and behavior in your organization. It is important to validate the programs and strategies that you define are consistent with the roles and responsibilities already identified.
- ❐ *Metrics.* These are the qualitative and quantitative measurements to evaluate the effectiveness of your enterprise knowledge portal change management programs and strategies.

An enterprise knowledge portal change management plan template is available in Figure 4-14. The template includes several enterprise knowledge portal–specific details to help you get started. You will want to prepare the complete enterprise knowledge portal change management plan document as an appendix to the enterprise knowledge portal program charter. An executive summary of the communication plan will be included in Section Eight of the program charter. Consider the following questions as you complete the enterprise knowledge portal change management plan:

- ☐ Why is the enterprise knowledge portal being implemented? What is the value proposition?
- ☐ Who are the stakeholders? What impact will the enterprise knowledge portal have on the stakeholders? Which stakeholders can make or break the enterprise knowledge portal?
- ☐ What does each identified stakeholder gain from an enterprise

Figure 4-14. Enterprise knowledge portal change management plan template.

Re: Enterprise Knowledge Portal Change Management Plan Template

How to Use This Template

Review the questions presented here to establish the enterprise knowledge portal change management plan. Add subsections or tables into each section to categorize the details. Consider changing or reducing the number of questions contained here to focus your change management plan on the most relevant change management efforts of the organization.

Section One: Why is the enterprise knowledge portal being implemented? What is the value proposition?

Section Two: What are the stakeholders? What impact will the enterprise knowledge portal have on the stakeholders? Which stakeholders can make or break the enterprise knowledge portal?

Section Three: For each identified stakeholder, what do they gain from an enterprise knowledge portal? What do they lose? What are the relationships of the stakeholders?

Section Four: What will a successful enterprise knowledge portal look like in your organization? What are the obstacles moving forward? How can these obstacles be minimized or eliminated?

Section Five: What individuals and teams in your organization are needed to implement a successful enterprise knowledge portal?

knowledge portal? What does each lose? What are the relationships of the stakeholders?

- ☐ What will a successful enterprise knowledge portal look like in your organization? What are the obstacles moving forward? How can these obstacles be minimized or eliminated?
- ☐ What individuals and teams in your organization are needed to implement a successful enterprise knowledge portal?

MYCOMPANY CASE STUDY

A detailed enterprise knowledge portal change management plan has been researched and completed by the enterprise knowledge portal team. Links and copies of the interviews and conversations were documented by the enterprise knowledge portal team and saved for discussion and review. The summarized enterprise knowledge portal change management plan is included in Section Eight of the enterprise knowledge portal program charter and can be seen in Figure 4-15. The details have been outlined and will be included as a supporting appendix to the enterprise knowledge portal program charter.

Enterprise Knowledge Portal Requirements

The enterprise knowledge portal requirements are the enterprise knowledge portal features and functions needed to create a solution that will meet your business objectives. You will need to collect and document enterprise knowledge portal requirements throughout your organization to gain a thorough understanding of the knowledge management similarities and differences between a significant sampling of business units and networks of users. The work you compiled in the enterprise knowledge portal IT–enabling framework report outlined the technology categories that collectively provide the tools of a complete knowledge management solution. You will want to identify enterprise knowledge portal features and functions within each technology category. As you implement your enterprise knowledge portal program, you will want to deploy features and functions from each of the technology categories to implement a knowledge management solution that meets the needs of employees, managers, cross-functional teams, individual contributors, and executives. The enterprise knowledge portal features and functions are mapped to your work processes and other job-related activities to produce the enterprise knowledge portal requirements report. The report identifies the technologies in each technology cat-

Figure 4-15. Enterprise knowledge portal program charter—Section Eight: Change Management Plan.

Re: Enterprise Knowledge Portal Program Executive Summary

Section Eight: Change Management Plan

There are several enterprise knowledge portal activities that need to be addressed and completed to ensure the enterprise knowledge portal initiative is successfully implemented and broadly accepted by users. Completing these change management activities will help the enterprise knowledge portal stakeholders to be effective and successful in moving forward. These change management activities make it possible for the enterprise knowledge portal organization to be effective generating a well-defined and well-accepted enterprise knowledge portal for users across your organization. These activities include:

- Identifying all enterprise portal and knowledge management applications and solutions in your organization
- Identifying overlapping functional and technical requirements
- Evaluating the work effort to establish a single enterprise knowledge portal
- Identifying work process integration requirements for the enterprise knowledge portal
- Establishing a methodology and owner for enterprise knowledge portal objects
- Establishing relationships with other corporate initiatives to ensure recognition and integration of the enterprise knowledge portal
- Coordinating with information technology teams to integrate several technologies and architecture planning issues
- Sponsoring and establishing an enterprise knowledge portal laboratory
- Establishing the enterprise knowledge portal framework
- Identifying unique enterprise knowledge portal requirements
- Creating the knowledge organization system

The change management plan will establish the roles and responsibilities for the following stakeholders to implement the enterprise knowledge portal at myCompany. The stakeholders identified include:

- Steering committee
- Stakeholders
- Knowledge expert community
- Enterprise knowledge portal program management
- Enterprise knowledge portal support and competency center
- Enterprise knowledge portal application development
- Enterprise knowledge portal architecture and infrastructure
- Information library services
- Subject matter experts

egory that will be required to support work processes throughout your organization. There are three steps outlined to establish your enterprise knowledge portal requirements report. They are:

1. *Modify the enterprise knowledge portal requirements template.* Using your enterprise knowledge portal value proposition and program charter information, review the enterprise knowledge portal requirements template and update to match your organization.
2. *Schedule interviews with the knowledge expert community.* Using the enterprise knowledge portal requirements template from the first step, interview targeted members of the knowledge expert community to identify the work processes that will benefit the most from the enterprise knowledge portal. Determine the enterprise knowledge portal features and functions that are critical to meet these work process requirements.
3. *Create the enterprise knowledge portal requirements report.* Summarize the results of the knowledge expert community interviews to generate what features and functions need to be available from the enterprise knowledge portal and an estimated time line of when these features and functions need to be available.

Modify the Enterprise Knowledge Portal Requirements Template

Purpose: Using your enterprise knowledge portal value proposition and program charter information, review the enterprise knowledge portal requirements template and update to match your organization.

The enterprise knowledge portal requirements template will provide a spreadsheet that outlines several enterprise knowledge portal features and functions. The spreadsheet will provide a standard way to collect and document enterprise knowledge portal requirements throughout your organization. To make certain you have a complete set of knowledge enterprise portal requirements that encompass most aspects of your organization, maintain the same categories used in the enterprise knowledge portal IT–enabling framework report. The enterprise knowledge portal requirements template can be seen in Figure 4-16. The enterprise knowledge portal features and functions make up the rows in the spreadsheet. You will want to add, edit, or delete the enterprise knowledge portal features based on your final enterprise knowledge portal IT–enabling framework report. The work processes and other job-related activities represented by the knowledge expert community members make up the columns in the spreadsheet and will be identified and added to the spreadsheet during the interviews with the knowledge expert community members.

Figure 4-16. Enterprise knowledge portal requirements template.

	Be Organized Around Work Processes	[Add enterprise knowledge portal projects]	Maintain Knowledge and Facilitate Communication	[Add enterprise knowledge portal projects]	Focus on the Future	[Add enterprise knowledge portal projects]	Support Your Organization's Business Objectives	[Add enterprise knowledge portal projects]	Promote Innovation	[Add enterprise knowledge portal projects]	Maintain a Knowledge-Creating Organization	[Add enterprise knowledge portal projects]
Enterprise Portal												
[Add IT–Enabling Framework Features]												
Business Intelligence												
[Add IT–Enabling Framework Features]												
Collaboration and Communities												
[Add IT–Enabling Framework Features]												
Content Management												
[Add IT–Enabling Framework Features]												
Learning												
[Add IT–Enabling Framework Features]												

MYCOMPANY CASE STUDY

The enterprise knowledge portal team has defined five unique information technologies that encompass all aspects of the enterprise knowledge portal features and functions being considered by myCompany. Using the five categories of the enterprise knowledge portal IT–enabling framework report as a way to group features and functions, the enterprise knowledge portal requirements template has been created. An example of the template can be seen in Figure 4-17. This document will be used to gather enterprise knowledge portal requirements as individual interviews with selected members of the knowledge expert community.

Schedule Interviews with the Knowledge Expert Community

Purpose: Using the enterprise knowledge portal requirements template from the first step, interview members of the knowledge expert community to identify the work processes that will benefit the most from the enterprise knowledge portal. Determine the enterprise knowledge portal features and functions that are critical to meet these work process requirements.

The enterprise knowledge portal team will need to collect require-

Figure 4-17. Enterprise knowledge portal requirements template (using five categories of enterprise knowledge portal IT–enabling framework).

	Be Organized Around Work Processes	[Add enterprise knowledge portal projects]	**Maintain Knowledge and Facilitate Communication**	[Add enterprise knowledge portal projects]	**Focus on the Future**	[Add enterprise knowledge portal projects]	**Support Your Organization's Business Objectives**	[Add enterprise knowledge portal projects]	**Promote Innovation**	[Add enterprise knowledge portal projects]	**Maintain a Knowledge-Creating Organization**	[Add enterprise knowledge portal projects]
Enterprise Portal												
Presentation												
Knowledge Organization System												
Search												
Plug and Play Functions												
Access and Integration												
Profiling and Personalization												
Business Intelligence												
Decision Support												
Performance-Based Metrics												
Process Management												
Balanced Scorecard												
Data Mining												
Information Mining												
Information Management												
Collaboration and Communities												
Electronic Messaging Management												
Discussion Groups												
Team-Based Collaboration												
Real-Time Collaboration												
Collaborative Commerce												
Communities												
Information Retrieval												
Content Management												
Structured Content												
Data Integration Services												
Unstructured Content												
Document Management												
Web Content Management												
Electronic Commerce												
Learning												
EPSS												
Video and Audio Conferencing												
Learning Management System												
Interactivity												

ments across the organization to make certain they understand 70 percent to 80 percent of the people, processes, and technologies the enterprise knowledge portal will need to deliver. Schedule interviews with members of the knowledge expert community that collectively provide a complete knowledge enterprise portal picture. Your goal is to understand the similarities and differences in your enterprise knowledge portal requirements across business units and other networks of users. The enterprise knowledge portal team will need to complete several activities to document the enterprise knowledge portal requirements interviews. You should:

- ❒ Hold a kick-off meeting with the selected knowledge expert community members and review the part of the organization they are representing for the requirements gathering effort, review the enterprise knowledge portal program charter, discuss the enterprise knowledge portal requirements template, and schedule interview times with each of the knowledge expert community members.
- ❒ Hold individual interview sessions to complete the enterprise knowledge portal requirements template, document the discussions, and post the results for the entire knowledge expert community members to read.
- ❒ Create a communication to share the highlights of the individual interviews and encourage knowledge expert community members to review details.

MYCOMPANY CASE STUDY

The enterprise knowledge portal team has scheduled interviews with each member of the knowledge expert community selected to complete the enterprise knowledge portal requirements template. The interviews allow the enterprise knowledge portal team to focus on specific work processes that will benefit significantly from features and functions available in the enterprise knowledge portal. The activities and tasks completed by the enterprise knowledge portal team included:

- ❒ A kick-off meeting that was held to introduce the knowledge expert community members and to review the part of the organization they represented for the requirements-gathering effort. The purpose of the meeting was to review the enterprise knowledge portal program charter, discuss the enterprise knowledge portal requirements template, and schedule interview times with each of the knowledge expert community members. (An example of a meeting invitation and a proposed agenda are presented in Figure 4-18.)

- Individual interview sessions that were held to complete the enterprise knowledge portal requirements template, document the discussions, and post the results for the entire knowledge expert community members to read.
- A communication (shown in Figure 4-19) that was distributed to members of the knowledge expert community to share the highlights of the individual interviews and encourage individual members to review details.

Create the Enterprise Knowledge Portal Requirements Report

Purpose: Summarize the results of the knowledge expert community interviews to generate what features and functions need to be available from the enterprise knowledge portal and an estimated time line of when these features and functions need to be available.

The enterprise knowledge portal requirements report is the summary of the enterprise knowledge portal requirements templates completed in the second step. You will want to share and review the results with the knowledge expert community. During this review you will be teaching as

Figure 4-18. A sample invitation and agenda for the enterprise knowledge portal requirements kick-off.

Agenda	**Enterprise Knowledge Portal Requirements Kick-Off** **Conference Room One**	
Type of meeting:	Enterprise Knowledge Portal Requirements Kick-Off Meeting	
Facilitator:	Heidi Collins	
Note taker:	David Kennedy	
Attendees:	Knowledge Expert Community Members	
	Agenda Topics	
15 Minutes	Knowledge Expert Community Members Introduction	Heidi Collins
45 Minutes	Review Enterprise Knowledge Portal Program Charter	Heidi Collins
15 Minutes	Break	
30 Minutes	Enterprise Knowledge Portal Requirements Template Review	Heidi Collins
15 Minutes	Schedule Enterprise Knowledge Portal Requirements Interviews	Heidi Collins

Figure 4-19. Knowledge expert community communication one.

Re: Knowledge Expert Community Interviews Available

Hello Knowledge Expert Community,

We would like to take the time to share the **Enterprise Knowledge Portal Requirements** interview results with you. The **Enterprise Knowledge Portal Team** has started the enterprise knowledge portal program definition and established the deliverables. They continue to monitor that the goals and objectives of the **Enterprise Knowledge Portal Program** definition are effectively being delivered on time and in budget. To review any status documents, research material, completed interviews, or other information, please visit:
www.myCompany.com/EKP/enterprise_knowledge_portal_program/material

The enterprise knowledge portal team members have completed several individual interviews with the knowledge expert community. This was the most effective approach to collect and understand myCompany's enterprise knowledge portal requirements. The information collected represents an enterprise sampling of enterprise knowledge portal requirements across myCompany to plan for the future. Please take the time to review the interviews in detail.

Once the enterprise knowledge portal requirements interviews are completed, a meeting will be scheduled to review the material followed by a discussion session to answer any questions and provide additional detail. Please attend or send a representative to the enterprise knowledge portal requirements review meeting. There will be AT&T conference call numbers and a videoconference set up for these sessions for anyone that cannot attend in person.

Please contact Heidi Collins or Michael Douglas if you have questions or need additional information.

---

much as sharing information as you walk through the enterprise knowledge portal requirements report. To teach and share the results effectively, you should consider bringing the knowledge expert community together in a meeting format. Create a supporting presentation to accompany the enterprise knowledge portal requirements report. You will want to have an open discussion of the summarized enterprise knowledge portal requirements and make any adjustments agreed on by the knowledge expert community to create the final version of the enterprise knowledge portal requirements report.

MYCOMPANY CASE STUDY

The enterprise knowledge portal requirements report has been created using the categories outlined in the enterprise knowledge

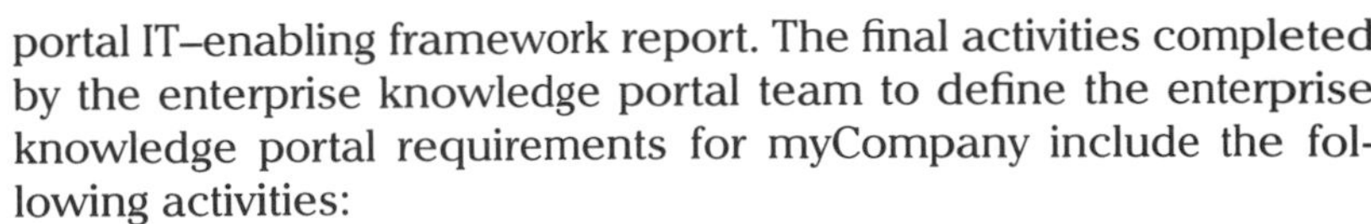

portal IT–enabling framework report. The final activities completed by the enterprise knowledge portal team to define the enterprise knowledge portal requirements for myCompany include the following activities:

- ❒ The enterprise knowledge portal team has summarized the interview results from the enterprise knowledge experts into the enterprise knowledge portal requirements report. This first release of the enterprise knowledge portal requirements report is shown in Figure 4-20.
- ❒ A supporting presentation has been created to accompany and explain the summarized results. The enterprise knowledge portal requirements report review presentation can be reviewed in Figure 4-21.
- ❒ A review meeting was held to discuss and clarify the results of the enterprise knowledge portal requirements report. An example of a meeting invitation and a proposed agenda are presented in Figure 4-22.
- ❒ The final version of the enterprise knowledge portal requirements report has been completed as a result of the review meeting and can be seen in Figure 4-23.
- ❒ A communication shown in Figure 4-24 was distributed to members of the knowledge expert community to share the final version of the enterprise knowledge portal requirements report and encourage individual members to review details with their business units.

Enterprise Knowledge Portal Strategy

The enterprise knowledge portal strategy outlines your available options to implement an enterprise knowledge portal that will achieve your value proposition. You will need to research, document, and compare the enterprise knowledge portal projects proposed for implementation. The priority and order you select to deploy the enterprise knowledge portal projects will provide different opportunities and emphasize different aspects of your value proposition. Your objective is to establish the most effective prioritization and deployment of your proposed enterprise knowledge portal projects and move forward. You will want to maintain the same categories you defined in the enterprise knowledge portal map report as you define your strategy to make certain you maintain a complete set of knowledge management objectives to meet the different uses of the enterprise knowledge

(text continues on page 212)

Figure 4-20. Enterprise knowledge portal requirements report (first release).

	Be Organized Around Work Processes	Sales and Distribution Work Process Improvement	Marketing Work Process Improvement	Operational Excellence Work Process Improvement	Functional Excellence Work Process Improvement	Service Work Process Improvement	Relationship Work Process Improvement	**Maintain Knowledge and Facilitate Communication**	Capture Integration	Subscribe to Integration	Collaborate Integration	**Focus on the Future**	Shareholder Value (Profitability)	Business-to-Consumer (Revenue Growth)	Business-to-Employee (Productivity)
Enterprise Portal															
Presentation		x	x	x	x	x	x		x	x	x		x	x	x
Knowledge Organization System		x	x	x	x	x	x		x	x	x		x	x	x
Search		x	x	x	x	x	x		x	x	x		x	x	x
Plug and Play Functions		x	x	x	x	x	x		x	x	x		x	x	x
Access and Integration		x	x	x	x	x	x		x	x	x		x	x	x
Profiling and Personalization		x	x	x	x	x	x		x	x	x		x	x	x
Business Intelligence															
Decision Support		x	x	x	x	x	x						x	x	x
Performance-Based Metrics		x	x	x	x	x	x						x	x	x
Process Management		x	x	x	x	x	x						x	x	x
Balanced Scorecard		x	x	x	x	x	x						x	x	x
Data Mining		x	x	x	x	x	x						x	x	x
Information Mining		x	x	x	x	x	x		x	x	x		x	x	x
Information Management		x	x	x	x	x	x		x	x	x		x	x	x
Collaboration and Communities															
Electronic Messaging Management		x	x	x	x	x	x		x	x	x		x	x	x
Discussion Groups		x	x	x	x	x	x		x	x	x				
Team-Based Collaboration		x	x	x	x	x	x		x	x	x		x	x	x
Real-Time Collaboration		x	x	x	x	x	x		x	x	x		x	x	x
Collaborative Commerce		x	x			x	x		x	x	x		x	x	x
Communities		x	x	x	x	x	x		x	x	x				
Information Retrieval		x	x	x	x	x	x		x	x	x		x	x	x
Content Management															
Structured Content		x	x	x	x	x	x						x	x	x
Data Integration Services		x	x	x	x	x	x						x	x	x
Unstructured Content		x	x	x	x	x	x		x	x	x		x	x	x
Document Management		x	x	x	x	x	x		x	x	x		x	x	x
Web Content Management		x	x	x	x	x	x		x	x	x		x	x	x
Electronic Commerce		x	x	x	x	x	x		x	x	x		x	x	x
Learning															
EPSS		x	x	x	x	x	x		x	x	x		x	x	x
Video and Audio Conferencing		x	x	x	x	x	x		x	x	x		x	x	x
Learning Management System		x	x	x	x	x	x						x	x	x
Interactivity		x	x	x	x	x	x		x	x	x		x	x	x

	Support Your Organization's Business Objectives	Personal Awareness	Personal Alignment	Employee Feedback	Personal Performance	**Promote Innovation**	Business Skills (Expert System)	Technical Skills (Expert System)	Productivity (Continuous Improvement)	**Maintain a Knowledge-Creating Organization**	Key Performance Indicators	Corporate Balanced Scorecard	Personal Balanced Scorecard
Enterprise Portal													
Presentation		x	x	x	x		x	x	x		x	x	x
Knowledge Organization System		x	x	x	x		x	x	x		x	x	x
Search		x	x	x	x		x	x	x		x	x	x
Plug and Play Functions		x	x	x	x		x	x	x		x	x	x
Access and Integration		x	x	x	x		x	x	x		x	x	x
Profiling and Personalization		x	x	x	x		x	x	x		x	x	x
Business Intelligence													
Decision Support			x		x				x		x	x	x
Performance-Based Metrics			x		x				x		x	x	x
Process Management					x		x	x	x		x	x	x
Balanced Scorecard			x		x				x		x	x	x
Data Mining									x				
Information Mining									x				
Information Management		x	x	x	x		x	x	x		x	x	x
Collaboration and Communities													
Electronic Messaging Management		x	x	x	x		x	x	x		x	x	x
Discussion Groups		x	x	x	x		x	x	x				
Team-Based Collaboration							x	x	x		x	x	x
Real-Time Collaboration		x	x	x	x		x	x	x		x	x	x
Collaborative Commerce							x	x	x		x	x	
Communities		x	x	x	x		x	x	x				
Information Retrieval		x	x	x	x		x	x	x		x	x	x
Content Management													
Structured Content			x		x				x		x	x	x
Data Integration Services			x		x				x		x	x	x
Unstructured Content		x	x	x	x		x	x	x		x	x	x
Document Management		x	x	x	x		x	x	x		x	x	x
Web Content Management		x	x	x	x		x	x	x		x	x	x
Electronic Commerce		x	x	x	x		x	x	x		x	x	x
Learning													
EPSS		x	x	x	x		x	x	x		x	x	x
Video and Audio Conferencing		x	x	x	x		x	x	x		x	x	x
Learning Management System		x	x	x	x				x		x	x	x
Interactivity		x	x	x	x		x	x	x		x	x	x

Figure 4-21. Enterprise knowledge portal requirements report review.

- The enterprise knowledge portal requirements were completed by the enterprise knowledge portal team with selected input from knowledge expert community members
- The enterprise knowledge portal features were pulled from the knowledge management IT–enabling framework and broken into rows on the spreadsheet:
  —Enterprise portal
  —Business intelligence
  —Collaboration and communities
  —Content management
  —Learning
- The enterprise knowledge portal projects were aligned to the knowledge management objectives and broken into columns on the spreadsheet:
  —Be organized around work processes
  —Maintain knowledge and facilitate communication
  —Focus on the future
  —Support your organization's business objectives
  —Promote innovations
  —Maintain a knowledge-creating organization
- Each enterprise knowledge portal IT–enabling framework feature needed for each enterprise knowledge portal project was identified with an "x" and will be prioritized as H-high, M-medium, or L-low depending on how critical the feature is for the project to meet user requirements
- The enterprise knowledge portal requirements report is available for review in the following spreadsheet:
  Enterprise Knowledge Portal Requirements Report (Excel spreadsheet)
- Open discussion of the enterprise knowledge portal requirements report
- Updates to the enterprise knowledge portal requirements report

- Note: Rows and columns can be added, updated, and removed from the enterprise knowledge portal requirements report to reflect the appropriate level of detail

portal by users in your organization. Your knowledge management objectives are mapped to your proposed enterprise knowledge portal projects to produce the enterprise knowledge portal strategy report. The report identifies the knowledge management objectives that will be implemented in the enterprise knowledge portal, as each enterprise knowledge portal project is successfully deployed. There are three steps outlined to establish your enterprise knowledge portal strategy report. They are:

1. *Modify the enterprise knowledge portal strategy template.* Using your enterprise knowledge portal program charter and the enterprise knowledge portal map report information, review the enterprise knowledge portal strategy template and update to match your organization.
2. *Schedule interviews with the knowledge expert community.* Using the enterprise knowledge portal strategy template from the previous step,

Figure 4-22. A sample invitation and agenda for the enterprise knowledge portal requirements report.

Agenda	**Enterprise Knowledge Portal Requirements Report**	
	Conference Room One	
Type of meeting:	Enterprise Knowledge Portal Requirements Report Review Meeting	
Facilitator:	Heidi Collins	
Note taker:	David Kennedy	
Attendees:	Knowledge Expert Community Members	
	Agenda Topics	
60 Minutes	The Enterprise Knowledge Portal Features identified from Knowledge Expert Community interviews are reviewed (rows in the template)	Heidi Collins
15 Minutes	Break	
60 Minutes	Enterprise Knowledge Portal Projects identified from Knowledge Expert Community interviews are reviewed (columns in the template)	Heidi Collins
15 Minutes	Break	
40 Minutes	Summarize and prioritize the relationships between enterprise knowledge portal features and enterprise knowledge portal projects	Heidi Collins
10 Minutes	Review action items	Heidi Collins
10 Minutes	Review Enterprise Knowledge Portal Program definition progress and discuss our next steps and activities	Heidi Collins

interview members of the knowledge expert community to generate open discussions around the value proposition of the enterprise knowledge portal for your organization. Explore the goals and methods required to achieve the value proposition.

3. *Create the enterprise knowledge portal strategy report*. Summarize the results of the knowledge expert community interviews to evaluate and prioritize the available options to marry the value proposition and the enterprise knowledge portal requirements together. Identify the advantages and disadvantages of your available options and recommend the best path forward for your organization.

Modify the Enterprise Knowledge Portal Strategy Template

Purpose: Using your enterprise knowledge portal program charter and the enterprise knowledge portal map report information, review the enterprise knowledge portal strategy template and update to match your organization.

(text continues on page 216)

Figure 4-23. Enterprise knowledge portal requirements report (final release).

	Be Organized Around Work Processes	Sales and Distribution Work Process Improvement	Marketing Work Process Improvement	Operational Excellence Work Process Improvement	Functional Excellence Work Process Improvement	Service Work Process Improvement	Relationship Work Process Improvement	**Maintain Knowledge and Facilitate Communication**	Capture Integration	Subscribe to Integration	Collaborate Integration	**Focus on the Future**	Shareholder Value (Profitability)	Business-to-Consumer (Revenue Growth)	Business-to-Employee (Productivity)
Enterprise Portal															
Presentation		H	H	H	H	H	H		H	H	H		H	H	H
Knowledge Organization System		H	H	H	H	H	H		H	H	H		H	H	H
Search		H	H	H	H	H	H		H	H	H		H	H	H
Plug and Play Functions		H	H	H	H	H	H		H	H	H		H	H	H
Access and Integration		H	H	H	H	H	H		M	M	M		H	H	H
Profiling and Personalization		H	H	H	H	H	H		H	H	H		H	H	H
Business Intelligence															
Decision Support		H	H	H	H	H	H						H	H	H
Performance-Based Metrics		H	H	H	H	H	H						H	H	H
Process Management		H	H	H	H	H	H						H	H	H
Balanced Scorecard		H	H	H	H	H	H						H	H	H
Data Mining		M	M	L	L	M	M						M	M	M
Information Mining		L	L	L	L	L	L		L	L	L		L	L	L
Information Management		M	M	M	M	M	M		M	M	M		M	M	M
Collaboration and Communities															
Electronic Messaging Management		H	H	H	H	H	H		M	M	M		H	H	H
Discussion Groups		H	H	H	H	H	H		H	H	H				
Team-Based Collaboration		H	H	H	H	H	H		H	H	H		H	H	H
Real-Time Collaboration		M	M	M	M	M	M		M	M	M		M	M	M
Collaborative Commerce		L	L			L	L		L	L	L		L	L	L
Communities		H	H	H	H	H	H		H	H	H				
Information Retrieval		H	H	H	H	H	H		H	H	H		H	H	H
Content Management															
Structured Content		H	H	H	H	H	H						H	H	H
Data Integration Services		H	H	H	H	H	H						H	H	H
Unstructured Content		H	H	H	H	H	H		H	H	H		H	H	H
Document Management		H	H	H	H	H	H		H	H	H		H	H	H
Web Content Management		H	H	H	H	H	H		H	H	H		H	H	H
Electronic Commerce		M	M	L	L	M	M		M	M	M		M	M	L
Learning															
EPSS		H	H	H	H	H	H		H	H	H		H	H	H
Video and Audio Conferencing		H	H	H	H	H	H		H	H	H		H	H	H
Learning Management System		M	M	M	M	M	M						M	M	M
Interactivity		H	H	H	H	H	H		H	H	H		H	H	H

	Support Your Organization's Business Objectives	Personal Awareness	Personal Alignment	Employee Feedback	Personal Performance	**Promote Innovation**	Business Skills (Expert System)	Technical Skills (Expert System)	Productivity (Continuous Improvement)	**Maintain a Knowledge-Creating Organization**	Key Performance Indicators	Corporate Balanced Scorecard	Personal Balanced Scorecard
Enterprise Portal													
Presentation		H	H	H	H		H	H	H		H	H	H
Knowledge Organization System		H	H	H	H		H	H	H		M	M	M
Search		H	H	H	H		H	H	H		H	H	H
Plug and Play Functions		H	H	H	H		H	H	H		H	H	H
Access and Integration		M	H	M	H		H	H	H		H	H	H
Profiling and Personalization		H	H	H	H		H	H	H		H	H	H
Business Intelligence													
Decision Support			H		H				H		H	H	H
Performance-Based Metrics			H		H				H		H	H	H
Process Management					H		H	H	H		H	H	H
Balanced Scorecard			H		H				H		H	H	H
Data Mining									M				
Information Mining									L				
Information Management		M	M	M	M		M	M	M		M	M	M
Collaboration and Communities													
Electronic Messaging Management		M	M	M	M		H	H	H		L	L	L
Discussion Groups		M	M	M	M		H	H	H				
Team-Based Collaboration							M	M	M		M	M	M
Real-Time Collaboration		L	L	L	L		L	L	L		L	L	L
Collaborative Commerce							L	L	L		L	I	
Communities		M	M	M	M		M	M	M				
Information Retrieval		H	H	H	H		H	H	H		H	H	H
Content Management													
Structured Content			H		H				H		H	H	H
Data Integration Services			H		H				H		H	H	H
Unstructured Content		H	H	H	H		H	H	H		H	H	H
Document Management		H	H	H	H		H	H	H		H	H	H
Web Content Management		H	H	H	H		H	H	H		H	H	H
Electronic Commerce		L	L	L	L		M	M	M		M	M	M
Learning													
EPSS		H	H	H	H		H	H	H		H	H	H
Video and Audio Conferencing		H	H	H	H		H	H	H		H	H	H
Learning Management System		M	M	M	M				M		M	M	M
Interactivity		H	H	H	H		H	H	H		H	H	H

Figure 4-24. Knowledge expert community communication two.

Re: Enterprise Knowledge Portal Requirements Report

Hello Knowledge Expert Community,

The final version of the **Enterprise Knowledge Portal Requirements** report is available. The **Enterprise Knowledge Portal Team** would like to thank each of you for your contribution in completing this effort. To review the final report, please visit:
Enterprise Knowledge Portal Requirements Report (Excel spreadsheet)

We are asking the **Knowledge Expert Community** members to share this information with other managers and teams in your business units. Review the **Enterprise Knowledge Portal Requirements Report** at team meetings or other events to begin to create awareness of myCompany's knowledge management objectives, corporate initiatives, and how knowledge management can support and improve our corporate initiatives. If you need additional presentation information or material, please let Heidi Collins, Michael Douglas, or David Kennedy know, and we will post it for everyone to use and access.

The enterprise knowledge portal strategy template will provide a document to prioritize available options to implement an enterprise knowledge portal to achieve your value proposition. The spreadsheet will provide a standard way to document and compare the options available to you. To make certain you have a complete set of knowledge management objectives that are tied closely to your value proposition, maintain the same categories used in the enterprise knowledge portal map report. The enterprise knowledge portal strategy template can be seen in Figure 4-25. The knowledge management objectives make up the rows in the spreadsheet. You will want to add, edit, or delete the knowledge management objectives based on your final enterprise knowledge portal map report. The enterprise knowledge portal projects that will deliver the value proposition make up the columns in the spreadsheet and will be identified and added to the spreadsheet during the interviews with the knowledge expert community members.

MYCOMPANY CASE STUDY

The enterprise knowledge portal team has defined six unique knowledge management categories that encompass all aspects of the organization that will benefit from the enterprise knowledge portal value proposition. Using the six categories of the enterprise knowledge portal map report as a way to group knowledge man-

Figure 4-25. Enterprise knowledge portal strategy template.

	Work Process Improvements	[Add enterprise knowledge portal projects]	Business-to-Employee Opportunities	[Add enterprise knowledge portal projects]	Business-to-Consumer Opportunities	[Add enterprise knowledge portal projects]
Be Organized Around Work Processes						
[Add knowledge management objectives]						
Maintain Knowledge and Facilitate Communication						
[Add knowledge management objectives]						
Focus on the Future						
[Add knowledge management objectives]						
Support Your Organization's Business Objectives						
[Add knowledge management objectives]						
Promote Innovations						
[Add knowledge management objectives]						
Maintain a Knowledge-Creating Organization						
[Add knowledge management objectives]						

agement objectives, the enterprise knowledge portal strategy template has been created. An example of the template can be seen in Figure 4-26. This document will be used to gather enterprise knowledge portal strategic options as individual interviews with selected members of the knowledge expert community are conducted.

Schedule Interviews with the Knowledge Expert Community

Purpose: Using the enterprise knowledge portal strategy template from step one, interview members of the knowledge expert community to generate open discussions around the value proposition of the enterprise knowledge portal for your organization. Explore the goals and methods required to achieve the value proposition.

The enterprise knowledge portal team will need to review knowledge management objectives across the organization to make certain they understand how the value proposition for the enterprise knowledge portal will benefit everyone throughout the organization. Schedule interviews with members of the knowledge expert community that collectively provide a complete knowledge enterprise portal picture for your organization. Your

Figure 4-26. Enterprise knowledge portal strategy with knowledge management objectives.

	Work Process Improvements	[Add enterprise knowledge portal projects]	Business-to-Employee Opportunities	[Add enterprise knowledge portal projects]	Business-to-Consumer Opportunities	[Add enterprise knowledge portal projects]	
Be Organized Around Work Processes							
Improve employee effectiveness							
Make better decisions faster							
Improve information availability and access							
Improve cycle times							
Embed knowledge management activities							
Improve response times							
Improve information reuse							
Maintain Knowledge and Facilitate Communication							
Improve communication between managers							
Improve alignment of management objectives							
Improve awareness of roles and responsibilities							
Improve strategic alignment							
Improve span of influence of human expertise							
Improve operational efficiencies through information reuse							
Focus on the Future							
Improve market knowledge business strategy effectiveness							
Improve work process innovation							
Improve product innovation							
Improve recruitment and succession							
Improve planning, budgeting, and forecasting processes							
Improve e-business opportunities and strategies							
Support Your Organization's Business Objectives							
Improve personal alignment to your business strategy							
Embed learning into doing							
Drive business value							
Promote Innovations							
Enrich employee work life experience							
Improve career development opportunities							
Improve employee autonomy							
Improve community involvement							
Maintain a Knowledge-Creating Organization							
Improve Web-centric business strategy							
Improve content management							
Improve enterprise search							
Improve user interface and usability consistency							
Improve cross-functional work processes							

goal is to understand the similarities and differences in value your enterprise knowledge portal will provide across business units and other networks of users. The enterprise knowledge portal team will need to complete several activities to complete the enterprise knowledge portal strategy interviews. They should:

- ❒ Hold a kick-off meeting with the selected knowledge expert community members and review the part of the organization they are representing for the strategic direction gathering effort, review the enterprise knowledge portal program charter, discuss the enterprise knowledge portal strategy template, and schedule interview times with each of the knowledge expert community members.
- ❒ Hold individual interview sessions to complete the enterprise knowledge portal strategy template, document the discussions, and post the results for the entire knowledge expert community members to read.
- ❒ Create a communication to share the highlights of the individual interviews and encourage knowledge expert community members to review details.

MYCOMPANY CASE STUDY

The enterprise knowledge portal team has scheduled interviews with each member of the knowledge expert community selected to complete the Enterprise Knowledge Portal Strategy template. The interviews allow the enterprise knowledge portal team to focus on specific projects that will tie directly into the value proposition of the enterprise knowledge portal. The activities and tasks completed by the enterprise knowledge portal team included:

- ❒ A kick-off meeting that was held to introduce the knowledge expert community members and to review the part of the organization they represented for the strategic direction gathering effort. The purpose of the meeting was to review the enterprise knowledge portal program charter, discuss the enterprise knowledge portal strategy template, and schedule interview times with each of the knowledge expert community members. (An example of a meeting invitation and a proposed agenda are presented in Figure 4-27.)
- ❒ Individual interview sessions that were held to complete the enterprise knowledge portal strategy template, document the discussions, and post the results for the entire knowledge expert community members to read.

Figure 4-27. A sample invitation and agenda for the enterprise knowledge portal strategy kick-off.

Agenda	**Enterprise Knowledge Portal Strategy Kick-Off** **Conference Room One**	
Type of meeting:	Enterprise Knowledge Portal Strategy Kick-Off Meeting	
Facilitator:	Heidi Collins	
Note taker:	David Kennedy	
Attendees:	Knowledge Expert Community Members	
	Agenda Topics	
15 Minutes	Knowledge Expert Community Members Introduction	Heidi Collins
45 Minutes	Review Enterprise Knowledge Portal Program Charter	Heidi Collins
15 Minutes	Break	
30 Minutes	Enterprise Knowledge Portal Strategy Template Review	Heidi Collins
15 Minutes	Schedule Enterprise Knowledge Portal Strategy Interviews	Heidi Collins

❒ A communication (shown in Figure 4-28) was distributed to members of the knowledge expert community to share the highlights of the individual interviews and encourage individual members to review details.

Create the Enterprise Knowledge Portal Strategy Report

Purpose: Summarize the results of the knowledge expert community interviews to evaluate and prioritize the available options to marry the value proposition and the enterprise knowledge portal requirements together. Identify the advantages and disadvantages of your available options and recommend the best path forward for your organization.

The enterprise knowledge portal strategy report is the summary of the enterprise knowledge portal strategy templates completed in step two. You will want to share and review the results with the knowledge expert community. During this review you will be teaching as much as sharing information as you walk through the enterprise knowledge portal strategy report. To teach and share the results effectively, you should consider bringing the knowledge expert community together in a meeting format. Create a supporting presentation to accompany the enterprise knowledge portal strategy report. You will want to have an open discussion of the summarized enterprise knowledge portal strategy and make any adjustments agreed on by the knowledge expert community to create the final version of the enterprise knowledge portal strategy report.

Figure 4-28. Knowledge expert community communication three.

Re: Knowledge Expert Community Interviews Available

Hello Knowledge Expert Community,

We would like to take the time to share the **Enterprise Knowledge Portal Strategy** interview results with you. The **Enterprise Knowledge Portal Team** has started the enterprise knowledge portal program definition and established the deliverables. They continue to monitor that the goals and objectives of the **Enterprise Knowledge Portal Program** definition are effectively being delivered on time and in budget. To review any status documents, research material, completed interviews, or other information, please visit: *www.myCompany.com/EKP/enterprise_knowledge_portal_program/material*

The enterprise knowledge portal team members have completed several individual interviews with the knowledge expert community. This was the most effective approach to collect and understand myCompany's enterprise knowledge portal strategy. The information collected represents an enterprise sampling of enterprise knowledge portal requirements across myCompany to plan for the future. Please take the time to review the interviews in detail.

Once the enterprise knowledge portal strategy interviews are completed, a meeting will be scheduled to review the material followed by a discussion session to answer any questions and provide additional detail. Please attend or send a representative to the enterprise knowledge portal strategy review meeting. There will be AT&T conference call numbers and a videoconference set up for these sessions for anyone that cannot attend in person.

Please contact Heidi Collins or Michael Douglas if you have questions or need additional information.

MYCOMPANY CASE STUDY

The enterprise knowledge portal strategy report has been created using the categories outlined in the enterprise knowledge portal map report. The final activities completed by the enterprise knowledge portal team to define the enterprise knowledge portal strategy for myCompany included the following activities:

- ❒ The enterprise knowledge portal team has summarized the interview results from the enterprise knowledge experts into the enterprise knowledge portal strategy report. This first release of the enterprise knowledge portal strategy report is shown in Figure 4-29.

(text continues on page 224)

Figure 4-29. Enterprise knowledge portal strategy report (first release).

	Work Process Improvements	Shareholder Value (Profitability)	Capture Integration	Subscribe To Integration	Collaborate Integration	**Business-to-Employee Opportunities**	Business-to-Employee (Productivity)	Operational Excellence Work Process Improvement	Functional Excellence Work Process Improvement	Personal Awareness	Personal Alignment	Employee Feedback	Personal Performance	Business Skills (Expert System)	Technical Skills (Expert System)	Productivity (Continuous Improvement)	Key Performance Indicators	Corporate Balanced Scorecard	Personal Balanced Scorecard	**Business-to-Consumer Opportunities**	Business-to-Consumer (Revenue Growth)	Sales and Distribution Work Process Improvement	Marketing Work Process Improvement	Service Work Process Improvement	Relationship Work Process Improvement
Be Organized Around Work Processes																									
Improve employee effectiveness		x	x	x	x		x	x	x	x	x	x	x	x	x	x	x	x	x		x	x	x	x	x
Make better decisions faster		x	x	x	x		x	x	x					x	x	x	x	x	x		x	x	x	x	x
Improve information availability and access		x	x	x	x		x	x	x	x	x	x	x	x	x	x	x	x	x		x	x	x	x	x
Improve cycle times		x	x	x	x		x	x	x					x	x	x	x	x	x		x	x	x	x	x
Embed knowledge management activities		x	x	x	x		x	x	x	x	x	x	x	x	x	x	x	x	x		x	x	x	x	x
Improve response times		x	x	x	x		x	x	x					x	x	x	x	x	x		x	x	x	x	x
Improve information reuse		x	x	x	x		x	x	x	x	x	x	x	x	x	x	x	x	x		x	x	x	x	x
Maintain Knowledge and Facilitate Communication																									
Improve communication between managers		x	x	x	x		x	x	x	x	x	x	x	x	x	x	x	x	x		x	x	x	x	x
Improve alignment of management objectives		x	x	x	x		x	x	x					x	x	x	x	x	x		x	x	x	x	x
Improve awareness of roles and responsibilities		x					x	x	x	x	x	x	x	x	x	x					x	x	x	x	x
Improve strategic alignment		x	x	x	x		x	x	x					x	x	x	x	x	x		x	x	x	x	x
Improve span of influence of human expertise		x	x	x	x		x	x	x	x	x	x	x	x	x	x	x	x	x		x	x	x	x	x
Improve operational efficiencies through information reuse		x	x	x	x		x	x	x	x	x	x	x	x	x	x	x	x	x		x	x	x	x	x
Focus on the Future																									
Improve market knowledge business strategy effectiveness		x	x	x	x		x	x	x	x	x	x	x	x	x	x	x	x	x		x	x	x	x	x
Improve work process innovation		x					x	x	x					x	x	x	x	x	x		x	x	x	x	x
Improve product innovation														x	x	x	x	x			x	x	x	x	x
Improve recruitment and succession			x	x	x					x	x	x	x	x	x				x						
Improve planning, budgeting, and forecasting processes		x	x	x	x		x	x	x					x	x	x	x	x	x		x	x	x	x	x
Improve e-business opportunities and strategies														x	x	x	x	x			x	x	x	x	x

	Work Process Improvements	Shareholder Value (Profitability)	Capture Integration	Subscribe To Integration	Collaborate Integration	**Business-to-Employee Opportunities**	Business-to-Employee (Productivity)	Operational Excellence Work Process Improvement	Functional Excellence Work Process Improvement	Personal Awareness	Personal Alignment	Employee Feedback	Personal Performance	Business Skills (Expert System)	Technical Skills (Expert System)	Productivity (Continuous Improvement)	Key Performance Indicators	Corporate Balanced Scorecard	Personal Balanced Scorecard	**Business-to-Consumer Opportunities**	Business-to-Consumer (Revenue Growth)	Sales and Distribution Work Process Improvement	Marketing Work Process Improvement	Service Work Process Improvement	Relationship Work Process Improvement
Support Your Organization's Business Objectives																									
Improve personal alignment to your business strategy			x	x	x					x	x	x	x				x	x	x						
Embed learning into doing		x					x	x	x				x	x	x	x	x	x	x		x	x	x	x	x
Drive business value		x	x	x	x		x	x	x	x	x	x	x	x	x	x	x	x	x		x	x	x	x	x
Promote Innovations																									
Enrich employee work life experience			x	x	x					x	x	x	x	x	x	x									
Improve career development opportunities										x	x	x	x	x	x	x									
Improve employee autonomy		x	x	x	x		x	x	x	x	x	x	x	x	x	x	x	x	x		x	x	x	x	x
Improve community involvement			x	x	x					x	x	x	x	x	x	x									
Maintain a Knowledge-Creating Organization																									
Improve Web-centric business strategy		x	x	x	x		x	x	x	x	x	x	x	x	x	x	x	x	x		x	x	x	x	x
Improve content management		x	x	x	x		x	x	x	x	x	x	x	x	x	x	x	x	x		x	x	x	x	x
Improve enterprise search		x	x	x	x		x	x	x	x	x	x	x	x	x	x	x	x	x		x	x	x	x	x
Improve user interface and usability consistency		x	x	x	x		x	x	x	x	x	x	x	x	x	x	x	x	x		x	x	x	x	x
Improve cross-functional work processes		x					x	x	x				x	x	x	x	x	x	x		x	x	x	x	x

- ❒ A supporting presentation has been created to accompany and explain the summarized results. The enterprise knowledge portal strategy report review presentation can be reviewed in Figure 4-30.
- ❒ A review meeting was held to discuss and clarify the results of the enterprise knowledge portal strategy report. An example of a meeting invitation and a proposed agenda are presented in Figure 4-31.
- ❒ The final version of the enterprise knowledge portal strategy report has been completed as a result of the review meeting and can be seen in Figure 4-32.
- ❒ A communication (shown in Figure 4-33) was distributed to members of the knowledge expert community to share the final version of the enterprise knowledge portal strategy report and to encourage individual members to review details with their business units.

Figure 4-30. Enterprise knowledge portal strategy report review.

- The enterprise knowledge portal strategy was completed by the enterprise knowledge portal team with selected input from knowledge expert community members.
- The knowledge management objectives were pulled from the enterprise knowledge portal map and broken into rows on the spreadsheet:
  —Be organized around work processes.
  —Maintain knowledge and facilitate communication.
  —Focus on the future.
  —Support your organization's business objectives.
  —Promote innovations.
  —Maintain a knowledge-creating organization.
- The enterprise knowledge portal projects were aligned to the corporate initiatives and broken into columns on the spreadsheet:
  —Work process improvements
  —Business-to-employee opportunities
  —Business-to-consumer opportunities
- Each knowledge management objective aligned to each enterprise knowledge portal project was identified with an "x" and will be prioritized as H-high, M-medium, or L-low depending on how critical the knowledge management objective is for the project to achieve the scope and objectives of the enterprise knowledge portal.
- The enterprise knowledge portal strategy report is available for review in the following spreadsheet:
  Enterprise Knowledge Portal Strategy Report (Excel spreadsheet)
- Open discussion of the enterprise knowledge portal strategy report.
- Updates to the enterprise knowledge portal strategy report.

- Note: Rows and columns can be added, updated, and removed from the enterprise knowledge portal strategy report to reflect the appropriate level of detail.

Figure 4-31. A sample invitation and agenda for the enterprise knowledge portal strategy report.

Agenda	**Enterprise Knowledge Portal Strategy Report** **Conference Room One**	
Type of meeting:	Enterprise Knowledge Portal Strategy Report Review Meeting	
Facilitator:	Heidi Collins	
Note taker:	David Kennedy	
Attendees:	Knowledge Expert Community Members	
	Agenda Topics	
60 Minutes	The Knowledge Management Objectives identified from Knowledge Expert Community interviews are reviewed (rows in the template)	Heidi Collins
15 Minutes	Break	
60 Minutes	Enterprise Knowledge Portal Projects identified from Knowledge Expert Community interviews are reviewed (columns in the template)	Heidi Collins
15 Minutes	Break	
40 Minutes	Summarize and prioritize the relationships between knowledge management objectives and enterprise knowledge portal projects	Heidi Collins
10 Minutes	Review action items	Heidi Collins
10 Minutes	Review Enterprise Knowledge Portal Program definition progress and discuss our next steps and activities	Heidi Collins

Enterprise Knowledge Portal Architecture and Infrastructure

The enterprise knowledge portal architecture and infrastructure outlines when enterprise knowledge portal features and functions need to be available in your information technology infrastructure. The work you completed in the enterprise knowledge portal requirements report outlines the enterprise knowledge portal features and functions targeted for implementation into the IT environment. Your objective is to identify the release schedule to deploy these applications, solutions, and services into the enterprise knowledge portal infrastructure that are needed in synchronization with the order enterprise knowledge portal projects are implemented. Your technology categories are mapped to your proposed enterprise knowledge portal projects to produce the enterprise knowledge portal architecture and infrastructure report. The report identifies the enterprise knowledge portal features and functions that will be implemented into your enterprise knowledge portal infrastructure, as each enterprise knowledge portal project is

Figure 4-32. Enterprise knowledge portal strategy report (final release).

	Work Process Improvements	Shareholder Value (Profitability)	Capture Integration	Subscribe To Integration	Collaborate Integration	**Business-to-Employee Opportunities**	Business-to-Employee (Productivity)	Operational Excellence Work Process Improvement	Functional Excellence Work Process Improvement	Personal Awareness	Personal Alignment	Employee Feedback	Personal Performance	Business Skills (Expert System)	Technical Skills (Expert System)	Productivity (Continuous Improvement)	Key Performance Indicators	Corporate Balanced Scorecard	Personal Balanced Scorecard	**Business-to-Consumer Opportunities**	Business-to-Consumer (Revenue Growth)	Sales and Distribution Work Process Improvement	Marketing Work Process Improvement	Service Work Process Improvement	Relationship Work Process Improvement
Be Organized Around Work Processes																									
Improve employee effectiveness		H	M	M	M		H	H	H	M	M	M	M	H	H	H	H	H	H		H	H	H	H	H
Make better decisions faster		H	H	H	H		H	H	H					H	H	H	H	H	H		H	H	H	H	H
Improve information availability and access		H	H	H	H		H	H	H	H	H	H	H	H	H	H	H	H	H		H	H	H	H	H
Improve cycle times		H	M	M	M		H	H	H					H	H	H	M	M	M		H	H	H	H	H
Embed knowledge management activities		H	H	H	H		H	H	H	M	M	M	H	H	H	H	H	H	H		H	H	H	H	H
Improve response times		M	M	M	M		M	M	M					M	M	M	M	M	M		M	M	M	M	M
Improve information reuse		H	H	H	H		H	H	H	H	H	H	H	H	H	H	H	H	H		H	H	H	H	H
Maintain Knowledge and Facilitate Communication																									
Improve communication between managers		M	H	H	H		M	H	H	L	L	L	H	H	H	H	H	H	H		M	H	H	H	H
Improve alignment of management objectives		H	H	H	H		H	H	H					H	H	H	H	H	H		H	H	H	H	H
Improve awareness of roles and responsibilities		H					H	H	H	H	H	H	H	H	H	H					H	H	H	H	H
Improve strategic alignment		H	M	M	M		H	H	H					M	M	H	H	H	H		H	H	H	H	H
Improve span of influence of human expertise		M	H	H	H		M	M	M	M	M	M	M	H	H	M	M	M	M		M	M	M	M	M
Improve operational efficiencies through information reuse		H	H	H	H		H	H	H	H	H	H	H	H	H	H	H	H	H		H	H	H	H	H
Focus on the Future																									
Improve market knowledge business strategy effectiveness		H	L	L	L		H	H	H	L	L	L	L	M	M	H	H	H	H		H	H	H	H	H
Improve work process innovation		H					H	H	H					H	H	H	H	H	H		H	H	H	H	H
Improve product innovation														H	H	H	H	H			H	H	H	H	H
Improve recruitment and succession			M	M	M					M	M	H	H	H	H				H						
Improve planning, budgeting, and forecasting processes		M	H	H	H		M	M	M					M	M	M	M	M	M		M	M	M	M	M
Improve e-business opportunities and strategies														M	M	M	M	M			M	M	M	M	M
Support Your Organization's Business Objectives																									
Improve personal alignment to your business strategy			M	M	M					H	H	H	M				M	M	H						
Embed learning into doing		H					H	H	H				H	H	H	H	H	H	H		H	H	H	H	H
Drive business value		H	H	H	H		H	H	H	H	H	H	H	H	H	H	H	H	H		H	H	H	H	H

	Work Process Improvements	Shareholder Value (Profitability)	Capture Integration	Subscribe To Integration	Collaborate Integration	Business-to-Employee Opportunities	Business-to-Employee (Productivity)	Operational Excellence Work Process Improvement	Functional Excellence Work Process Improvement	Personal Awareness	Personal Alignment	Employee Feedback	Personal Performance	Business Skills (Expert System)	Technical Skills (Expert System)	Productivity (Continuous Improvement)	Key Performance Indicators	Corporate Balanced Scorecard	Personal Balanced Scorecard	Business-to-Consumer Opportunities	Business-to-Consumer (Revenue Growth)	Sales and Distribution Work Process Improvement	Marketing Work Process Improvement	Service Work Process Improvement	Relationship Work Process Improvement
Promote Innovations																									
Enrich employee work life experience			M	M	M					H	H	H	H	M	M	M									
Improve career development opportunities										H	H	H	H	H	H	H									
Improve employee autonomy		M	H	H	H		H	H	H	M	M	H	H	H	H	M	M	M	M		M	H	H	H	H
Improve community involvement			M	M	M					H	H	H	L	H	H	L									
Maintain a Knowledge-Creating Organization																									
Improve Web-centric business strategy		H	H	H	H		H	H	H	H	H	H	H	H	H	H	H	H	H		H	H	H	H	H
Improve content management		H	H	H	H		H	H	H	H	H	H	H	H	H	H	H	H	H		H	H	H	H	H
Improve enterprise search		H	H	H	H		H	H	H	H	H	H	H	H	H	H	H	H	H		H	H	H	H	H
Improve user interface and usability consistency		H	H	H	H		H	H	H	H	H	H	H	H	H	H	H	H	H		H	H	H	H	H
Improve cross-functional work processes		H					H	H	H				H	H	H	H	H	H	H		H	H	H	H	H

Figure 4-33. Knowledge expert community communication four.

Re: Enterprise Knowledge Portal Strategy Report

Hello Knowledge Expert Community,

The final version of the **Enterprise Knowledge Portal Strategy** report is available. The **Enterprise Knowledge Portal Team** would like to thank each of you for your contribution in completing this effort. To review the final report, please visit:
Enterprise Knowledge Portal Strategy Report (Excel spreadsheet)

We are asking the **Knowledge Expert Community** members to share this information with other managers and teams in your business units. Review the **Enterprise Knowledge Portal Strategy Report** at team meetings or other events to begin to create awareness of myCompany's knowledge management objectives, corporate initiatives, and how knowledge management can support and improve our corporate initiatives. If you need additional presentation information or material, please let Heidi Collins, Michael Douglas, or David Kennedy know, and we will post it for everyone to use and access.

successfully deployed. There are three steps outlined to establish your enterprise knowledge portal architecture and infrastructure report. They are:

1. *Modify the enterprise knowledge portal architecture and infrastructure template.* Using your enterprise knowledge portal IT–enabling framework report and enterprise knowledge portal requirements report information, review the enterprise knowledge portal architecture and infrastructure template and update to match your organization.
2. *Schedule interviews with the chief technology office.* Using the enterprise knowledge portal architecture and infrastructure template from step one, interview members of your information technology department to identify the existing applications, solutions, and services that will be integrated with the enterprise knowledge portal. Determine the enterprise knowledge portal applications, solutions, and services that will need to be added or upgraded to your existing architecture and infrastructure.
3. *Create the enterprise knowledge portal architecture and infrastructure report.* Summarize the results of the information technology interviews to document the current architecture and infrastructure that is available in your organization to support the enterprise knowledge portal. You will want to include information about how the enterprise knowledge portal infrastructure and architecture will evolve to meet your enterprise knowledge portal requirements report.

Modify the Enterprise Knowledge Portal Architecture and Infrastructure Template

Purpose: Using your enterprise knowledge portal IT–enabling framework report and enterprise knowledge portal requirements report information, review the enterprise knowledge portal architecture and infrastructure template and update to match your organization.

The enterprise knowledge portal architecture and infrastructure template will provide a spreadsheet that outlines when enterprise knowledge portal features and functions need to be available in your information technology infrastructure. The spreadsheet will provide a standard way to outline the applications, solutions, and services to be deployed in your organization. The release schedule to deploy these applications, solutions, and services needs to tie directly to the recommended enterprise knowledge portal strategy report. The Enterprise knowledge portal architecture and infrastructure template can be seen in Figure 4-34. The enterprise knowledge portal features and functions make up the rows in the spreadsheet. You will want to add, edit, or delete the enterprise knowledge portal features based on your final enterprise knowledge portal IT–enabling framework report. The enterprise knowledge portal projects that will de-

Figure 4-34. Enterprise knowledge portal architecture and infrastructure template.

	Work Process Improvements	[Add enterprise knowledge portal projects]	**Business-to-Employee Opportunities**	[Add enterprise knowledge portal projects]	**Business-to-Consumer Opportunities**	[Add enterprise knowledge portal projects]
Enterprise Portal						
[Add IT-enabling framework features]						
Business Intelligence						
[Add IT-enabling framework features]						
Collaboration and Communities						
[Add IT-enabling framework features]						
Content Management						
[Add IT-enabling framework features]						
Learning						
[Add IT-enabling framework features]						

liver the value proposition make up the columns in the spreadsheet and will be identified and added to the spreadsheet during the interviews with the chief technology office.

MYCOMPANY CASE STUDY

The enterprise knowledge portal team has defined five unique technology categories that encompass all aspects of the organization that will benefit from the enterprise knowledge portal value proposition. Using the five categories of the enterprise knowledge portal IT–enabling framework report as a way to group enterprise knowledge portal projects, the enterprise knowledge portal architecture and infrastructure template has been created. An example of the template can be seen in Figure 4-35. This document will be used to gather enterprise knowledge portal architecture and infrastructure requirements as individual interviews with selected members of the chief technology office.

Schedule Interviews with the Chief Technology Office

Purpose: Using the enterprise knowledge portal architecture and infrastructure template from step one, interview members of your information technology department to identify the existing applications, solutions, and services that will be integrated with the enterprise knowledge portal. Determine the enterprise knowledge portal applications, solutions, and services that will need to be added or upgraded to your existing architecture and infrastructure.

The enterprise knowledge portal team will need to review knowledge management objectives across the organization to make certain they understand how the value proposition for the enterprise knowledge portal will benefit everyone throughout the organization. Schedule interviews with members of the knowledge expert community that collectively provide a complete knowledge enterprise portal picture for your organization. Your goal is to understand the similarities and differences in value your enterprise knowledge portal will provide across business units and other networks of users. The enterprise knowledge portal team will need to complete several activities to complete the enterprise knowledge portal strategy interviews. They should:

- ❒ Hold a kick-off meeting with the selected knowledge expert community members and review the part of the organization they are representing for the strategic direction gathering effort, review the enterprise knowl-

Figure 4-35. Enterprise knowledge portal architecture and infrastructure template.

	Work Process Improvements	[Add enterprise knowledge portal projects]	**Business-to-Employee Opportunities**	[Add enterprise knowledge portal projects]	**Business-to-Consumer Opportunities**	[Add enterprise knowledge portal projects]	
Enterprise Portal							
Presentation							
Knowledge Organization System							
Search							
Plug and Play Functions							
Access and Integration							
Profiling and Personalization							
Business Intelligence							
Decision Support							
Performance-Based Metrics							
Process Management							
Balanced Scorecard							
Data Mining							
Information Mining							
Information Management							
Collaboration and Communities							
Electronic Messaging Management							
Discussion Groups							
Team-Based Collaboration							
Real-Time Collaboration							
Collaborative Commerce							
Communities							
Information Retrieval							
Content Management							
Structured Content							
Data Integration Services							
Unstructured Content							
Document Management							
Web Content Management							
Electronic Commerce							
Learning							
EPSS							
Video and Audio Conferencing							
Learning Management System							
Interactivity							

edge portal program charter, discuss the enterprise knowledge portal strategy template, and schedule interview times with each of the knowledge expert community members.

- ❒ Hold individual interview sessions to complete the enterprise knowledge portal strategy template, document the discussions, and post the results for the entire knowledge expert community members to read.
- ❒ Create a communication to share the highlights of the individual interviews and encourage knowledge expert community members to review details.

MYCOMPANY CASE STUDY

The enterprise knowledge portal team has scheduled interviews with the chief technology office to complete the enterprise knowledge portal architecture and infrastructure template. The interviews allow the enterprise knowledge portal team to focus on specific projects that will require additional applications, solutions, and services from information technology. As part of the enterprise knowledge portal architecture and infrastructure report deliverable, a proposed timeline is included to enhance the information technology applications, solutions, and services that are synchronized with the enterprise knowledge portal strategy report. The activities and tasks completed by the enterprise knowledge portal team included:

- ❒ A kick-off meeting that was held to review the enterprise knowledge portal program charter, discuss the enterprise knowledge portal architecture and infrastructure template, and schedule interview times with each of the chief technology office members. (An example of a meeting invitation and a proposed agenda are presented in Figure 4-36.)
- ❒ Individual interview sessions that were held to complete the enterprise knowledge portal architecture and infrastructure template, document the discussions, and post the results for all the knowledge expert community members to read.
- ❒ A communication (shown in Figure 4-37) that was distributed to members of the chief technology office to share the highlights of the individual interviews and encourage individual members to review details.

Figure 4-36. A sample invitation and agenda for the enterprise knowledge portal architecture and infrastructure kick-off.

Agenda	**Enterprise Knowledge Portal Architecture and Infrastructure Kick-Off** **Conference Room One**	
Type of meeting:	Enterprise Knowledge Portal Architecture and Infrastructure Kick-Off Meeting	
Facilitator:	Heidi Collins	
Note taker:	David Kennedy	
Attendees:	Knowledge Expert Community Members	
	Agenda Topics	
15 Minutes	Knowledge Expert Community Members Introduction	Heidi Collins
45 Minutes	Review Enterprise Knowledge Portal Program Charter	Heidi Collins
15 Minutes	Break	
30 Minutes	Enterprise Knowledge Portal Architecture and Infrastructure Template Review	Heidi Collins
15 Minutes	Schedule Enterprise Knowledge Portal Architecture and Infrastructure Interviews	Heidi Collins

Create the Enterprise Knowledge Portal Architecture and Infrastructure Report

Purpose: Summarize the results of the information technology interviews to document the current architecture and infrastructure that is available in your organization to support the enterprise knowledge portal. You will want to include information about how the enterprise knowledge portal infrastructure and architecture will evolve to meet your enterprise knowledge portal requirements report.

The enterprise knowledge portal architecture and infrastructure report is the summary of the enterprise knowledge portal architecture and infrastructure templates completed in step two. You will want to share and review the results with the chief technology office. You should consider bringing the members of the chief technology office together in a meeting format. Create a supporting presentation to accompany the enterprise knowledge portal architecture and infrastructure report. You will want to have an open discussion of the summarized enterprise knowledge portal applications, solutions, and services and make any adjustments agreed on by the chief technology office to create the final version of the enterprise knowledge portal architecture and infrastructure report.

Figure 4-37. Knowledge expert community communication five.

Re: Knowledge Expert Community Interviews Available

Hello Knowledge Expert Community,

We would like to take the time to share the **Enterprise Knowledge Portal Architecture and Infrastructure** interview results with you. The **Enterprise Knowledge Portal Team** has started the enterprise knowledge portal program definition and established the deliverables. They continue to monitor that the goals and objectives of the **Enterprise Knowledge Portal Program** definition are effectively being delivered on time and in budget. To review any status documents, research material, completed interviews, or other information, please visit: *www.myCompany.com/EKP/enterprise_knowledge_portal_program/material*

The enterprise knowledge portal team members have completed several individual interviews with the knowledge expert community. This was the most effective approach to collect and understand myCompany's enterprise knowledge portal architecture and infrastructure requirements. The information collected represents an enterprise sampling of enterprise knowledge portal architecture and infrastructure available to support myCompany's enterprise knowledge portal. Please take the time to review the interviews in detail.

Once the enterprise knowledge portal architecture and infrastructure interviews are completed, a meeting will be scheduled to review the material followed by a discussion session to answer any questions and provide additional detail. Please attend or send a representative to the enterprise knowledge portal architecture and infrastructure review meeting. There will be AT&T conference call numbers and a videoconference set up for these sessions for anyone that cannot attend in person.

Please contact Heidi Collins or Michael Douglas if you have questions or need additional information.

MYCOMPANY CASE STUDY

The enterprise knowledge portal architecture and infrastructure report was created using the categories outlined in the enterprise knowledge portal IT–enabling framework report. The final activities completed by the enterprise knowledge portal team to define the enterprise knowledge portal applications, solutions, and services for myCompany included:

- ❒ A summarization of the interview results from the chief technology office into the enterprise knowledge portal architecture and infrastructure report by the enterprise knowledge portal team. (This first release of the enterprise knowledge portal infrastructure report is shown in Figure 4-38.)

- A supporting presentation created to accompany and explain the summarized results. (The enterprise knowledge portal architecture and infrastructure report review presentation can be reviewed in Figure 4-39.)
- A review meeting to discuss and clarify the results of enterprise knowledge portal architecture and infrastructure report. (An example of a meeting invitation and a proposed agenda are presented in Figure 4-40.)
- Completion of the final version of the enterprise knowledge portal architecture and infrastructure report as a result of the review meeting. (The report can be seen in Figure 4-41.)
- A communication (shown in Figure 4-42) that was distributed to members of the chief technology office to share the final version of the enterprise knowledge portal architecture and infrastructure report and encourage individual members to review details with the information technology departments.

Enterprise Knowledge Portal Program Plan

Your program plan is a well-outlined sequence of events with an identifiable beginning and ending. The focus of the enterprise knowledge program plan is to define the effort required to meet the objectives and value proposition identified in the program charter using the established parameters, such as time, cost, and resources. The program plan is different from a work process. When the activities outlined in the program plan are completed, the enterprise knowledge portal organization and identified projects will be implemented and the objective will have been met. A work process is a reoccurring sequence of events. For example, if your job is to create test plans for new releases of the enterprise knowledge portal, the activities and tasks are familiar to you and are repeatable. A detailed plan that outlines the steps and activities you need to complete are not necessary. On the other hand, each of the enterprise knowledge portal projects identified to implement the enterprise knowledge program will require a detailed plan. The plan is necessary to manage the changing membership and objectives of the cross-functional teams unfamiliar with information technology work processes to develop, deploy, and manage the new enterprise knowledge portal functionality.

Third-party project management software applications are excellent

(text continues on page 239)

Figure 4-38. Enterprise knowledge portal architecture and infrastructure (first release).

	Work Process Improvements	Shareholder Value (Profitability)	Capture Integration	Subscribe To Integration	Collaborate Integration	**Business-to-Employee Opportunities**	Business-to-Employee (Productivity)	Operational Excellence Work Process Improveme	Functional Excellence Work Process Improvement	Personal Awareness	Personal Alignment	Employee Feedback	Personal Performance	Business Skills (Expert System)	Technical Skills (Expert System)	Productivity (Continuous Improvement)	Key Performance Indicators	Corporate Balanced Scorecard	Personal Balanced Scorecard	**Business-to-Consumer Opportunities**	Business-to-Consumer (Revenue Growth)	Sales and Distribution Work Process Improvement	Marketing Work Process Improvement	Service Work Process Improvement	Relationship Work Process Improvement
Enterprise Portal																									
Presentation		2	2	2	2		2	2	2	2	2	2	2	2	2	2	2	2	2		2	2	2	2	2
Knowledge Organization System		1	1	1	1		1	1	1	1	1	1	1	1	1	1	1	1	1		1	1	1	1	1
Search		2	2	2	2		2	2	2	2	2	2	2	2	2	2	2	2	2		2	2	2	2	2
Plug and Play Functions		3	3	3	3		3	3	3	3	3	3	3	3	3	3	3	3	3		3	3	3	3	3
Access and Integration		4	4	4	4		4	4	4	4	4	4	4	4	4	4	4	4	4		4	4	4	4	4
Profiling and Personalization		1	1	1	1		1	1	1	1	1	1	1	1	1	1	1	1	1		1	1	1	1	1
Business Intelligence																									
Decision Support		4	4	4	4		4	4	4	4	4	4	4	4	4	4	4	4	4		4	4	4	4	4
Performance-Based Metrics		4	4	4	4		4	4	4	4	4	4	4	4	4	4	4	4	4		4	4	4	4	4
Process Management		4	4	4	4		4	4	4	4	4	4	4	4	4	4	4	4	4		4	4	4	4	4
Balanced Scorecard		4	4	4	4		4	4	4	4	4	4	4	4	4	4	4	4	4		4	4	4	4	4
Data Mining		2	2	2	2		2	2	2	2	2	2	2	2	2	2	2	2	2		2	2	2	2	2
Information Mining		4	4	4	4		4	4	4	4	4	4	4	4	4	4	4	4	4		4	4	4	4	4
Information Management		3	3	3	3		3	3	3	3	3	3	3	3	3	3	3	3	3		3	3	3	3	3
Collaboration and Communities																									
Electronic Messaging Management		3	3	3	3		3	3	3	3	3	3	3	3	3	3	3	3	3		3	3	3	3	3
Discussion Groups		4	4	4	4		4	4	4	4	4	4	4	4	4	4	4	4	4		4	4	4	4	4
Team-Based Collaboration		4	4	4	4		4	4	4	4	4	4	4	4	4	4	4	4	4		4	4	4	4	4
Real-Time Collaboration		3	3	3	3		3	3	3	3	3	3	3	3	3	3	3	3	3		3	3	3	3	3
Collaborative Commerce		2	2	2	2		2	2	2	2	2	2	2	2	2	2	2	2	2		2	2	2	2	2
Communities		3	3	3	3		3	3	3	3	3	3	3	3	3	3	3	3	3		3	3	3	3	3
Information Retrieval		3	3	3	3		3	3	3	3	3	3	3	3	3	3	3	3	3		3	3	3	3	3

	Content Management	Structured Content	Data Integration Services	Unstructured Content	Document Management	Web Content Management	Electronic Commerce	Learning	EPSS	Video and Audio Conferencing	Learning Management System	Interactivity
Work Process Improvements												
Shareholder Value (Profitability)		4	4	3	3	3	1		3	4	1	0
Capture Integration		4	4	3	3	3	1		3	4	1	0
Subscribe To Integration		4	4	3	3	3	1		3	4	1	0
Collaborate Integration		4	4	3	3	3	1		3	4	1	0
Business-to-Employee Opportunities												
Business-to-Employee (Productivity)		4	4	3	3	3	1		3	4	1	0
Operational Excellence Work Process Improveme		4	4	3	3	3	1		3	4	1	0
Functional Excellence Work Process Improvement		4	4	3	3	3	1		3	4	1	0
Personal Awareness		4	4	3	3	3	1		3	4	1	0
Personal Alignment		4	4	3	3	3	1		3	4	1	0
Employee Feedback		4	4	3	3	3	1		3	4	1	0
Personal Performance		4	4	3	3	3	1		3	4	1	0
Business Skills (Expert System)		4	4	3	3	3	1		3	4	1	0
Technical Skills (Expert System)		4	4	3	3	3	1		3	4	1	0
Productivity (Continuous Improvement)		4	4	3	3	3	1		3	4	1	0
Key Performance Indicators		4	4	3	3	3	[illegible]		3	4	[illegible]	0
Corporate Balanced Scorecard		4	4	3	3	3	1		3	4	1	0
Personal Balanced Scorecard		4	4	3	3	3	1		3	4	1	0
Business-to-Consumer Opportunities												
Business-to-Consumer (Revenue Growth)		4	4	3	3	3	1		3	4	1	0
Sales and Distribution Work Process Improvement		4	4	3	3	3	1		3	4	1	0
Marketing Work Process Improvement		4	4	3	3	3	1		3	4	1	0
Service Work Process Improvement		4	4	3	3	3	1		3	4	1	0
Relationship Work Process Improvement		4	4	3	3	3	1		3	4	1	0

Figure 4-39. Enterprise knowledge portal architecture and infrastructure report review.

- The enterprise knowledge portal architecture and infrastructure was completed by the enterprise knowledge portal team with selected input from knowledge expert community members.
- The enterprise knowledge portal features were pulled from the knowledge management IT–enabling framework and broken into rows on the spreadsheet:
  —Enterprise portal
  —Business intelligence
  —Collaboration and communities
  —Content management
  —Learning
- The enterprise knowledge portal projects were aligned to the corporate initiatives and broken into columns on the spreadsheet:
  —Work process improvements
  —Business-to-employee opportunities
  —Business-to-consumer opportunities
- Each enterprise knowledge portal IT–enabling framework feature was ranked against each enterprise knowledge portal project to meet the intent of what the project is expected to deliver. Values between 0 and 5 were assigned. The higher the value, the more likely the current IT environment can meet the intent of the objective.
- In the enterprise knowledge portal requirements report each enterprise knowledge portal IT–enabling framework feature was assigned a value of importance that the feature brings to accomplishing the enterprise knowledge portal project. Values of H-high, M-medium, and L-low were assigned. The higher the value, the more critical the feature is for the project to meet user requirements. The enterprise knowledge portal requirements information will be mapped to the enterprise knowledge portal architecture and infrastructure to establish a baseline for the enterprise knowledge portal program.
- The enterprise knowledge portal architecture and infrastructure report (Excel spreadsheet) is available for review in the following spreadsheet:
  Enterprise Knowledge Portal Architecture and Infrastructure Report
- Open discussion of the enterprise knowledge portal architecture and infrastructure report
- Updates to the enterprise knowledge portal architecture and infrastructure report

tools for establishing an initial program plan. These applications can quickly recalculate schedules and allow the enterprise knowledge portal program management team to see how changes in one part of the program will affect the overall enterprise knowledge portal implementation. Reviewing the credibility of tasks, adjusting schedule dates, and juggling available resources can be done quickly with project management applications. The enterprise knowledge portal program plan will be a master plan with several work categories. Each work category will outline a specific amount of work required to implement the enterprise knowledge portal. The complete collection of work categories will outline the effort to accomplish the objectives outlined in the enterprise knowledge portal project charter. The

Figure 4-40. A sample invitation and agenda for the enterprise knowledge portal architecture and infrastructure report.

Agenda	**Enterprise Knowledge Portal Architecture and Infrastructure Report** **Conference Room One**	
Type of meeting:	Enterprise Knowledge Portal Architecture and Infrastructure Report Review Meeting	
Facilitator:	Heidi Collins	
Note taker:	David Kennedy	
Attendees:	Knowledge Expert Community Members	
	Agenda Topics	
60 Minutes	The Enterprise Knowledge Portal Features identified from Knowledge Expert Community interviews are reviewed (rows in the template)	Heidi Collins
15 Minutes	Break	
60 Minutes	Enterprise Knowledge Portal Projects are mapped from the Enterprise Knowledge Portal Requirements report and are reviewed (columns in the template)	Heidi Collins
15 Minutes	Break	
40 Minutes	Summarize and prioritize the relationships between enterprise knowledge portal features available in myCompany's IT environment and enterprise knowledge portal projects	Heidi Collins
10 Minutes	Review action items	Heidi Collins
10 Minutes	Review Enterprise Knowledge Portal Program definition progress and discuss our next steps and activities	Heidi Collins

enterprise knowledge portal program plan is outlined in four steps. They are:

1. Identify activities and tasks. Using the goals and objectives from the enterprise knowledge portal program charter, create the project schedule by identifying the tasks necessary to implement the enterprise knowledge portal. Categorize the tasks into defined categories of work.
2. Outline the task list. Organize common activities and tasks into groups with the task list. The categorized groups created in the task list represent phases of the enterprise knowledge portal program. The final hierarchical structure establishes a logical organization of the components of work required to meet the objectives defined in the enterprise knowledge portal program charter.

(text continues on page 242)

Figure 4-41. Enterprise knowledge portal architecture and infrastructure report (final release).

	Work Process Improvements	Shareholder Value (Profitability)	Capture Integration	Subscribe To Integration	Collaborate Integration	**Business-to-Employee Opportunities**	Business-to-Employee (Productivity)	Operational Excellence Work Process Improveme	Functional Excellence Work Process Improvement	Personal Awareness	Personal Alignment	Employee Feedback	Personal Performance	Business Skills (Expert System)	Technical Skills (Expert System)	Productivity (Continuous Improvement)	Key Performance Indicators	Corporate Balanced Scorecard	Personal Balanced Scorecard	**Business-to-Consumer Opportunities**	Business-to-Consumer (Revenue Growth)	Sales and Distribution Work Process Improvement	Marketing Work Process Improvement	Service Work Process Improvement	Relationship Work Process Improvement
Enterprise Portal																									
Presentation		H-2	H-2	H-2	H-2		H-2	H-2	H-2	H-2	H-2	H-2	H-2	H-2	H-2	H-2	H-2	H-2	H-2		H-2	H-2	H-2	H-2	H-2
Knowledge Organization System		H-1	H-1	H-1	H-1		H-1	H-1	H-1	H-1	H-1	H-1	H-1	H-1	H-1	H-1	M-1	M-1	M-1		H-1	H-1	H-1	H-1	H-1
Search		H-2	H-2	H-2	H-2		H-2	H-2	H-2	H-2	H-2	H-2	H-2	H-2	H-2	H-2	H-2	H-2	H-2		H-2	H-2	H-2	H-2	H-2
Plug and Play Functions		H-3	H-3	H-3	H-3		H-3	H-3	H-3	H-3	H-3	H-3	H-3	H-3	H-3	H-3	H-3	H-3	H-3		H-3	H-3	H-3	H-3	H-3
Access and Integration		H-4	H-4	H-4	H-4		H-4	H-4	H-4	H-4	H-4	H-4	H-4	H-4	H-4	H-4	H-4	H-4	H-4		H-4	H-4	H-4	H-4	H-4
Profiling and Personalization		H-1	H-1	H-1	H-1		H-1	H-1	H-1	H-1	H-1	H-1	H-1	H-1	H-1	H-1	H-1	H-1	H-1		H-1	H-1	H-1	H-1	H-1
Business Intelligence																									
Decision Support		H-4					H-4	H-4	H-4		H-4		H-4			H-4	H-4	H-4	H-4		H-4	H-4	H-4	H-4	H-4
Performance-Based Metrics		H-4					H-4	H-4	H-4		H-4		H-4			H-4	H-4	H-4	H-4		H-4	H-4	H-4	H-4	H-4
Process Management		H-4					H-4	H-4	H-4				H-4	H-4	H-4	H-4	H-4	H-4	H-4		H-4	H-4	H-4	H-4	H-4
Balanced Scorecard		H-4					H-4	H-4	H-4		H-4		H-4			H-4	H-4	H-4	H-4		H-4	H-4	H-4	H-4	H-4
Data Mining		M-2					M-2	L-2	L-2							M-2					M-2	M-2	M-2	M-2	M-2
Information Mining		L-4	L-4	L-4	L-4		L-4	L-4	L-4							L-4					L-4	L-4	L-4	L-4	L-4
Information Management		M-3	M-3	M-3	M-3		M-3	M-3	M-3	M-3	M-3	M-3	M-3	M-3	M-3	M-3	M-3	M-3	M-3		M-3	M-3	M-3	M-3	M-3
Collaboration and Communities																									
Electronic Messaging Management		H-3	M-3	M-3	M-3		H-3	H-3	H-3	M-3	M-3	M-3	M-3	H-3	H-3	H-3	L-3	L-3	L-3		H-3	H-3	H-3	H-3	H-3
Discussion Groups			H-4	H-4	H-4			H-4	H-4	M-4	M-4	M-4	M-4	H-4	H-4	H-4						H-4	H-4	H-4	H-4
Team-Based Collaboration		H-4	H-4	H-4	H-4		H-4	H-4	H-4					M-4	M-4	M-4	M-4	M-4	M-4		H-4	H-4	H-4	H-4	H-4
Real-Time Collaboration		M-3	M-3	M-3	M-3		M-3	M-3	M-3	L-3	L-3	L-3	L-3	L-3	L-3	L-3	L-3	L-3	L-3		M-3	M-3	M-3	M-3	M-3
Collaborative Commerce		L-2	L-2	L-2	L-2		L-2							L-2	L-2	L-2	L-2	L-2			L-2	L-2	L-2	L-2	L-2
Communities			H-3	H-3	H-3			H-3	H-3	M-3	M-3	M-3	M-3	M-3	M-3	M-3						H-3	H-3	H-3	H-3
Information Retrieval		H-3	H-3	H-3	H-3		H-3	H-3	H-3	H-3	H-3	H-3	H-3	H-3	H-3	H-3	H-3	H-3	H-3		H-3	H-3	H-3	H-3	H-3

	Work Process Improvements	Shareholder Value (Profitability)	Capture Integration	Subscribe To Integration	Collaborate Integration	Business-to-Employee Opportunities	Business-to-Employee (Productivity)	Operational Excellence Work Process Improveme	Functional Excellence Work Process Improvement	Personal Awareness	Personal Alignment	Employee Feedback	Personal Performance	Business Skills (Expert System)	Technical Skills (Expert System)	Productivity (Continuous Improvement)	Key Performance Indicators	Corporate Balanced Scorecard	Personal Balanced Scorecard	Business-to-Consumer Opportunities	Business-to-Consumer (Revenue Growth)	Sales and Distribution Work Process Improvement	Marketing Work Process Improvement	Service Work Process Improvement	Relationship Work Process Improvement
Content Management																									
Structured Content		H-4					H-4	H-4	H-4		H-4		H-4			H-4	H-4	H-4	H-4		H-4	H-4	H-4	H-4	H-4
Data Integration Services		H-4					H-4	H-4	H-4		H-4		H-4			H-4	H-4	H-4	H-4		H-4	H-4	H-4	H-4	H-4
Unstructured Content		H-3	H-3	H-3	H-3		H-3	H-3	H-3	H-3	H-3	H-3	H-3	H-3	H-3	H-3	H-3	H-3	H-3		H-3	H-3	H-3	H-3	H-3
Document Management		H-3	H-3	H-3	H-3		H-3	H-3	H-3	H-3	H-3	H-3	H-3	H-3	H-3	H-3	H-3	H-3	H-3		H-3	H-3	H-3	H-3	H-3
Web Content Management		H-3	H-3	H-3	H-3		H-3	H-3	H-3	H-3	H-3	H-3	H-3	H-3	H-3	H-3	H-3	H-3	H-3		H-3	H-3	H-3	H-3	H-3
Electronic Commerce		M-1	M-1	M-1	M-1		L-1	L-1	L-1	L-1	L-1	L-1	L-1	M-1	M-1	M-1	M-1	M-1	M-1		M-1	M-1	M-1	M-1	M-1
Learning																									
EPSS		H-3	H-3	H-3	H-3		H-3	H-3	H-3	H-3	H-3	H-3	H-3	H-3	H-3	H-3	H-3	H-3	H-3		H-3	H-3	H-3	H-3	H-3
Video and Audio Conferencing		H-4	H-4	H-4	H-4		H-4	H-4	H-4	H-4	H-4	H-4	H-4	H-4	H-4	H-4	H-4	H-4	H-4		H-4	H-4	H-4	H-4	H-4
Learning Management System		M-1					M-1	M-1	M-1	M-1	M-1	M-1	M-1			M-1	M-1	M-1	M-1		M-1	M-1	M-1	M-1	M-1
Interactivity		H-0	H-0	H-0	H-0		H-0	H-0	H-0	H-0	H-0	H-0	H-0	H-0	H-0	H-0	H-0	H-0	H-0		H-0	H-0	H-0	H-0	H-0

Figure 4-42. Knowledge expert community communication six.

Re: Enterprise Knowledge Portal Architecture and Infrastructure Report

Hello Knowledge Expert Community,

The final version of the **Enterprise Knowledge Portal Architecture and Infrastructure** report is available. The **Enterprise Knowledge Portal Team** would like to thank each of you for your contribution in completing this effort. To review the final report, please visit: *Enterprise Knowledge Portal Architecture and Infrastructure Report*

We are asking the **Knowledge Expert Community** members to share this information with other managers and teams in your business units. Review the **Enterprise Knowledge Portal Architecture and Infrastructure Report** at team meetings or other events to begin to create awareness of myCompany's knowledge management objectives, corporate initiatives, and how knowledge management can support and improve our corporate initiatives. If you need additional presentation information or material, please let Heidi Collins, Michael Douglas, or David Kennedy know, and we will post it for everyone to use and access.

3. Assign resources, roles, and team members to activities and tasks. Assign the appropriate equipment, location, and people required to the activities and tasks identified in the program plan. At a minimum you will want to identify at least one role to each task. This will identify the skill set required to complete individual tasks.
4. Determine the relationships between activities and tasks. Establish the dependencies between tasks to determine the sequence of how work will need to be completed. The dependency of tasks will modify the duration of the effort required to complete the objectives and goals of the enterprise knowledge portal program.

Identify Activities and Tasks

Purpose: Using the goals and objectives from the enterprise knowledge portal program charter, create the project schedule by identifying the tasks necessary to implement the enterprise knowledge portal. Categorize the tasks into defined categories of work.

After identifying the objectives and goals of the enterprise knowledge portal, you will need to decompose the enterprise knowledge portal program into tasks and milestones. The enterprise knowledge portal team will need to establish a high-level set of tasks. The result is a list of tasks that define the work necessary to complete the objectives and goals of the enterprise knowledge portal program. Be sure to include all tasks that require planning, estimating, or special arrangements. With each task, you need to consider the time estimate it will take to accomplish the task. You will only want to identify working time that is bound by the hours of the day and number of days that someone will be dedicated to the task. The purpose of estimating the duration of each task allows you to quickly add additional tasks, remove tasks, and edit the scope of the effort for each task to understand the impact each task has on the overall program effort. A milestone is a special type of task. Milestone tasks represent the completion of an event, group of tasks, or other measurable accomplishment within the program. Add milestones at logical breaks between tasks. These milestones give you the opportunity to evaluate the quality, effectiveness, and appropriateness of the complete tasks. When necessary you will need to add, remove, or update tasks to reduce the risk, improve the quality, and increase the effectiveness of the execution of the enterprise knowledge portal program.

MYCOMPANY CASE STUDY

The initial set of activities and tasks that can be defined for the enterprise knowledge portal program are identified and shown in Figure 4-13. They include tasks to establish the enterprise knowledge portal organization, identify and prioritize the first enterprise knowledge projects targeted to develop, and implement the first enterprise knowledge portal projects.

Outline the Task List

Purpose: Organize common activities and tasks into groups with the task list. The categorized groups created in the task list represent phases of the enterprise knowledge portal program. The final hierarchical structure establishes a logic organization of the components of work required to meet the objectives defined in the enterprise knowledge portal program charter.

Creating a hierarchical outline organizes the project tasks list into groups of tasks. Each group of tasks is preceded by a summary task that describes the tasks within the group. Each level within the outline provides an additional level of detail for the tasks included in the group. An outline might be created to make a long list of tasks easier to read, to divide the program into distinct phases, or to create a high-level view of the program for management. Outlining the enterprise knowledge portal program will give you an idea of the schedule and timeline required to implement the solution in your organization.

The outline of your enterprise knowledge portal program generally starts with a main summary task. The main summary task is a brief description of the program. All tasks are subordinate to the main summary task.

Figure 4-43. Enterprise knowledge portal program plan activities and tasks.

Enterprise Knowledge Portal Porgam
Determine enterprise knowledge portal scope
Document high-level enterprise knowledge portal requirements including resources
Justify the enterprise knowledge portal via business model
Secure executive sponsorship
Review enterprise knowledge portal documentation
Establish a management framework
Analyze business objectives
Define mission statement
Define goals
Establish communications plan
Secure enterprise knowledge portal core resources
Define work processes
Define technologies
Define techniques
Establish resource relationships
Define compliance criteria
Define project test processes
Define reporting requirements
Define enterprise knowledge portal priorities
Define security/roles/responsibilities
Define system parameters
Create the change management plan
Define budgeting and funding
Identify program categories for template creation
Create enterprise knowledge portal templates
Empower enterprise knowledge portal organization
Announce enterprise knowledge portal organization
Staff enterprise knowledge portal personnel
Determine enterprise knowledge portal projects
Audit projects
Modify projects for compliance
Manage enterprise knowledge portal projects
Identify new projects for the enterprise knowledge portal organization
Create project using established templates
Establish monitoring criteria
Establish performance metrics
Establish budget guidelines
Enter project into enterprise knowledge portal management
Review business priorities applicable to projects
Perform risk assessment
Evaluate risk assessment against project priorities
Prepare contingency plans
Prepare project review meeting agenda
Conduct project review meetings
Create reports for critical issues, budgets, allocating resources, tracking progress, etc.
Work to mitigate critical Issues
Assist with allocating resources
Freeze/release project baselines
Establish change management control
Freeze/release project budgets

Establish project archives
Establish lessons learned repository
Manage project archives
Obtain user feedback
Evaluate lessons learned
Modify Items as necessary
Enterprise Knowledge Portal Program Complete

The enterprise knowledge portal program main summary task is useful to quickly identify the program. It can be useful if multiple plans are compiled to define the complete enterprise knowledge portal program plan.

MYCOMPANY CASE STUDY

Using the initial set of activities and tasks defined in step one, additional categories of work are outlined to create logical groups of tasks. The first version of the enterprise knowledge portal program is an organized overview of the work effort myCompany expects to exert to meet the program charter goals and objectives. An example of the outlined enterprise knowledge portal program plan can be seen in Figure 4-44.

Assign Resources, Roles, and Team Members to Activities and Tasks

Purpose: Assign the appropriate equipment, location, and people required to the activities and tasks identified in the program plan. At a minimum you will want to identify at least one role to each task. This will identify the skill set required to complete individual tasks.

Each task within the program plan needs to be assigned all the resources necessary to complete the task. If assigning individuals or teams is not possible at the time the enterprise knowledge portal program is being defined, you will want to identify at least one role as a resource to define the skills required to complete the task. A task might require a single resource to be completed or it might require several resources. A resource can be the equipment or other unique tools and utilities to achieve a task. For example, video equipment might be required to complete an identified task. You might want to include the video equipment as a resource if special reservations or rental of the equipment will be needed.

MYCOMPANY CASE STUDY

Using the outlined enterprise knowledge portal program plan from step two, the roles required to complete each identified task are added. (An example of the roles identified for the enterprise knowledge portal program plan can be seen in Figure 4-45.)

Figure 4-44. Enterprise knowledge portal program plan task outline.

Enterprise Knowledge Portal Porgam
Scope
Determine enterprise knowledge portal scope
Document high-level enterprise knowledge portal requirements including resources
Justify the enterprise knowledge portal via business model
Secure executive sponsorship
Scope Complete
Planning
Analysis/Logistics
Review enterprise knowledge portal documentation
Establish a management framework
Analyze business objectives
Define mission statement
Define goals
Establish communications plan
Secure enterprise knowledge portal core resources
Logistics Complete
Policies and Procedures
Define work processes
Define technologies
Define techniques
Establish resource relationships
Define compliance criteria
Define project test processes
Define reporting requirements
Define enterprise knowledge portal priorities
Policies and Procedures Complete
Program Standards and Controls
Define security/roles/responsibilities
Define system parameters
Create the change management plan
Define budgeting and funding
Identify program categories for template creation
Create enterprise knowledge portal templates
Program standards and controls complete
Empower enterprise knowledge portal organization
Announce enterprise knowledge portal organization
Planning Complete
Initiate Enterprise Knowledge Portal Organization
Staff enterprise knowledge portal personnel
Enterprise Knowledge Portal Support for Planned Projects
Determine enterprise knowledge portal projects
Audit projects
Modify projects for compliance
Manage enterprise knowledge portal projects
Enterprise Knowledge Portal Support for Existing Projects Complete

Enterprise Knowledge Portal Support for New Projects
Create project using established templates
Establish monitoring criteria
Establish performance metrics
Establish budget guidelines
Enter project into enterprise knowledge portal management
Enterprise knowledge portal organization support for new projects complete
Initiate Enterpirse Knowledge Portal Organization Complete
Management (ongoing)
Review business priorities applicable to projects
Risk Assessment
Perform risk assessment
Evaluate risk assessment against project priorities
Prepare contingency plans
Risk Assessment Complete
Monitoring
Prepare project review meeting agenda
Conduct project review meetings
Create reports for critical issues, budgets, allocating resources, tracking progress, etc.
Work to mitigate critical Issues
Assist with allocating resources
Freeze/release project baselines
Establish change management control
Freeze/release project budgets
Monitoring Complete
Historical/Archival
Establish project archives
Establish lessons learned repository
Manage project archives
Historical Complete
Post Implementation Review
Obtain user feedback
Evaluate lessons learned
Modify Items as necessary
Post Implementation Review Complete
Enterprise Knowledge Portal Program Complete

Determine the Relationships Between Activities and Tasks

Purpose: Establish the dependencies between tasks to determine the sequence of how work will need to be completed. The dependency of tasks will modify the duration of the effort required to complete the objectives and goals of the enterprise knowledge portal program.

Once the activities, tasks, durations, and resources are outlined, you will want to establish the relationships between the individual tasks. The dependencies between the tasks will either lengthen or shorten the enterprise knowledge portal program schedule duration. For example, if one task must be completed before another task can begin, the overall program schedule will be longer than if the tasks could be completed concurrently.

Figure 4-45. Enterprise knowledge portal program plan roles assigned.

	Roles Assigned
Enterprise Knowledge Portal Program	
Scope	
Determine enterprise knowledge portal scope	Enterprise Knowledge Portal Team
Document high-level enterprise knowledge portal requirements including resources	Enterprise Knowledge Portal Team, Executive Sponsor
Justify the enterprise knowledge portal via business model	Enterprise Knowledge Portal Team, Executive Sponsor
Secure executive sponsorship	Enterprise Knowledge Portal Team, Executive Sponsor
Scope Complete	
Planning	
Analysis/Logistics	
Review enterprise knowledge portal documentation	Executive Sponsor
Establish a management framework	Enterprise Knowledge Portal Team, Executive Sponsor
Analyze business objectives	Executive Sponsor
Define mission statement	Executive Sponsor
Define goals	Executive Sponsor
Establish communications plan	Executive Sponsor
Secure enterprise knowledge portal core resources	Executive Sponsor
Logistics Complete	
Policies and Procedures	
Define work processes	Executive Sponsor, Analyst
Define technologies	Executive Sponsor, Analyst
Define techniques	Executive Sponsor, Analyst
Establish resource relationships	Executive Sponsor, Analyst
Define compliance criteria	Executive Sponsor, Analyst
Define project test processes	Executive Sponsor, Analyst
Define reporting requirements	Executive Sponsor, Analyst
Define enterprise knowledge portal priorities	Executive Sponsor, Analyst
Policies and Procedures Complete	
Program Standards and Controls	
Define security/roles/responsibilities	Executive Sponsor, Analyst
Define system parameters	Executive Sponsor, Analyst
Create the change management plan	Executive Sponsor, Analyst
Define budgeting and funding	Executive Sponsor, Analyst
Identify program categories for template creation	Executive Sponsor, Analyst
Create enterprise knowledge portal templates	Developer
Program standards and controls complete	
Empower enterprise knowledge portal organization	Enterprise Knowledge Portal Team, Executive Sponsor
Announce enterprise knowledge portal organization	Enterprise Knowledge Portal Team, Executive Sponsor
Planning Complete	
Initiate Enterprise Knowledge Portal Organization	
Staff enterprise knowledge portal personnel	Executive Sponsor
Enterprise Knowledge Portal Support for Planned Projects	
Determine enterprise knowledge portal projects	Executive Sponsor, Knowledge Expert Community
Audit projects	Knowledge Expert Community
Modify projects for compliance	Knowledge Expert Community
Manage enterprise knowledge portal projects	Knowledge Expert Community
Enterprise Knowledge Portal Support for Existing Projects Complete	
Enterprise Knowledge Portal Support for New Projects	
Create project using established templates	Executive Sponsor, Knowledge Expert Community
Establish monitoring criteria	Knowledge Expert Community
Establish performance metrics	Knowledge Expert Community
Establish budget guidelines	Knowledge Expert Community
Enter project into enterprise knowledge portal management	Knowledge Expert Community
Enterprise knowledge portal organization support for new projects complete	Knowledge Expert Community
Initiate Enterpirse Knowledge Portal Organization Complete	

The dependencies between the tasks will either lengthen or shorten the enterprise knowledge portal program schedule duration. For example, if one task must be completed before another task can begin, the overall program schedule will be longer than if the tasks could be completed concurrently.

The enterprise knowledge portal program plans and their associated schedules should be created as a deliverable for the enterprise knowledge

	Roles Assigned
Management (ongoing)	
Review business priorities applicable to projects	Knowledge Expert Community
Risk Assessment	
Perform risk assessment	Knowledge Expert Community
Evaluate risk assessment against project priorities	Knowledge Expert Community
Prepare contingency plans	Knowledge Expert Community
Risk Assessment Complete	
Monitoring	
Prepare project review meeting agenda	Knowledge Expert Community
Conduct project review meetings	Knowledge Expert Community
Create reports for critical issues, budgets, allocating resources, tracking progress, etc.	Knowledge Expert Community
Work to mitigate critical Issues	Knowledge Expert Community
Assist with allocating resources	Knowledge Expert Community
Freeze/release project baselines	Knowledge Expert Community
Establish change management control	Knowledge Expert Community
Freeze/release project budgets	Knowledge Expert Community
Monitoring Complete	
Historical/Archival	
Establish project archives	Executive Sponsor, Knowledge Expert Community
Establish lessons learned repository	Knowledge Expert Community
Manage project archives	Knowledge Expert Community
Historical Complete	
Post Implementation Review	
Obtain user feedback	Executive Sponsor, Knowledge Expert Community
Evaluate lessons learned	Executive Sponsor, Knowledge Expert Community
Modify Items as necessary	Executive Sponsor, Knowledge Expert Community
Post Implementation Review Complete	
Enterprise Knowledge Portal Program Complete	

portal program. Once execution of the enterprise knowledge portal program begins, the program manager can oversee the tasks as they occur and make adjustments to the schedule as required. When adjustments to the schedule are necessary, the results and changes must be communicated to everyone in the organization associated with the enterprise knowledge portal program.

MYCOMPANY CASE STUDY

Using the enterprise knowledge portal program plan template in progress from step three, the relationships between tasks are added. (An example of the overall schedule of the enterprise knowledge portal program outlined in the plan can be seen in Figure 4-46.)

Executive Approval

The enterprise knowledge portal program provides the scope for the enterprise knowledge portal in terms specific to your organization. The research, documents, and reports delivered describe different elements of the enterprise knowledge portal you expect to implement. The enterprise knowl-

(text continues on page 253)

Figure 4-46. Enterprise knowledge portal program plan task relationships assigned.

	Roles Assigned	Task Number	Predecessors
Enterprise Knowledge Portal Progam		1	
Scope		2	
Determine enterprise knowledge portal scope	Enterprise Knowledge Portal Team	3	
Document high-level enterprise knowledge portal requirements including resources	Enterprise Knowledge Portal Team, Executive Sponsor	4	3
Justify the enterprise knowledge portal via business model	Enterprise Knowledge Portal Team, Executive Sponsor	5	4
Secure executive sponsorship	Enterprise Knowledge Portal Team, Executive Sponsor	6	5
Scope Complete		7	6
Planning		8	
Analysis/Logistics		9	
Review enterprise konwledge portal documentation	Executive Sponsor	10	7
Establish a management framework	Enterprise Knowledge Portal Team, Executive Sponsor	11	10
Analyze business objectives	Executive Sponsor	12	11
Define mission statement	Executive Sponsor	13	12
Define goals	Executive Sponsor	14	13
Establish communications plan	Executive Sponsor	15	14
Secure enterprise knowledge portal core resources	Executive Sponsor	16	15
Logistics Complete		17	16
Policies and Procedures		18	
Define work processes	Executive Sponsor, Analyst	19	16
Define technologies	Executive Sponsor, Analyst	20	16
Define techniques	Executive Sponsor, Analyst	21	16
Establish resource relationships	Executive Sponsor, Analyst	22	16
Define compliance criteria	Executive Sponsor, Analyst	23	16
Define project test processes	Executive Sponsor, Analyst	24	19,20,21,22,23
Define reporting requirements	Executive Sponsor, Analyst	25	24
Define enterprise knowledge portal priorities	Executive Sponsor, Analyst	26	25
Policies and Procedures Complete		27	26

	Roles Assigned	Task Number	Predecessors
Program Standards and Controls		28	
Define security/roles/responsibilities	Executive Sponsor, Analyst	29	27
Define system parameters	Executive Sponsor, Analyst	30	29
Create the change management plan	Executive Sponsor, Analyst	31	30
Define budgeting and funding	Executive Sponsor, Analyst	32	31
Identify program categories for template creation	Executive Sponsor, Analyst	33	32
Create enterprise knowledge portal templates	Developer	34	33
Program Standards and Controls Complete		35	34
Empower enterprise knowledge portal organization	Enterprise Knowledge Portal Team, Executive Sponsor	36	35
Announce enterprise knowledge portal organization	Enterprise Knowledge Portal Team, Executive Sponsor	37	36
Planning Complete		38	37
Initiate Enterprise Knowledge Portal Organization		39	
Staff enterprise knowledge portal personnel	Executive Sponsor	40	38
Enterprise Knowledge Portal Support for Planned Projects		41	
Determine enterprise knowledge portal projects	Executive Sponsor, Knowledge Expert Community	42	40
Audit projects	Knowledge Expert Community	43	42
Modify projects for compliance	Knowledge Expert Community	44	43
Manage enterprise knowledge portal projects	Knowledge Expert Community	45	44
Enterprise knowledge portal support for existing projects complete		46	45
Enterprise Knowledge Portal Support for New Projects		47	
Create project using established templates	Executive Sponsor, Knowledge Expert Community	48	38
Establish monitoring criteria	Knowledge Expert Community	49	48
Establish performance metrics	Knowledge Expert Community	50	49
Establish budget guidelines	Knowledge Expert Community	51	50
Enter project into enterprise knowledge portal management	Knowledge Expert Community	52	51
Enterprise knowledge portal organization support for new projects complete	Knowledge Expert Community	53	52
Initiate Enterpirse Knowledge Portal Organization Complete		54	45,53
Management (ongoing)		55	
Review business priorities applicable to projects	Knowledge Expert Community	56	54
Risk Assessment		57	
Perform risk assessment	Knowledge Expert Community	58	56
Evaluate risk assessment against project priorities	Knowledge Expert Community	59	58
Prepare contingency plans	Knowledge Expert Community	60	59
Risk assessment complete		61	60

(continues)

Figure 4-46. (Continued).

	Roles Assigned	Task Number	Predecessors
Monitoring		62	
Prepare project review meeting agenda	Knowledge Expert Community	63	61
Conduct project review meetings	Knowledge Expert Community	64	63
Create reports for critical issues, budgets, allocating resources, tracking progress, etc.	Knowledge Expert Community	65	64
Work to mitigate critical Issues	Knowledge Expert Community	66	65
Assist with allocating resources	Knowledge Expert Community	67	66
Freeze/release project baselines	Knowledge Expert Community	68	67
Establish change management control	Knowledge Expert Community	69	68
Freeze/release project budgets	Knowledge Expert Community	70	69
Monitoring Complete		71	70
Historical/Archival		72	
Establish project archives	Executive Sponsor, Knowledge Expert Community	73	71
Establish lessons learned repository	Knowledge Expert Community	74	73
Manage project archives	Knowledge Expert Community	75	74
Historical Complete		76	75
Post Implementation Review		77	
Obtain user feedback	Executive Sponsor, Knowledge Expert Community	78	76
Evaluate lessons learned	Executive Sponsor, Knowledge Expert Community	79	78
Modify Items as necessary	Executive Sponsor, Knowledge Expert Community	80	79
Post Implementation Review Complete		81	80
Enterprise Knowledge Portal Program Complete		82	81

edge portal program charter describes how the enterprise knowledge portal will be integrated into corporate initiatives, how the solution will be funded and resourced, and what the benefits and risks are expected to be. The program charter includes a communication plan and change management plan to address acceptance, culture, and behavior issues to implement the enterprise knowledge portal. The enterprise knowledge portal requirements report summarizes the knowledge management objectives and work processes that can benefit from the enterprise knowledge portal. The goals and methods to achieve the value proposition are outlined as enterprise knowledge portal projects and are summarized in the enterprise knowledge portal strategy report. The enterprise knowledge portal architecture and infrastructure report summarizes the architecture and infrastructure updates and enhancements required to support the enterprise knowledge portal. The enterprise knowledge portal program plan takes the information from the enterprise knowledge portal requirements report, the enterprise knowledge portal strategy report, and the enterprise knowledge portal architecture and infrastructure report and creates a timeline that describes what and when to deploy the enterprise knowledge portal.

The executive sponsor working with the enterprise knowledge portal team needs to agree that the enterprise knowledge portal program is well understood, clearly states the scope of the enterprise knowledge portal, and provides a successful path forward to implement the enterprise knowledge portal in your organization. You can use this opportunity to either approve or cancel the enterprise knowledge portal in your organization. If the executive sponsor and enterprise knowledge portal team agree with the value proposition of the enterprise knowledge portal and approve to continue with the program, you have the approval to continue when the executive sponsor accepts the final version of the enterprise knowledge portal program.

MYCOMPANY CASE STUDY

The enterprise knowledge portal program is a collection of the program charter, requirements report, strategy report, architecture and infrastructure report, and program plan. The enterprise knowledge portal team will share and review the results with the executive sponsor, knowledge expert community, and stakeholders. During this review you will be making decisions as much as sharing information as you walk through the enterprise knowledge portal program. To review the results effectively, you should consider bringing the decision makers together in a meeting format. Create a supporting presentation to accompany the enterprise knowledge

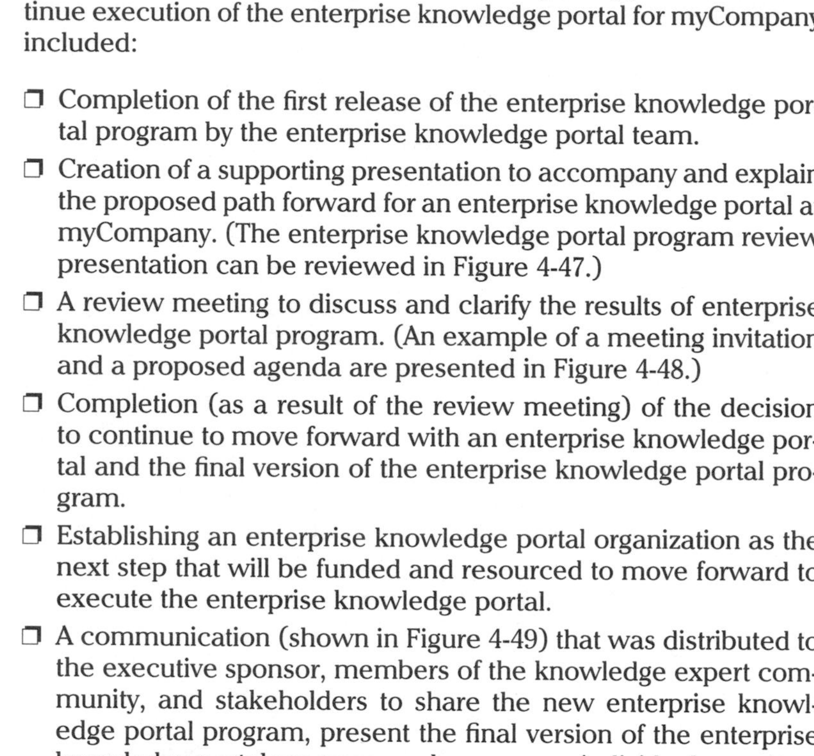

portal program. Any adjustments agreed on by the decision makers will be incorporated into the final enterprise knowledge portal program to create the final version. The final activities completed by the enterprise knowledge portal team to gain approval and continue execution of the enterprise knowledge portal for myCompany included:

- ❐ Completion of the first release of the enterprise knowledge portal program by the enterprise knowledge portal team.
- ❐ Creation of a supporting presentation to accompany and explain the proposed path forward for an enterprise knowledge portal at myCompany. (The enterprise knowledge portal program review presentation can be reviewed in Figure 4-47.)
- ❐ A review meeting to discuss and clarify the results of enterprise knowledge portal program. (An example of a meeting invitation and a proposed agenda are presented in Figure 4-48.)
- ❐ Completion (as a result of the review meeting) of the decision to continue to move forward with an enterprise knowledge portal and the final version of the enterprise knowledge portal program.
- ❐ Establishing an enterprise knowledge portal organization as the next step that will be funded and resourced to move forward to execute the enterprise knowledge portal.
- ❐ A communication (shown in Figure 4-49) that was distributed to the executive sponsor, members of the knowledge expert community, and stakeholders to share the new enterprise knowledge portal program, present the final version of the enterprise knowledge portal program, and encourage individual members to review details with their business units.

Figure 4-47. Enterprise knowledge portal program review.

- The enterprise knowledge portal program was completed by the enterprise knowledge portal team with selected input from knowledge expert community members
- The enterprise knowledge portal program is a compilation of several documents:
  —Enterprise knowledge portal program charter
  —Enterprise knowledge portal requirements report
  —Enterprise knowledge portal strategy report
  —Enterprise knowledge portal architecture and infrastructure report
  —Enterprise knowledge portal program plan
- The enterprise knowledge portal program material is available for review in the following directory:
  Enterprise Knowledge Portal Program Material
- Open discussion of the enterprise knowledge portal program material
- Updates to the enterprise knowledge portal program material

Figure 4-48. A sample invitation and agenda for the enterprise knowledge portal program review.

Agenda	Enterprise Knowledge Portal Program Review Conference Room One	
Type of meeting:	Enterprise Knowledge Portal Program Review Meeting	
Facilitator:	Heidi Collins	
Note taker:	David Kennedy	
Attendees:	Executive Management	
	Agenda Topics	
45 Minutes	The Enterprise Knowledge Portal Charter Overview and Discussion	Heidi Collins
15 Minutes	Break	
30 Minutes	Enterprise Knowledge Portal Requirements Report Overview and Discussion	Heidi Collins
30 Minutes	Enterprise Knowledge Portal Strategy Report Overview and Discussion	Heidi Collins
10 Minutes	Break	
30 Minutes	Enterprise Knowledge Portal Architecture and Infrastructure Report Overview and Discussion	Heidi Collins
30 Minutes	Enterprise Knowledge Portal Program Plan Overview and Discussion	Heidi Collins
10 Minutes	Break	
20 Minutes	Executive Approval for the Enterprise Knowledge Portal Program	Heidi Collins
10 Minutes	Review action items	Heidi Collins
10 Minutes	Review Enterprise Knowledge Portal Program next steps and activities	Heidi Collins

Key Points

The enterprise knowledge portal program is a series of future events that clarify the scope of the enterprise knowledge portal; the roles and responsibilities within your organization reserved to create and maintain the enterprise knowledge portal; the methodology and supporting work processes to maintain the solution; and a timeline describing how, what, and when the enterprise knowledge portal will be implemented. Your knowledge management objectives and enterprise knowledge portal vision from your enterprise knowledge portal map report create a one-, three-, or five-year picture and plan to implement your enterprise knowledge portal. The completed enterprise knowledge portal program provides a clear definition of

Figure 4-49. Knowledge expert community communication seven.

Re: An Approved Enterprise Knowledge Portal Program

Hello Knowledge Expert Community,

Congratulations! The enterprise knowledge portal has been approved as an initiative moving forward at myCompany. The final version of the **Enterprise Knowledge Portal Program** and supporting documentation is available for distribution. The **Enterprise Knowledge Portal Team** would like to thank each of you for your contribution in the successful completion of this effort. To review the final documents, please visit:
Enterprise Knowledge Portal Program Material

We are asking the **Knowledge Expert Community** members to share this information with other managers and teams in your business units. Review the **Enterprise Knowledge Portal Program** information at team meetings or other events to begin to generate awareness of myCompany's enterprise knowledge portal initiative. If you need additional presentation information or material, please let Heidi Collins, Michael Douglas, or David Kennedy know, and we will post it for everyone to use and access.

an enterprise knowledge portal that outlines a better way to locate, learn, capture, and reuse information and human expertise throughout your organization. A collection of templates has been created to document your enterprise knowledge portal program. These include:

The Enterprise Knowledge Portal Program Charter

- ❐ The enterprise knowledge portal program charter template
- ❐ The enterprise knowledge portal risks spreadsheet
- ❐ The enterprise knowledge portal communication plan template
- ❐ The enterprise knowledge portal change management plan template

The Enterprise Knowledge Portal Requirements

- ❐ The enterprise knowledge portal requirements template

The Enterprise Knowledge Portal Strategy

- ❐ The enterprise knowledge portal strategy template

The Enterprise Knowledge Portal Architecture and Infrastructure

- ❐ The enterprise knowledge portal architecture and infrastructure template

The Enterprise Knowledge Portal Program Plan

- ❒ The enterprise knowledge portal program plan template

Using the enterprise knowledge portal map report as a starting point to establish the value proposition, you will have some perspective of your business strategy. Look across employee, customer, supplier, and partner-user communities for broad opportunities across your organization. The value proposition will be unique for every organization, based on your business strategy and enterprise knowledge portal priorities. Several value propositions include:

- ❒ Competitive advantage
- ❒ Change management
- ❒ Knowledge management
- ❒ Intellectual growth
- ❒ Partnership development
- ❒ Early adopter advantages

The enterprise knowledge portal should be implemented from the beginning as part of your business strategy. Corporate initiatives are complex; if executives can understand how the enterprise knowledge portal integrates and enhances existing efforts, they will be able to incorporate the knowledge portal into the existing business strategy, understand the value proposition to the organization, and want to be involved in the enterprise knowledge portal initiative. The enterprise knowledge portal program that you create provides a well-understood path forward for the enterprise knowledge portal as a cohesive and comprehensive solution. The activities to establish the enterprise knowledge portal program include:

- ❒ Defining your enterprise knowledge portal value proposition
- ❒ Documenting your enterprise knowledge portal program charter
  1. Document scope and objectives
  2. Identify team members and stakeholders
  3. Define strategic relationships to other corporate initiatives
  4. Add benefits
  5. Add risks
  6. Document budgets and funding
  7. Document the communication plan
  8. Document the change management plan

- ❒ Documenting your enterprise knowledge portal requirements
    1. Modify the enterprise knowledge portal requirements template
    2. Schedule interviews with the knowledge expert community
    3. Create the enterprise knowledge portal requirements report
- ❒ Documenting your enterprise knowledge portal strategy
    1. Modify the enterprise knowledge portal strategy template
    2. Schedule interviews with the knowledge expert community
    3. Create the enterprise knowledge portal strategy report
- ❒ Documenting your enterprise knowledge portal architecture and infrastructure
    1. Modify the enterprise knowledge portal architecture and infrastructure template
    2. Schedule interviews with the chief technology office
    3. Create the enterprise knowledge portal architecture and infrastructure report
- ❒ Documenting your enterprise knowledge portal program plan
    1. Identify activities and tasks
    2. Outline the task list
    3. Assign resources, roles, and team members to activities and tasks
    4. Determine the relationships between activities and tasks
- ❒ Obtaining executive approval for the enterprise knowledge portal program

Once you have executive approval and sponsorship for the enterprise knowledge portal program, the next effort of the enterprise knowledge portal is to establish the enterprise knowledge portal organization and governance. Chapter 5 provides suggestions for organizational structure, team membership, and associated skills that you should consider to create and continue to expand to design, build, and successfully support your enterprise knowledge portal initiative.

5

The Enterprise Knowledge Portal Organization

". . . [T]he information revolution favors and strengthens network forms of organization, while making life difficult for hierarchical forms . . . It means conflicts will increasingly be waged by "networks," rather than by "hierarchies." It means that whoever masters the network form stands to gain major advantages in the new epoch."

John Arquilla and David Ron, *In Athena's Camp: Preparing for Conflict in the Information Age*

The people that make up the teams in your organization assigned to the enterprise knowledge portal will become the soul and passion of your enterprise knowledge portal. The quality of the individuals will determine your success. The effectiveness of your change management plan and acceptance of the enterprise knowledge portal by knowledge workers throughout your organization will be directly affected by the strength of the people involved. The experience, skills, and personalities of the team members aligned with the enterprise knowledge portal will have a greater impact on the long-term success of the actual solution delivered. For this reason, you should carefully scrutinize the qualifications of the people behind the enterprise knowledge portal. Compile the teams with the appropriate expertise that will be able to maximize the talents of the individual team members.

Another important consideration when pulling together your enterprise knowledge portal organization is management styles that motivate employees. People will do their best work when they are encouraged, recognized, and rewarded for their achievements. As you develop your enterprise knowledge portal teams, look for strong leaders to establish process and governance and the appropriate management structure and style to define the appropriate culture and behavior in your organization. With the right mix of leadership and management styles, you will be able to create clear lines of organizational responsibility.

The most important person assigned to the enterprise knowledge portal is the executive sponsor. This individual will serve as the top manager and exercise day-to-day control over the enterprise knowledge portal. The executive sponsor who worked with the enterprise knowledge portal team to develop the enterprise knowledge portal program will usually continue in this role. This person will also position and champion the relationship of the enterprise knowledge portal initiative with all other corporate initiatives in your organization. The enterprise knowledge portal team, knowledge expert community, and stakeholders will be redeployed into the more permanent enterprise knowledge portal organization moving forward. The kinds of permanent enterprise knowledge portal teams that will be resourced include:

- The steering committee
- The stakeholders
- The knowledge expert community
- The enterprise knowledge portal program management
- The enterprise knowledge portal support and competency center
- The enterprise knowledge portal application development team
- The enterprise knowledge portal architecture and infrastructure team
- The information library services
- The subject matter experts

To begin to define your enterprise knowledge portal organization, start with your enterprise knowledge portal program charter, analyze your business processes, and define your roles and responsibilities. The overview of your vision and what to consider as you deploy and implement your enterprise knowledge portal can be reviewed in your enterprise knowledge portal program charter. You will need to evaluate the work processes needed to achieve your expected benefits from the enterprise knowledge portal program. Once the business processes have been identified, you will be able to define roles and responsibilities. A role is the complete set of knowledge, skills, and activities needed for one person to execute her assigned responsibilities in a given work process. The details around the process and governance, as well as the culture and behavior of your enterprise knowledge portal organization, are discussed in detail throughout this chapter.

Process and Governance

When examining your organization, managers usually begin with the formal structure that outlines the official lines of authority. It is important to think about how employees will be supervised and how job functions will be allocated. Clear lines of authority are important so all team members and managers can easily delineate areas of responsibility and decision making between each other. There are several questions to consider as you decide your company's enterprise knowledge portal structure. These include:

- Should responsibilities be allocated between functional areas or geographic divisions?
- What will each team be responsible for? How will the different teams share work processes?
- Will you use a production line or team approach to complete the assigned responsibilities within the different enterprise knowledge portal teams? Will each team member be responsible for one particular task, or will each team be responsible for many tasks?

The quickest and clearest way to communicate your management structure is through a graphic organizational flow chart. You can use two kinds of charts: one describing areas of responsibility, and the other outlining reporting or supervisory relationships. A proposed enterprise knowledge portal organization is presented as an example. The enterprise knowledge portal areas of responsibility are shown in Figure 5-1. You will notice that this is very different from the functional areas by business unit reporting relationships shown in Figure 5-2.

The areas of responsibility for the enterprise knowledge portal are the relationships that need to be explored in more detail. A short narrative description explaining the roles, objectives, guiding principles, and the work processes for each individual and team are included to provide more information as you think through the appropriate areas of responsibility for your company. The individuals and teams to review include:

- The executive sponsor
- The steering committee
- The stakeholders
- The knowledge expert community
- The enterprise knowledge portal program management
- The enterprise knowledge portal support and competency center
- The enterprise knowledge portal application development team
- The enterprise knowledge portal architecture and infrastructure team

Figure 5-1. Enterprise knowledge portal areas of responsibility.

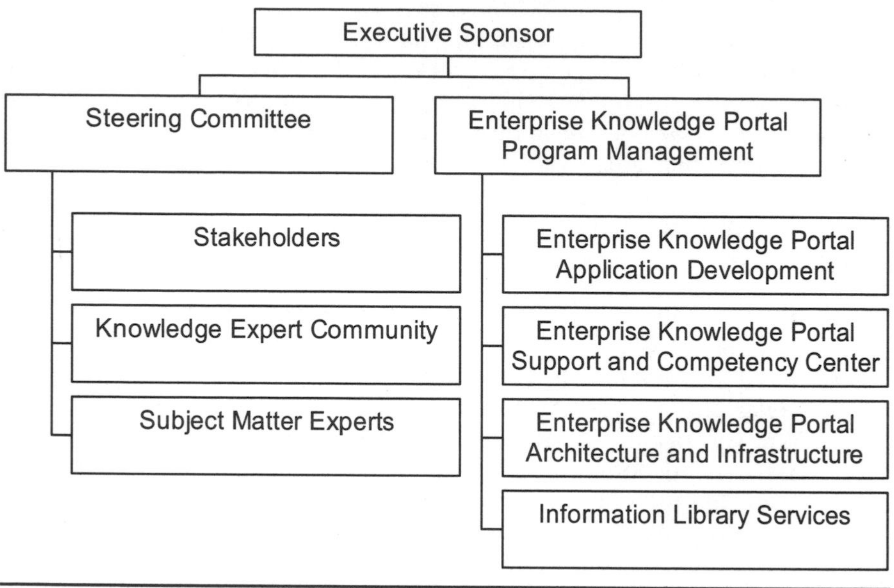

Figure 5-2. Functional areas by business unit reporting relationships.

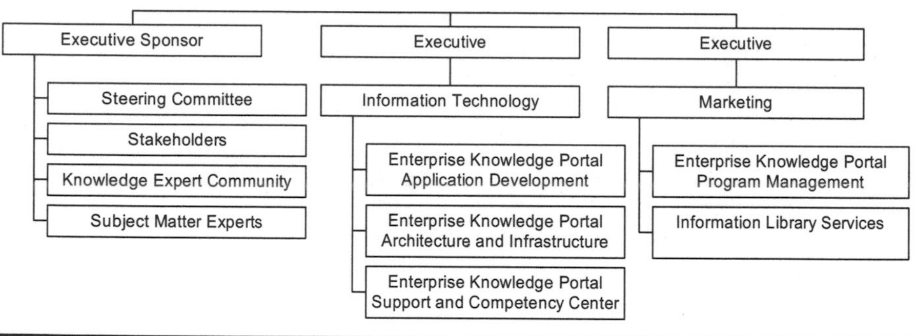

- The information library services
- The subject matter experts

The Executive Sponsor

The executive sponsor is the most senior decision maker for the day-to-day enterprise knowledge portal activities and tasks. This person will champion establishing relationships between the enterprise knowledge portal and other corporate initiatives. The executive sponsor will work closely with the steering committee and the enterprise knowledge portal program management team to secure funding and resources for the enterprise knowledge portal program.

Objectives

The following objectives are outlined to provide direction in developing the executive sponsor structure:

- ❒ Approve and support the enterprise knowledge portal program.
- ❒ Approve the high-level business case model to be used in subsequent design and implementation of enterprise knowledge portal efforts.
- ❒ Provide funding and resources to establish the appropriate process and governance required to implement the enterprise knowledge portal program.

Guiding Principles

The executive sponsor structure is developed using these guiding principles:

- ❒ Be responsible for making executive decisions required to support the enterprise knowledge portal program, projects, and work processes.
- ❒ Work with other senior executives to integrate the enterprise knowledge portal into other corporate initiatives.
- ❒ Secure funding and resources for the enterprise knowledge portal program, projects, and work processes.

Work Processes

There are several work processes identified for the executive sponsor structure:

- ❒ The enterprise knowledge portal program development and approval process

- The planning, budgeting, and forecasting process
- The communication process
- The change management process

The Steering Committee

The steering committee consists of several representatives from your organization's senior management team. The steering committee is the enterprise knowledge portal program sponsor. They will serve as the overall decision maker and governing body for the enterprise knowledge portal. The group monitors program and project progress and makes global strategic decisions to coordinate and manage the enterprise knowledge portal investment.

Objectives

The following objectives are outlined to provide direction in developing the steering committee structure:

- Ensure the enterprise knowledge portal initiative is consistent with corporate and business unit goals and objectives.
- Provide administrative, functional direction, and support to the enterprise knowledge portal program management team.
- Approve the enterprise knowledge portal program scope and continually assesses the program's viability.
- Resolve corporate issues.
- Provide formal approval or rejection to proceed through each stage of the enterprise knowledge portal program.

Guiding Principles

The steering committee structure is developed using these guiding principles:

- Act as the corporate sponsor for the enterprise knowledge portal.
- Act as the governing body for global strategic decisions associated with the enterprise knowledge portal.
- Monitor enterprise knowledge portal program and project progress.

Work Processes

There are several work processes identified for the steering committee structure:

- ❐ The enterprise knowledge portal program approval process
- ❐ The planning, budgeting, and forecasting process
- ❐ The communication process
- ❐ The change management process

The Stakeholders

Stakeholders will represent all the functional areas of your organization. They provide usability, functionality, and feedback necessary to develop an enterprise knowledge portal that the full user community will accept. The stakeholders will be instrumental in the execution of your change management and communications plans.

Objectives

The following objectives are outlined to provide direction in developing the stakeholders structure:

- ❐ Contribute to the enterprise knowledge portal vision, program, and objectives.
- ❐ Assume ownership of the enterprise knowledge portal vision and objectives.
- ❐ Demonstrate ownership through active and visible participation of the enterprise knowledge portal.
- ❐ Identify cross-functional and business unit enterprise knowledge portal similarities and differences.
- ❐ Review key enterprise knowledge portal program and project deliverables.

Guiding Principles

The stakeholders structure is developed using these guiding principles:

- ❐ Be responsible for working closely with the enterprise knowledge portal program management team to develop and deliver the enterprise knowledge portal program, projects, and work processes.
- ❐ Work with managers throughout the organization to educate and successfully implement the enterprise knowledge portal.
- ❐ Secure resources for the knowledge expert community to work on enterprise knowledge portal project teams.

Work Processes

There are several work processes identified for the stakeholders structure:

- The enterprise knowledge portal program approval process
- The enterprise knowledge portal project process
- The planning, budgeting, and forecasting process
- The communication process
- The change management process

The Knowledge Expert Community

The knowledge expert community is composed of people from information technology and each of the business units involved in the enterprise knowledge portal program and projects. The business unit representatives understand and improve work processes and help document architecture and work flow. The information technology members are responsible for validating the enterprise knowledge portal requirements for the enterprise knowledge portal projects, providing information and research as needed. You should expect knowledge expert community team members to dedicate at least 60 percent of their time to the enterprise knowledge portal projects they are involved in.

Objectives

The following objectives are outlined to provide direction in developing the knowledge expert community structure:

- Work with the enterprise knowledge portal program management team and subject matter experts on enterprise knowledge portal projects.
- Provide a global communication bridge between business end-users, the enterprise knowledge portal program management team, and the enterprise knowledge portal architecture and infrastructure team around the enterprise knowledge portal projects being deployed.
- Ensure that global user needs are understood and properly represent business drivers to the enterprise knowledge portal program management team.
- Document the business requirements definition for the enterprise knowledge portal projects.

Guiding Principles

The knowledge expert community structure is developed using these guiding principles:

- ❐ Be responsible for integrating locate, learn, capture, and reuse business opportunities into the enterprise knowledge portal.
- ❐ Work with the enterprise knowledge portal program management team to successfully define and deploy the enterprise knowledge portal.
- ❐ Work with managers and users throughout the organization to educate and successfully implement the enterprise knowledge portal.

Work Processes

There are several work processes identified for the knowledge expert community structure:

- ❐ The enterprise knowledge portal project process
- ❐ The communication process
- ❐ The change management process

The Enterprise Knowledge Portal Program Management

The enterprise knowledge portal program management office reports on status and raises issues to the steering committee. Team membership requires both business and technical areas of expertise. This team is responsible for maintaining the enterprise knowledge portal program, planning projects, reporting program and project status, assigning resources, monitoring the progress against the program plan, and managing multiple teams. This team will also identify and resolve issues independently and with the project leaders. It is responsible for delivering the enterprise knowledge portal on time, within a way that meets user expectations. A critical competence for the members of the program management office is prior experience or training in the management of complex enterprise systems development.

Objectives

The following objectives are outlined to provide direction in developing the enterprise knowledge portal program management structure:

- Be responsible for overall enterprise knowledge portal program and associated project planning and coordination.
- Assume ownership of the project deliverables and responsibility for day-to-day project management.
- Proactively anticipate project deviations and be responsible for taking immediate corrective action.
- Set enterprise knowledge portal project standards and milestones and monitor work against those standards to ensure on-time completion.
- Monitor and report progress against milestones for the enterprise knowledge portal program and projects.
- Manage and communicate scope and potential scope changes for the enterprise knowledge portal program and projects.
- Assume overall coordination of all activities to ensure proper communication.

Guiding Principles

The enterprise knowledge portal program management structure is developed using these guiding principles:

- Create, develop, and maintain the enterprise knowledge portal program.
- Manage enterprise knowledge portal projects working with knowledge expert community team members and subject matter experts.
- Provide overall communication for the enterprise knowledge portal program and projects.
- Provide overall change management for the enterprise knowledge portal program and projects.
- Maintain progress reports for the enterprise knowledge portal program and projects.

Work Processes

There are several work processes identified for the enterprise knowledge portal program management structure:

- The enterprise knowledge portal program development and approval process

- The enterprise knowledge portal project process
- The planning, budgeting, and forecasting process
- The communication process
- The change management process

The Enterprise Knowledge Portal Support and Competency Center

The support and competency center will maintain and support the production releases of the enterprise knowledge portal. They will champion the best practices, standards, and guidelines to be understood and used consistently across the organization. This team will maintain the enterprise knowledge portal library of development objects, documentation, and other information that needs to be centralized to effectively manage the enterprise knowledge portal.

Objectives

The following objectives are outlined to provide direction in developing the enterprise knowledge portal support and competency center structure:

- Maintain a stable enterprise knowledge portal environment that supports the daily production activities, enterprise knowledge portal project team activities, and other preimplementation activities.
- Support users in their use of the enterprise knowledge portal.
- Resolve user questions, problems, and requests in a timely manner as defined by defined service-level agreements.
- Implement and manage maintenance and other approved production releases of the enterprise knowledge portal.
- Maintain the enterprise knowledge portal library of documentation, enterprise knowledge portal objects, and other centralized information that needs to be managed and communicated.

Guiding Principles

The enterprise knowledge portal support and competency center structure is developed using these guiding principles:

- Provide seamless end-to-end support for enterprise knowledge portal users, project teams, and enterprise knowledge portal teams.
- Communicate, teach, and share the enterprise knowledge portal library.

- Leverage the existing support applications and solutions where applicable.

Work Processes

There are several work processes identified for the enterprise knowledge portal support and competency center structure:

- The call management process
- The problem management process
- The enterprise knowledge portal library management process
- The enterprise knowledge portal project process
- The communication process
- The change management process

The Enterprise Knowledge Portal Application Development Team

The application development teams support the enterprise knowledge portal program management team and the enterprise knowledge portal architecture and infrastructure team in managing and implementing the enterprise knowledge portal. This team is responsible for building and testing the features to meet the specification and customer expectations. They participate in the design of the enterprise knowledge portal and estimate the time and effort to complete each feature. Make sure to include the enterprise knowledge portal application development team in defining the quality bar for the enterprise knowledge portal.

Objectives

The following objectives are outlined to provide direction in developing the enterprise knowledge portal application development team structure:

- Provide consistent portal objects for the enterprise knowledge portal using a well-defined and organized rapid application development environment.
- Provide portal objects that meet quality assurance standards for deployment and inclusion for reuse in the enterprise knowledge portal library.
- Establish regression, system, integrity, integration, and other test plans to maintain the enterprise knowledge portal.

- Leverage the existing enterprise knowledge portal library where applicable.

Guiding Principles

The enterprise knowledge portal application development team structure is developed using these guiding principles:

- Be responsible for the design, development, and deployment of the enterprise knowledge portal.
- Work with the enterprise knowledge portal program management team to successfully define and deploy the enterprise knowledge portal.
- Work with the enterprise knowledge portal support and competency center and information technology teams throughout the organization to register enterprise knowledge portal objects into production and the enterprise knowledge portal library.

Work Processes

There are several work processes identified for the enterprise knowledge portal application development team structure:

- The enterprise knowledge portal project process
- The communication process
- The change management process

The Enterprise Knowledge Portal Architecture and Infrastructure Team

The architecture and infrastructure team is responsible for ensuring that the enterprise knowledge portal technical solution satisfies the organization's present and future business requirements. This team sets the direction and establishes the approach to select technical platforms, network architecture, and system software. They work closely with the enterprise knowledge portal program management team to plan effectively for the current and future enterprise knowledge portal projects.

Objectives

The following objectives are outlined to provide direction in developing the enterprise knowledge portal architecture and infrastructure team structure:

- Work with the enterprise knowledge portal program management team and subject matter experts on enterprise knowledge portal projects.
- Provide a global communication bridge between information technology, the enterprise knowledge portal program management team, and the knowledge expert community around the enterprise knowledge portal projects being deployed.
- Ensure that information technology needs are understood and properly representative of infrastructure requirements to the enterprise knowledge portal program management team.
- Document the technology requirements definition for the enterprise knowledge portal projects.

Guiding Principles

The enterprise knowledge portal architecture and infrastructure team structure is developed using these guiding principles:

- Be responsible for integrating enterprise portal, business intelligence, content management, collaboration, and learning features and functions into the enterprise knowledge portal.
- Work with the enterprise knowledge portal program management team to successfully define and deploy the enterprise knowledge portal.
- Work with the enterprise knowledge portal support and competency center and information technology teams throughout the organization to educate and successfully implement the enterprise knowledge portal.

Work Processes

There are several work processes identified for the enterprise knowledge portal architecture and infrastructure team structure:

- The enterprise knowledge portal project process
- The communication process
- The change management process

The Information Library Services

Information library services is a special team of subject matter experts to establish the corporate knowledge organization system. This collection of term lists, relationship lists, and data dictionaries used to manage indexes and catalogs, taxonomies, and category schemes will ensure integrity and interoperability for the enterprise knowledge portal. Information library services will work closely with the steering committee to maintain your organization's knowledge organization system.

Objectives

The following objectives are outlined to provide direction in developing the information library services structure:

- Work with the enterprise knowledge portal program management team and the knowledge expert community on enterprise knowledge portal projects.
- Provide enterprise taxonomy and categorization schemes for the enterprise knowledge portal.
- Ensure that search, index, and cataloging features are understood by the enterprise knowledge portal project teams and the enterprise knowledge portal support and competency center.
- Document the taxonomy and categorization scheme requirements definition for the enterprise knowledge portal projects.

Guiding Principles

The information library services structure is developed using these guiding principles:

- Be responsible for integrating federated search and the knowledge organization system into the enterprise knowledge portal.
- Work with the enterprise knowledge portal program management team to successfully define and deploy the enterprise knowledge portal.
- Work with the enterprise knowledge portal support and competency center and information technology teams throughout the organization to educate and successfully implement the taxonomy and categorization schemes for the enterprise knowledge portal.

Work Processes

There are several work processes identified for the information library services structure:

- ❒ The enterprise knowledge portal project process
- ❒ The communication process
- ❒ The change management process

The Subject Matter Experts

The subject matter experts have special skills in technical solutions or business systems. They provide insight and experience in setting the direction and establishing the approach for the enterprise knowledge portal. Technical experts provide insight into selecting technical platforms, network architecture, and system software. Subject matter experts should be involved in designing the enterprise knowledge portal's conceptual architecture, quality standards, and performance metrics. Business experts can help in identifying and solving business issues and problems, developing business models, and providing guidance to the enterprise knowledge portal program management team.

Objectives

The following objectives are outlined to provide direction in developing the subject matter experts structure:

- ❒ Work with the enterprise knowledge portal program management team and knowledge expert community on enterprise knowledge portal projects.
- ❒ Provide insight and expertise around business issues and technical requirements for enterprise knowledge portal projects.

Guiding Principles

The subject matter experts structure is developed using these guiding principles:

- ❒ Be responsible for providing experience and expertise to enterprise knowledge portal project teams.
- ❒ Work with the enterprise knowledge portal program management team to successfully define and deploy the enterprise knowledge portal.

Work Processes

There are several work processes identified for the subject matter experts structure:

- The enterprise knowledge portal project process
- The communication process
- The change management process

Culture and Behavior

There are several enterprise knowledge portal activities that need to addressed and completed as soon as your enterprise knowledge portal organization is formed. Completing these activities will help the enterprise knowledge portal organization be effective and successful in moving forward. They will also make it possible for the enterprise knowledge portal organization to be effective in generating a well-defined and well-accepted enterprise knowledge portal for users across your organization. These activities include:

- *Identifying all enterprise portal and knowledge management applications and solutions in your organization.* There will be several business unit solutions that exist in your organization for enterprise portals and knowledge management. You will need to spend some time researching the majority of the resources involved in these business unit applications and solutions.
- *Identifying overlapping functional and technical requirements.* Once the enterprise portal and knowledge management applications and solutions have been identified, take some time to review the functionality and technology. This research will help you identify the redundancies in the solutions and the work processes that exist in the current applications, solutions, and services.
- *Evaluating the work effort to establish a single enterprise knowledge portal.* Your previous efforts to create the enterprise knowledge portal map report and the enterprise knowledge portal program charter have framed the benefits of a single enterprise knowledge portal. Use this information to research what obsolescence and migration plans for applications, solutions, data, and services need to be established to standardize on a single enterprise knowledge portal.
- *Identifying work process integration requirements for the enterprise knowledge portal.* Work with business units throughout your organization to define end-to-end work processes, the roles and responsibilities involved in the work processes, and the relationships between business units that share these work processes. This information will help you anticipate enterprise knowledge portal integration issues that will need to be included in the long-term enterprise knowledge portal program.

- *Establishing a methodology and owner for enterprise knowledge portal objects*. The enterprise knowledge portal will consist of several development and documentation objects. An enterprise knowledge portal library will need to be established and an owner identified. Several templates, development objects, best practices, guidelines, and standards will be generated and made available to be used consistently by enterprise knowledge portal project teams.
- *Establishing relationships with other corporate initiatives to ensure recognition and integration of the enterprise knowledge portal*. Leaders of other corporate initiatives in your organization may not have recognized the enterprise knowledge portal as an enabling technology for their individual efforts. In order to facilitate wide adoption of the solution, you must integrate the enterprise knowledge portal into your other corporate initiatives.
- *Coordinating with information technology teams to integrate several technologies and architecture planning issues*. The enterprise knowledge portal requires significant integration with related technologies such as business intelligence, content management, collaboration, and learning. Make certain all the appropriate teams are aware of the enterprise knowledge portal program requirements.
- *Sponsoring and establishing an enterprise knowledge portal laboratory*. An enterprise knowledge portal laboratory provides a proven approach to defining and maintaining architectural integrity and application interoperability. Business units can use the enterprise knowledge portal lab to carry out the initial evaluation of different requirements and other enterprise knowledge portal–related activities.
- *Establishing the enterprise knowledge portal framework*. The requirements that are common across all business units, cross-functional teams, work processes, and external groups are the enterprise standards and become the framework of your enterprise knowledge portal best practices, guidelines, and standards.
- *Identifying unique enterprise knowledge portal requirements*. Apply the enterprise knowledge portal framework and determine the unique requirements of a particular area implementing these unique requirements using the same process in a similar manner each time.
- *Creating the knowledge organization system*. For enterprise knowledge portal access across the organization, standard naming conventions, taxonomies, categorization, rules, and information technology architecture standards will be required.

The enterprise knowledge portal organization needs to execute the change management plan to modify the culture and behavior of people throughout your organization. Your culture represents the accepted practices and politics that define how work gets done. Behavior is how people respond and interact within the corporate culture. The enterprise knowledge portal will identify new practices to be adopted by your organization. The change management plan will be a way to change the behavior of the employees to adopt and accept these new practices.

Knowledge management has been adopted to promote locating, learning, capturing, and reusing information and best practices. When the process works and employees begin working on collaborative teams, their normal work behaviors are changed and, over time, the culture begins to change. The purpose of the enterprise knowledge portal is to bring these knowledge management best practices and work processes into everything employees and knowledge workers do. There are several opportunities available in your organization to work on changing behavior. These include:

- *Enterprise Knowledge Portal Structure*. Look for opportunities in work processes and relationships to influence behavior.
- *Coercion*. Look for small teams with opportunities to implement unique ways of working together and force them to work differently from the status quo.
- *Rewards and Recognition*. Make certain that how employees are recognized and what reward system is used are tied directly to desired behaviors.
- *Setting Expectations*. Manage expectations for enterprise knowledge portal users so the solution is successful and matches their requirements and knowledge management objectives.
- *Role Modeling*. Look to showcase successful enterprise knowledge portal implementations and model new releases after proven success stories.
- *Participation*. Include as many stakeholders, knowledge expert community members, subject matter experts, and other people in your enterprise knowledge portal projects as possible so they feel ownership of the enterprise knowledge portal deployed.

Key Points

To begin to define your enterprise knowledge portal organization, start with your enterprise knowledge portal program charter, analyze your business processes, and define your roles and responsibilities. You will need to evaluate the work processes needed to achieve your expected benefits from the enterprise knowledge portal program. Once the business processes have been identified, you will be able to define roles and responsibilities. A role is the complete set of knowledge, skills, and activities needed for one person to execute his assigned responsibilities in a given work process. The details around the process and governance, as well as the culture and behavior of your enterprise knowledge portal organization, need to be well defined and comprehended. A proposed enterprise knowledge portal organization to be resourced includes:

- The executive sponsor
- The steering committee
- The stakeholders
- The knowledge expert community
- The enterprise knowledge portal program management
- The enterprise knowledge portal support and competency center
- The enterprise knowledge portal application development team
- The enterprise knowledge portal architecture and infrastructure team
- The information library services
- The subject matter experts

There are several enterprise knowledge portal activities that need to be addressed and completed as soon as your enterprise knowledge portal organization is formed. Completing these activities will help the enterprise knowledge portal organization be effective and successful in moving forward. They will also make it possible for the enterprise knowledge portal organization to be effective in generating a well-defined and well-accepted enterprise knowledge portal for users across your organization. These activities include:

- Identifying all enterprise portal and knowledge management applications and solutions in your organization
- Identifying overlapping functional and technical requirements
- Evaluating the work effort to establish a single enterprise knowledge portal
- Identifying work process integration requirements for the enterprise knowledge portal
- Establishing a methodology and owner for enterprise knowledge portal objects
- Establishing relationships with other corporate initiatives to ensure recognition and integration of the enterprise knowledge portal

- ❒ Coordination with information technology teams to integrate several technologies and architecture planning issues
- ❒ Sponsoring and establishing an enterprise knowledge portal laboratory
- ❒ Establishing the enterprise knowledge portal framework
- ❒ Identifying unique enterprise knowledge portal requirements
- ❒ Creating the knowledge organization system

The enterprise knowledge portal program will be implemented in your organization as a series of enterprise knowledge portal development projects and infrastructure projects. You will want to establish an enterprise knowledge portal methodology to deploy a consistent and cohesive solution. Chapter 6 identifies a series of activities and tasks as well as templates you can use or modify to create a methodology to successfully implement each of your enterprise knowledge portal projects.

III

The Enterprise Knowledge Portal Projects

6

The Enterprise Knowledge Portal Methodology

"You will want to establish a methodology that can be followed for the corporate portal project. A methodology is a collection of techniques for building models that are applied across the development of a software system (i.e., software life cycle)."

HEIDI COLLINS, *CORPORATE PORTALS*

The enterprise knowledge portal program outlines the scope of the overall investment that will be made in managing knowledge and creating your enterprise knowledge portal. The program is achieved as a series of enterprise knowledge portal projects. Each project is more than a software or technical solution. It encompasses four components:

- People
- Process
- Content
- Technology

The enterprise knowledge portal is a single infrastructure solution that supports the distributed knowledge management objectives of business units throughout your organization and brings these components together in a powerful working relationship. The enterprise knowledge portal methodology provides templates and techniques to design and organize content in the enterprise knowledge portal. Knowledge workers throughout your organization will be required to analyze and supply the business requirements, work processes, and content for the enterprise knowledge portal. The enterprise knowledge portal will provide access to all the application screens, documents, and functionality required by your work processes from a single user interface. Using the enterprise knowledge portal, employees are capable of auditing and documenting the knowledge that is available throughout the organization that can then be assessed as information. Understanding the work processes and the content is the responsibility of the knowledge workers. Making sure the enterprise knowledge portal functionalities like search, connectivity to data sources, security to access and work with the enterprise portal, and several other enterprise knowledge portal services meet performance expectations is the responsibility of information technology and the enterprise knowledge portal support and competency center.

The enterprise knowledge portal project needs to be a well-established sequence of activities with a recognized beginning and ending. You will need to define and staff enterprise knowledge portal project teams. These teams will use project management practices to implement the enterprise knowledge portal. Project management practices allow the enterprise knowledge portal project team to deliver a complete solution with the appropriate documentation, on schedule and within budget. The best practices your project teams adopt include project integrity, construction integrity, and solution integrity and stability. Each project team will need to create a project charter that is supported by a project plan and associate timeline. Several deliverables include:

- *The Enterprise Knowledge Portal Project Charter.* The enterprise knowledge portal project scope and objectives are outlined, budgets and funding are identified, and benefits and risks are documented. The project charter will be reviewed to verify that it maps appropriately into the enterprise knowledge portal program.
- *The Enterprise Knowledge Portal Project Plan.* A detailed list of tasks to be completed to implement the enterprise knowledge portal will provide the information needed to allocate the appropriate resources and follow the progress of the project. Each task can consist of several steps that must be completed before the task is considered complete. You will want to define the relationships and dependencies these tasks have with each other.
- *The Enterprise Knowledge Portal Quality Assurance Plan.* A definition of the quality characteristics needed for the enterprise knowledge portal should exist for each project team to use. This information will allow the types of quality tasks needed for the enterprise knowledge portal project to be added to the project plan.

You should review the project management methodology used in your organization and incorporate it into the enterprise knowledge portal design methodology presented throughout this chapter. It is important that you include consistent project management best practices into your overall enterprise knowledge portal design methodology best practices. These will allow the enterprise knowledge portal program management team to communicate and work consistently with managers and employees throughout your organization. An example of the enterprise knowledge portal projects and their relationship to program management, project management, change management, communication, and education and training are diagrammed in Figure 6-1. Additional sources of project management information can be found in Appendix C: Recommended Reading.

The enterprise knowledge portal methodology is an orderly procedure to collect and document the information needed to design, build, deploy, and maintain an effective enterprise knowledge portal. The methodology is focused on supporting information and the flow of information and delivering all of it into the enterprise knowledge portal. There are several elements to define and document in the enterprise knowledge portal methodology. These include:

❐ *Defining Business Objects*. A business object is a collection of information designed to achieve a specific business purpose. Examples include invoices, product catalogs, and medical insurance claims.

Figure 6-1. Enterprise knowledge portal project management.

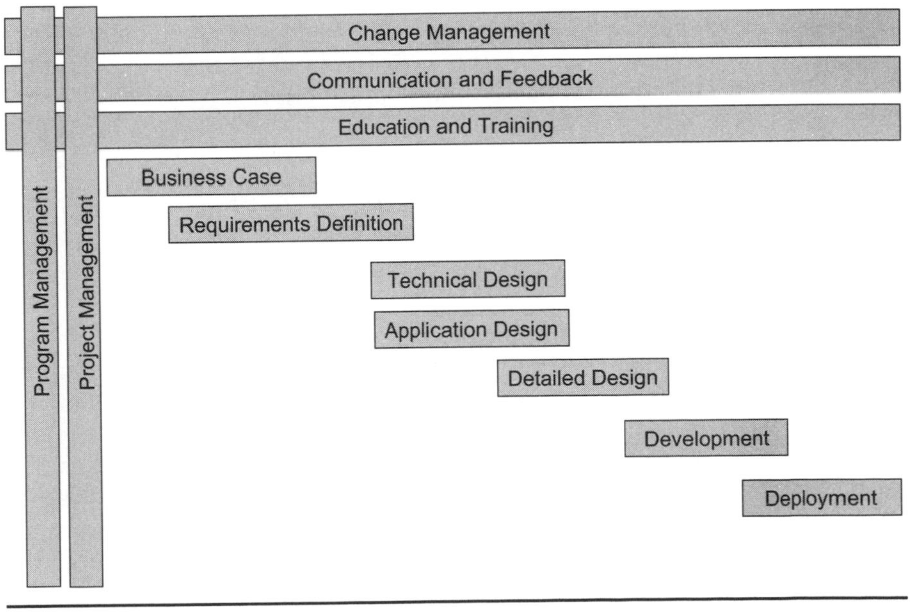

- ❒ *Breakdown Into Content Elements*. Multiple content elements form a business object. Content elements are stored in different systems and can be structured or unstructured.
- ❒ *Outlining Work Flow Systems.* This element electronically stores business object content elements. Codify the rules for dynamic assembly of business objects, do work flow processing, and deliver these business objects in the appropriate context for customer use.
- ❒ *Documenting Business Object Context.* This element breaks down into five subcategories:

    1. *Work Process Diagrams.* These complete the documentation that defines the structure and purpose of the business object.
    2. *Focus Area Diagrams.* These diagrams document information about the activities, tasks, and user roles associated with the business object.
    3. *The Content Network.* Content network documents the enterprise entities that provide content to the business objects and assign information owners to manage and maintain the information.
    4. *User Context.* This structures the business object as appropriate for delivery via the enterprise information portal.
    5. *The Presentation Filter.* The filter documents how the presentation of the business object will be made to the individual, encompassing the user role and security requirements.

- ❒ *Identifying Business Rules*. A business rule engine dynamically assembles business objects, controls the work flow and processing of business objects, and enforces role assignment and security.
- ❒ *Designing the System.* Remember to design the system to meet any regulatory and content retention requirements.
- ❒ *Integrating the Enterprise Knowledge Portal.* Integrate the enterprise knowledge portal with key systems, e-mail (automatic notification), and office document creation.

The template collection presented here is used to provide the details needed to capture the information critical to designing a logical enterprise knowledge portal based on integrating your work processes and personalized content. The enterprise knowledge portal methodology will be integrated into the execution of your enterprise knowledge portal projects. The enterprise knowledge portal methodology will provide the details to design a work process–centric solution. Your project management and system development life cycle systems are not represented in this material but are necessary to deploy a cohesive and consistent enterprise knowledge portal for users. Details around the enterprise knowledge portal infrastructure and environment are included in Part IV of the book. The enterprise activities and deliverables to outline the enterprise knowledge portal methodology are presented in Figure 6-2 and covered in detail throughout the remaining sections.

Figure 6-2. Enterprise knowledge portal project activities and deliverables.

Activities	Deliverables
Enterprise Knowledge Portal Business Objects	• Enterprise Knowledge Portal Work Process Template ▪ Map Targeted Activities into the Work Process • Enterprise Knowledge Portal Focus Area Diagram Template ▪ Create Focus Area Diagrams for Each Targeted Activity ▪ Add Focus Area Diagrams for Each User Role Included in the Targeted Activity
Enterprise Knowledge Portal Content Elements	• Enterprise Knowledge Portal Content Network ▪ Create a Content Network Logical Model of the Organization ▪ Add Enterprise Entities to the Content Network Logical Model ▪ Assign Information Owners to the Content Network Logical Model
Enterprise Knowledge Portal Business Object Context	• Enterprise Knowledge Portal Business Object Context ▪ Add User Context into the Enterprise Knowledge Portal Focus Area Diagrams ▪ Add Presentation Filters into the Enterprise Knowledge Portal Focus Area Diagrams ▪ Add Business Rules into the Enterprise Knowledge Portal Focus Area Diagrams
Enterprise Knowledge Portal Storyboards and Scripts	• Enterprise Knowledge Portal Storyboards and Scripts ▪ Create the Portal Banner ▪ Create the Portal Menu ▪ Create the Content Page ▪ Create the Content Page Tabs ▪ Create the Content Windows ▪ Create the Content-Relevant Information ▪ Create the Storyboard Frame

MyCompany Case Study Introduction

MyCompany has established its enterprise knowledge portal program and has targeted several enterprise knowledge portal projects to meet its vision and objectives. The team has reviewed their organization and has decided to focus on a business-to-employee solution as the first implementation of the enterprise knowledge portal. The enterprise knowledge portal program will be implemented as a combined series of application development projects and infrastructure projects. The enterprise knowledge portal organization has been established to maintain the appropriate organization governance and change management effort, methodology, measurements, technical architecture, and support services.

MyCompany's vice president of human resources is the executive sponsor for the enterprise knowledge portal initiative and understands that all team members involved in the same work processes will have to use the same technologies to work together effectively and electronically. The first enterprise knowledge portal project will focus on capturing objective information as well as subjective information to guide the effectiveness of managers and knowledge workers in myCompany. The employee performance-management project was selected as the first project and will be designed to create a consistent way of improving employee performance throughout myCompany. Specific objectives of the employee performance management project include: Define key performance indicators that focus on myCompany corporate objectives; establish a deliberate plan to place the most qualified individuals in jobs that best match their abilities and accomplishments; and define a career development program for each employee focused on evaluating results, analyzing needs, setting objectives, determining accountability, measuring progress, appraising performance, recognizing improvement, and projecting the future. Future releases of the enterprise knowledge portal will link training and education opportunities into the employee performance-management work processes.

The activities to create an overview of myCompany by mapping its knowledge management objectives into an enterprise knowledge portal have been completed. The enterprise knowledge portal program has been approved, and the organization to support the enterprise knowledge portal is in place. The next activities that will be completed include:

- ❒ Creating the employee performance management enterprise knowledge portal project charter, project plan, and quality assurance plan
- ❒ Establishing the enterprise knowledge portal IT–enabling framework requirements
- ❒ Identifying unique enterprise knowledge portal requirements
- ❒ Creating the knowledge organization system

- Defining the business objects: completing the work process diagrams and related focus area diagrams
- Breaking down into content elements: completing the content network diagrams
- Documenting business object context: outlining work process scenarios, adding content to the focus area diagrams, adding relevant links to the focus area diagrams, and adding presentation features to the focus area diagrams
- Identifying business rules: completing the environment diagrams
- Creating the storyboards and scripts: completing the enterprise knowledge portal storyboards and accompanying enterprise knowledge portal scripts

Business Objects

Begin each new iteration of the enterprise knowledge portal by selecting the work processes most positively influenced by delivering focused content and bringing managers and knowledge workers together more effectively. If the work processes selected have an external focus, you may concentrate on speeding up the assimilation of partners into your work processes, or you may decide that delivering competitive intelligence to sales representatives can help significantly compress the sales cycle. The point is to pick a definable issue or collection of work processes and focus on improving them with better content delivery.

The enterprise knowledge portal must have the appropriate function and structure to support your work processes. The enterprise knowledge portal business object diagrams break out the tasks of a targeted activity and illustrate how they are related to each other from the user's point of view. The business object diagrams outline each task of the activity, the work flow of the business object, and how each task connects to other tasks in the work process–targeted activities. The enterprise knowledge portal business object diagrams will validate that the work flow structure is correct for the users involved in the work process.

Two types of diagrams are created once the business objects have been identified to be part of the current enterprise knowledge portal release. The first diagram is a work process diagram showing the complete set of activities and tasks to be included in the enterprise knowledge portal. The second series of work process diagrams are called focus area diagrams and are created to illustrate just the focus areas of the targeted activities and work processes specified to be included in the current delivery phase of the enterprise knowledge portal project. The first focus area diagram illustrates what the enterprise knowledge portal project team intends to deliver and is used to determine if the proposed deliverable is self-contained and represents a coherent collection of targeted activities. You will want to create additional focus area diagrams for each role involved in the work process. These focus area diagrams are used to discuss the delivery phase with users, to validate that the work processes and targeted activities are an encapsulated solution for each user role, and to run scenarios against the work processes identified and incorporate any missed details. The enterprise knowledge portal work process diagram and focus area diagrams involve completing three steps:

1. *Map targeted activities into the work process.* Create a work process diagram that describes the business object. Include a high-level description of the targeted activities and the user role responsible for completing the activities.
2. *Create the focus area diagrams for each targeted activity.* Create a collection of focus area diagrams of the selected targeted activities to be included in the enterprise knowledge portal. Determine if the focus area is self-contained and represents a coherent collection of targeted activities.
3. *Add focus area diagrams for each user role.* Each role that interacts with the targeted activities will require a unique perspective or work flow of the business object. Create a focus area diagram for each role identified in the work process diagram, if needed, to clarify the interactions between the multiple roles involved in the targeted activities.

Map Targeted Activities into the Work Process

Purpose: Create a work process diagram that describes the business object. Include a high-level description of the targeted activities and the user role responsible for completing the activities.

The work process diagram creates a concrete representation of the purpose and existing activities that are included in your work processes. In terms of targeted activities, the diagram will remain specific to the work process selected. The work process diagram will concentrate on the sequential flow, purpose, and other functional details associated with the targeted activities to be included in the enterprise knowledge portal. You will want to keep the user interface requirements separate at this point.

Focus on the work processes outlined in the enterprise knowledge portal project charter. The goal is to map the relationships of the targeted activities for the selected work processes. Use the enterprise knowledge portal work process template shown in Figure 6-3 to identify each targeted activity and briefly outline the purpose of the activity. There are several validations

Figure 6-3. Enterprise knowledge portal work process template.

Re: How to Diagram an Enterprise Knowledge Portal Work Process

How to Use This Template

Review the steps defined here to create an outline of the work process targeted to be included in the enterprise knowledge portal. The concept is to break the targeted work process down into understandable activities. Once the activities have been identified, the order in which they will logically be completed is added to the enterprise knowledge portal work process template. The final step is to append additional notes to clarify the activities identified as part of the work process being documented. You will want to create a work processes diagram for each work process to be added to the enterprise knowledge portal.

Step One: Identify the Enterprise Knowledge Portal Work Processes Diagrams to Be Completed

Using the enterprise knowledge portal project charter that defines the scope of the work, determine the work processes targeted to be delivered in this release of the enterprise knowledge portal. You will want to complete an individual Enterprise Knowledge Portal Work Process Template for each work process identified.

Example:
The personal performance enterprise knowledge portal project charter is reviewed and several business-to-employee work processes are identified to be included in the enterprise knowledge portal. The employee performance management work process was targeted to document in the enterprise knowledge portal work process template.

Step Two: Identify the High-Level Activities that Comprise the Work Process

For the targeted work process from step one, identify the second level of detail. This detail will be the high-level activities associated with the targeted work process.

Example:
The activities that comprise the employee performance management work process include:

- Organization performance objectives
- Resource planning
- Employee performance objectives
- Employee self-appraisal
- Employee tentative evaluation
- One-on-one interviews
- Performance evaluation
- Compensation evaluation

(continues)

Figure 6-3. (Continued).

Each activity is added to an individual row in the enterprise knowledge portal work process template.

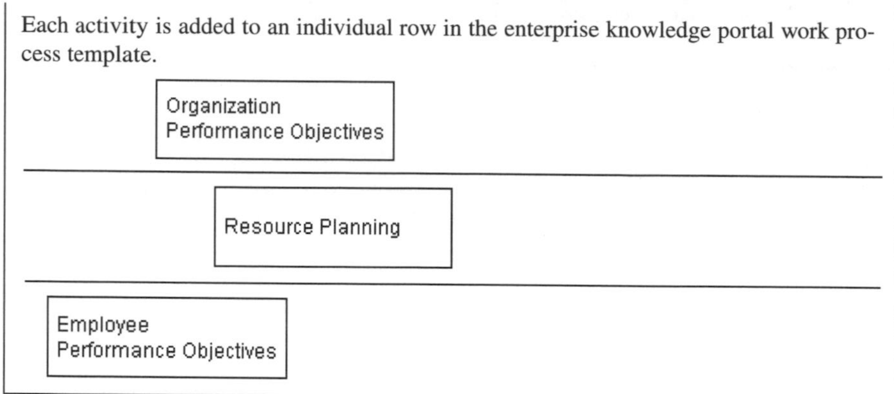

Step Three: Identify the Logical Order in which Activities Will Be Completed

For the activities from Step Two, identify the logical order in which the activities will be completed to successfully accomplish the objective of the targeted work process.

Example:
Walk through the activities and determine the logical start to finish of the activities within the work process. Reorganize the activities in the rows from step two to reflect any changes in the order in which the activities will occur.

Step Four: Identify the Relationships Between the Activities

Once the activities are outlined in their logical order from Step Three, add the links that define the relationships between the individual activities. These links visually show the activity that begins the process and illustrates the activities that are used as input to the activities that follow.

Example:
The links are added to the individual activities in the enterprise knowledge portal work process template.

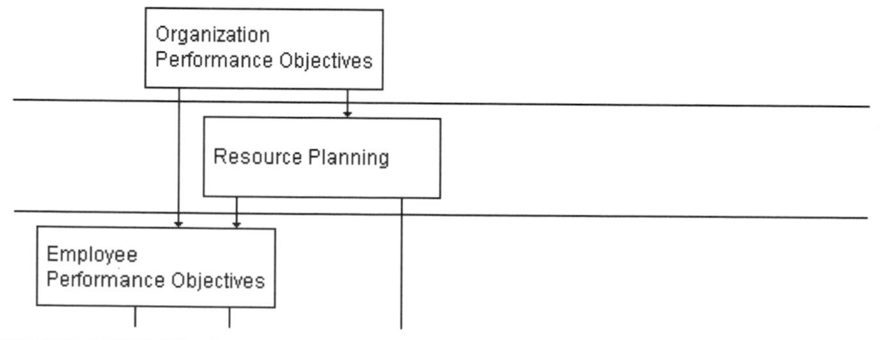

Step Five: Add Clarification or Supporting Documentation to the Activities Included in the Work Process

Once the relationships between activities are outlined in Step Four, add any notes or additional information to clarify the targeted work process or individual activities.

Example:
Additional notes to clarify the details are added to the individual activities in the enterprise knowledge portal work process template.

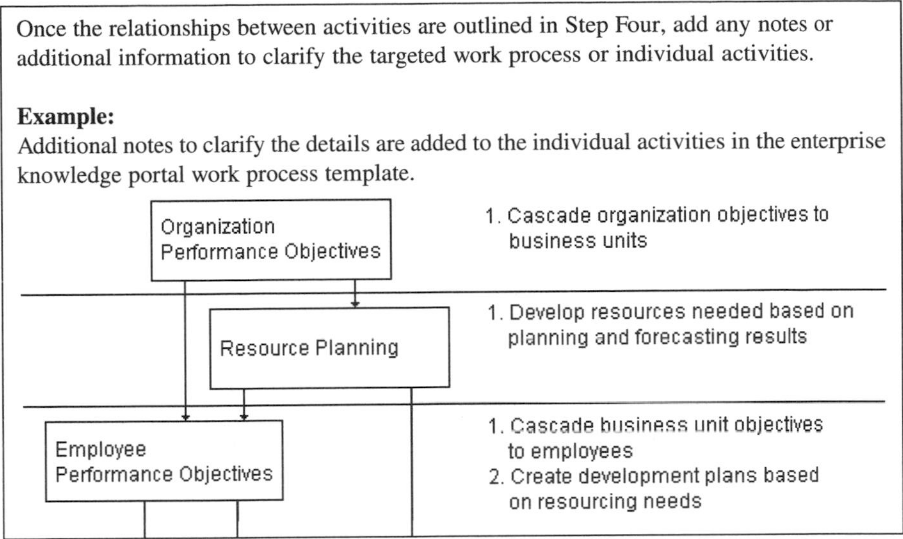

to complete once the enterprise knowledge portal work process diagram is documented from the template. These include:

- *Validating that the Targeted Activities Are Coherent.* The work process should represent the targeted activities for a single work process. The work process should contain a title and purpose statement to identify how the targeted activities are used.
- *Validating that the Targeted Activities Support Real Work.* Look for targeted activities that are not connected or support a coherent work process.
- *Validating that the Targeted Activities Are Distinct.* Collect the targeted activities that support the same work processes or the same type of work or role, and compare them. Determine whether they are distinct or if they need to be recombined in some way.

MYCOMPANY CASE STUDY

Using the information available from the enterprise knowledge portal project charter, the project team has created the enterprise knowledge portal work process diagram for the employee performance management work process–targeted activities. This can be reviewed in Figure 6-4. There are several activities identified that

Figure 6-4. Employee performance management: work process.

Process Step	Activities
Organization Performance Objectives	1. Cascade organization objectives to business units
Resource Planning	1. Develop resources needed based on planning and forecasting results
Employee Performance Objectives	1. Cascade business units objectives to employees 2. Create development plans based on resourcing needs
Employee Self-Appraisal	1. Allow employees to create a self-appraisal to match personal goals with organizational needs
Employee Tentative Evaluation	1. Allow managers to evaluate employees matching available skills to meet business unit objectives
One-on-One Interviews	1. Establish a set of objectives that employees and managers agree to 2. Continue to monitor progress against objectives set
Performance Evaluation	1. Document results of employee accomplishments and file
Compensation Evaluation	1. Based on resource planning and employee accomplishments adjust compensation 2. Submit appropriate documents to human resources

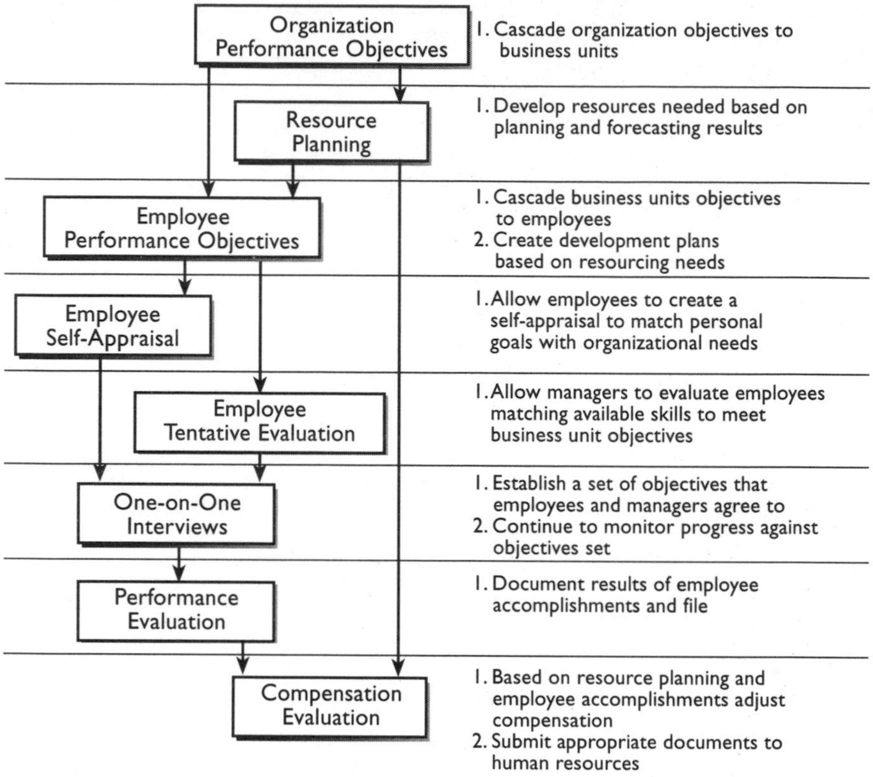

have to be consistently completed to meet the objectives of the employee performance management work process. These include:

- ❒ Cascading the organization's objectives to the business units
- ❒ Developing resources needed based on planning, budgeting, and forecasting results
- ❒ Cascading business units objectives to employees
- ❒ Creating individual employee development plans based on resources needed
- ❒ Linking training and education opportunities into employee development plans
- ❒ Allowing employees to create a self-appraisal to match personal goals with organizational needs
- ❒ Allowing managers to evaluate employees matching available skills to meet business unit objectives

- ❒ Establishing a set of objectives that employees and managers agree to
- ❒ Continuing to monitor progress against objectives set
- ❒ Documenting results of employee accomplishments and file
- ❒ Adjusting compensation, based on resource planning and employee accomplishments
- ❒ Submitting appropriate documents to human resources

Create the Focus Area Diagrams for Each Targeted Activity

Purpose: Create a collection of focus area diagrams of the selected targeted activities to be included in the enterprise knowledge portal. Determine if the focus area is self-contained and represents a coherent collection of targeted activities.

The focus area diagrams include the key concepts for designing the work model. Focus areas show the coherent places in the targeted activity that support doing tasks. The individual tasks need to identify the functions that are supported. The model allows the relationship between tasks to be clearly defined in a way that best fits the context of the work to be completed. The structure of the work flow diagram must be designed to fit the structure of how users interact with the individual tasks.

Focus on the activities identified in the enterprise knowledge portal work process diagram from step one. The goal is to identify a subset of the activities from the enterprise knowledge portal work process diagram to implement in the enterprise knowledge portal. Use the enterprise knowledge portal focus area template shown in Figure 6-5 to identify the subset of targeted activities. There are several validations to complete once the enterprise knowledge portal focus area diagram has been created from the template. These include:

- ❒ *Validating that Functions Are Correct*. Review functions to verify that they support the purpose of the task. If separate activities are required, create another work process diagram and focus area diagram.
- ❒ *Validating that Links Make Sense*. Make certain that the links to switch between activities or tasks make sense.
- ❒ *Validating that the Work Processes Are Supported.* Make certain that the sequential flow of tasks for the targeted activity is correct from the point of view of the different roles and activities.

MYCOMPANY CASE STUDY

Using the information available from the enterprise knowledge portal work process diagram created in step one, create a focus area

(text continues on page 299)

Figure 6-5. Enterprise knowledge portal focus area template.

Re: How to Diagram an Enterprise Knowledge Portal Focus Area

How to Use This Template

Review the steps defined here to document the details of each activity identified in the enterprise knowledge portal work process diagram. The concept is to create a diagram that is focused on the individual activities identified in the targeted work process down into understandable tasks. You will want to create a focus area diagram for each activity identified in the enterprise knowledge portal work process diagrams. Each row of the focus area diagram is for a user role involved in the activity. The tasks associated with each role are added to the appropriate rows. Once the tasks have been added, the order in which they will logically be completed is included in the enterprise knowledge portal focus area template. The final step is to append a description of the function of each task being documented. If the activity being diagramed is complicated, you will want to create an individual focus area diagram for each user role involved in the activity.

Step One: Identify the Enterprise Knowledge Portal Focus Area Diagrams to Be Completed

Using the enterprise knowledge portal project work process diagrams, you will want to complete an individual enterprise knowledge portal focus area template for each activity identified in the enterprise knowledge portal work process diagrams. Depending on the level of detail and sophistication of the targeted activity, it might take several focus area diagrams to complete the documentation of each activity. To reduce the complexity of the focus area diagram is to create several focus area diagrams for each user role involved in the activity.

Example:
The employee performance management enterprise knowledge portal work process diagram is reviewed and several activities are identified to be included in the enterprise knowledge portal. The enterprise knowledge portal focus area diagrams to be created include:

- Organization performance objectives
- Resource planning
- Employee performance objectives
- Employee self-appraisal
- Employee tentative evaluation
- One-on-one interviews
- Performance evaluation
- Compensation evaluation

The employee performance objectives activity is selected to review in detail.

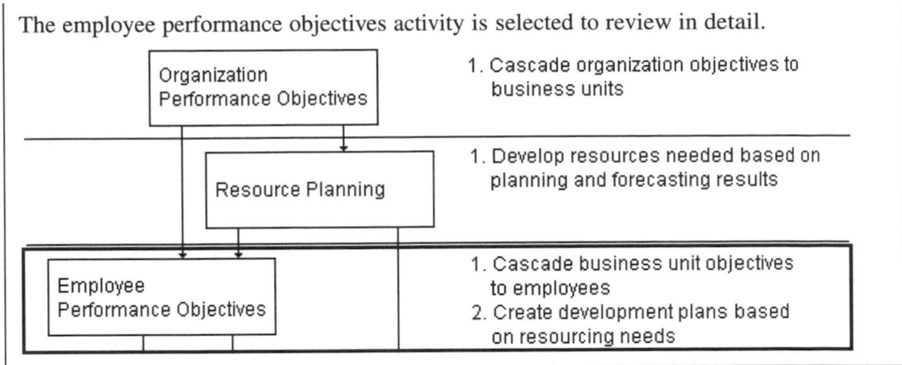

Step Two: Identify All User Roles Associated with the Targeted Activity

For the targeted activity from step one, identify the user roles required to successfully complete the individual tasks. Each user role will become a row in the enterprise knowledge portal focus area diagram. Create an individual focus area diagram for each user role involved in the activity if there are a significant number of tasks associated with each role or if there are a significant number of roles accountable for completing the activity.

Example:
Continuing to review the employee performance objectives activity as an example, the user roles involved to successfully complete the activity are identified to include:

- Employee
- Manager

Each user role is added to an individual row in the enterprise knowledge portal focus area template.

Employee

Manager

(continues)

Figure 6-5. (Continued).

Step Three: Identify the Individual Tasks that Comprise the Activity

The next step to complete the enterprise knowledge portal focus area diagram is to identify all the tasks that you will need to accomplish to successfully complete the targeted activity. Add each task in the enterprise knowledge portal focus area diagram template in the appropriate user role row.

Example:
The tasks that comprise the employee performance objectives activity include:
- Review cascaded objectives
- Create performance plan
- Review performance plan
- Approve performance plan

The employee user role is involved in all four tasks. The manager user role's assigned tasks include review performance plan and approve performance plan task.

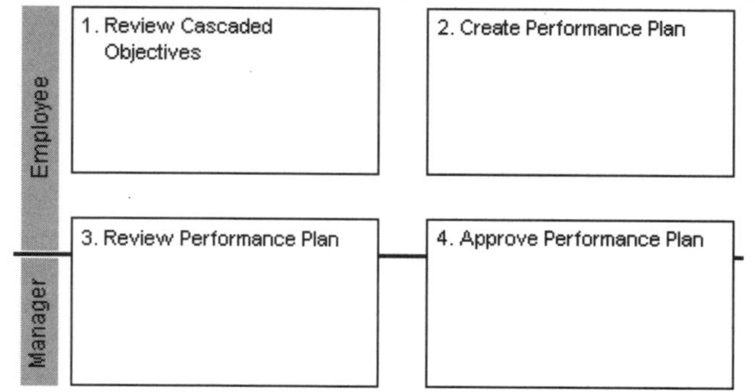

Step Four: Identify the Logical Order in which Tasks Will Be completed

For the tasks from step three, identify the logical order in which the tasks will be completed to successfully accomplish the objective of the targeted activity.

Example:
Walk through the tasks and determine the logical start to finish of the tasks within the activity. Reorganize the tasks in the rows from step three to reflect any changes in the order the tasks will occur.

Step Five: Identify the Relationships Between the Tasks

Once the tasks are outlined in their logical order from step four, add the links that define the relationships between the individual tasks. These links visually show the task that begins the process and illustrates the tasks that are used as input to the tasks that follow.

Example:
The links are added to the individual tasks in the enterprise knowledge portal work focus area template.

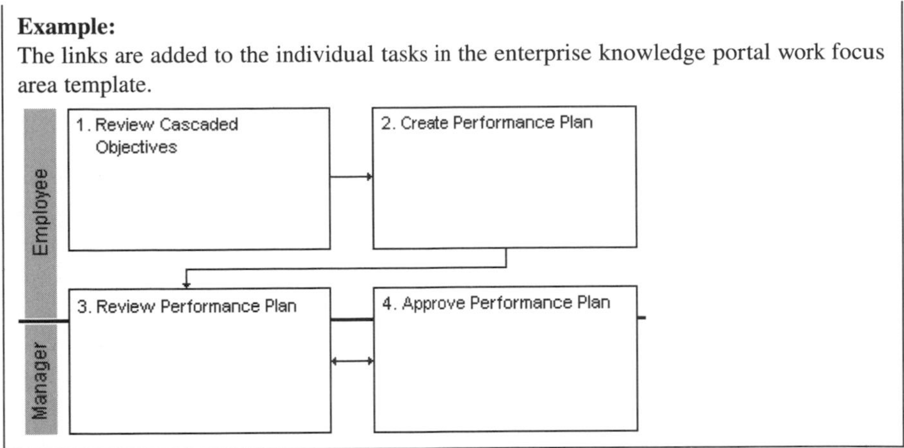

Step Six: Add Clarification or Supporting Documentation to the Tasks Included in the Activity

Once the relationships between tasks are outlined in step five, add any notes or additional information to clarify the targeted activity or individual tasks.

Example:
Additional notes to clarify the function of each task is added to the enterprise knowledge portal focus area template.

Employee

1. Review Cascaded Objectives

Function - Review objectives in the organization to create performance plans

2. Create Performance Plan

Function - Create the employee's personal performance plan

Manager

3. Review Performance Plan

Function - The employee and manager review the personal performance plan and agree to modifications

4. Approve Performance Plan

Function - The final version of the personal performance plan is approved by the employee and manager

diagram for each targeted activity to be incorporated into the enterprise knowledge portal as part of the current project. The employee performance management work process includes the following targeted activities:

- ❐ Organization performance objectives
- ❐ Resource planning
- ❐ Employee performance objectives
- ❐ Employee self-appraisal

- ❒ Employee tentative evaluation
- ❒ One-on-one interviews
- ❒ Performance evaluation
- ❒ Compensation evaluation

The employee performance objectives activity has been selected to illustrate what a focus area diagram would look like. The focus area diagram documents the employee performance objectives activity from the employee and management role perspectives. The purpose of the enterprise knowledge portal focus area diagram is to outline the objectives of each task required to complete the employee performance objectives activity. The final enterprise knowledge portal focus area diagram for the employee performance objectives activity is shown in Figure 6-6.

Add Focus Area Diagrams for Each User Role

Purpose: Each role that interacts with the targeted activities will require a unique perspective or work flow of the business object. Create a focus area diagram for each role identified in the work process diagram, if needed, to clarify the interactions between the multiple roles involved in the targeted activities.

Figure 6-6. Employee performance management work process: focus area diagram—employee objectives activity functions.

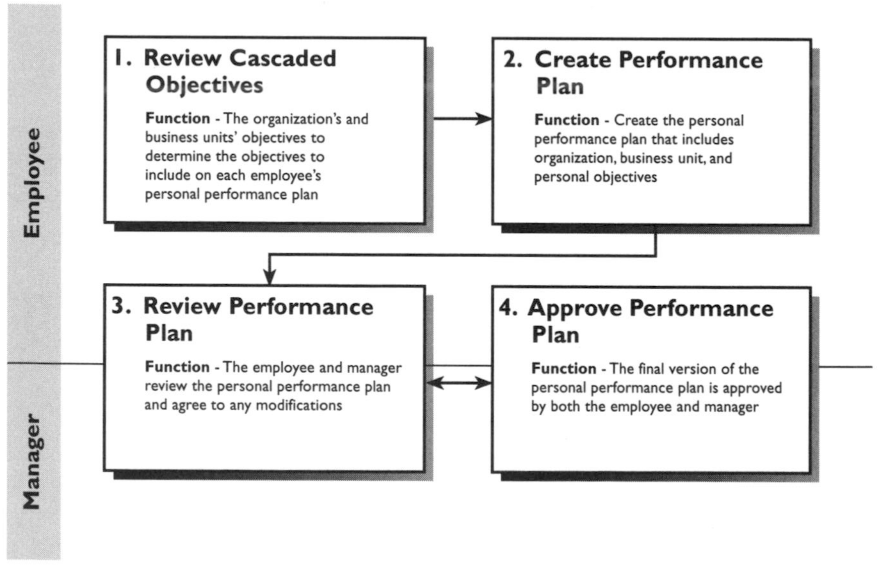

Once the enterprise knowledge portal focus area diagram from step two is complete, continue to create focus area diagrams from the perspective of each user role involved in the work process. You want to create one focus area diagram from the perspective of each role that is involved in the identified activities and tasks. There are several validations to complete once the entire collection of enterprise knowledge portal focus area diagrams has been created. These include:

- *Validating that the Focus Areas Are Coherent.* The focus area should represent the tasks for a single activity.
- *Validating that the Focus Areas Support Real Work.* Look for focus areas that are not connected or support a coherent activity.
- *Validating that the Focus Areas Are Distinct.* Collect the focus areas that support the same work processes or the same targeted activities or role, and compare them. Determine whether they are distinct or if they need to be recombined in some way.
- *Validating that Functions Are Correct.* Review functions to verify that they support the purpose of the task. If separate activities are required, create another work process diagram and focus area diagrams.
- *Validating that Links Make Sense.* Review that the links to switch between activities or tasks make sense.
- *Validating that the Work Processes Are Supported.* Review that the sequential flow of tasks for the targeted activity is correct from the point of view of the different roles and activities.

MYCOMPANY CASE STUDY

Using the information available from the enterprise knowledge portal focus area diagrams created in step two, create a focus area diagram for each user role involved in the targeted activity to make sure the individual roles and responsibilities are coherent, not redundant, and efficient. The purpose of the enterprise knowledge portal focus area diagram for each role is to outline all the tasks the employee, manager, or human resource representative would be responsible for completing as part of the employee performance objectives activity.

Content Elements

Traditional business unit structures have worked as independently as possible within your organization and as a result have created an inefficient flow of information, data, and knowledge to people in other parts of your organization. The intranet and e-mail have created a new paradigm where individuals no longer care about the departmental or business unit origins of content, they simply need to get to it. Content often resides in several different business units, and the enterprise knowledge portal will allow you to make the information accessible from a single location and help to establish desired team behavior.

The objective of mapping your content network is to visualize the knowledge in your organization and begin assigning information ownership to people who maintain different kinds of content. You will be able to see the complexity of the information and knowledge you are seeking to continue to maintain and manage. The content network diagram will help you identify the business analysts and content authors you will need to maintain the information required for the enterprise knowledge portal. The resource questions to be answered include:

- What additional roles and responsibilities are created?
- Where will you need to focus resources to ensure that content gets captured and delivered?
- How will you distribute your knowledge management effort throughout the organization?

The content network focuses on the content or information requirements associated with the work processes defined in the enterprise knowledge portal work flow diagrams. The content network diagram has three sections. The steps involved in diagramming the content network include:

1. *Create the content network.* Document a series of logical models to capture how content is organized throughout your organization. This information is used for managing information and identifying ownership of content.
2. *Identify enterprise entities.* Establish a collection of entities that need to be defined and managed at the enterprise level. Expand the content network diagrams created in step one to include the enterprise entities.
3. *Assign information owners.* These are the individuals with expertise over each high-level category in the content network. They are responsible for the accuracy and consistency of the information in their assigned sections of the content network.

The challenge is to create a content network that combines the best of the existing hierarchy and blends it with new, network-based forms of organization, in terms of identifying and maintaining information. Creating the content network diagrams will help assign the information ownership to transform your organization from a traditional corporate hierarchy into a powerful and flexible knowledge-sharing and continuous learning, changing, and improving organization.

Create the Content Network

Purpose: Document a series of logical models to capture how content is organized throughout your company. This information is used for managing information and identifying ownership of content.

Think about the hierarchical organization charts and what information these business units are responsible for managing. Consider the categories or containers as the focal points that information, data, and knowledge can be organized around. Many business units will contribute to these centers. The design is to be a logical model for organizing information by function or work process. This collection of logical models defines the content network and provides you the basis for supporting the work processes in your organization and delivering the information required. This logical modeling effort will yield significant benefits as the enterprise knowledge portal continues to grow. The first is to facilitate improved searching over information throughout the enterprise. Additional benefits include subscription and personalization of content.

Begin with your organization and consider what you do. For example, the company owns fixed assets, does business from several locations, is the parent company, provides feedback, agrees to contracts, and is a member of competitive intelligence. Continue to drill into the logical model of how information is used in your organization. The logical model will allow you to uncover the complexity of the information and knowledge you are attempting to manage. As you develop the logical model, consider how the organization, partners, and customers work. Are you product-centric or customer-centric? Are you organized by project or by business processes? Addressing these questions will drive you to a solution that places your highest-level activities into the content network.

MYCOMPANY CASE STUDY

MyCompany has created a content network diagram to capture the high-level model of entities for their ability to represent the key concepts of the organization. See Figure 6-7 to review the content network for myCompany. On the content network diagram an open circle indicates that there is only one instance of the entity. A closed circle indicates that there are many instances of the entity. A line is

Figure 6-7. Content network diagram: organization.

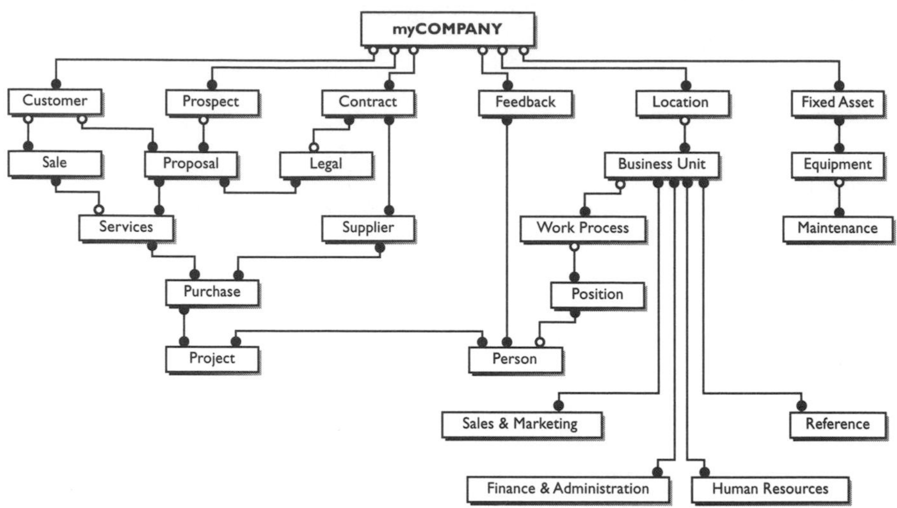

drawn to show the connection to the entities with a verb (not shown) to describe the relationship between the entities.

Identify Enterprise Entities

Purpose: Establish a collection of entities that need to be defined and managed at the enterprise level. Expand the content network diagrams created in step one to include the enterprise entities.

Below each primary content network entities are additional enterprise entities. These additional logical models represent additional details of information. For example, in the fixed asset entity a second content network diagram is created to describe land, buildings, and equipment. The point is to make your company look like the knowledge it produces and not the business units that produce the knowledge. You must decide where additional information is needed to support additional enterprise entities. The goal is to establish a manageable logical model of your organization. As the collection of enterprise entities to manage grows, it is likely that you will create a spreadsheet or relational database to store the details about your enterprise entities. To help you work through the creation of your content network diagrams, consider the following:

- ❐ Focus on content and not on business units.
- ❐ Rely on your identified business objects to help you start testing the validity of your high-level content network nodes.

- ❒ You should group lower levels of enterprise entities into additional content network diagrams such as sales and marketing, human resources, fixed assets, administration and finance, and product.
- ❒ Each content network diagram center will become a managed domain for a single information owner who can oversee the content.

MYCOMPANY CASE STUDY

The secondary content network diagrams for myCompany have been identified.
They include:

- ❒ Sales and marketing
- ❒ Procurement
- ❒ Fixed assets
- ❒ Services
- ❒ Finance and administration
- ❒ Human resources
- ❒ Reference

The sales and marketing, services (Figure 6-8), finance and administration (Figure 6-9), human resources (Figure 6-10), and reference (Figure 6-11) content network diagrams have been included for your review.

Figure 6-8. Content network diagram: sales and marketing.

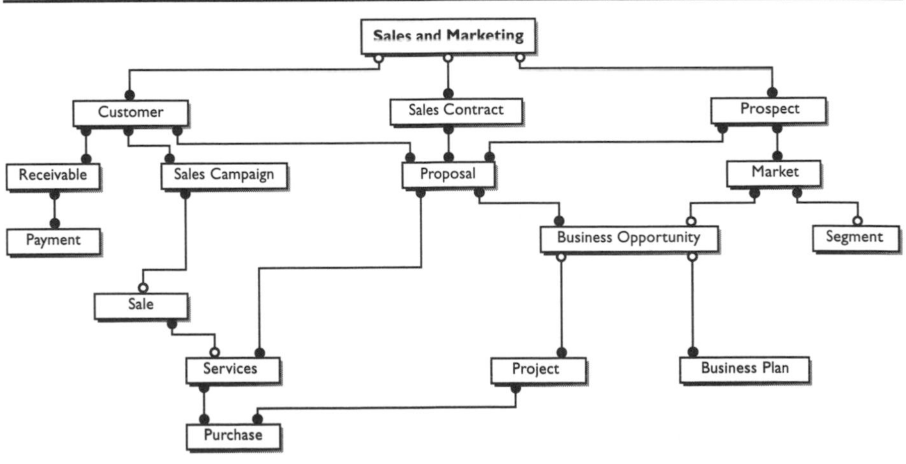

Figure 6-9. Content network diagram: finance and administration.

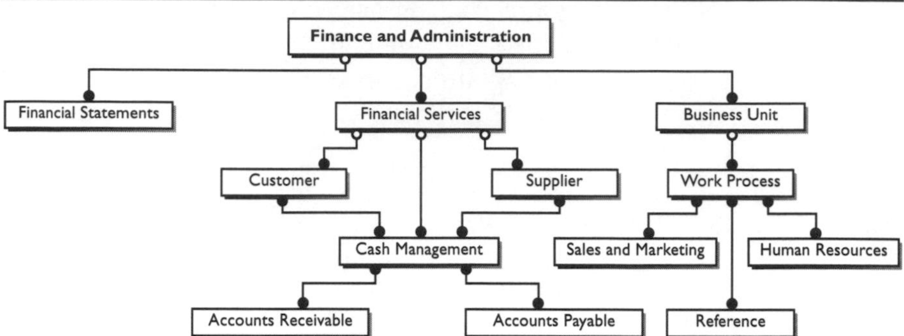

Figure 6-10. Content network diagram: human resources.

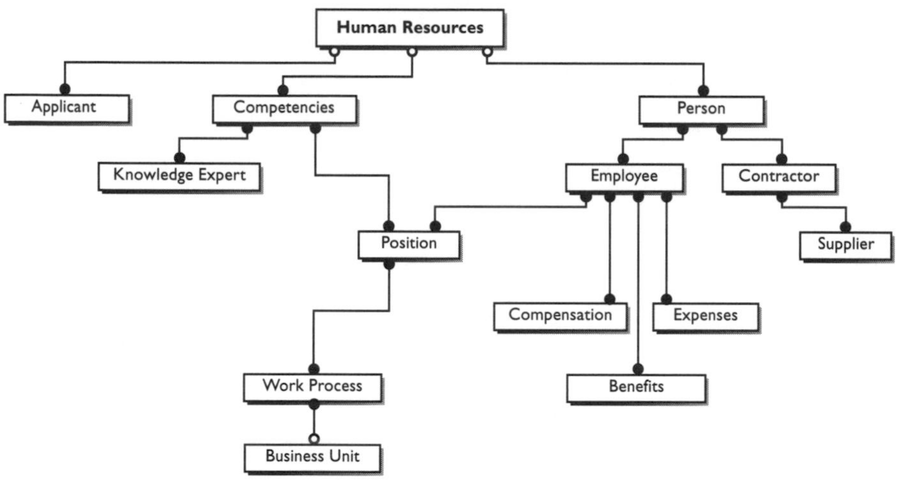

Assign Information Owners

Purpose: These are the individuals with expertise over each high-level category in the content network. They are responsible for the accuracy and consistency of the information in their assigned sections of the content network.

The final step in your content network diagram is assigning ownership of the information and knowledge you have identified. This is where the hierarchical structure of your organization needs to be considered. You are combining the organization's hierarchical structure into the content knowledge structure you are creating. The objective here is to write data sources

Figure 6-11. Content network diagram: reference.

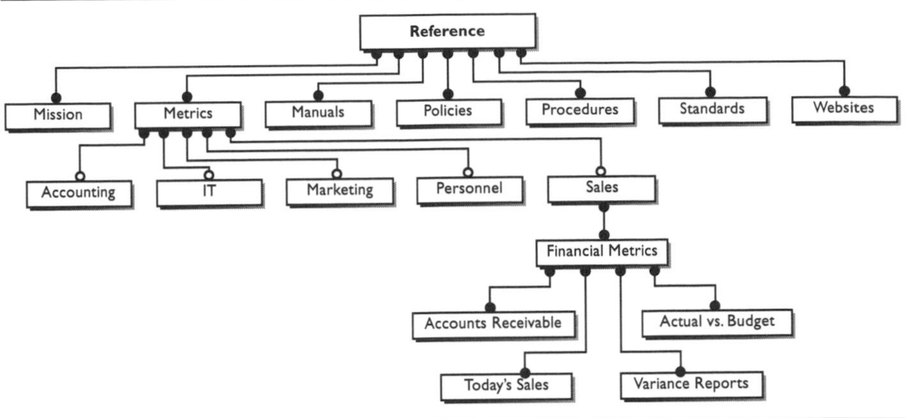

and names of owners into the primary content and secondary content centers. This will create the appropriate level of accountability required to maintain and manage the information used in the enterprise knowledge portal.

Owners of information are assigned for each content network and should be managers in your organization. This is essential for furthering organizational change, as well as ensuring that content authors keep electronic or Web and traditional information up-to-date and accurate. These managers of knowledge management content need to hold people accountable to the content network. More important, announcing ownership is a key principle of knowledge management to further the connection between people over these collections of information. No matter how well defined the collection and presentation of useful information is within the enterprise knowledge portal, when users need additional details, more information, or modifications to the content items provided, they can call or e-mail the information owner.

MYCOMPANY CASE STUDY

Ownership assignments have been established for each content network diagram. These owners are all managers within myCompany. A spreadsheet has been created to document the enterprise entities, descriptions, information owner, and knowledge expert with e-mail address and phone number. The sample content network spreadsheet can be seen in Figure 6-12.

(text continues on page 310)

Figure 6-12. Sample content network (spreadsheet version).

myCompany Content Network					
	Descriptions	**Information Owner**	**Knowledge Expert**	**e-Mail**	**Phone Number**
myCompany Organization	Logical model of how information is accessed throughout the organization				
Customer	Customer information is managed for Sales, Proposal, Services, Purchase, and Project entities	Nancy Harrison	David Cooper	dcooper@mycompany.com	555-2783
Prospect	Prospect information is managed for Proposal, Legal, Services, Purchase, and Project entities	Richard Ward	Daniel Nelson	dnelson@mycompany.com	555-2346
Contract	Contract information is managed for Legal, Supplier, Purchase, and Project entities	Tom Black	Eric Wagner	ewagner@mycompany.com	555-9824
Feedback	Feedback information is managed for Person entities	Alice Moore	Alice Moore	amoore@mycompany.com	555-2378
Location	Location information is managed for Business Unit, Work Process, Position, Person, Sales and Marketing, Finance and Administration, Human Resources, and Reference entities	David Easton	David Easton	deaston@mycompany.com	555-9078
Fixed Asset	Fixed Asset information is managed for Equipment and Maintenance entities	Richard Morris	Ellen Baker	ebaker@mycompany.com	555-2145
Sales and Marketing	Logical model of how information is accessed in the Sales and Marketing business unit				
Customer	Customer information is managed for Receivable, Sales Campaign, Proposal, Payment, Sales, Services, Purchase, and Project entities	Nancy Harrison	Martin Smith	msmith@mycompany.com	555-0987
Sales Contract	Sales Contract is managed for Proposal, Business Opportunity, Services, Project, Business Plan, and Purchase entities	Tom Black	Elizabeth Lineman	elineman@mycompany.com	555-2984
Prospect	Prospect information is managed for Proposal, Market, Business Opportunity, Segment, Project, Business Plan, and Purchase entities	Richard Ward	Daniel Nelson	dnelson@mycompany.com	555-2375

myCompany Content Network					
	Descriptions	**Information Owner**	**Knowledge Expert**	**e-Mail**	**Phone Number**
Finance and Administration	Logical model of how information is accessed in the Finance and Administration business unit				
Financial Statements	Financial Statements information is managed as a single entity	Chris Harris	Chris Harris	charris@mycompany.com	555-1234
Financial Services	Financial Services information is managed for Customer, Supplier, Cash Management, Accounts Receivable, and Accounts Payable entities	Allen Pierce	Mark Newton	mnewton@mycompany.com	555-2943
Business Unit	Business Unit information is managed for Work Process, Sales and Marketing, Human Resources, and Reference entities	Caroline Davis	Helen Jeffreys	hjeffreys@mycompany.com	555-9982
Human Resources	Logical model of how information is accessed in the Human Resources business unit				
Applicant	Applicant information is managed as a single entity	Elizabeth Myers	Elizabeth Myers	emyers@mycompany.com	555-4554
Competencies	Competencies information is managed for Knowledge Expert, Employee, Position, Work Process, and Business Unit entities	Gus Edwards	Tim Green	tgreen@mycompany.com	555-7732
Person	Person information is managed for Employee, Contractor, Position, Supplier, Work Process, Compensation, Expenses, Business Unit, and Benefits entities	Robert Back	Greg Johnson	gjohnson@mycompany.com	555-8823
Reference	Logical model of how information is accessed in the Reference business unit				
Mission	Mission information is managed as a single entity	John Jacob	John Jacob	jjacob@mycompany.com	555-1193
Metrics	Metrics information is managed for Accounting, IT, Marketing, Personnel, Sales, Financial Metrics, Accounts Receivable, Acutal vs. Budget, Today's Sales and Variance Reports entities	Steve Miller	Theresa Brown	tbrown@mycompany.com	555-4442
Manuals	Manuals information is managed as a single entity	Ellen Thomas	Ellen Thomas	ethomas@mycomany.com	555-9090
Policies	Policies information is managed as a single entity	Clayton Carson	Clayton Carson	ccarson@mycompany.com	555-7111
Procedures	Procedures is managed as a single entity	Dennis Allen	Dennis Allen	dallen@mycompany.com	555-8225
Standards	Standards is managed as a single entity	Karen Stanley	Karen Stanley	kstanley@mycompany.com	555-0096
Websites	Websites is managed as a single entity	Steve Collins	Steve Collins	scollins@mycompany.com	555-1030

Business Object Context

With the business object context documents you will be able to identify where you are currently doing well in managing knowledge, and you will also be able to understand where you need improvement. These items sharpen your understanding and are your guides to identifying and providing the right information to knowledge workers so they can effectively do their jobs and make decisions. The final documentation will outline the enterprise knowledge portal objects needed to deliver necessary information. The business object context documents are included in the enterprise knowledge portal methodology for defining how knowledge management objectives will map to work processes. In the next few steps, how to identify and document knowledge management elements of the enterprise knowledge portal methodology are discussed in detail.

Success in the emerging information economy is based on effective packaging and delivery of content to the managers and knowledge workers who must use it. This should be done logically. You need to recognize the steps to be completed and then formalize your efforts as part of the enterprise knowledge portal methodology. The enterprise knowledge portal methodology represents the process your organization will formalize and follow to recognize the experience and expertise that must be preserved and used to your corporate advantage.

It is important to realize that the technology identified for the enterprise knowledge portal solution is only as good as the people who use and manage the content. Building a successful enterprise knowledge portal solution means assessing the important content for the success of your organization, then putting the people, work processes, and technology behind that information. The enterprise knowledge portal methodology identifies the scope of the investment required to document your enterprise portal solution and to begin to understand what the initial time and investment will be. The techniques for building the business object context are outlined in the following three steps:

1. *Document user context.* Outline the structure to deliver the targeted business objects into the enterprise knowledge portal.
2. *Determine the presentation filters.* Identify the presentation and delivery capabilities that will be provided to display the targeted business objects into the enterprise knowledge portal.
3. *Outline the business rules.* Document the business rules to assemble business objects, control work flow and processing of business objects, and enforce role assignment and security for targeted business objects that are being integrated into the enterprise knowledge portal.

Document User Context

Purpose: Outline the structure to deliver the targeted business objects into the enterprise knowledge portal.

Review the work process diagrams to be incorporated into the enterprise knowledge portal. Determine when multiple roles are exchanging information or decisions are being made. These are the critical points in the work process that you will want to incorporate into the enterprise knowledge portal. There will be several different types of information and views of information that will need to be available for the roles outlined in the focus area diagrams.

Outline two or three scenarios that the work process is designed to address. Using the scenarios you define, walk through the work process from the perspective of each role involved. At each step in the work process, define the content and links to content that need to be available for each role to complete their assigned tasks. Identify that the content currently exists in your organization and how accurate and current the content will need to be for the user to effectively complete the work process scenario. You will have to research the specific content and content attributes that apply to the work process and navigation links used to access additional information that might be relevant. The work process scenarios allow you to validate that the tasks to be completed are closely related to the content that best fits the context of the work.

The presentation of the targeted business objects into the enterprise knowledge portal must closely match how users work and what users expect to see. The creation and validation of work process scenarios allow you to verify that the correct information is presented at the right time in the work process. You will be able to confirm that the context of information and the links to switch between business objects and tasks provided to each role involved in the work process support the purpose of the business objects. If you determine that separate activities are required, create additional work process diagrams and focus area diagrams to fill the gap. Working with knowledge expert community members, review the sequential flow of tasks for the business objects to verify that they are correct from the point of view of the different roles. Once the presentation requirements of the business objects are confirmed, it is important to assign and document information owners for the content that is targeted to be included in the enterprise knowledge portal for the targeted work process.

MYCOMPANY CASE STUDY

The focus area diagrams are enhanced to include the content and relevant links required to support the business objects. Two scenarios of the employee performance objectives activity have been identified to validate the review of the work process diagram. For the employee and manager focus area diagrams, the employee performance objectives activity scenarios have been walked through, and the content and links to information that need to be available for each step of the employee performance objectives activity have been confirmed. In addition, the information owners have been identified for the targeted content. The activities completed include a review of the employee performance objectives activity scenarios, identification of the content and content format for the manager and employee roles, definition of the links to relevant information to support the targeted work process, and assignment of the information owners for the targeted content. The focus area diagrams are updated to include targeted content in Figure 6-13. Content-relevant links are added to the focus area diagrams in Figure 6-14.

Determine the Presentation Filters

Purpose: Identify the presentation and delivery capabilities that will be provided to display the targeted business objects in the enterprise knowledge portal.

A typical enterprise knowledge portal content page is comprised of a

Figure 6-13. Employee performance management work process: focus area diagram—employee performance objectives activity content.

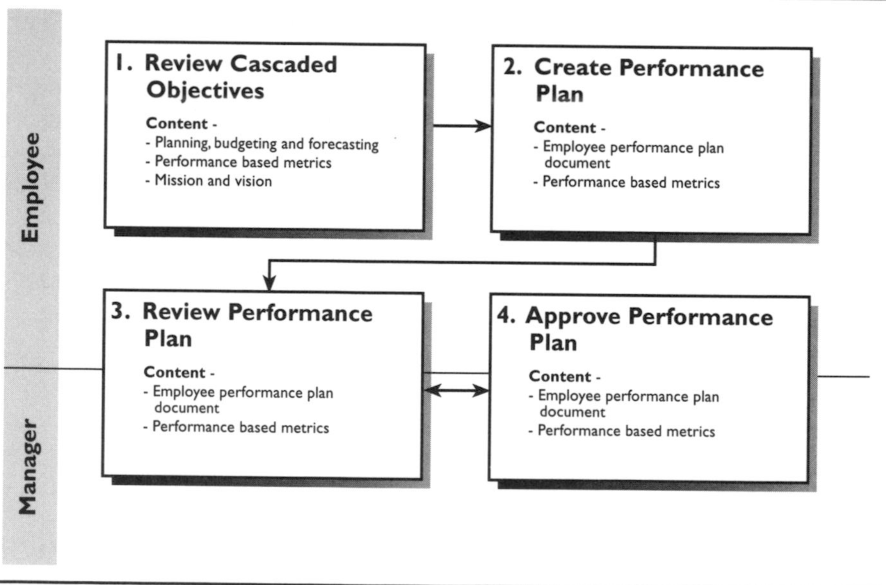

Figure 6-14. Employee performance management work process: focus area diagram—employee performance objectives activity links.

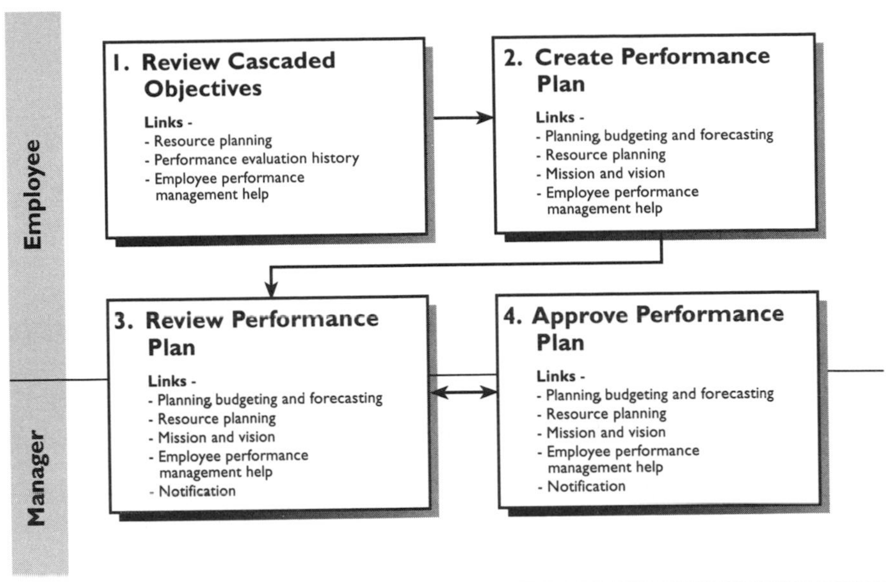

number of reusable information components and portal objects. Each portal object is responsible for capturing and delivering information back to the enterprise knowledge portal from the targeted information sources identified in step one. Individual content windows are then displayed on the content page to present information into the enterprise knowledge portal. A majority of the work designing the enterprise knowledge portal is the ability to build and maintain individual content windows. The presentation of information for the enterprise knowledge portal must be fluid and dynamic to support your knowledge management and work processes requirements. Your portal objects need to meet the following design standards:

- *They must dynamically build the content into the portal content windows when the user opens the portal page.* The information the user has requested will continue to reside and be maintained in the data source it originates from. The portal object will attach to the data source, retrieve the content requested, and present the information into a content window. This process guarantees that every user has access to the same single source of information, provided they have the security rights to interact with the information.
- *They must have content that is relevant, timely, and provides accurate information, making the enterprise knowledge portal an interactive envi-*

ronment for users. Providing a user interface that brings content from legacy systems, applications, websites, documents, reports, and spreadsheets into a unified view for users will bring significant value and return on investment to your organization.

There are several features you will want to build into the presentation layer to provide the services and dynamic presentation that information users require. Users will need to interact with screens to enter and submit information. They will need to easily navigate and link to additional content pages and content windows. An individual content window needs to be able to expand to take over the entire content page, the content needs to reformatted to fit the screen, and the content window needs to be able to be minimized back to the original size. Content windows need to be able to be collapsed to a title bar and expanded back to their default size. When the user selects a specific set of values from the corporate taxonomy and submits the request, the information on the content page and in the content windows will be filtered to present the information relative to the values selected. Users need to be able to configure content windows to different formats or different slices and dices of information by default when they are dynamically built to the page. Users need to be able to rearrange content windows on the same portal page or move to additional portal pages that they add. Users need to add or remove content windows from portal pages. The user needs to be able to set notification and alert parameters, subscribe to information that is delivered at some regular interval to content windows, and access other customization functionality designed into the enterprise knowledge portal. The user will require a broad and narrow navigation scheme to get to content pages and content windows. There are additional features you might want to include in your enterprise knowledge portal or features that the vendor provides as part of their enterprise portal software solution.

MYCOMPANY CASE STUDY

The focus area diagrams are enhanced to include the enterprise knowledge portal features. The presentation features and functions that will be available in the enterprise knowledge portal and how they will be integrated with the targeted content of the employee performance objectives activity are outlined. The navigation scheme, the content window configuration options, the customization features, and other enterprise knowledge portal features and functions that add value to the user are documented. The presentation details are documented in Figure 6-15.

Figure 6-15. Employee performance management work process: presentation filters—employee performance objectives activity.

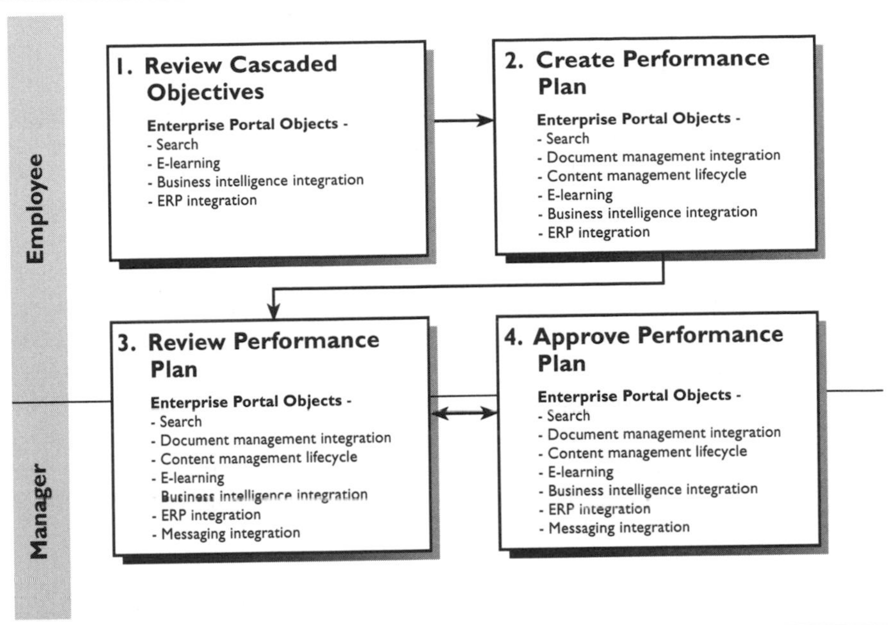

Outline the Business Rules

Purpose: Document the business rules to assemble business objects, control work flow and processing of business objects, and enforce role assignment and security for targeted business objects that are being integrated into the enterprise knowledge portal.

The focus area diagrams are enhanced to include the nonpresentation portal object details. The goal is to overlay the focus area diagram with enterprise knowledge portal objects. Enterprise knowledge portal objects are the integration components and other enterprise knowledge portal features that will be used to develop the final solution. User interface technical considerations can also be added to the environmental overlay. By diagramming the structure of the overall system, the environmental overlay details provide a map to the enterprise knowledge portal implementation considerations. The collection of enterprise knowledge portal objects is designed to pull together the applications and content required to support the targeted activities of the user's work processes and tie these point solutions together into one comprehensive working environment. The enterprise knowledge portal objects provide seamless support to the work processes. It is important to validate the environmental overlay diagram for missing links between components, duplicated objects, missing objects, and inconsistencies.

The actual enterprise knowledge portal objects that you are going to annotate will require some understanding of the enterprise knowledge portal software and other services included in the architecture to complete the environment diagram. Our recommendation is to refer to enterprise knowledge portal object libraries of existing functions to use or reuse and your enterprise knowledge portal considerations outlined in step two. Several enterprise knowledge portal objects to consider referencing in the environment diagram include:

- *The Presentation Requirements for Functions, Content, and Links.* Reuse enterprise knowledge portal objects that already exist in the library for connecting to data sources, presenting applications, and hyperlinks. Create enterprise knowledge portal objects to support parameters stored in the enterprise portal metadata repository giving them a more universal use. A subscription or maintenance contract for new and updated portal objects, available through software vendors, is a valuable way to get started with your portal object library.
- *The Taxonomy or Knowledge Organization System Scheme Associated with the Content.* The knowledge organization schemes applied to content provide additional flexibility to create relationships and interactions between content windows and enterprise knowledge portal features. Enterprise knowledge portal objects are constructed using these logic maps allowing disparate data sources to work together.
- *The Search and Index Features, Application, and Automatic Queries Requirements.* The search and index features, application, or automatic queries requirements can be included in the environment diagram.
- *The Process and Action or Work Flow Features.* The process and action or work flow features included in or accessed from other sources by enterprise knowledge portal objects should be considered.
- *The User Profile or Role Attributes.* The user profile or role attributes that are available or that will created to be used as parameters in enterprise knowledge portal objects can be included.
- *The Personalization Attributes.* Consider the personalization attributes (i.e., delete, add, move, create) that will be applied to content and menu options for enterprise knowledge portal users, and whether personalization will be available from the personalize features in the enterprise portal software or designed and included as part of the content window functions.
- *The Integration Services and Applications.* The integration services and applications that support these services need to be reviewed to support

multilanguage, peer-to-peer services, Web services, process integration, multiple repository support, and other application integration requirements.

- *Objects That Support the Same Functionality, Integration, or Connectivity.* Collect the objects identified that support the same type of functionality, integration, or connectivity to the same data source or application, or profile or metadata repository attributes, and compare them. Determine whether they are distinct or if they need to be recombined in some way.

MYCOMPANY CASE STUDY

Using the information available from the focus area diagrams enhanced in step two, create the environment diagram for the employee performance objectives activity. This environment diagram overlays the focus area diagrams with the enterprise knowledge portal objects that will provide the business rules to assemble portal pages and content windows, control work flow and processing of the work processes, and enforce role assignment and security for the enterprise knowledge portal. The environment diagrams are shown in Figure 6-16.

Storyboards and Scripts

A storyboard contains several screen shots or pictures of the proposed enterprise knowledge portal desktop. These screen shots demonstrate how the work processes and enterprise knowledge portal software features are integrated into the user interface. You might create two or three different layouts to present how the user interface can be presented to the user. Getting the user interface correct is an important part of the design process. A few principles around the user interface design to consider include:

- *Follow a defined process*. It is possible to approach the user interface design task much like visioning by sketching several alternative approaches to the user interface, evaluating their effectiveness, and synthesizing a single-user interface theme from the best of the alternatives. The user interface vision ties the enterprise knowledge portal work processes together at the user interface level.
- *Base your design on the work process diagrams*. The work process diagrams and the focus area diagrams help guide the user interface design.

Figure 6-16. Employee performance management work process: environment diagram—employee performance objectives activity.

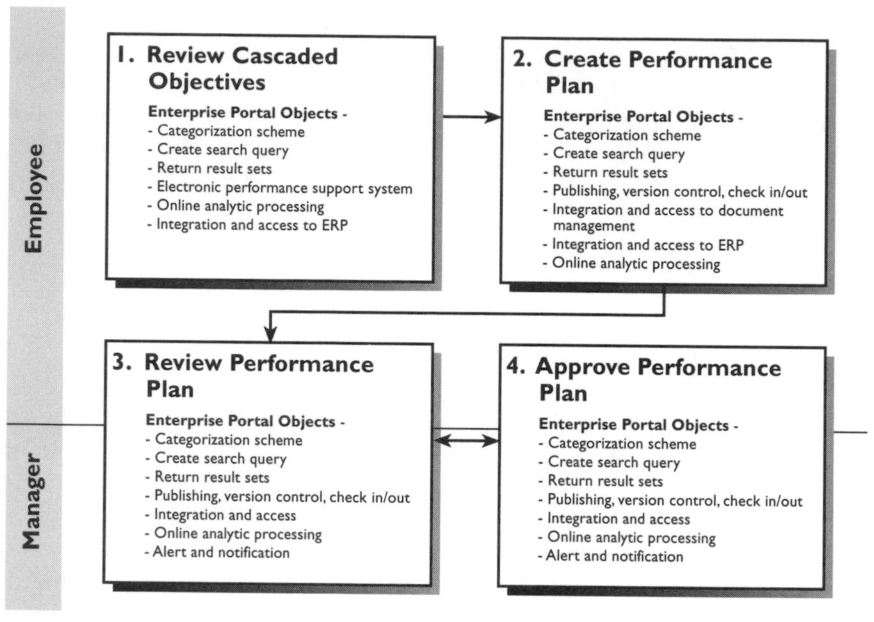

The different roles involved in the same phase of a work process need consistent and common content and enterprise knowledge portal features. The work process diagram and focus area diagrams show work broken up into multiple activities and tasks. Design the user interface to fit the work process and focus areas defined.

User interface design and implementation considerations for the portal pages included in the enterprise knowledge portal solution are represented as a storyboard. Each page will include details for the portal banner, portal menus, personalization, content page tabs, content windows, and content-relevant information. The user interface designer will incorporate color, packaging, and style to match your branding image. The collection of created storyboards shows how the enterprise knowledge portal hangs together. These pages capture the focus areas and enterprise knowledge portal objects into a single picture, showing all parts of the enterprise knowledge solution together. It might be necessary to annotate content windows by creating a series of storyboard frames to demonstrate the use of the portal page. The result demonstrates how specific targeted activities in work processes will be represented in the enterprise knowledge portal solution. Each portal page is a frame in the storyboard and captures a single scene. The portal pages or storyboard frames follow the structure of the focus area diagrams. The portal pages define what the enterprise knowledge portal is like and the consolidated sequences define the structure that underlies the work process. Walking through the storyboard's user interface will reveal problems users will have interacting with the enterprise knowledge portal. The enterprise knowledge portal storyboarding process involves seven steps:

1. *Create the portal banner.* The portal banner incorporates the organization's logo as well as other branding information or mantras that help define the organization's image. Additional content might be added to personalize the user interface with the user's name or include the path from the homepage to the portal page presented in the user interface as a navigation tool.
2. *Create the portal menu.* The portal menu is used to implement the pervasive features or portal pages frequently accessed by users. The enterprise knowledge portal features to consider include help, search, and personalization.
3. *Create the content page.* Each content page becomes a single storyboard frame. The content page contains a logical collection of the tasks contained in the focus area diagram.
4. *Create the content page tabs.* The content page tabs define a secondary portal menu. The content page tabs are the complete set of content pages used to compile the complete set of tasks identified in the focus area diagram.
5. *Create the content windows.* Each content window contains a logical subset of the collection of information contained on the content page. Content windows contain reports, documents, graphs, or links to applications or additional data points. Configuration or setup options can be made available for personalization of the content window information.
6. *Create the content-relevant information.* For each tabbed page the content-relevant information is available to provide additional navigation and detail surrounding the context of the information available in the content page. Content-relevant information can contain links to other portal pages in the enterprise knowledge portal, Internet websites, related reports, and knowledge experts. Communication, collaboration, intelligent agents, and other enterprise knowledge portal services can be made available from the content-relevant information section of the user interface.
7. *Create the storyboard frame.* Compile the portal banner, portal menu, content page, content page tabs, content windows, and content-relevant information to create a single storyboard frame. It might be useful to annotate how a user would interact with the enterprise knowledge

portal by creating a series of storyboard frames to demonstrate a user scenario.

Create the Portal Banner

Purpose: The portal banner incorporates the organization's logo as well as other branding information or mantras that help define the organization's image. Additional content might be added to personalize the user interface with the user's name or include the path from the homepage to the portal page presented in the user interface as a navigation tool.

A consistent location, look, and feel of the portal banner in the enterprise knowledge portal will create a sense of familiarity and harmony, which adds a sense of order and everything fitting together. A lack of consistency in the user interface will create a sense of disorganization and confusion. The types of design elements that should be predefined include the types of controls to be included. You want to establish standards for size, font choices, and groupings. The portal banner will provide familiarity and connection to your organization for users. Unless the user maximizes a content window, navigates away from the enterprise knowledge portal website, or opens another content window to launch a second application or other activity, the portal banner should always be on the portal page anchored in the same location.

Create a general layout for the storyboard frame and determine where the enterprise knowledge portal banner will be located in the layout. Look at Internet websites and other examples of portals to determine what users like and dislike. You will want to determine the color scheme and establish the graphics for the company logo and other graphic icons and elements to be used in the user interface. Identify the content to be included in the enterprise knowledge portal banner and where it will be included in the layout. Create several general layouts and portal banner samples to be used in variations of the storyboard frames to be reviewed and approved by users. An example is available that includes a company logo, a personalized welcome message, and a portal navigation message to show the user what portal page is currently visible and how many pages deep they are in the enterprise knowledge portal. See Figure 6-17.

Figure 6-17. Enterprise knowledge portal storyboards and scripts: portal banner.

myCOMPANY Welcome Heidi Collins

Navigation: Corporate Portal >> Home >> Business Unit >> Information Technology

Create the Portal Menu

Purpose: The portal menu is used to implement the pervasive features or portal pages frequently accessed by users. The enterprise knowledge portal features to consider include help, search, and personalization.

Menus in the enterprise knowledge portal can be a single menu item or a menu item that includes a submenu. If you need to support submenu options, consider cascading them from the higher-level menu to display a new collection of menu items. Menu names should be unique within a menu and may be repeated in different menus to represent the same action in another location or second menu. You might create a submenu when the primary menu is full, to provide a function or feature that is used infrequently, or to emphasize the relationship between menus. An ellipsis (. . .) should follow menu items that require more information before they can be completed. Menu names may be single, compound, or multiple words. A simple rule to follow is that menu names should be short. Each menu name should have a keyboard access character. The access character should be the first letter of the menu title (each menu title needs a unique keyboard option per menu). There are several ways to get started that include:

- ❒ Using the general layout for the storyboard frame and determining where the portal menu will be located in the layout.
- ❒ Determining the portal menu and submenu names.
- ❒ Establishing the behavior of the portal menu and submenus. (For example, the submenu might drop down from the main menu when the mouse is laid over the main menu option.)
- ❒ Determining the organization of the portal menu and submenus and identifying where they will be included in the layout.
- ❒ Diagramming the portal menus and submenus.

The example includes a main or primary portal menu that will open the selected enterprise knowledge portal feature or portal page when the option is clicked on. See Figure 6-18. Discussion forums, communities, and other facilitated shared communication work processes and features are

Figure 6-18. Enterprise knowledge portal storyboards and scripts: portal menu.

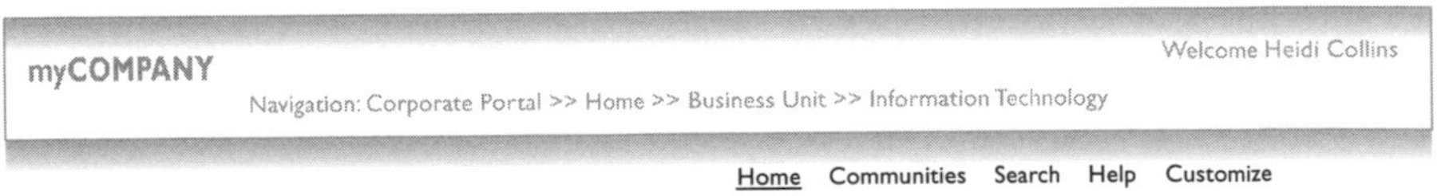

myCOMPANY

Welcome Heidi Collins

Navigation: Corporate Portal >> Home >> Business Unit >> Information Technology

Home Communities Search Help Customize

available from the "communities" menu option. There are several opportunities for team members to join in discussions or collaborate with other knowledge workers familiar with your work process, documentation, and best practices to follow.

Create the Content Page

Purpose: Each content page becomes a single storyboard frame. The content page contains a logical collection of the tasks contained in the focus area diagram.

The usability of the enterprise knowledge portal desktop depends on users' acceptance of the interface. A number of decisions must be made about the interface. As you evaluate the work processes, activities, tasks, and functions you want added to the enterprise knowledge portal, you also want several features in the user interface to be consistent. The requirements are different for activities whose primary purpose is displaying information and those activities that gather information or provide data input screens. The employee roles intended to interact with each content window or data object also influence the design of the user interface. A targeted activity that is aimed at users less familiar with a task in your organization will require more help features than a targeted activity designed to be used by experienced users. If the enterprise knowledge portal solution will be distributed internationally, language and culture considerations need to be evaluated. The design of the user interface is best approached as an iterative process. The perfect design will evolve over time.

The implementation of comfort and familiarity of features in the enterprise knowledge portal solution will determine the level of knowledge and understanding users gain from their experience interacting with the user interface. Create a collection of standards, guidelines, and best practices to be used in the overall design of the enterprise knowledge portal. Publish this information. Include a user interface designer as a member of the enterprise knowledge portal project team. Make sure you add the graphics and other user interface objects in the enterprise knowledge portal object library. The consistency of menus and toolbars across content pages as fixed user interface features is important. Knowledge workers in your organization will view the enterprise knowledge portal as the solution to accomplish work processes and will insist that the individual tasks are easy to understand and perform. Schedule walkthroughs to confirm that user interface standards are being applied consistently before portal pages are released into production. Your goal is to determine what controls are needed, the relative importance of the different elements, and the relationships between controls. Several composition issues to consider include:

- *Toolbars*. A toolbar contains buttons that provide quick access to frequently used commands and can enhance the menu interface, content windows, and other features included in the enterprise knowledge portal solution.

- *Positioning of Controls.* Not all the design elements are of equal importance in the enterprise knowledge portal. The focus of your design ensures that the most important elements are apparent to enterprise knowledge portal users. How the elements and controls are grouped together is important and should be established logically according to function or relationship. Buttons used for navigation should be grouped together to indicate their relationship to each other.
- *Form Follows Function.* The user interface should include visual clues to the function of the elements included. You might include buttons that have a three-dimensional effect to look like they should be pushed. All the buttons should have the same form throughout the enterprise knowledge portal solution.
- *Use of White Space.* To emphasize elements and improve usability, blank space should be used. This area of blank space is referred to as white space. The use of white space will remove clutter from the user interface and add focus to design elements. Consistent spacing and alignment of vertical and horizontal elements will make the design more appealing and readable.
- *Simplicity.* Divide the functionality throughout menus, submenus, toolboxes, and content page tabs to keep the individual content pages simple to use. A simple, logically organized design is always preferable. Creating groupings of information with similar purpose or functionality and minimal scrolling requirements will reduce the amount of searching and typing required by the enterprise knowledge portal users.
- *Use of Color and Images*. For applications that are going to be accessed by a large number of users, it is usually best to use neutral (conservative) colors. Small amounts of bright color can be used to emphasize or draw attention to important areas on content pages. You will want to limit the number of colors in the enterprise knowledge portal to create a consistent color scheme. Enterprise knowledge portal users will need to readily identify a function that is represented by icons or images.
- *Readability.* The font selected for use in the enterprise knowledge portal solution should be readable at different resolutions and on different types of displays. Avoid decorative fonts since they are hard to read at smaller point sizes. Once again consistency is important in the choice of fonts. Try to stick to one or two fonts in two or three different point sizes to make the enterprise knowledge portal look cohesive.

In our example, marketing team members are responsible for identifying the strategic requirements of customers, suppliers, and other external users. Additional applications and services, infrastructure and architecture, and technologies that are required to meet the organization's strategic and operational objectives are reviewed as part of the information technology responsibilities. The enterprise knowledge portal content pages will contain different content windows that are most useful for the specific responsibilities of each business unit and knowledge worker.

Create the Content Page Tabs

Purpose: The content page tabs define a secondary portal menu. The content page tabs are the complete set of content pages used to compile the complete set of tasks identified in the focus area diagram.

The content page tabs represent a secondary menu in the enterprise knowledge portal. The content page tabs are available once a portal page or a portal menu option has been selected. In several cases there are additional levels of breakout for items presented in the enterprise knowledge portal desktop. Depending on the users' role, as defined by a metadata repository attribute value or personalization settings created and saved by the user, a unique collection of content page tabs will be presented in the content page. The example includes content page tabs for projects, applications, services, infrastructure, and knowledge base. See Figure 6-19.

Create the Content Windows

Purpose: Each content window contains a logical subset of the collection of information contained on the content page. Content windows contain reports, documents, graphs, or links to applications or additional data points. Configuration or setup options can be made available for personalization of the content window information.

The next element to create is the content windows that will be included in the content page area of the portal page. You will want to consider a content window a unique design element. In many cases a content window can logically belong on more than one portal page. Users might add the same content window to multiple portal pages or the content window might be included on several different portal pages due to the relation-

Figure 6-19. Enterprise knowledge portal storyboards and scripts: content page tabs.

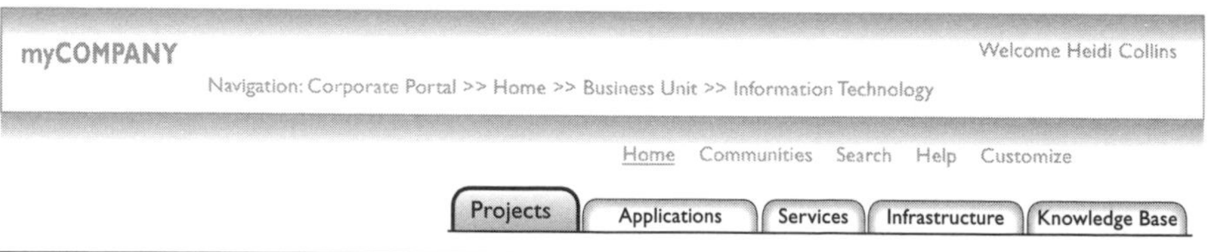

ship the content has with the surrounding content windows. It is much easier for users to navigate the enterprise knowledge portal and locate information if material, reports, and links can be found in several locations. Some best practices to consider are to establish a set of standard sizes for content windows and create a collection of standards, guidelines, and best practices to be used in the development of content windows. Add the content windows enterprise knowledge portal objects and other supporting enterprise knowledge portal objects that provide connectivity to data sources or other services in the enterprise knowledge portal object library.

There are several formats and uses for how information is presented in content windows. In most cases hyperlinks are contained within content windows to perform an action or drill into additional information. Many content windows contain report summary information with hyperlinks to continue to focus on a dimension and drill into the details. Hyperlinks can behave in other ways. They might be configured to navigate to other sections in the same document or open new content windows with new information. Users will interact with content information to submit requests and complete online forms. The content window will contain a title bar that includes a toolbar or drop-down menu to provide additional functionality. These include collapsing the content window to a title bar or expanding to display the entire content window. Maximizing and minimizing allow the content window to fill the user screen or return to the standard content window within the content page. Additional features that are common include forwarding mail, creating discussion documents, notifying a knowledge expert associated with the content, and refreshing to update the information presented in the content window. There are several ways to get started that include:

- ❐ Creating a content window for each task in the focus area diagram mockup.
- ❐ Creating additional views of the same content window to annotate the functions and links where additional detail is needed to illustrate the behavior and features of the task. (Complete this process for each task in the focus area diagram that requires additional detail.)
- ❐ Establishing the collection and behavior of content window toolbar features. (For example, the maximize feature might expand the content window to fill the screen or open a second content window to present a larger or expanded image of the content.)
- ❐ Identifying the size and location of content windows in the layout of the content page.
- ❐ Diagramming the content windows.

The example includes content windows for an information technology review task. See Figure 6-20. To demonstrate peer-to-peer computing or

Figure 6-20. Enterprise knowledge portal storyboards and scripts: content windows.

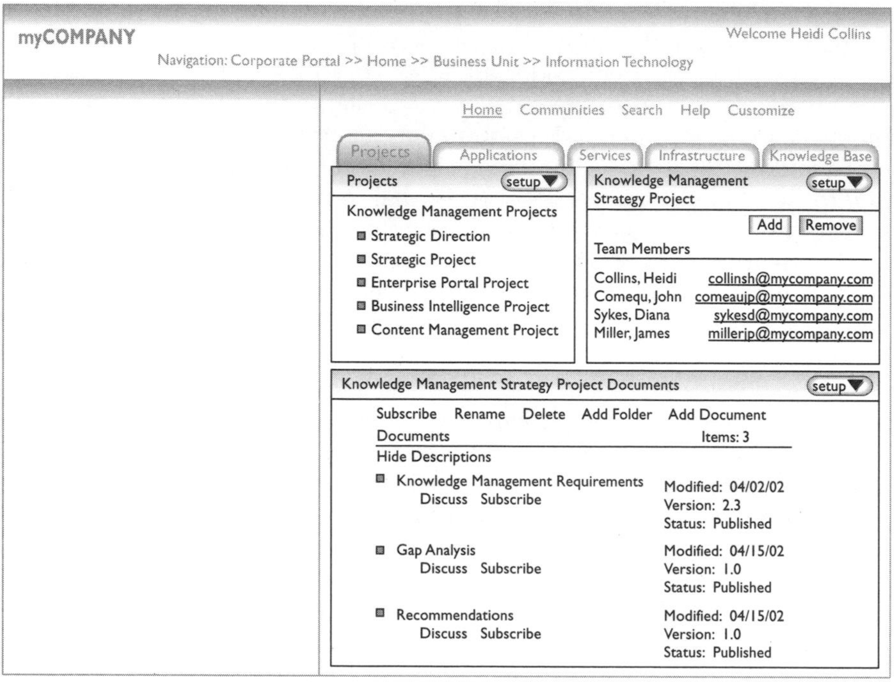

myCOMPANY
Welcome Heidi Collins
Navigation: Corporate Portal >> Home >> Business Unit >> Information Technology

Home Communities Search Help Customize

Projects | Applications | Services | Infrastructure | Knowledge Base

Projects (setup▼)
Knowledge Management Projects
- Strategic Direction
- Strategic Project
- Enterprise Portal Project
- Business Intelligence Project
- Content Management Project

Knowledge Management Strategy Project (setup▼)
Add | Remove
Team Members

Collins, Heidi	collinsh@mycompany.com
Comequ, John	comeaujp@mycompany.com
Sykes, Diana	sykesd@mycompany.com
Miller, James	millerjp@mycompany.com

Knowledge Management Strategy Project Documents (setup▼)
Subscribe Rename Delete Add Folder Add Document
Documents Items: 3
Hide Descriptions

- Knowledge Management Requirements — Discuss Subscribe — Modified: 04/02/02 Version: 2.3 Status: Published
- Gap Analysis — Discuss Subscribe — Modified: 04/15/02 Version: 1.0 Status: Published
- Recommendations — Discuss Subscribe — Modified: 04/15/02 Version: 1.0 Status: Published

other online review work processes, additional storyboard frames can be annotated. You will need to determine when supporting storyboard frames are required to explain the work process in the appropriate level of detail. When the content is different you will want to create multiple sets of storyboard frames to illustrate how a collection of user roles interact in the enterprise knowledge portal looking at unique content.

Create the Content-Relevant Information

Purpose: For each tabbed page the content-relevant information is available to provide additional navigation and detail surrounding the context of the information available in the content page. Content-relevant information can contain links to other portal pages in the enterprise knowledge portal, Internet websites, related reports, and knowledge experts. Communication, collaboration, intelligent agents, and other enterprise knowledge portal services can be made available from the content-relevant information section of the user interface.

Based on the context of the information available in the content windows of the portal page, the content-relevant information of the enterprise knowledge portal offers a wide variety of content and services. The content-relevant information is unique for each role involved in the task and focuses on specific information needed to complete responsibilities. Before the advent of the enterprise knowledge portal, knowledge workers had to open several applications from their workstations to complete different activities. The enterprise knowledge portal desktop brings the ability to complete a variety of activities from a single location.

The content-relevant information provides an additional benefit by bringing new procedures, tips and tricks, lessons learned, and related material to users while they are doing their job. The interactive mapping of menus and content with all information contained in the content windows allows content to pivot or focus on a single customer or any other selection made by the user as he requires different levels of detail to perform his job. In addition there will be a collection of links that open applications, navigate to other content pages, navigate to websites, and access other documents and services that are included as content-relevant information in the portal page. You want the collection of material that can be accessed from the content-relevant information section to be context-sensitive to the content page and content windows on the screen. Since the content-relevant information is based on the context of the current portal page, the categories available in the content-relevant information section can be static or dynamic, depending on the requirements of the roles using the portal page. There are several ways to get started that include:

- ❐ Using the general layout for the storyboard frame and determining the layout options for the content-relevant information section. (In some enterprise portal products an icon will expand and collapse the content-relevant information section when clicked to provide additional screen area for users to work with content windows.)
- ❐ Determining the organization and naming of the hyperlinks in the content-relevant information.
- ❐ Establishing the behavior of the content-relevant information hyperlinks. (For example, an icon might be clicked to expand and collapse categories of options available in the content-relevant information.)
- ❐ Determining the organization of the content-relevant information. (Identify where they will be included in the layout.)
- ❐ Adding personal information management collection of enterprise knowledge portal objects. (These elements might allow users to add links or shortcuts to their favorite portal pages and other intranet and Internet URLs, organize personal agents that perform actions frequently used for notification or run queries to update or gather information, or switch between several predefined portal page configurations. These personal information management requirements

could be constructed as a content window that a user could add, move, or remove on content pages rather than fixed in the content-relevant information section of the portal page.)

❒ Diagramming the content-relevant information section of the storyboard frame.

The example is updated to include the content-relevant information section. The content-relevant information section can be collapsed and expanded using the icon to the left of the primary portal menu. Collapsing the content-relevant information section provides additional screen space for the content page and content windows. See Figure 6-21.

Create the Storyboard Frame

Purpose: Compile the portal banner, portal menu, content page, content page tabs, content windows, and content-relevant information to create a single storyboard frame. It might be useful to annotate how a user would interact with the enterprise knowledge portal by creating a series of storyboard frames to demonstrate a user scenario.

Figure 6-21. Enterprise knowledge portal storyboards and scripts: content-relevant information.

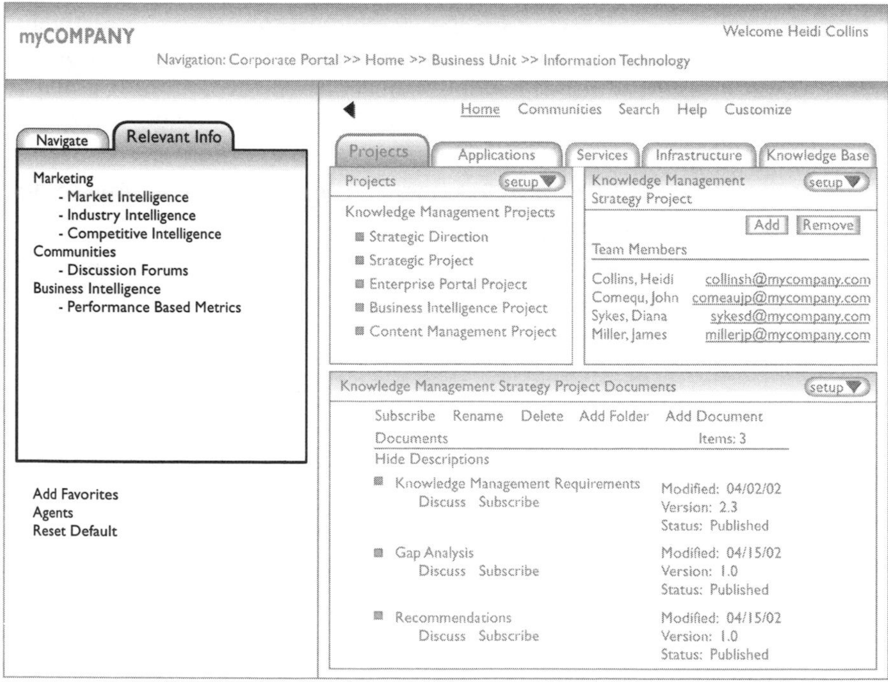

The storyboard defines how the enterprise knowledge portal will behave and organizes functions in a way that makes sense for the user. Based on this, you can refine the overall methodology for additional details that are not clear or that are invalid. A typical storyboard will incorporate all of the following elements:

- Work process diagrams
- Focus area diagrams
- Content network diagrams
- Focus area diagrams with targeted content overlaid
- Focus area diagrams with targeted content links overlaid
- Focus area diagrams with presentation features overlaid
- Environment diagrams

The collection of portal objects used to manage the enterprise knowledge portal is documented in the enterprise knowledge portal object library. The meaning and usage of the portal objects including their relationship to work process diagrams, focus area diagrams, and content network diagrams are cataloged in the library. The collection of enterprise knowledge portal methodology diagrams will document the enterprise knowledge portal solution and provide a map to knowledge throughout your organization.

You will need to compile the collection of storyboard frames to demonstrate the functionality outlined in the work process and focus area diagrams. Review the storyboard frames with the users to validate that the enterprise knowledge portal solution will meet expectations and objectives. The example includes the following collection of storyboard frames to complete a project initiation activity. These include:

- Identify organization objectives. (See Figure 6-22.)
- Prioritize organization objectives. (See Figure 6-23.)
- Review applications and services. (See Figure 6-24.)
- Review infrastructure and architecture. (See Figure 6-25.)
- Identify technology requirements. (See Figure 6-26.)
- Identify vendors in the market. (See Figure 6-27.)
- Information technology review. (See Figure 6-28.)

MYCOMPANY CASE STUDY

The storyboard frames have been created for the employee performance objectives activity. These included the following activities:

Figure 6-22. Project initiation activity: identify organization objectives task.

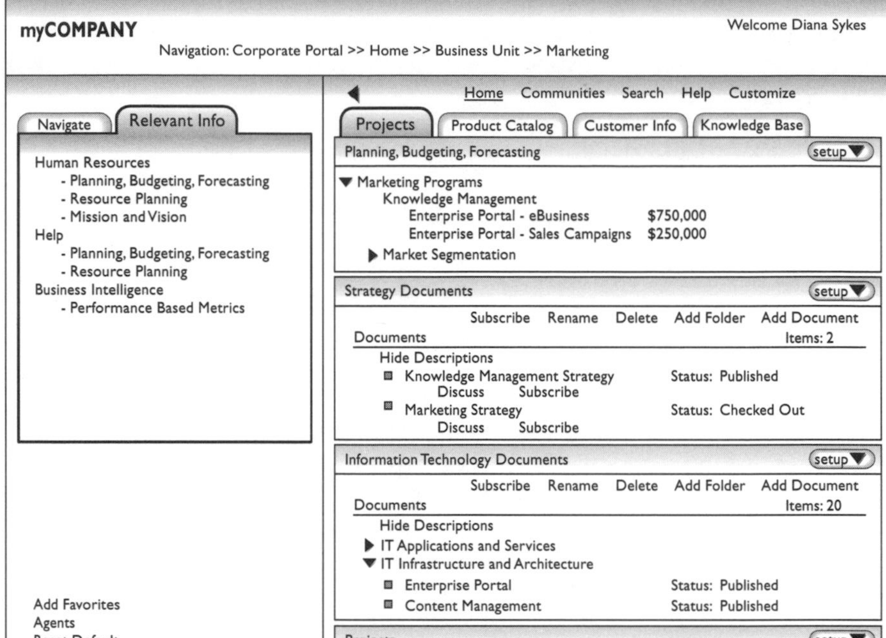

❒ *Review cascaded objectives task*. The knowledge worker opens the enterprise knowledge portal to the human resources portal page and selects the performance enhancement content page tab. The first content window illustrates the employee performance management work process. The knowledge worker clicks on the targeted activity, in this case the employee performance objectives activity. Content windows that are associated with the employee performance objectives task are displayed on the content page. These include:

1. *The First Content Window.* The first content window shows the employee performance management documents (collapsed content window). Performance management documents include completed performance plan documents from previous years, completed performance evaluation documents from previous years, and one-on-one interviews completed throughout the year. Only the documents that are specific to the knowledge worker will appear in the content window. The example performance plan documents to use when creating the current year performance plan will appear

Figure 6-23. Project initiation activity: prioritize organization objectives task.

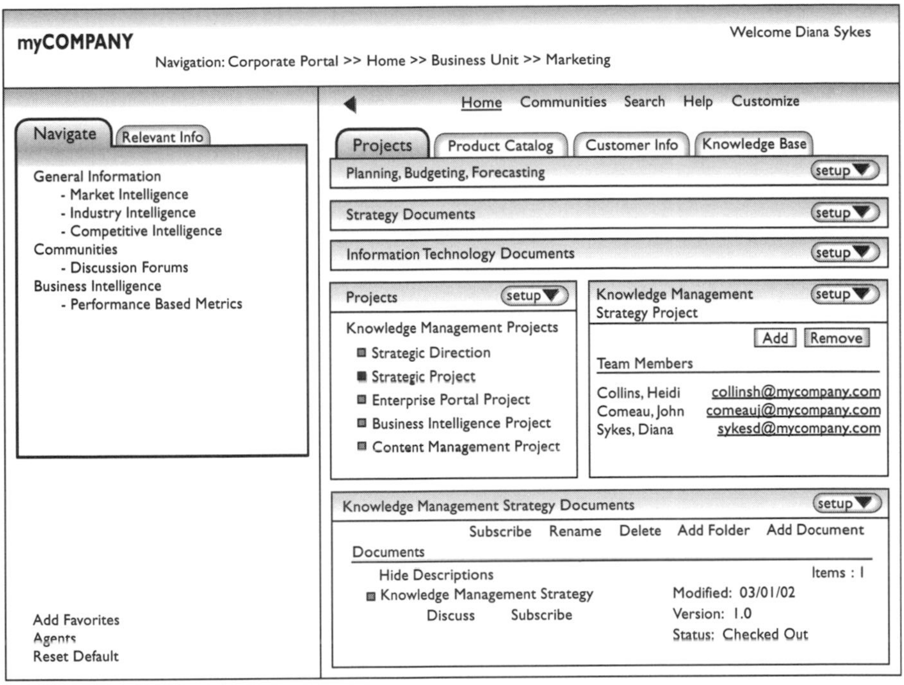

myCOMPANY
Welcome Diana Sykes
Navigation: Corporate Portal >> Home >> Business Unit >> Marketing

Home Communities Search Help Customize

Navigate | Relevant Info

General Information
- Market Intelligence
- Industry Intelligence
- Competitive Intelligence
Communities
- Discussion Forums
Business Intelligence
- Performance Based Metrics

Add Favorites
Agents
Reset Default

Projects | Product Catalog | Customer Info | Knowledge Base

Planning, Budgeting, Forecasting (setup)

Strategy Documents (setup)

Information Technology Documents (setup)

Projects (setup)
Knowledge Management Projects
- Strategic Direction
- Strategic Project
- Enterprise Portal Project
- Business Intelligence Project
- Content Management Project

Knowledge Management Strategy Project (setup)
Add Remove
Team Members
Collins, Heidi collinsh@mycompany.com
Comeau, John comeauj@mycompany.com
Sykes, Diana sykesd@mycompany.com

Knowledge Management Strategy Documents (setup)
Subscribe Rename Delete Add Folder Add Document
Documents
Hide Descriptions Items : 1
- Knowledge Management Strategy Modified: 03/01/02
Discuss Subscribe Version: 1.0
Status: Checked Out

in the content window for everyone with access to employee performance management documents.

2. *The Second Content Window.* The second content window contains the planning, budgeting, and forecasting documents to review the cascaded objectives for the organization and the individual business units.
3. *The Third Content Window.* The third content window contains the performance-based metrics for the knowledge worker. This information is focused for the knowledge worker to review her current skills and ratings. Each skill can be drilled down into to see the specific gaps the knowledge worker should focus on to include in her next performance plan.

In the relative-content information section of the portal page, there are hyperlinks to quickly access resource planning information created in a previous task of the work process, navigate to performance evaluation history in one quick click, review the mission and vision of the organization and the business units, or navigate to the employee performance management help solution for additional assistance using the

Figure 6-24. Project initiation activity: review applications and services task.

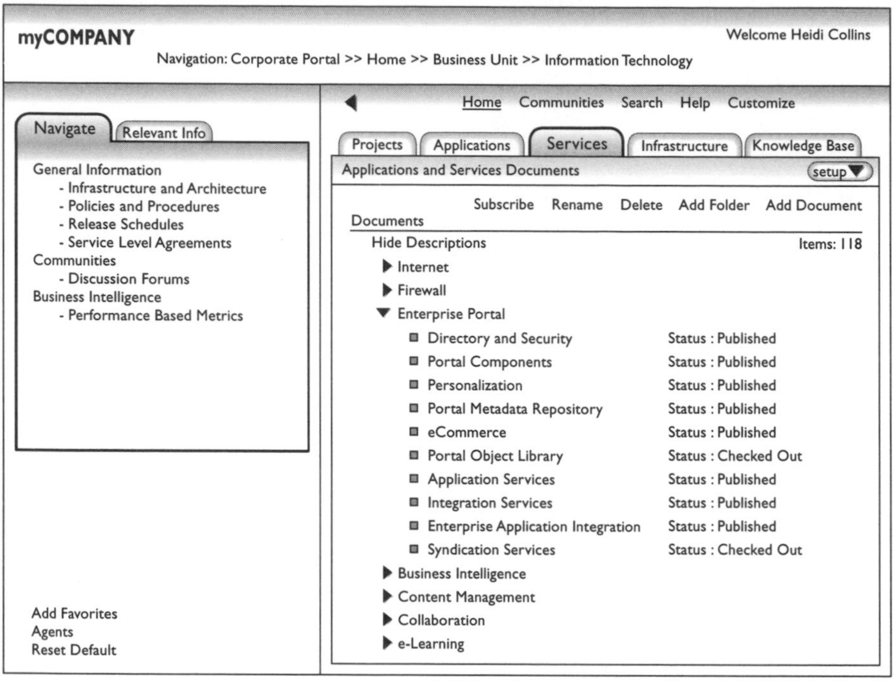

employee performance management work process. See Figure 6-29.

- *Create a performance plan task.* The knowledge worker opens the employee performance management documents content window and clicks on "add document" to create the new year's performance plan. The content window to complete the performance plan document is displayed on the desktop for the knowledge worker to complete. The performance plan document can be saved and revisited as the knowledge worker thinks through his objectives for the coming year or reviews the additional information that helps him clarify his objectives. Once the knowledge worker has completed his performance plan document, he clicks "submit" for the manager to be able to read and edit the document. Additionally, a notification is sent to the manager that the document is available in the employee performance management documents to review. See Figure 6-30.
- *Review the performance plan.* The manager clicks on the notification from the navigation tab of the content-relevant informa-

Figure 6-25. Project initiation activity: review infrastructure and architecture task.

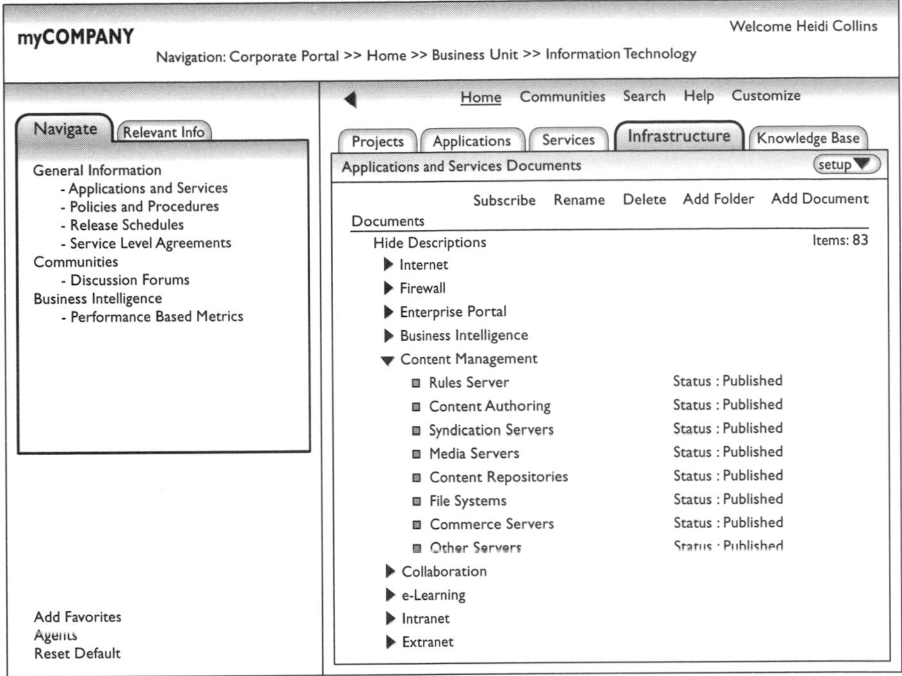

tion section to navigate to the employee performance management documents and review the submitted performance plan or she can follow the similar process that the knowledge worker followed in the first storyboard frame. The manager will have access to all the performance plans that have been submitted by the knowledge workers that she manages. When a performance plan is selected, a content window will display the selected performance plan document. The manager will be able to suggest modifications and click "submit" to start the review process over with the knowledge worker or click "approve" to accept the performance plan document. See Figure 6-31.

- *Approve the performance plan.* The storyboard frame continues to follow the manager to illustrate additional content windows available to verify that a match between skills and resource planning requirements and approved performance plans will allow the business unit and organization objectives to be achieved. The performance-based metrics content window can be drilled into to see additional details on skills found throughout the organization. See Figure 6-32.

Figure 6-26. Project initiation activity: identify technology requirements task.

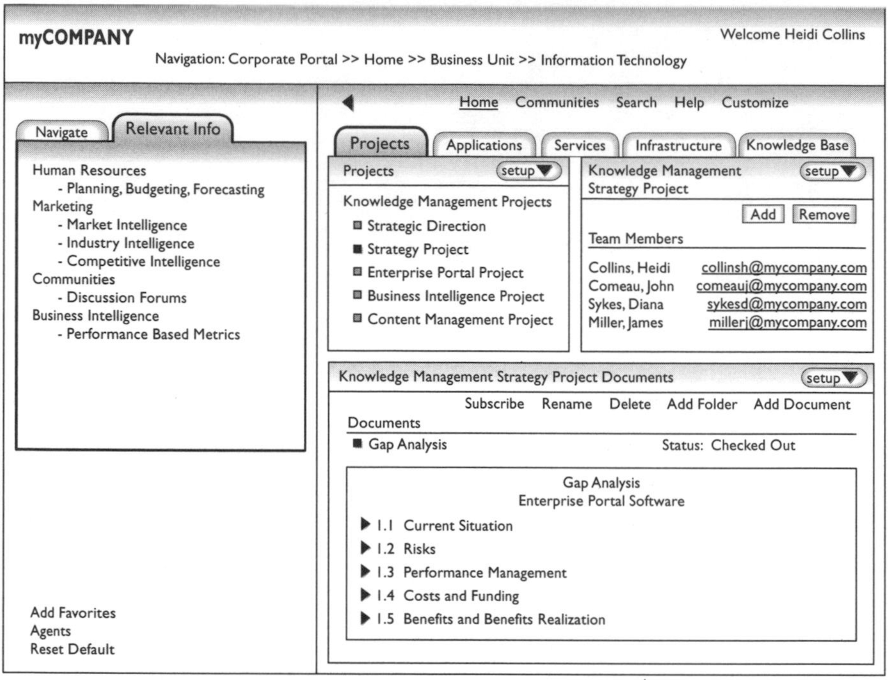

myCOMPANY
Welcome Heidi Collins
Navigation: Corporate Portal >> Home >> Business Unit >> Information Technology

Home Communities Search Help Customize

Navigate | Relevant Info

Human Resources
- Planning, Budgeting, Forecasting
Marketing
- Market Intelligence
- Industry Intelligence
- Competitive Intelligence
Communities
- Discussion Forums
Business Intelligence
- Performance Based Metrics

Add Favorites
Agents
Reset Default

Projects | Applications | Services | Infrastructure | Knowledge Base

Projects (setup)
Knowledge Management Projects
- Strategic Direction
- Strategy Project
- Enterprise Portal Project
- Business Intelligence Project
- Content Management Project

Knowledge Management Strategy Project (setup)
Add Remove
Team Members

Collins, Heidi	collinsh@mycompany.com
Comeau, John	comeauj@mycompany.com
Sykes, Diana	sykesd@mycompany.com
Miller, James	millerj@mycompany.com

Knowledge Management Strategy Project Documents (setup)
Subscribe Rename Delete Add Folder Add Document
Documents
- Gap Analysis Status: Checked Out

Gap Analysis
Enterprise Portal Software
- 1.1 Current Situation
- 1.2 Risks
- 1.3 Performance Management
- 1.4 Costs and Funding
- 1.5 Benefits and Benefits Realization

Key Points

The enterprise knowledge portal methodology is an orderly procedure to collect and document the information needed to design, build, deploy, and maintain an effective enterprise knowledge portal. The methodology is focused on supporting information and the flow of information and delivering all of it into the enterprise knowledge portal. There are several elements to define and document in the enterprise knowledge portal methodology. These include:

- *Defining Business Objects*. A business object is a collection of information designed to achieve a specific business purpose. Examples include invoices, product catalogs, and medical insurance claims.
- *Breakdown into Content Elements*. Multiple content elements form a business object. Content elements are stored in different systems and can be structured or unstructured.
- *Outlining Work Flow Systems*. This element electronically stores business object content elements. Codify the rules for dynamic assembly of business objects, do work flow processing, and deliver these business objects in the appropriate context for customer use.

Figure 6-27. Prospecting activity: identify vendors in the market task.

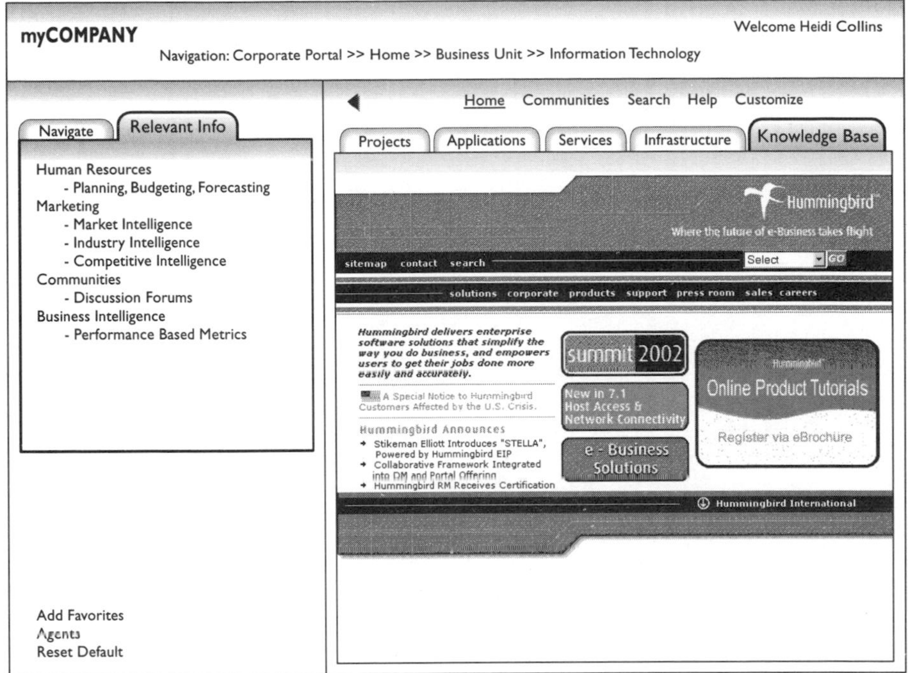

❐ *Documenting Business Object Context.* This element breaks down into five subcategories:

1. *Work Process Diagrams.* These complete the documentation that defines the structure and purpose of the business object.
2. *Focus Area Diagrams.* These diagrams document information about the activities, tasks, and user roles associated with the business object.
3. *The Content Network.* The content network documents the enterprise entities that provide content to the business objects and assign information owners to manage and maintain the information.
4. *User Context.* This structures the business object as appropriate for delivery via the enterprise information portal.
5. *The Presentation Filter.* The filter documents how the presentation of the business object will be made to the individual, encompassing the user role and security requirements.

❐ *Identifying Business Rules.* A business rule engine dynamically assembles business objects, controls the work flow and processing of business objects, and enforces role assignment and security.

Figure 6-28. Project initiation activity: IT review task.

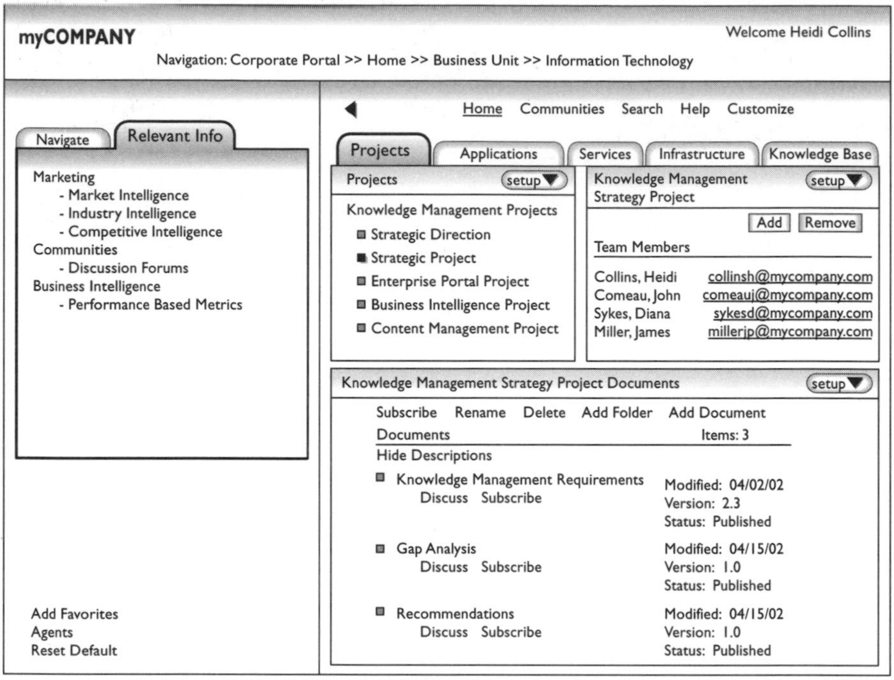

- *Designing the System.* Remember to design the system to meet any regulatory and content retention requirements.

- *Integrating the Enterprise Knowledge Portal.* Integrate the enterprise knowledge portal with key systems, e-mail (automatic notification), and office document creation.

The execution of the enterprise knowledge portal methodology will be integrated into the execution of your enterprise knowledge portal projects. The enterprise knowledge portal methodology will provide the details needed to deploy a cohesive and consistent enterprise knowledge portal for users to work effectively with information and each other. The template collection is used to provide the details needed to outline a logical path forward to implement your enterprise knowledge portal. These include:

- Business objects
  1. Work process diagram template
  2. Focus area diagram template
- Content elements
  1. Content network spreadsheet

Figure 6-29. Enterprise performance management work progress: employee performance objectives activity—review created objectives task.

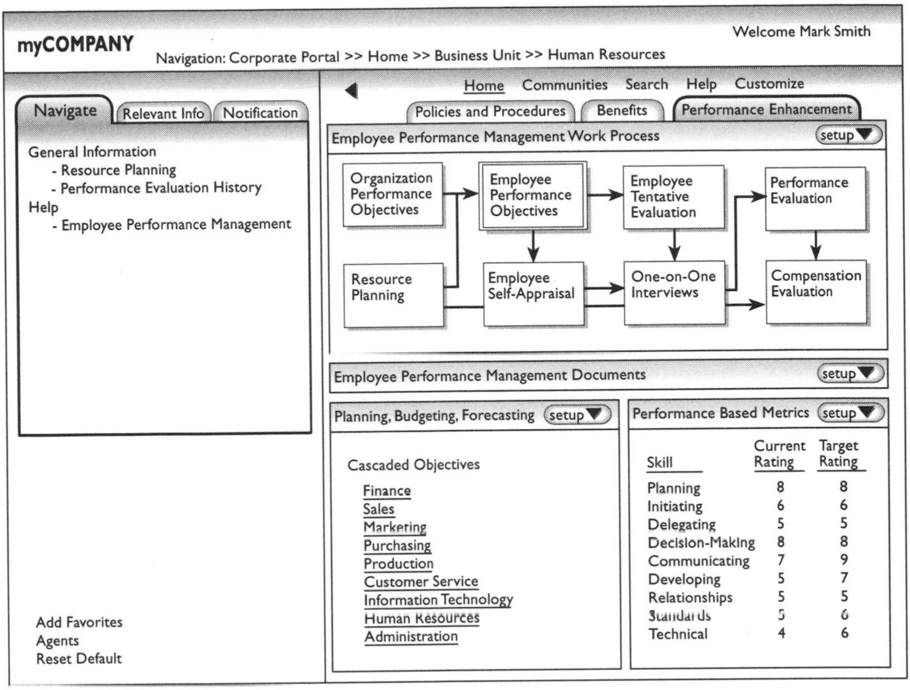

- ❒ Business object context
  1. Focus area diagram with content overlaid
  2. Focus area diagram with content links overlaid
  3. Focus area diagram with presentation filters overlaid
- ❒ Business rules
  1. Environment diagram template
- ❒ Storyboards and scripts
  1. Enterprise knowledge portal storyboard template

The activities to create your enterprise knowledge portal map are complete. Your enterprise knowledge portal program has been approved and the organization to support the enterprise knowledge portal is in place. The enterprise knowledge portal program outlined several development and infrastructure projects to successfully implement the enterprise knowledge portal. You will use standard project management and system development life cycle best practices combined with the enterprise knowledge portal methodology to complete individual projects. The activities you will have

Figure 6-30. Enterprise performance management work progress: employee performance objectives activity—create performance plan task.

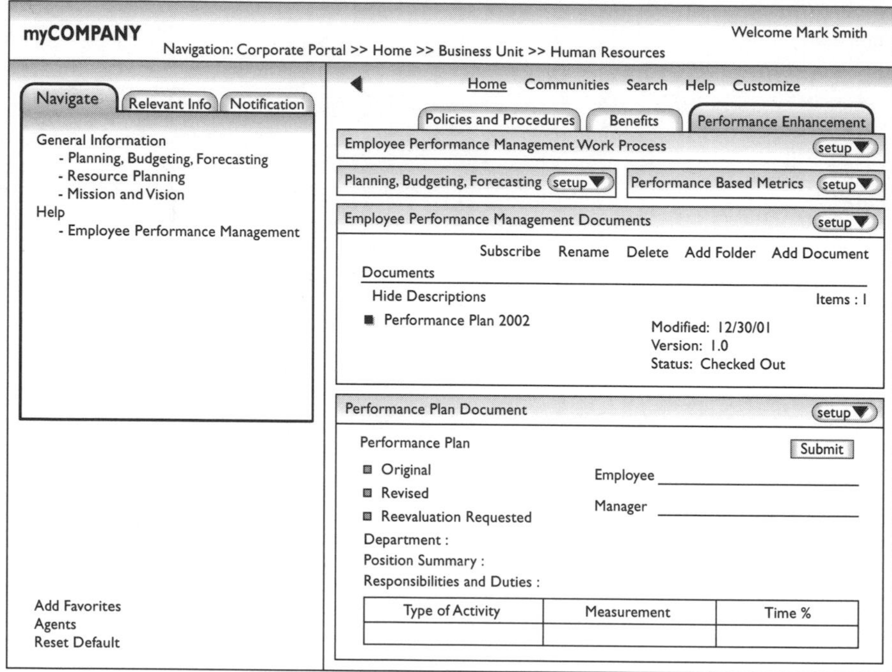

completed before applying the enterprise knowledge portal methodology include:

- Creating the employee performance management enterprise knowledge portal project charter, project plan, and quality assurance plan
- Establishing the enterprise knowledge portal IT–enabling framework requirements
- Identifying unique enterprise knowledge portal requirements
- Creating the knowledge organization system

The activities to apply the enterprise knowledge portal methodology include:

- Documenting your business objects
  1. Map targeted activities into the work process
  2. Add focus area diagrams for each targeted activity
  3. Add focus area diagrams for each user role

Figure 6-31. Enterprise performance management work progress: employee performance objectives activity—review performance plan task.

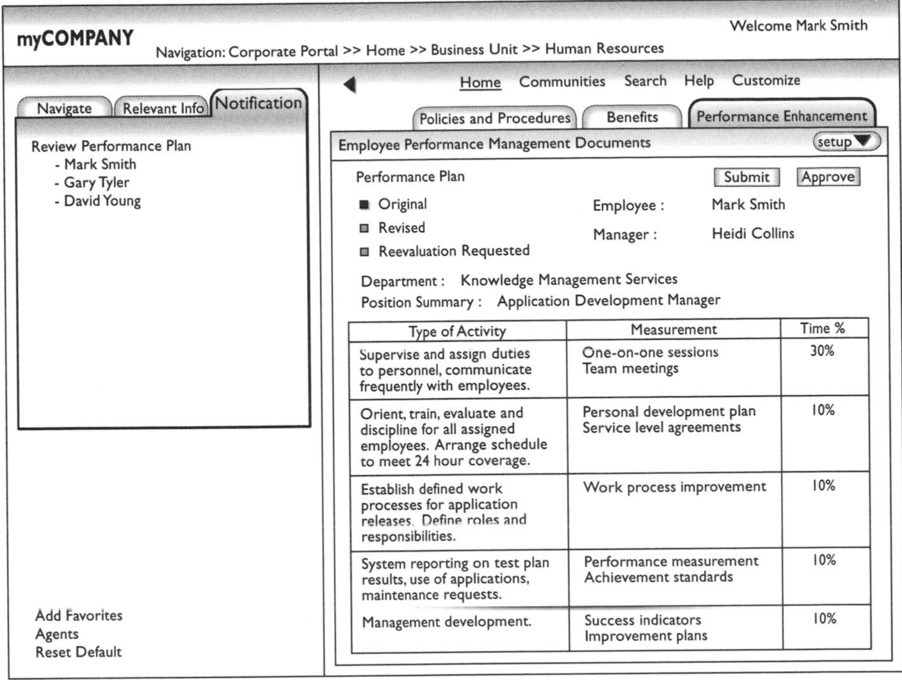

Type of Activity	Measurement	Time %
Supervise and assign duties to personnel, communicate frequently with employees.	One-on-one sessions Team meetings	30%
Orient, train, evaluate and discipline for all assigned employees. Arrange schedule to meet 24 hour coverage.	Personal development plan Service level agreements	10%
Establish defined work processes for application releases. Define roles and responsibilities.	Work process improvement	10%
System reporting on test plan results, use of applications, maintenance requests.	Performance measurement Achievement standards	10%
Management development.	Success indicators Improvement plans	10%

- ❒ Documenting your content elements
  1. Create the content network
  2. Identify enterprise entities
  3. Assign information owners
- ❒ Documenting your business object context
  1. Document user context
  2. Determine the presentation filters
  3. Outline the business rules
- ❒ Documenting your storyboards and scripts
  1. Create the portal banner
  2. Create the portal menu
  3. Create the content page
  4. Create the content page tabs
  5. Create the content windows
  6. Create the content-relevant information
  7. Create the storyboard frame

Figure 6-32. Enterprise performance management work progress: employee performance objectives activity—approve performance plan task.

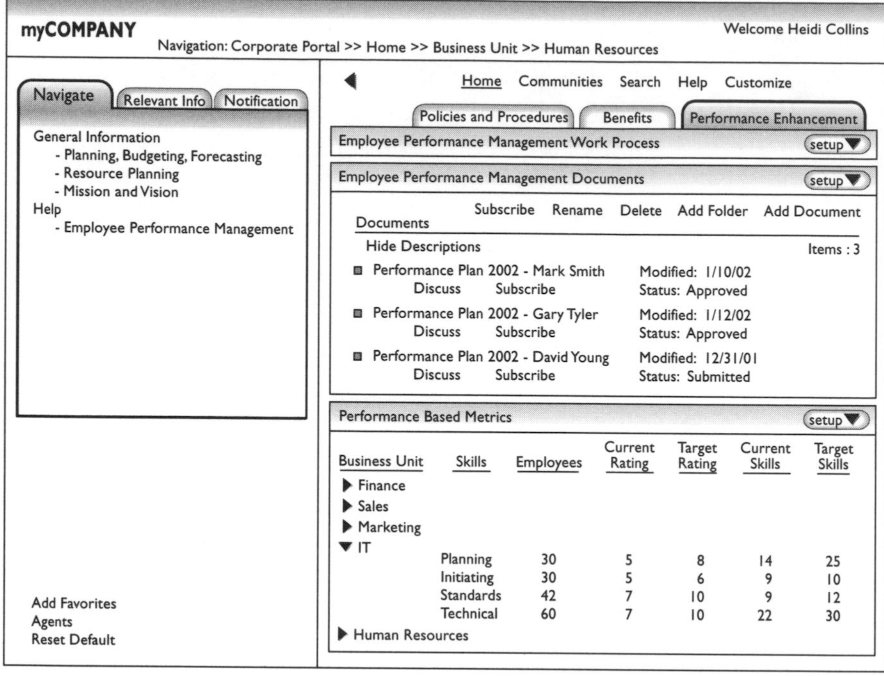

Once you have completed the design of the enterprise knowledge portal for the scope outlined in the enterprise knowledge portal project charter, the next effort is to establish the associated financial metrics. Chapter 7 provides a series of spreadsheets for establishing a return on investment for the enterprise knowledge portal project.

7

Financial Metrics

"Knowledge assets, like money or equipment, exist and are worth cultivating only in the context of strategy."

Thomas A. Stewart, *Intellectual Capital: The New Wealth of Organizations*

There are three inevitable questions that will arise when developing your enterprise knowledge portal initiative: What is this going to cost? Will the enterprise knowledge portal be worth the investment? How can I measure my results to determine if the enterprise knowledge portal solution has been effective? These can be difficult questions to answer. You will want to include some information on the return for "managing knowledge." This is even more difficult because the benefits are much less classically measurable. These benefits include:

- Faster, simplified partnering strategies
- Greater retention of expertise
- Better and more effective frontline decision making

You will want to continually develop, deploy, and measure versions of the enterprise knowledge portal. Each iterative deployment will include improvements identified by existing users and additions of new work processes. You will want to analyze the number of expected users inside and outside your organization, labor savings, direct reduction in expenses, direct increases in revenue, and project costs. You can optionally include a cost and benefit analysis to measure increased satisfaction and soft dollar benefits.

The return on investment spreadsheet focuses on the ratio of the estimated total positive benefits to the estimated total costs of the enterprise knowledge portal project. You will usually create the ROI analysis for the first year. You will want to create an ROI analysis for each phase or iteration of the enterprise knowledge portal solution. This will allow you to follow and track the financial results associated with your knowledge management initiatives to present to management and support your continuous improvement efforts. The ROI analysis consists of two primary calculations: ROI and payback period. Each is defined as follows:

- *Return on Investment.* Return on investment is the percentage of benefit relative to total cost over a period of time (usually a year). Most organizations look for at least an annualized ROI of 20 percent, although some ROI calculations may reach 200 percent or more. The calculation is as follows:

  ROI = estimate total positive benefits / estimated total costs.

- *Payback Period.* Payback period is the length of time required for the benefits to exceed the costs. It represents the budgetary cycle or cash flow of your organization. The payback period calculation is often valuable in helping your organization decide when to begin a project or discussing when to begin any subsequent phases of the enterprise knowledge portal solution. A very rapid payback period is three to four months; your organization should expect a payback period of nine to ten months.

A second ROI analysis is conducted at the conclusion of the enterprise knowledge portal project phase to verify that your organization is receiving the benefits that were originally estimated. On large projects, an interim ROI analysis is also run in order to:

- Evaluate if project costs are rising.
- Reevaluate if the business requirements or environment is changing.
- Determine if the benefits for the enterprise knowledge portal project are over- or underestimated.

The ROI spreadsheet has six sections. The steps involved in creating a simple ROI calculation include:

1. *Human Resources Information.* Identify the user community, human resource, and payroll information that will benefit from the enterprise knowledge portal solution.

2. *Labor Savings.* Outline in detail the measurements defined to reduce labor costs through the implementation of the enterprise knowledge portal and your knowledge management initiatives.
3. *Cost Savings.* Add the target areas controlled by your organization that will be focused on to reduce expenses.
4. *Increased Revenue.* Define how revenue will be increased from new sources within the first year. In addition, you will want to include how revenue will increase from existing sources in the first year.
5. *Project Costs.* Identify the one-time project implementation and development costs. It is also important to include recurring support and maintenance costs that will be incurred after the first year.
6. *Analysis and Results.* Summarize the ROI results to determine the expected ROI percentage and payback period or breakeven date. You will want to include expected benefits, investment, and cash flow.

There are different approaches, each with a variety of definitions that can be used to evaluate the financial consequences of implementing an enterprise knowledge portal. It is important that the enterprise knowledge portal project is represented in financial terms. To incorporate this information you will have to know the time period evaluated and the assumptions used to calculate the financial metrics. The result is an effective conclusion used to support the objectives of the enterprise knowledge portal project. The conclusions and formal recommendations are used to track total benefits and total costs associated with the enterprise knowledge portal project. The benefits and costs include:

Total Benefits

- Direct increases in revenue
- Direct reduction in expenses
- Increased satisfaction of key stakeholders (measured through surveys and usability acceptance of the enterprise knowledge portal)

Total Costs

- Direct costs (e.g., software, hardware, services, training)
- Indirect costs (e.g., decreased productivity during system changeover, parallel system support)

Human Resources Information

The human resources business unit can usually provide the information you need to complete this section of the return on investment spreadsheet.

If you need to provide details with respect to soft benefits or nonfinancial benefits associated with knowledge management initiatives and the enterprise knowledge portal solution, you will want to consider creating a cost and benefit analysis to supplement the ROI spreadsheet. You are looking for the following human resources information, so be certain to:

- ❒ Enter the attributes or metadata used to uniquely identify your ROI calculation spreadsheet.
- ❒ Identify the expected number of internal users for the enterprise portal (employees, contractors, knowledge workers, etc.). Enter this information as a number.
- ❒ Identify the expected number of external users (suppliers, partners, customers, etc.). Enter this information as a number.
- ❒ Include standard benefit costs that include benefits, Social Security taxes, workers' compensation, insurance, allocated administrative overhead, etc. This information is entered as a percentage of overall compensation.
- ❒ Include average compensation for users of the enterprise portal solution. Compensation includes salary, overtime, and bonuses. This information is entered as a dollar figure.

Human Resources Information—The First Step

Purpose: Identify the user community, human resource, and payroll information that will benefit from the enterprise knowledge portal solution.

The human resources information targets the number of users impacted or targeted to use the enterprise knowledge portal solution. Several formulas created as quick ROI calculations are derived from the human resources information provided. If you are planning to reference these ROI spreadsheets as you continue to deploy new iterations of the enterprise knowledge portal, you will want to summarize the information from individual ROI spreadsheets to understand the benefits and costs that the collection of enterprise knowledge portal project phases have had on your organization.

The total user community is the number of internal users added to the number of external users. The formula is represented as:

$$\text{User community} = \text{internal users} + \text{external users}$$

The human resources information or total compensation is the average compensation for one user added to the standard benefit overhead cost. The standard benefit overhead cost is usually derived as a percentage of the average compensation. The formula is represented as:

Total compensation = (1 + standard benefit overhead cost) × average compensation.

MYCOMPANY CASE STUDY

The user community is targeted to be all internal users. There are no external users that will have access to the employee performance management work process. An example of the human resources information for the employee performance management work process ROI calculation is shown in Figure 7-1.

Labor Savings

Review templates in your organization for ROI or other financial metrics and use these to present financial metrics for the enterprise knowledge portal solution. Determine if additional or a different cross-section of labor savings metrics need to be tracked and managed by your organization. You are looking for the following labor savings information, so be certain to follow these six steps:

Figure 7-1. Employee performance management ROI: human resources information.

Return On Investment
Version 1.0

Basic Information

Project Name	B2E: Employee Performance Management
Estimated Project Start Date	1-Jan-2002
Internal Project Leader	Heidi Collins

User Community

Expected number of Internal Users (employees, contractors, knowledge workers, etc.)	2,500
Expected number of External Users (suppliers, partners, customers, etc.)	0
Total	2,500

Human Resources Information

		Typical Range
What is the standard benefit overhead cost? Includes: benefits, Social Security taxes, workman's compensation, insurance, allocated administrative overhead, etc.	35%	35% to 50%
What is the average compensation (salary, overtime and bonuses) for the users of this solution?	$35,000	$30,000 to $100,000
Total	$47,250	

1. *Enter fewer full-time employees (FTE) as a number.* This number includes how many FTEs can be reduced through natural attrition, redeployment within the organization, reduced support and administration for FTEs, reduced future hiring, and lower payroll costs. Total benefit received is equal to: Total benefit = A × fewer full-time employees.
   (A) Human resources worksheet: total compensation. (See Step One.)
2. *Enter fewer steps as a percentage of productivity.* This percentage is an average increase in productivity for all users, associated with easier and faster data entry methods, eliminated or faster approvals, automated steps, online analysis, faster access to information, faster decision making, faster methods of communication, less time educating a customer, less time spent updating information, and other related items. Total benefit received is equal to: Total benefit = A × B × fewer steps.
   (A) Human resources worksheet: internal users. (See Step One.)
   (B) Human resources worksheet: total compensation. (See Step One.)
3. *Enter fewer errors as a percentage of productivity.* This percentage is an increase in productivity associated with spending less time in identifying and correcting errors. Total benefit received is equal to: Total benefit = A × B × fewer errors.
   (A) Human resources worksheet: internal users. (See Step One.)
   (B) Human resources worksheet: total compensation. (See Step One.)
4. *Enter fewer customer inquiries as a percentage of productivity.* This percentage is an increase in productivity associated with less time receiving and processing customer inquiries, resolving customer inquiries, and communicating resolution to key stakeholders. Total benefit received is equal to: Total benefit = A × B × fewer customer inquiries.
   (A) Human resources worksheet: Internal Users. (See Step One.)
   (B) Human resources worksheet: Total Compensation. (See Step One.)
5. *Enter less expensive resources as a dollar figure.* This number is the reduced labor costs associated with leveraging less expensive internal resources, activities leveraged to the customer or supplier or other third parties.
6. *Enter faster time to proficiency as a dollar figure.* This number represents the reduced labor costs associated with less training time, less training support, and fewer instructor expenses.
7. *Total reduced labor cost is equal to the sum of the following:*
   - ❒ Total benefit full-time employees
   - ❒ Total benefit fewer steps
   - ❒ Total benefit fewer errors
   - ❒ Total benefit fewer customer inquiries

- ❒ Total benefit less expensive resources
- ❒ Total benefit faster time to proficiency

Labor Savings—The Second Step

Purpose: Outline in detail the measurements defined to reduce labor costs through the implementation of the enterprise knowledge portal and your knowledge management initiatives.

Labor savings are achieved in several measurements that include fewer full-time employees, fewer steps in a work process, fewer errors in the overall deliverables, fewer customer inquiries, less expensive resources, and faster time to proficiency.

MYCOMPANY CASE STUDY

The labor savings will be realized through increased productivity of users. An example of the labor savings information for the employee performance management work process ROI calculation is shown in Figure 7-2.

Cost Savings

Review templates in your organization for ROI or other financial metrics and use these to present financial metrics for the enterprise knowledge portal solution. Determine if additional or a different cross-section of cost

Figure 7-2. Employee performance management ROI: labor savings.

Reduced Labor Cost

Metric	Number	Benefit	Typical Range
Fewer Full Time Employees -- how many FTE's can be reduced thru natural attrition, redeployed within the organization, reduced support and administration FTE's, reduced future hiring, and lower payroll costs	0	$0	0 to 50+
	% Productivity Gain		
Fewer Steps -- average increase in productivity for all users; associated with easier, faster data entry methods, eliminated or faster approvals, automated steps, online analysis, faster access to information, faster decision making, faster methods of communication, less time educating a customer, less time spent updating information, etc.	4%	$4,725,000	4% to 14%
Fewer Errors -- increase in productivity associated with spending less time in identifying and correcting errors	0%	$0	1% to 10%
Fewer Customer [Internal or External] Inquiries -- increase in productivity associated with less time receiving & processing customer inquiries, resolving customer inquiries, and communicating resolution to key stakeholders	0%	$0	3% to 12%
Less Expensive Resources -- reduced labor costs associated with leveraging less expensive internal resources, activities leveraged to the customer or supplier or other 3rd parties		$0	$0 to $100,000
Faster Time-to-Proficiency -- reduced labor costs associated with less training time, less training support, fewer instructor expenses		$0	$0 to $100,000
	Total	$4,725,000	

savings metrics need to be tracked and managed by your organization. You are looking for the following cost savings information, so be certain to take the following five steps:

1. Enter reduced intermediate costs in the value chain, through reductions in distributor mark-ups, transportation costs, licensing expenses, or costs required to set up and maintain the channel as a dollar figure.
2. Enter reduced delivery expenses and charges, including express delivery services and postage expenses as a dollar figure.
3. Enter reduced communication costs through reductions in printing and publication costs, telephone and fax charges, travel costs for meetings, and other associated expenses as a dollar figure.
4. Enter reduced training costs through reductions in travel costs associated with training, training materials, training room expenses, instructor fees, and other associated costs as a dollar figure.
5. Enter reduced procurement costs as a result of lower bids from new suppliers as a dollar figure.

The total reduced expenses or cost savings are equal to the sum of the following:

- ❒ Estimated benefit for reduced costs in the value chain
- ❒ Estimated benefit for reduced delivery expenses and charges
- ❒ Estimated benefit for reduced communication costs
- ❒ Estimated benefit for reduced training costs
- ❒ Estimated benefit for reduced procurement costs

Cost Savings—The Third Step

Purpose: Add the target areas controlled by your organization that will be focused on to reduce expenses.

Cost savings are achieved by reducing expenses and are tracked in several measurements that include reduced costs in the value chain, reduced delivery expenses and charges, reduced communication costs, reduced training costs, and reduced procurement costs.

MYCOMPANY CASE STUDY

The cost savings will be realized through reduced communication and training costs. There will be initial training to understand the

employee performance management work process. Several wizards to walk users through the process and submitting forms will be delivered through the enterprise knowledge portal solution. An example of the cost-savings information for the employee performance management work process ROI calculation is shown in Figure 7-3.

Revenue

Review templates in your organization for ROI or other financial metrics and use these to present financial metrics for the enterprise knowledge portal solution. Determine if additional or a different cross-section of increased revenue metrics need to be tracked and managed by your organization. You are looking for the following revenue information, so be certain to follow these nine steps:

1. Enter increased revenue from first-time customers, customers in untapped global markets, e-business and Internet customers, and other new customers as a dollar figure.
2. Enter increased revenue from new products offered through the enterprise knowledge portal as a dollar figure.
3. Enter increased revenue from advertising over the new enterprise knowledge portal as a dollar figure.
4. The total new revenue from the first year is the sum of the following:
   - Estimated benefit for new customers
   - Estimated benefit for new products
   - Estimated benefit for enterprise portal advertising revenue
5. Enter the estimated change during the second year from new revenue sources as a percentage of the first year total new revenue.

Figure 7-3. Employee performance management ROI: cost savings.

Reduced Expenses

Metric	Estimated Benefit	Typical Range
Reduced intermediate costs in the value chain, through reductions in distributor mark-ups, transportation costs, licensing expenses, costs required to setup and maintain the channel.	$0	$0 to $100,000+
Reduced delivery expenses and charges, including express (FedEx) and postage expenses.	$0	$10,000 to $50,000+
Reduced communication costs, through reductions in printing and publication costs, telephone and fax charges, travel costs for meetings, etc.	$500,000	$10,000 to $50,000+
Reduced training costs, through reductions in travel costs associated with training, training materials, training room expenses, instructor fees, etc.	$500,000	$0 to $100,000+
Reduced procurement costs as a result of lower bids from new suppliers.	$0	$0 to $10,000+
Total	$1,000,000	

6. Enter the estimated change during the third year from new revenue sources as a percentage of the first year total new revenue.
7. Enter increased revenues from customers buying more products and services through increased volume and increased total revenue from existing customers processed through the enterprise knowledge portal solution as a dollar figure.
8. Enter increased revenue from cross-selling products to existing customers as a dollar figure.
9. Enter increased revenue in targeted areas where market share, follow-on sales, or strategic relationships are specifically important as a dollar figure.

   The total existing revenue from the first year is the sum of the following:

   - Estimated benefit for customers buying more products
   - Estimated benefit for cross-selling products to existing customers
   - Estimated benefit for revenue generated from strategic partnerships

Increased Revenue—The Fourth Step

Purpose: Define how revenue will be increased from new sources within the first year. In addition, you will want to include how revenue will increase from existing sources in the first year.

Revenue expansion is defined from both new and existing sources. New sources include more customers, new products, and advertising revenue received by the enterprise knowledge portal solution. Existing revenue sources include customers buying more products, cross-selling products to existing customers, and additional revenue generated from strategic partnerships. You will also want to determine an estimated change in increased revenue for the second and third years of the enterprise knowledge portal.

MYCOMPANY CASE STUDY

There is no expected revenue to be generated from the employee performance management work processes. An example of the increased revenue information for the employee performance management work process ROI calculation is shown in Figure 7-4.

Project Costs

Review templates in your organization for ROI or other financial metrics and use these to present financial metrics for the enterprise knowledge

Figure 7-4. Employee performance management ROI: increased revenue.

Revenue Expansion

Increased Revenue from New Sources (1st Year)

Metric	Estimated Benefit
Increased revenue from more customers, through more first-time customers, customers in untapped markets (global), customers outside of standard operating hours, etc.	$0
Increased revenue from new products offered via the application.	$0
Increased revenue from advertising over the new portal.	$0
Total 1st Year	$0

Estimated Change During 2nd Year	5%
Estimated Change During 3rd Year	2%

Increased Revenue from Existing Sources (1st Year)

Metric	Estimated Benefit
Increased revenues from customers buying more products and services through increased volume and increased total revenue from existing customers processed through the enterprise portal solution.	$0
Increased revenue from cross-selling products to existing customers.	$0
Increased revenue in targeted areas where market share, follow-on sales, or strategic relationships are specifically important.	$0
Total 1st Year	$0

Estimated Change During 2nd Year	5%
Estimated Change During 3rd Year	2%

portal solution. Determine if additional or a different cross-section of project costs metrics need to be tracked and managed by your organization. You are looking for the following project costs information, so be sure to follow these fifteen steps:

1. Enter the solution implementation estimate for the identification of business requirements, enterprise knowledge portal architecture, development, and deployment as an estimated cost.

2. Enter the customer labor costs associated with managing the project, participating in the development and design effort for the initial development, and implementation of the enterprise knowledge portal project as an estimated cost.

3. Enter software costs, either purchase costs or first-year subscription costs, as an estimated cost.

4. Enter other software costs that include client access licenses and server costs for new, related, accessed, or integrated applications as an estimated cost.

5. Enter training costs including administrator, developer, and end-user training as an estimated cost.

6. Enter the technical support contract for the first year as an estimated cost.

7. Enter server-related costs such as server hardware, OS (operating system) upgrades, RAM (random access memory) upgrades, or other costs as an estimated cost.

8. Enter network-related costs such as network OS upgrades, network cards, gateways, hubs, routers, switches, remote access, or other costs as an estimated cost.

9. Enter client-related costs such as client hardware, RAM upgrades, or other costs as an estimated cost.

10. The total project implementation and development costs are a sum of the following:
    - ❒ Estimated costs for solution implementation
    - ❒ Estimated costs for customer labor costs
    - ❒ Estimated costs for software costs
    - ❒ Estimated costs for other software costs
    - ❒ Estimated costs for training costs
    - ❒ Estimated costs for the first-year technical support contract
    - ❒ Estimated costs for server-related costs
    - ❒ Estimated costs for network-related costs
    - ❒ Estimated costs for client-related costs

11. Enter customer internal recurring labor costs associated with providing technical support, administration of the system, and recurring training on the system as an estimated cost.

12. Enter software costs, either software maintenance or software subscription costs, as an estimated cost.

13. Enter other software costs, either software maintenance or software subscription costs, as an estimated cost.

14. Enter technical support contract renewals as an estimated cost.

15. The recurring total support and maintenance costs are the sum of the following:
    - Estimated costs for customer internal recurring labor costs
    - Estimated costs for software costs
    - Estimated costs for other software costs
    - Estimated costs for technical support contract renewals

Project Costs—The Fifth Step

Purpose: Identify the one-time project implementation and development costs. It is also important to include recurring support and maintenance costs that will be incurred after the first year.

Project costs are defined from both one-time implementation and development costs and recurring support and maintenance costs. Implementation and development costs include solution implementation costs, customer labor costs, software costs, training costs, the technical support contract for the first year, server-related costs, network-related costs, and client-related costs. Support and maintenance costs include customer internal recurring labor costs, software costs, and technical support contract renewal.

MYCOMPANY CASE STUDY

There will be several project implementation and development costs. Recurring costs include administration, support, maintenance, and training for new employees and managers. An example of the project costs information for the employee performance management work process ROI calculation is shown in Figure 7-5.

Return on Investment

Review templates in your organization for ROI or other financial metrics and use these to present financial metrics for the enterprise knowledge portal solution. Determine if additional or a different cross-section of analy-

Figure 7-5. Employee performance management ROI: project costs—project implementation and development costs (one time).

Project Implementation and Development Costs (one-time)

Metric	Estimated Costs
Solution Implementation -- estimate for Solution Plan, Architecture, Development and Deployment	$500,000
Customer Labor Costs associated with managing the project, participating in development and design effort for the initial development and implementation of the enterprise portal project.	$150,000
Software Costs -- either purchase costs or 1st year subscription costs	$250,000
Other Software Costs -- client access licenses and server costs for new, related, accessed, or integrated applications.	$250,000
Training Costs -- including administrator, developer, and end-user training.	$2,500,000
Technical Support Contract for 1st Year	$125,000
Server related costs - such as Server Hardware, OS upgrades, RAM upgrades, etc.	$200,000
Network related costs - such as network OS upgrades, network cards, gateways, hubs, routers, switches, remote access, etc.	$150,000
Client related costs - such as client hardware, RAM upgrades, etc.	$0
Total Project Implementation & Development Costs	$4,125,000

Recurring Support and Maintenance Costs (after 1st year)

Metric	Estimated Costs
Customer Internal Recurring Labor Costs associated with providing technical support, administration of the system, and recurring training on the system	$1,250,000
Software Costs - either software maintenance or software subscription costs	$100,000
Other Software Costs - either software maintenance or software subscription costs	$100,000
Technical Support Contract Renewal	$125,000
Total Recurring Support and Maintenance Costs	$1,575,000

sis and results metrics need to be tracked and managed by your organization. You are looking for the following information to complete the ROI spreadsheet:

Financial Assumptions Section

1. Enter the cost of capital (assumed interest rate) as a percentage.
2. Enter the reinvestment interest rate as a percentage.
3. Enter the inflation rate as a percentage.

Investment Section

1. The initial project investment is equal to the project costs worksheet: Total project implementation and development costs. (See Step Five.)
2. The recurring investment year two is equal to the project costs worksheet: Total recurring support and maintenance costs. (See Step Five.)
3. The recurring investment in year three is equal to the project costs worksheet: Total recurring support and maintenance costs. (See Step Five.)

4. The total investment over a three-year period is equal to the sum of the following:
   - ❐ Total initial project investment
   - ❐ Total recurring investment for year two
   - ❐ Total recurring investment for year three

Benefits Section (Year One)

1. The reduced labor costs are equal to labor savings worksheet: Total labor savings. (See Step Two.)
2. The reduced expenses are equal to cost savings worksheet: Total cost savings. (See Step Three.)
3. The increased revenue from new sources is equal to revenue worksheet: Total increased revenue from new sources. (See Step Four.)
4. The increased revenue from existing sources is equal to revenue worksheet: Total increased revenue from existing sources. (See Step Four.)

Benefits Section (Year Two)

1. The reduced labor costs are equal to labor savings worksheet: Total labor savings. (See Step Two.)
2. The reduced expenses are equal to cost savings worksheet: Total cost savings. (See Step Three.)
3. The increased revenue from new sources is equal to the following formula: Total increased revenue from new sources = A × (1 + B − C).
   (A) The revenue worksheet: Total increased revenuc from new sources. (See Step Four.)
   (B) The revenue worksheet: Estimated change during second year for increased revenue from new sources. (See Step Four.)
   (C) The investment section inflation rate.
4. The increased revenue from existing sources is equal to the following: Total increased revenue from existing sources = A × (1 + B − C).
   (A) The revenue worksheet: Total increased revenue from existing sources. (See Step Four.)
   (B) The revenue worksheet: Estimated change during second year for increased revenue from existing sources. (See Step Four.)
   (C) The investment section inflation rate.

Benefits Section (Year Three)

1. The reduced labor costs are equal to labor savings worksheet: Total labor savings. (See Step Two.)

2. The reduced expenses are equal to cost savings worksheet: Total cost savings. (See Step Three.)
3. The increased revenue from new sources is equal to the following: Total increased revenue from new sources = A × (1 + B − C).
   (A) The revenue worksheet: Total increased revenue from new sources. (See Step Four.)
   (B) The revenue worksheet: Estimated change during third year for increased revenue from new sources. (See Step Four.)
   (C) The investment section inflation rate.
4. The increased revenue from existing sources is equal to the following: Total increased revenue from existing sources = A × (1 + B − C).
   (A) The revenue worksheet: Total increased revenue from existing sources. (See Step Four.)
   (B) The revenue worksheet: Estimated change during third year for increased revenue from existing sources. (See Step Four.)
   (C) The investment section inflation rate.

Cash Flow Section (Year One)

1. The cumulative benefits are equal to the sum of the following:
   - ❒ Benefits section (Year One) reduced labor costs
   - ❒ Benefits section (Year One) reduced expenses
   - ❒ Benefits section (Year One) increased revenue from new sources
   - ❒ Benefits section (Year One) increased revenue from existing sources
2. The cumulative investment is equal to the sum of the following:
   - ❒ Investment section initial project investment
3. The cumulative cash flow is equal to the following:
   (A) Cash flow section (Year One) cumulative benefits
   (B) Cash flow section (Year One) cumulative investment
   Cumulative cash flow = A − B
4. The annual benefits are equal to the sum of the following:
   - ❒ Benefits section (Year One) reduced labor costs
   - ❒ Benefits section (Year One) reduced expenses
   - ❒ Benefits section (Year One) increased revenue from new sources
   - ❒ Benefits section (Year One) increased revenue from existing sources
5. The annual investment is equal to the following:
   Annual investment = investment section initial project investment × −1

6. The annual cash flow is equal to sum of the following:
   - ❒ Cash flow section (Year One) annual benefits
   - ❒ Cash flow section (Year One) annual investment

Cash Flow Section (Year Two)

1. The cumulative benefits is equal to the sum of the following:
   - ❒ Cash flow section (Year One) cumulative benefits
   - ❒ Benefits section (Year Two) reduced labor costs
   - ❒ Benefits section (Year Two) reduced expenses
   - ❒ Benefits section (Year Two) increased revenue from new sources
   - ❒ Benefits section (Year Two) increased revenue from existing sources
2. The cumulative investment is equal to the sum of the following:
   - ❒ Cash flow section (Year One) cumulative investment
   - ❒ Investment section recurring investment (Year Two)
3. The cumulative cash flow is equal to the following:
   (A) Cash flow section (Year Two) cumulative benefits
   (B) Cash flow section (Year Two) cumulative investment
   Cumulative cash flow = A − B
4. The annual benefits are equal to the sum of the following:
   - ❒ Benefits section (Year Two) reduced labor costs
   - ❒ Benefits section (Year Two) reduced expenses
   - ❒ Benefits section (Year Two) increased revenue from new sources
   - ❒ Benefits section (Year Two) increased revenue from existing sources
5. The annual investment is equal to the following:
   Annual investment = investment section recurring investment Year Two × −1
6. The annual cash flow is equal to sum of the following:
   - ❒ Cash flow section (Year Two) annual benefits
   - ❒ Cash flow section (Year Two) annual investment

Cash Flow Section (Year Three)

1. The cumulative benefits is equal to the sum of the following:
   - ❒ Cash flow section (Year Two) cumulative benefits
   - ❒ Benefits section (Year Three) reduced labor costs
   - ❒ Benefits section (Year Three) reduced expenses
   - ❒ Benefits section (Year Three) increased revenue from new sources

- ❒ Benefits section (Year Three) increased revenue from existing sources

2. The cumulative investment is equal to the sum of the following:
   - ❒ Cash flow section (Year Two) cumulative investment
   - ❒ Investment section (Year Three) recurring investment
3. The cumulative cash flow is equal to the following:
   (A) Cash flow section (Year Three) cumulative benefits
   (B) Cash flow section (Year Three) cumulative investment
   Cumulative cash flow = A − B
4. The annual benefits are equal to the sum of the following:
   - ❒ Benefits section (Year Three) reduced labor costs
   - ❒ Benefits section (Year Three) reduced expenses
   - ❒ Benefits section (Year Three) increased revenue from new sources
   - ❒ Benefits section (Year Three) increased revenue from existing sources
5. The annual investment is equal to the following:
   Annual investment = investment section recurring investment Year Three × −1
6. The annual cash flow is equal to sum of the following:
   - ❒ Cash flow section (Year Three) annual benefits
   - ❒ Cash flow section (Year Three) annual investment

Results Section

1. The return on investment Year One is equal to the following:
   (A) Cash flow section (Year One) cumulative benefits
   (B) Cash flow section (Year One) cumulative investment
   Return on investment (Year One) = A / B
2. The return on investment (Three Years) is equal to the following:
   (A) Cash flow section (Year Three) cumulative benefits
   (B) Cash flow section (Year Three) cumulative investment
   Return on investment (Three Years) = A / B
3. The breakeven analysis (Years) is equal to the following:
   (A) Results section (Year One) return on investment
   Breakeven analysis (Years) = 1 / A
4. The breakeven date is equal to the following:
   (A) Human resources worksheet: Estimated project start date. (See Step One.)
   (B) Results section breakeven analysis (Years)
   Breakeven date = A + (B × 365.25)

Analysis and Results—The Sixth Step

Purpose: Summarize the ROI results to determine the expected ROI percentage and payback period or breakeven date. You will want to include expected benefits, investment, and cash flow.

The analysis and results of the ROI spreadsheet are a collection of calculations based on the estimates and percentages included in the previous steps. The analysis and results page is broken into several sections that include financial assumptions, benefits, investments, cash flow, ROI, and payback period or breakeven results.

MYCOMPANY CASE STUDY

The breakeven date is realized approximately ten months after the project is initiated. The ROI is expected to be 139 percent in the first year. An example of the analysis and results information for the employee performance management work process ROI calculation is shown in Figure 7-6.

Key Points

You will want to continually develop, deploy, and measure versions of the enterprise knowledge portal. Each iterative deployment will include im-

Figure 7-6. Employee performance management ROI: analysis and results.

Results

Return On Investment Year 1	139%
Return On Investment 3 Years	236%

Breakeven Analysis (Years)	0.721
Breakeven Date	09/21/02

Investment

Initial Project Investment	$4,125,000
Recurring Investment Year 2	$1,575,000
Recurring Investment Year 3	$1,575,000
Total Investment Over 3-Year Period	$7,275,000

Benefits Estimates in Present Dollar Terms

Year 1		
	Reduced Labor Costs	$4,725,000
	Reduced Expenses	$1,000,000
	Increased Revenue from New Sources	$0
	Increased Revenue from Existing Sources	$0
Year 2		
	Reduced Labor Costs	$4,725,000
	Reduced Expenses	$1,000,000
	Increased Revenue from New Sources	$0
	Increased Revenue from Existing Sources	$0
Year 3		
	Reduced Labor Costs	$4,725,000
	Reduced Expenses	$1,000,000
	Increased Revenue from New Sources	$0
	Increased Revenue from Existing Sources	$0
	Total Benefits Over 3-Year Period	$17,175,000

Financial Assumptions

Cost of Capital (assumed interest rate)	10%
Reinvestment Interest Rate	8%
Inflation Rate	3%

Cash Flow

	Year 1	Year 2	Year 3
Cumulative Benefits	$5,725,000	$11,450,000	$17,175,000
Cumulative Investment	$4,125,000	$5,700,000	$7,275,000
Cumulative Cash Flow	$1,600,000	$5,750,000	$9,900,000
Annual Benefits	$5,725,000	$5,725,000	$5,725,000
Annual Investment	($4,125,000)	($1,575,000)	($1,575,000)
Annual Cash Flow	$1,600,000	$4,150,000	$4,150,000

provements identified by existing users and additions of new work processes. You will want to analyze the number of expected users inside and outside your organization, labor savings, direct reduction in expenses, direct increases in revenue, and project costs. You can optionally include a cost and benefit analysis to measure increased satisfaction and soft dollar benefits.

The cost and benefit analysis presents a collection of positive and negative impacts that are weighed against each other and summarized. This type of analysis is commonly used to evaluate projects. The cost and benefit analysis must clearly identify the timing of expected inflows and outflows as well as their costs and benefits. The cost and benefit analysis is a mechanism for including discussion regarding nonquantified benefits or costs. The research done to define the benefits of an enterprise knowledge portal should be included as part of the cost and benefit analysis. For example, the ability to make better, more informed decisions is a benefit of the enterprise knowledge portal, but it is difficult to apply a monetary value. These types of cost and benefit items require that the enterprise knowledge portal project team determine exactly how a monetary value will be assigned.

The return on investment spreadsheet focuses on the ratio of the estimated total positive benefits to the estimated total costs of the enterprise knowledge portal project. You will usually create the ROI analysis for the first year. You will want to create an ROI analysis for each phase or iteration of the enterprise knowledge portal. This will allow you to follow and track the financial results associated with your knowledge management initiatives to present to management and support your continuous improvement efforts. The ROI spreadsheet has six sections. The six steps involved in creating a simple ROI calculation include:

1. *Human Resources Information.* Identify the user community, human resource, and payroll information that will benefit from the enterprise knowledge portal solution.
2. *Labor Savings.* Outline in detail the measurements defined to reduce labor costs through the implementation of the enterprise knowledge portal and your knowledge management initiatives.
3. *Cost Savings.* Add the target areas controlled by your organization that will be focused on to reduce expenses.
4. *Increased Revenue.* Define how revenue will be increased from new sources within the first year. In addition, you will want to include how revenue will increase from existing sources in the first year.
5. *Project Costs.* Identify the onetime project implementation and development costs. It is also important to include recurring support and maintenance costs that will be incurred after the first year.

6. *Analysis and Results.* Summarize the ROI results to determine the expected ROI percentage and payback period or breakeven date. You will want to include expected benefits, investment, and cash flow.

You are going to need a centralized infrastructure and architecture to deliver a centralized configuration of enterprise knowledge portal hardware, software, administration, and security to support a decentralized collection of work processes and content. Chapter 8 describes common enterprise knowledge portal technologies that will need to be supported in your infrastructure environment and identifies the information technology personnel that will be necessary to plan, design, develop, and maintain an enterprise knowledge portal in your organization.

IV

The Enterprise Knowledge Portal Infrastructure and Environment

8

Enterprise Knowledge Portal Technical Architecture

"Computers communicate faster and better than layers of middle management. They also demand knowledgeable users who can transform their data into information."

Peter F. Drucker, *The Coming of the New Organization*

The information technology requirements for the enterprise portal do not focus on a specific product. The information technology environment described here sketches out a way to architect your enterprise knowledge portal solution and understand the types of deployment decisions that will be required as you move forward. There is no one single technology that supports the scope of enterprise knowledge management outlined in this book. The challenge you are faced with is to incorporate a variety of Internet and application-related technology components to create a comprehensive enterprise knowledge portal. The list of possible technologies you will utilize in your enterprise knowledge portal is outlined in your enterprise knowledge portal IT–enabling framework report. Technology is constantly evolving. The information presented here is a good introduction to the most common technologies included in enterprise knowledge portal solutions. Several technologies to be familiar with include:

- *Application Servers*. These are computers in a distributed network that provide business logic for an application program. They are frequently viewed as part of a three-tier application. The first-tier, front-end, is a Web-based user interface that is usually a personal computer or workstation. The middle-tier business logic application or set of business rules and applications usually runs on the network or intranet server. The third-tier, back-end, is a database or transaction server that runs on the network, mainframe, or large server.

- *Web Server*. A Web server is a program that understands and presents the files that form Web pages to users. Every computer that hosts a Web site must have a Web server program.
- *Relational Databases*. A relational database is a collection of data items organized as a set of tables from which data can be accessed or reassembled in many different ways without having to reorganize the original database tables. It is a set of tables containing information fitted into predefined categories. Each table contains one or more data categories in columns. Each row contains a unique instance of data for the categories defined in the columns.
- *Metadata Repository*. A metadata repository contains the definition or description of data about the content and the structure of the content. This includes metadata about relational databases and taxonomy, as well as individual documents. For example, each document stored in a customer folder might have a metadata field called "customer" that would have one or more values. The value of the customer field for a particular document is metadata about that document.
- *Taxonomy*. The taxonomy is the classification of information according to a predefined system. The resulting catalog is used to provide a conceptual framework for discussion, analysis, or information retrieval.
- *Categorization Engine*. The categorization engine is used for sorting documents and information into taxonomy. The categorization engine may do this based on metadata in the documents, business rules, the content of the document, search criteria, and filters.
- *Index*. An index is a collection of information that allows for fast query and retrieval. An index is usually a combination of a full-text index and a metadata repository to be considered for inclusion in result sets.
- *Crawler*. A crawler is a program that searches Web pages and other information on many servers to create entries for a search engine index. Search engines use these programs. They are often called "spider" or "bot" programs. These programs crawl through a website a page at a time, following the links to other pages on the site until all pages have been read and indexed.
- *Portal Objects*. The portal objects are enterprise knowledge portal building blocks. They exist in the user interface and present data and functionality from multiple applications into a single Web page. They

encompass the presentation layer and the business rules, and tie into back-end data sources. The enterprise knowledge portal will be designed, developed, and deployed as a collection of portal objects. Many enterprise portal vendors have several prebuilt portal objects for connecting to enterprise systems and services.

- *Web Services.* A Web service is a program that accepts and responds to requests over the Internet. They include some combination of programming and data that is made available for a Web server, users, and other Web-connect programs. Web services include storage management, customer relationship management, stock quotes, and checking bids for an auction item.

The purpose of the enterprise knowledge portal technical architecture analysis is to organize your infrastructure planning and documentation activities for the enterprise knowledge portal. The information collected will allow you to clarify the technologies common to your infrastructure environment and identify the information technology personnel that will be necessary to plan, design, develop, and maintain an enterprise knowledge portal in your organization. The steps outlined and the sections included throughout this chapter will give you the details needed to build the enterprise knowledge portal infrastructure.

Enterprise Knowledge Portal Information Technology Environment

The enterprise knowledge portal technical architecture is a federation of technologies running on top of your existing network. You may think of these components as layers of technology. An overview of these layers can be visualized in Figure 8-1. When laid on top of each other, the available technologies form a cohesive foundation for additional applications and services to use as a platform and user interface. The enterprise knowledge portal technical architecture layers include:

- *Layer One—Extranet and Internet.* The Internet layer is the interface to external customers and partners. The presentation to the user is to multiple devices that include Web browsers, personal data assistant (PDA) handheld or palmtop devices, cellular phones, and other electronic devices.
- *Layer Two—Firewall and Demilitarized Zone.* The network security policy, software, and architecture that allow users to access resources in your organization.

Figure 8-1. Enterprise knowledge portal information technology environment.

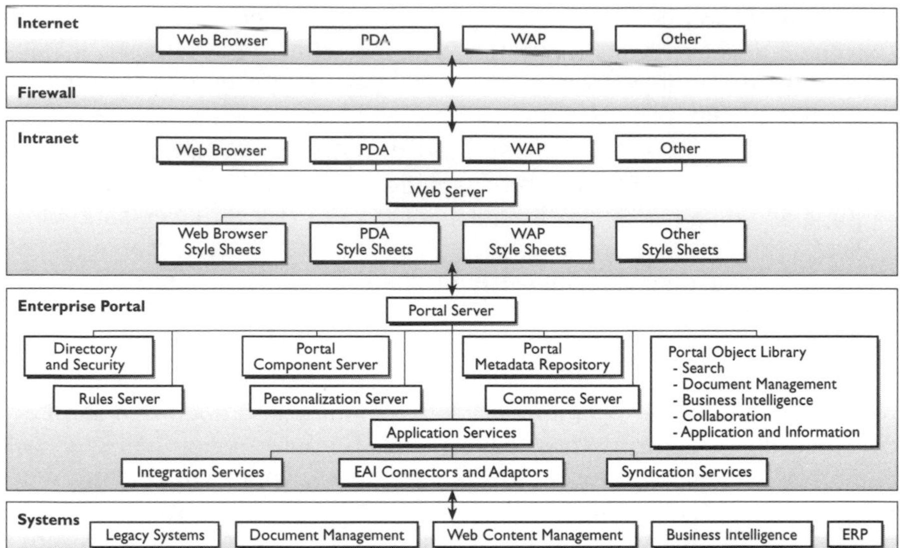

- *Layer Three—Intranet.* The intranet layer is the interface to managers and knowledge workers. The presentation to the user is made possible through a collection of stylesheet templates that present information to the different devices. The interface provides a universal view to documents, e-mail, calendars, and people.
- *Layer Four—Enterprise Knowledge Portal.* A software solution that provides a personalized interface to online resources for employees and customers that integrates and organizes data and applications. Features and functions supported by the enterprise knowledge portal include presentation, knowledge organization systems, search and index, personalization and roles, integration, and technical architecture supporting application and integration services.
- *Layer Five—Application and Integration Services.* These are the services that provide the plans, methods, and tools used to consolidate and coordinate the applications and systems in an enterprise.
- *Layer Six—Applications and Systems.* The collection of content repositories and applications within your organization that include legacy systems, document management systems, Web content management systems, business intelligence applications, enterprise resource planning (ERP) systems, and others.

Layer One—Extranet and Internet

Purpose: The Internet layer is the interface to external customers and partners. The presentation to the user is to multiple devices that include Web browsers, personal data assistant (PDA) handheld or palmtop devices, cellular phones, and other electronic devices.

The interface into your organization for customers, partners, and suppliers will be through the Internet. Providing content that is effective is your objective. All website visitors should not be treated the same. Potential customers have needs and viewpoints different from longtime valued customers. Personalization is an important technique to make each site visitor's experience useful and satisfying. Content can be tailored for a particular site visitor or a category of visitor. They tailor the content and the site themselves by selecting preferences, which are stored in their user profile. Employees and business partners will be able to personalize content using intelligent agents or business rules. The user can activate intelligent agents and business rules by clicking on them or they can be designed into the user experience. An example of an automated business rule is that any visitor shopping for flowers should also be shown vases. Viewer expectations for Internet users can be reviewed several ways including:

- *User Interface*. User interface includes shortcuts for frequently used features, custom screen layout, links to frequently accessed sites, and navigation controls.
- *Content*. This includes customized content, such as information about accounts or the status of the most recent purchases, notification of related material, or content the user subscribed to.
- *Delivery Channel*. This includes choice of e-mail, Web, pager, CD-ROM, personal data assistant, cellular telephone, and other delivery options.

Extranet and Internet Discussion Questions

- ☐ Do you have a single, centralized Internet connection, or do the various sites have their own direct Internet connections?
- ☐ What is the bandwidth of your various Internet and extranet connections?
- ☐ What projects are currently in process or planned to improve, add to, or change your Internet and extranet connectivity?
- ☐ What are your Internet and extranet security models and structure?
- ☐ Will your current Internet and extranet configuration meet the needs of your enterprise knowledge portal Internet and extranet user requirements?

Layer Two—Firewall or Demilitarized Zone

Purpose: The network security policy, software, and architecture that allow users to access resources in your organization.

A firewall is a set of programs located on your network that protect the resources of your local area network (LAN) and wide area network (WAN) from users outside your organization. The configuration of the firewall establishes your security policy. A small computer network that is created between your organization's network and the outside public network is called a demilitarized zone (DMZ). This configuration creates an environment for outside users to only access information in this private network area or DMZ. The DMZ will contain Web pages and other content that can be shared with people outside your organization. Managers and knowledge workers inside your organization will pass into the DMZ through the firewall facing the private network. Outside users will pass into the DMZ through the firewall facing the public network. In the event that an unwelcome user penetrates the DMZ's security, only the information in the DMZ would be exposed. There are several topics to consider when dealing with Internet security. These include:

- ❒ Authentication
- ❒ Firewall server hardware and software
- ❒ Internet security software
- ❒ Network management
- ❒ Network security
- ❒ Proxy server software
- ❒ Web applications management

Additional sources of Internet security information can be found in Appendix C: Recommended Reading.

Firewall or Demilitarized Zone Discussion Questions

- ☐ Do you have any private networks or demilitarized zones set up and in place?
- ☐ What is the bandwidth of these private network connections?
- ☐ Do you have any plans for setting up, improving, or adding to your existing private network infrastructure, including setting up a virtual private network (VPN) over the Internet?
- ☐ What is your firewall configuration and security policy?
- ☐ What is the Internet security architecture and infrastructure?
- ☐ Will your current Internet security architecture and infrastructure meet the needs of your enterprise knowledge portal requirements?

Layer Three—Intranet

Purpose: The intranet layer is the interface to managers and knowledge workers. The presentation to the user is made possible through a collection of stylesheet templates that present information to the different devices. The interface provides a universal view to documents, e-mail, calendars, and people.

A presentation requirement for delivering content to your browser on your desktop and other devices is the ability to allow data to be separated from the presentation rules or instructions. Extensible markup language (XML) and extensible stylesheet language transformation (XSLT) are a common way to use templates that provide a common look and feel for different types of content. Using templates is an effective way to gather metadata that can then be used to add new content and content sources into the overall knowledge organization system and present it into the user interface. It is critical that only one instance of the content exists to be managed and updated while templates can deliver this same information in multiple formats through multiple channels. For example, as new databases are identified to be included in the enterprise knowledge portal, the existing templates can be reused to point to the new data source and present the new data in the user interface. The speed of delivery is important, and different alternatives for improving performance need to be considered as you develop and reuse enterprise knowledge portal templates. The alternatives to review include:

- *Replication.* This involves making multiple copies of the content for clustering and load-balancing purposes.
- *Application Hosting Services.* This involves leveraging a separate organization to host high-performance servers and network capabilities to deliver content.
- *Caching.* Caching takes information that is compiled and stored in memory on a server to present to the user on request in the least amount of time.
- *Syndication.* Syndication is a publish-and-subscribe model to make content available to the users that have requested the content through personalization or receive the information automatically based on their roles and profile settings.

Intranet Discussion Questions on User Population and Organizational Environment

- ☐ What is the total number of locations or offices and where are they geographically located?
- ☐ How many employees or users are at each of the above listed locations?
- ☐ How many of these locations are connected to your wide area network (WAN)?

- ☐ How many report locations are there with either dial-up or no access to the corporate network?
- ☐ How many employees or users are there at each location?
- ☐ How many remote employees or users are there?

Intranet Discussion Questions on Networking Infrastructure

- ☐ Which network protocols do you support within your organization (e.g., TCP/IP, SPX, NetBIOS)?
- ☐ Which network operating systems (NOS) do you support within your organization (e.g., NetWare, Windows XP, Windows 2000, Windows NT, UNIX)?
- ☐ Which directory services (DS) do you support within your organization (e.g., NDS, Active Directory, LDAP)?
- ☐ What tools or network operating system do you use to manage your network, including the directory and address structure?
- ☐ What is the network bandwidth of the local area networks (LANs) at your various sites?
- ☐ What is the bandwidth of the WAN connecting to your various sites?
- ☐ What are the known problems with the LAN/WAN at the current time?
- ☐ What projects are currently in process or planned to improve, add to, or change the current LAN/WAN infrastructure?

Intranet Discussion Questions on Remote Access

- ☐ How do remote users connect to the network?
- ☐ Approximately how many remote users are there, and what information systems do they commonly use?

Intranet Discussion Questions on Strategies

- ☐ What is your intranet strategy?
- ☐ What is your Internet presence strategy?
- ☐ Do you host your own site or is this contracted out?
- ☐ Which Web browsers (e.g., Microsoft IE, Netscape, Mosaic) do you use? (Include version numbers.)
- ☐ How many users are currently using each browser?
- ☐ If you have multiple browsers, do you have any plans to standardize?
- ☐ Which Web servers (e.g., Microsoft Site Server/IIS, Lotus Domino, Netscape) do you use? (Include version numbers.)
- ☐ What operating system platforms do they run on?
- ☐ Do you use any application servers, transaction servers, or active

application servers (e.g., Microsoft Transaction Server, Net Dynamics, Web Sphere) that may be used to process the business logic or rules in a three-tier or multiple-tier architecture system?

- ☐ What tools do you use for creating your intranet?
- ☐ How are decisions about your intranet made? Is there an oversight board?
- ☐ What tools do you use for creating your Internet site?
- ☐ How are decisions about your Internet presence made? Is there an oversight board?

Layer Four—Enterprise Knowledge Portal

Purpose: A software solution that provides a personalized interface to online resources for employees and customers that integrates and organizes data and applications. Features and functions supported by the enterprise knowledge portal include presentation, knowledge organization systems, search and index, personalization and roles, integration, and technical architecture supporting application and integration services.

Using the extranet, Internet, and intranet as the user interface to deliver information throughout the enterprise means that high-quality content is available in your organization and on your website. The strategy, technologies, and work processes included make quality the most important factor. The technical architecture used to manage content through the enterprise knowledge portal will need to be developed. The architecture should support adding and replacing content and related application services individually. Modularity allows syndication, personalization, and other services to be added or updated without reengineering the solution. You can scale individual components without having to scale all components. You should:

- ❒ Adopt XML-based or other open standards and industry-wide data models.
- ❒ Manage content creation and maintenance responsibilities through the content network.
- ❒ Separate the content from the user interface presentation so it can be easily reused and enhanced.

Enterprise Knowledge Portal Discussion Questions on Software Considerations

- ☐ What is the portal software application's name, manufacturer, and version number?
- ☐ Briefly describe the benefits provided.
- ☐ Briefly describe the weaknesses.

- ☐ What operating system platforms does it run on?
- ☐ What database or data storage platform does it use?
- ☐ What is the current status and plan for this system? If the system is planned or in the process of being implemented, what is the targeted production date?
- ☐ How many users access the enterprise knowledge portal system and how useful is the information provided by the system? Where does it provide good information, bad information, or no information?
- ☐ What are the known external interfaces with this system and the types of interface available (e.g., batch, text file, pumping technology, CORBA/COM interface, real time)?
- ☐ What features and services will be available for enterprise knowledge portal users and application services?
- ☐ Please submit any current documentation or diagrams that would be helpful in detailing, describing, or clarifying any of your organization's topologies, systems, or strategies.

Enterprise Knowledge Portal Discussion Questions on Administration

- ☐ Which administrator will be responsible for establishing default user interfaces?
- ☐ Who will be responsible for ongoing maintenance and customization to the user interfaces?
- ☐ What skills are needed to manage and maintain the enterprise knowledge portal solution? (Include all functions of the system, administration requirements, procedures and processes to follow, system maintenance, and common problems.)
- ☐ What are the methods for delivering training (e.g., classroom, online computer-based training, deskside)?
- ☐ What are the required training materials (e.g., handouts, guides, quick reference material, e-learning features through the enterprise knowledge portal)?
- ☐ What are the logistics for training (e.g., length, topics, location requirements, method of instruction)?

Enterprise Knowledge Portal Discussion Questions on Security

- ☐ What are the overall security requirements for each work process included in the enterprise knowledge portal?
- ☐ What (if any) are the criteria that each work process must meet in order to be certified and accredited for security purposes?
- ☐ What safeguards are required for each work process security?

- ☐ What are the overall privacy requirements for each work process?
- ☐ Does your organization have a standard policy on privacy, both in the workplace and from a business perspective (e.g., regarding customers, vendors, other suppliers)?
- ☐ What information is considered to be sensitive or private information?
- ☐ What safeguards need to be in place to ensure that private or sensitive information remains that way?

Layer Five—Application and Integration Services

Purpose: These are the services that provide the plans, methods, and tools used to consolidate and coordinate the applications and systems in an enterprise.

Application and integration services are required to develop a complete view of your organization's business. The solution provides a way to look at how existing applications and content work together to create an enterprise-wide content and data distribution network. The integration network created needs to be based on open standards for a high level of flexibility. There are several enterprise application integration services to consider. These include:

- ❐ *Platform Integration.* Platform integration provides connectivity between heterogeneous hardware, operating systems, and application platforms. Technologies that provide platform integration include messaging, object request brokers (ORB), and remote procedure calls (PRC). The enterprise knowledge portal will use these technologies to provide asynchronous and synchronous connectivity between platforms. Additional functionality is required for connecting to applications and reconciling differences in data representation between systems.
- ❐ *Component Integration.* Application servers and application integration products provide data access to a variety of relational database sources. There are some solutions that provide access to nonrelational and mainframe data. Other solutions provide application adapters to packaged applications and middleware services.
- ❐ *Application Integration.* This is the collection of technologies that together provide platform integration, event integration using message brokers to provide data translation, transformation and rules-based routing, application interface integration using application adapters, and custom applications.
- ❐ *Process Integration.* Process integration solutions enable users and administrators to define, monitor, and change work processes through a graphical modeling interface. Work process integration requires all the

underlying integration services. Work process modeling enables managers and analysts to define how information flows across systems and organizational boundaries in a graphical model declarative language instead of through programming. The result is an integration solution that is generated from the model. When work processes or rules change, these updates are made to the model and the solution is regenerated.

- *Business-to-Business Integration.* Business-to-business integration takes application integration beyond the walls of your organization and delivers the full promise of integrating customers, suppliers, and partners. There are several business-to-business approaches that include XML, process integration, and technology for brokering exchanges in online trading communities.

Application and Integration Services Discussion Questions

- What underlying platform integration technology is available in your organization?
- What technologies or services are available to provide data translation?
- What standards and guidelines are established for transformation and rules-based routing?
- What application interface integration services are provided through application adapters or the enterprise knowledge portal?
- What custom applications are available for application and integration services in your organization?
- What application and integration services are required to meet the enterprise knowledge portal requirements?

Layer Six—Applications and Systems

Purpose: The collection of content repositories and applications within your organization that include legacy systems, document management systems, Web content management systems, business intelligence applications, enterprise resource planning (ERP) systems, and others.

The enterprise knowledge portal will require that extranet, Internet, and intranet users can access the complete collection of applications and systems identified during the enterprise knowledge portal design methodology through the channels outlined. The enterprise knowledge portal IT–enabling framework report should provide the list of applications and systems that will need to be supported. For each application and system it is important to establish the best practices and available options for making the data from the application or the entire application available through a browser or other distribution channel. If there are integration requirements between these applications and services, you will want to evaluate whether to manage these requirements through application and integration services in the enterprise knowledge portal or through enterprise application integration (EAI) software packages that will be configured to work with the enterprise knowledge portal solution. Establishing the standards, guidelines, and best practices for coordinating the enterprise knowledge portal with applications and systems throughout your organization will define several of the connection and other portal objects that will need to be available in the enterprise knowledge portal library.

Applications and Systems Discussion Questions

For each enterprise system or application (e.g., business intelligence, content management, e-learning, collaboration, ERP, other) to be included in the enterprise knowledge portal solution consider the following:

- ☐ What operating system platforms does it run on?
- ☐ Which database or data storage platform does it use?
- ☐ What is the current status and plan for the system? If the system is planned or in the process of being implemented, what is the targeted production date?
- ☐ How many users access the system? How useful is the information provided by the system?
- ☐ Where does it provide good information, bad information, or no information?
- ☐ What are the known external interfaces with this system or application and the types of interface available (e.g., batch, text file, CORBA/COM interface, real time)?
- ☐ What features and services will be available for enterprise knowledge portal users and work processes?
- ☐ Please submit any current documentation or diagrams that would be helpful in detailing, describing, or clarifying any of your organization's topologies, systems, or strategies.

Enterprise Knowledge Portal Information Technology Staff

Staffing demands on an extranet, intranet, and Internet vary based on a number of factors. The total number of users and sites served, the number and complexity of applications, the number of servers, and the degree of centralized application development are the primary variables. In general, a decentralized, multiple site enterprise knowledge portal solution requires more staff to support it than a highly centralized, single site. Your Internet or intranet staff will generally be the same staff that support the enterprise knowledge portal solution and must foresee, plan, manage, create, and support the growth inside your organization. These demands call for distinct skills defined by several roles.

Roles and Responsibilities

The enterprise knowledge portal technical staff requires a significant number of skills and people to run and maintain a mature system as a stable, reliable, and responsive service. The enterprise knowledge portal solution presents additional complexities when required to connect and integrate existing systems into your organization's complete solution. It is important to identify and train, or possibly hire and outsource, the resources necessary for the enterprise knowledge portal's beginning and ongoing infrastructure development and growth. It consists of the following core team.

Web Access Architects

The Web access architect is an infrastructure expert responsible for intranet, extranet, Internet, and enterprise knowledge portal services. This person or persons oversee the technical architecture, maintenance of hardware and software, and service level agreements to maintain the solutions. Responsibilities include:

- Leading and planning new services and system expansion
- Managing expansion and upgrade projects
- Establishing service levels for system availability
- Defining the performance requirements of existing intranet, extranet, Internet, and enterprise knowledge portal services for the wide area network
- Setting standards for performance, accessibility, scalability, security, and maintainability

Site Managers

Site managers are responsible for configuration and administrative responsibilities for a subset of the intranet, extranet, Internet, and enterprise knowledge portal infrastructure. Responsibilities include:

- Managing expansion and upgrade projects for subnetworks, local area networks, or remote sites

- Establishing and maintaining service levels for system availability
- Installing and configuring application servers and Web servers
- Applying consistent use of performance, accessibility, scalability, security, maintainability, and extensibility standards

Server Administrators

Server administrators are responsible for the technical operation and security of intranet, extranet, Internet, and enterprise knowledge portal servers. They need to be well trained on server operating systems and know the particulars of each type of server they administer. If you do not use a site manager role, the server administrator may perform those responsibilities as well. Responsibilities include:

- Providing expertise on the operating systems and associated applications of the servers maintained
- Ensuring that server security allows remote access only to authorized personnel
- Providing hardware and software maintenance
- Conducting security checks
- Providing log analysis and user management
- Conducting preventative maintenance
- Conducting regular backups
- Providing consistent monitoring
- Providing emergency fallback planning

Support and Competency Center Staff

The support and competency center staff must be trained to support enterprise knowledge portal and browser users. They will also be trained as enterprise knowledge portal developers to maintain the viability of the enterprise knowledge portal. Support and competency center team members will thoroughly understand browser use, searching, and enterprise knowledge portal features. Additionally, support and competency center team members will be able to provide assistance to developers that submit technical questions and other design questions. The support and competency center will need to manage and maintain the metadata associated with the enterprise knowledge portal and the enterprise knowledge portal library to promote and reuse programming code and development standards. Responsibilities include:

- Providing an online knowledge base of frequently asked questions for employees
- Providing telephone or peer-to-peer support for employees that have enterprise knowledge portal questions
- Providing escalation paths to knowledge expert community members or other employees who can answer questions or provide direction
- Establishing and maintaining service-level agreements for enterprise knowledge portal users
- Defining and executing enhancement and maintenance releases of the enterprise knowledge portal
- Managing and maintaining enterprise knowledge portal metadata
- Managing and maintaining the portal object library to promote and reuse programming code and development standards for the enterprise knowledge portal

Technical Analysts

The technical analyst is responsible for ensuring that the enterprise knowledge portal technical solution satisfies the enterprise's present and future business requirements. These individuals set the direction and establish the approach for the technical solution. Technical analysts provide insight into selecting technical platforms, network architecture, and system software. They lead the effort in designing the enterprise knowledge portal's conceptual architecture, quality standards, and performance metrics. Responsibilities include:

- Coordinating, collating, and disseminating of the enterprise knowledge portal architecture and supporting infrastructure
- Working with project team members, support and competency center team members, business analysts, and executives to define the objectives and priorities of the enterprise knowledge portal architecture and supporting infrastructure
- Establishing a plan to accomplish the selected objectives
- Supervising the progress of the enterprise knowledge portal architecture and infrastructure
- Analyzing the impact of schedule variations
- Collecting enhancements to be integrated into future enterprise knowledge portal architecture and infrastructure

Application Developers

Application developers are accountable for building and maintaining dynamic applications for intranet, extranet, and Internet solutions including the enterprise knowledge portal. These applications may be built using HTML, DHTML, XML, XSL, XSLT, C++, Perl, Visual Basic, Visual Basic Script, JavaScript, Java, ActiveX, COM objects, SOAP, and other tools. Application developers need to be trained according to the types of applications they expect to create and project teams they expect to be members of. They will work closely with the support and competency center to create, edit, and enhance the enterprise knowledge portal library.

User Interface Designer

The user interface designer provides specialty consulting and development for knowledge delivery media. This person is responsible for all functions of information design, site architecture, interface design, multimedia design, and graphic design for the enterprise knowledge portal and other knowledge management related applications and solutions.

Multimedia Coordinators

This person or group develops, directs, and researches multimedia applications, including animation, voice, video, and just-in-time communications. Multimedia coordinators also provide consulting expertise in the use of related authoring tools and technology. They must also coordinate network infrastructure and all necessary support to ensure successful implementation of these knowledge management solutions.

Key Points

The purpose of the enterprise knowledge portal technical architecture analysis is to organize your infrastructure planning and documentation activities for the enterprise knowledge portal. The information collected will allow you to clarify the technologies common to your infrastructure environment and identify the information technology personnel that will be necessary to plan, design, develop, and maintain an enterprise knowledge portal in your organization. The steps outlined and the sections included throughout this chapter will give you the details needed to build the enterprise knowledge portal infrastructure. The list of possible technologies you will utilize in your enterprise knowledge portal is outlined in your enterprise knowledge portal IT–enabling framework report. Technology is constantly evolving. The information presented here is a good introduction to the most common technologies included in enterprise knowledge portal solutions. Several technologies to be familiar with include:

- ❒ Application servers
- ❒ Web servers
- ❒ Relational databases
- ❒ Metadata repository
- ❒ Taxonomy
- ❒ Categorization engine
- ❒ Index
- ❒ Crawler
- ❒ Portal objects
- ❒ Web services

The enterprise knowledge portal technical architecture is a federation of technologies running on top of your existing network. You may think of these components as layers of technology. An overview of these layers can be visualized in Figure 8-1. When laid on top of each other, the available technologies form a cohesive foundation for additional applications and services to use as a platform and user interface. The enterprise knowledge portal technical architecture layers include:

- ❒ *Layer One—Extranet and Internet.* The Internet layer is the interface to external customers and partners. The presentation to the user is to multiple devices that include Web browsers, personal data assistant (PDA) handheld or palmtop devices, cellular phones, and other electronic devices.
- ❒ *Layer Two—Firewall and Demilitarized Zone.* The network security policy, software, and architecture that allow users to access resources in your organization.
- ❒ *Layer Three—Intranet.* The intranet layer is the interface to managers and knowledge workers. The presentation to the user is made possible through a collection of stylesheet templates that present information to the different devices. The interface provides a universal view to documents, e-mail, calendars, and people.
- ❒ *Layer Four—Enterprise Knowledge Portal.* A software solution that provides a personalized interface to online resources for employees and customers that integrates and organizes data and applications. Features and functions supported by the enterprise knowledge portal include pre-

sentation, knowledge organization systems, search and index, personalization and roles, integration, and technical architecture supporting application and integration services.

- *Layer Five—Application and Integration Services.* These are the services that provide the plans, methods, and tools used to consolidate and coordinate the applications and systems in an enterprise.
- *Layer Six—Applications and Systems.* The collection of content repositories and applications within your organization that include legacy systems, document management systems, Web content management systems, business intelligence applications, enterprise resource planning (ERP) systems, and others.

The enterprise knowledge portal technical staff requires a significant number of skills and people to run and maintain a mature system as a stable, reliable, and responsive service. The enterprise knowledge portal solution presents additional complexities when required to connect and integrate existing systems into your organization's complete solution. It is important to identify and train, or possibly hire and outsource, the resources necessary for the enterprise knowledge portal's beginning and ongoing infrastructure development and growth. It consists of the following core team:

- Web access architects
- Site managers
- Server administrators
- Support and competency center staff
- Technical analysts
- Application developers
- User interface designer
- Multimedia coordinators

You are going to need a support and competency center team for the success of a long-term enterprise knowledge portal in your organization. There are several services that the support and competency center will establish to be effective managing and maintaining the enterprise knowledge portal. Chapter 9 describes common enterprise knowledge portal services that will need to be defined and supported. This is the organizational structure necessary to manage problem resolution work processes, maintain the enterprise knowledge portal library of reusable development objects and documentation, and other activities associated with your enterprise knowledge portal's continued success.

9

Support and Competency Center Services

"How groups communicate is as important as the knowledge each center of excellence may have."

James Brian Quinn, Philip Anderson, and Sydney Finkelstein,
Managing Professional Intellect: Making the Most of the Best

The enterprise knowledge portal support and competency center is critical to the success of a long-term enterprise knowledge portal for your organization. There are several services that the support and competency center will establish to be effective in managing and maintaining the enterprise knowledge portal. The standards around the services provided by the support and competency center will define the policies and procedures that frame the system boundaries. The best practices and guidelines will define how to best apply the standards for each service. The overall structure and responsibilities of the support and competency center involve the collaboration and shared work processes of knowledge experts throughout the organization. You will want to review and analyze the information structure and create a structure that best fits your organization. The information provided here is one possible set of services with identified roles and responsibilities to manage those services. You will want to modify the scenario to more closely match your organization.

Enterprise Knowledge Portal Support and Competency Center Services

Once the enterprise knowledge portal has been deployed, the support and competency center will take over the day-to-day maintenance of services.

This team will create a service level agreement that defines the performance and availability of the enterprise knowledge portal for users in your organization. Performance is critical to the enterprise knowledge portal. You will need to establish what the response time is from the user interface to users and monitor the enterprise knowledge portal solution to meet this expectation. The enterprise knowledge portal will need to be available during the hours outlined in the service level agreement. There might be times that the enterprise knowledge portal is unavailable for maintenance, backup, new releases, and other identified outages.

There are additional enterprise knowledge portal infrastructure issues. These include being able to scale to accommodate a growing number of enterprise knowledge portal users and being able to extend across a growing number of applications, solutions, and services. The security model you establish is critical to ensure that the right people have access to the right information. It takes on two aspects: one that responds to authenticating to the organization and the second that responds to the authentication and access of users in the organization. The maintainability issues of the enterprise knowledge portal are covered in detail as a collection of services. This type of organization allows you to break up the enterprise knowledge portal solution into subsets of activities, best practices, and guidelines for more effective management, support, and maintenance. The enterprise knowledge portal services are owned by the support and competency center. The services include:

- Presentation services
- Information services
- Infrastructure services
- Identity management services
- Administration services
- Access and integration services
- Content services
- Collaboration services
- Development services

Presentation Services

The presentation services deal with the user interface elements of the enterprise knowledge portal. The browser interface is segmented into frames where each personalized application or a new browser window can be launched when a new application is initiated. The enterprise knowledge portal is a collection of different panes that contain portal objects. In a majority of enterprise portal solutions the portal objects function as a Web service that transforms the back-end data and business logic to the final presentation format. It is possible to design relationships between the portal objects. For example, you might select customers that have purchased a specific service in the last quarter from the enterprise knowledge portal taxonomy. When the user submits his request, all the enterprise knowledge portal content windows presented in the user interface pivot to present the information specific to the query selected by the user. The utility of the enterprise knowledge portal is its ability to integrate multiple technologies within a single Web screen. These enterprise knowledge portal pages support the integration of technologies over multiple platforms in a highly available solution. Standards, service levels, best practices, and guidelines to establish include:

- *Usability Standards, Best Practices, and Guidelines.* The support and competency center will need to work closely with enterprise knowledge portal users and enterprise knowledge portal project teams to maintain an intuitive user interface. Document and publish your usability standards.
- *User Interface Standards, Best Practices, and Guidelines.* Personalized user interfaces will provide new challenges in your organization. It will be possible for users to create unique user experiences. The support and competency center will need to know how to support this environment and will need to work closely with corporate communications and other Web user interface owners to agree to the standards that will apply to your organization. Document and publish your user interface standards.
- *Standard User Interface Templates.* You will need to create a collection of user interface templates that incorporate your usability and user interface standards. Enterprise knowledge portal developers on the enterprise knowledge portal project team and the enterprise knowledge portal support and competency center team will use these templates to develop new releases of the solution and to learn and understand your user interface and usability corporate standards.

Information Services

An information service deals with managing the content that is presented in the enterprise knowledge portal. The content might originate from a structured data source, an unstructured data source inside your organization, or external information available on public or private websites. The information may be coming from third-party sources in the form of a Web service (e.g., syndicated content), or might be provided in the form of documents. Enterprise knowledge portal users can then subscribe to one or more information services on a personalized basis as part of their customization functionality. Standards, service levels, best practices, and guidelines to establish include:

- *Content Network*. Create the content network diagrams for your organization. Publish and continue to maintain the content network diagrams.
- *Content Registry.* Establish a database that documents the content being accessed in the enterprise knowledge portal. Document information owners and knowledge experts for the content. Identify how often the content is updated for enterprise knowledge portal users.

Infrastructure Services

The enterprise knowledge portal is constructed as multiple levels of infrastructure services that provide a comprehensive unification and integration platform. It is important to know the network platforms, applications, and services that are working together to provide enterprise knowledge portal features and functions. You will want to include services related to load balancing, caching, high availability, and performance that are provided by the Web server environment. The infrastructure services issues are focused on performance, accessibility, scalability, security, maintainability, and extensibility of the enterprise knowledge portal solution. Standards, service levels, best practices, and guidelines to establish include:

- *Platform Standards, Best Practices, and Guidelines.* There will be standards for the operating system as well as client services for e-mail, groupware, and Web browsers. You will create additional standards for presentation servers, application servers, integration servers, and data servers. Work with information technology in your organization to identify and publish your platform standards. Learn the best practices and guidelines to use your platform standards.
- *Systems Management Standards, Best Practices, and Guidelines.* There will be standards created for day-to-day operations required to maintain the enterprise knowledge portal and planning for future enhancements and upgrades that will be required. Document your systems management standards and share them with the support and competency center.
- *Service-Level Agreements.* You will want to document and publish the proper levels of service for the enterprise knowledge portal. This is a list of performance and availability specifications based on certain workloads. Measure the performance and availability of the enterprise knowledge portal.

- *Operational Level Agreements.* The enterprise knowledge portal support and competency center will have response and other agreements with users. You will want to document, publish, and measure any operational agreements your organization implements.

Identity Management Services

The identity management services deal with authentication issues that map the roles and privileges of end users to individual security policies and domains of content within the enterprise knowledge portal. The security elements to be dealt with as a part of identity management services include secure access (e.g., firewalls), directory synchronization, authentication (e.g., user name and password management), and single sign-on that tie directly to infrastructure services. There are additional security issues at the individual portal objects that will tie directly to administration services and content services. A well-integrated set of identity management services will tie the administration and content services with an independent set of corporate information technology security services. Standards, service levels, best practices, and guidelines to establish include:

- *User Profiles.* The enterprise knowledge portal will keep a profile for each user. This profile is used for customization and personalization features. Each of the portal objects has access to the individual user profiles and uses them to store preference information about a user or role. The support and competency center will need to manage enhancements, updates, and maintenance of user profiles for the enterprise knowledge portal.
- *Role and Group Definitions.* Roles are organized collections of capabilities that are utilized by developers. Roles can have groups or individual users as members. The role members will have access to the capabilities defined by enterprise knowledge portal developers. Groups are organized collections of identities that are configured and managed by administrators. Groups are an efficient way to manage the privacy, integrity, and access to data. The support and competency center will need to maintain the role and group definitions used in the enterprise knowledge portal.
- *Directory Structure.* The enterprise knowledge portal will use a common structure to maintain user information, organizational information, and access control and certificate information. This information is used to manage authentication and sign-on to the enterprise knowledge portal. It will also be used to pass authentication information to applications and systems accessed by users while they interact with the enterprise

knowledge portal. The support and competency center will work with information technology to manage and maintain the directory structure.

- *Single Sign-On Strategy.* The enterprise knowledge portal will coordinate information from several websites, data stores, applications, and systems. Each of these environments has different security paradigms that your single sign-on technologies will address. You will need to establish and document a single sign-on strategy for your organization. This strategy will be owned by the information technology security team and used by the enterprise knowledge portal.

Administration Services

The administration services are necessary for the enterprise knowledge portal to be easily managed, maintained, and supported. This is necessary if you want to delegate parts of the configuration to the enterprise knowledge portal knowledge workers and members of the information technology organization. Administration services are often offered through a Web interface and might include taxonomy management, role management, user management, configuration management, and registration of portal objects. Standards, service levels, best practices, and guidelines to establish include:

- *Delegated Management.* Your support and competency center will want to identify knowledge expert community members to configure access for roles and groups or other activities for the enterprise knowledge portal users. The support and competency center will need to establish standards and publish the delegated management policies and procedures to be used throughout your organization.
- *Certification of Enterprise Knowledge Portal Objects.* The support and competency center will want to review the portal objects created by enterprise knowledge portal development teams. They will validate that usability, user interface, and programming standards were followed. They will verify that as often as possible, portal objects were used from the reusable library. Setting up code review sessions as part of the enterprise knowledge portal development schedule will resolve issues as soon as possible during the development process.
- *Registration of Enterprise Knowledge Portal Objects.* As part of the deployment process for the enterprise knowledge portal, the appropriate documentation, updates to the roles and groups, updates to the user profile, and additions to the reusable portal object library need to be completed. The support and competency center will work with enterprise knowledge portal project teams to make sure they are aware of the registration requirements.

Access and Integration Services

A comprehensive enterprise knowledge portal solution will provide the access and integration services required to work directly with databases and applications. The access and integration services deal with these issues for the enterprise knowledge portal and portal objects. You will also tie existing enterprise application integration (EAI) solutions to gain access to back-end adapters or application programming interfaces (API). The access and integration services deal with issues associated with application programming interfaces or enterprise application integration functionality. Access and integration services include interfaces and connectivity to enterprise resource planning (ERP) software packages such as SAP. They can also provide access to legacy systems, content management, document management, and collaboration. A well-designed access and integration services solution will allow for the development of additional adapters for new systems, databases, and applications as needed. Standards, service levels, best practices, and guidelines to establish include:

- *Enterprise Application Integration Standards, Best Practices, and Guidelines.* You will need to create a set of standards that will accept and coordinate queries that produce consolidated results from one or many back-end systems. Enterprise knowledge portal developers on the enterprise knowledge portal project team and the enterprise knowledge portal support and competency center team will use these access and integration standards to develop portal objects. Your EAI standards need to be published and communicated.
- *Connectivity Standards, Best Practices, and Guidelines.* You will need to create a collection of standards that define how to link the enterprise knowledge portal to back-end systems and data sources. Enterprise knowledge portal developers on the enterprise knowledge portal project team and the enterprise knowledge portal support and competency center team will use these connectivity standards to create connectivity portal objects.
- *Access and Integration Enterprise Knowledge Portal Objects.* The portal objects that are created that comply with your EAI and connectivity standards will be added to the enterprise knowledge portal library and reused by developers throughout your organization.

Content Services

The content services deal with the management of unstructured digital assets within the enterprise knowledge portal. This will include a fill-text indexing engine, a set of crawlers that are capable of navigating and indexing existing content, a metadata repository, and a content management system to allow for the submittal and approval of content into the enterprise knowledge portal. It is important to include information library services or a taxonomy manager to effectively deal with your content services issues. Standards, service levels, best practices, and guidelines to establish include:

- *Knowledge Organization System Standards, Best Practices, and Guidelines.* The knowledge organization system consists of the content directory, term lists, classification hierarchies, and other structures you define. The taxonomy directory will be used to tag content throughout the organization into a hierarchy of categories. The knowledge organization system elements locate content and navigate the directory structure from within the enterprise knowledge portal. The categorization schemes and other knowledge organization system elements need to be published to set standards, best practices, and guidelines for how they will be used.
- *Federated Search Standards, Best Practices, and Guidelines.* Search functionality is a fundamental capability. Search includes a set of indexes that allow users to browse and retrieve content based on selection criteria. The federated search will be able to retrieve information across multiple data sources and their integrated applications. The user will be able to specify the search criteria once, and retrieve relevant content links from multiple repositories targeted in the search request. Your organization will need to document and publish search functionality and standards that will be used by the enterprise knowledge portal.
- *Enterprise Knowledge Portal Library Standards, Best Practices, and Guidelines.* A complete collection of portal objects that are used in your enterprise knowledge portal are registered as part of the library. The registered objects are validated to verify compliance with your collection of enterprise knowledge portal standards, best practices, and guidelines. Development teams and the support and competency center will use the reusable enterprise knowledge portal library to continue to deploy consistent functionality for enterprise knowledge portal users that meet their requirements and objectives. For example, there will be user interface templates, connectivity objects, and taxonomy objects that are available for development teams to deploy to meet the requirements and objectives of their current enterprise knowledge portal projects. If the enterprise knowledge portal library is captured and maintained appropriately, it will produce a knowledge map of information and show how people use that information for your organization.

Collaboration Services

Collaboration services allow enterprise knowledge portal users to work together more effectively by establishing shared workspaces, shared document repositories, real-time interactions, and shared discussion forums. Collaboration services will sponsor the definition and execution of work flow across the organization and to the extranet to include external content, systems, and services. You should consider opportunities that allow users to subscribe to information, to be notified of status changes in information, and to set up personal or broadcast alerts. Standards, service levels, best practices, and guidelines to establish include:

- *Discussion Forums Standards, Best Practices, and Guidelines.* For networks of users to come together briefly and permanently to meet their objectives, you will need some standards and best practices for implementing and using discussion forums in your organization. You will want to publish these standards to establish the policy and procedure around discussion forums. This will allow best practices and guidelines to be consistent between discussion forums for the dynamic addition and removal of users to work effectively.
- *Subscription Standards, Best Practices, and Guidelines.* Users will want to request information be forwarded to them as it becomes available in your organization. To do this, users will be able to subscribe to receive information on certain topics. Using the categorization schemes outlined as part of your knowledge organization system, you can provide user customization and configuration to provide subscription features and functionality to enterprise knowledge portal users. You will want to publish your subscription standards, best practices, and guidelines for your organization.
- *Alert and Notification Standards, Best Practices, and Guidelines.* The enterprise knowledge portal can forward information to users based on one or more conditions occurring in one or many application sources. These alerts and notifications can be delivered within the enterprise knowledge portal as well as by e-mail or wireless devices. Alerts and notifications usually accommodate individual user preferences, such as deliver mechanism and format, the conditions that trigger an alert, and the frequency of notifications. You will need to establish templates and other standards, best practices, and guidelines to effectively manage alerts and notifications for your organization.

Development Services

The development services create an environment that allows for the development of portal objects, components, and modules. In most cases these portal objects are implemented as Web services. The development services deal with issues around creating, testing, registering, and deploying these portal objects, components, and modules. Standards, service levels, best practices, and guidelines to establish include:

- *Programming Standards, Best Practices, and Guidelines.* There will need to be best practices for how to organize code for the enterprise knowledge portal. These programming standards will define your policies and procedures around organizing and creating code. The best practices and guidelines will be used to help developers apply your programming standards. Make certain developers have good code samples from the portal object library to learn and execute their enterprise knowledge portal project.
- *Quality Assurance Standards, Best Practices, and Guidelines.* You will want to establish measurements for your enterprise knowledge portal that define the effectiveness of the solution. Apply quality assurance standards, code reviews, test plans, integrity testing, and system integration testing that will help assure that you are producing a high-quality enterprise knowledge portal. You will want to document and publish your quality assurance standards.

Enterprise Knowledge Portal Support and Competency Center Staff

The enterprise knowledge portal support and competency center staff requires a significant number of skills and people to provide seamless end-to-end support processes for users. They will leverage the current support and help desk structure in your organization. There will be several levels of support established. The first level will be the knowledge expert community to answer questions in their own business units. They will review work processes and explain data, reports, and usability of the enterprise knowledge portal. The second level will be the call center, where all queries and problems will be recorded, resolved, or escalated to the enterprise knowledge portal support and competence center. The third level of support will be the support and competency team to resolve problems that were promoted from the second level. The fourth level of support will be enterprise knowledge portal experts throughout the organization. They might reside in the support and competency center or on enterprise knowledge portal project teams. This collection of corporate experts will work with the support and competency center to resolve the issue. An overview of the support levels follows:

- *First Level.* The knowledge expert community where the users work and work processes are performed. The knowledge expert community extends the understanding of the enterprise knowledge portal beyond the project team and the support and competency center. They will be available to answer questions relative to the work process and use of the enterprise knowledge portal. They will refer questions they are unable to resolve to the call center for resolution and proper escalation. They will assist business analysts and provide communications to their business units relevant to support issues. The knowledge expert community can assist in the definition of business requirements and testing of enterprise knowledge portal enhancements, upgrades, and fixes that affect their business unit.

- *Second Level.* Enterprise knowledge portal users and knowledge expert community members will submit enterprise knowledge portal issues to the call center. The call center is a tracking system to capture user queries and problems. A knowledge base will accompany the call tracking system to proved answers where possible. The call center will receive and log calls. They will provide assistance in the basic concepts, navigation, categorization and file management, print management, and other enterprise knowledge portal functions. The call center will resolve or escalate queries and problems to the support and competency center established by the service level agreements.
- *Third Level.* The support and competency center will fix issues and communicate to the appropriate teams. They will own the problems and ensure that the users are kept updated on the status until there is a resolution. They have expertise in enterprise knowledge portal services, communications, and learning information.
- *Fourth Level.* The final level of support will be provided from within the support and competency center. Enterprise knowledge portal experts throughout the organization will be utilized to fix or make progress on any identified configuration or program changes and provide more in-depth analysis of problems that are not easily resolved at third-level support. The level three support and competency center resource will remain the main contact to the user for communication of status and resolution of the problem.

Roles and Responsibilities

The roles identified are not necessarily full-time activities. The roles ensure that the skill sets and responsibilities are well defined. These clear definitions of what is needed to fill the role assists the support and competency center management in synchronizing the skills of the team members to get the job done effectively. It consists of the following core team roles:

Knowledge Expert Community (First-Level Support)

The knowledge expert community members have a strong understanding of the enterprise knowledge portal and business processes in their business unit. They have excellent communication and facilitation skills. These individuals are responsive and cooperative. The knowledge expert community members do not work in the support and competency center. Responsibilities include:

- Using their enterprise knowledge portal functional knowledge and business unit work process knowledge
- Assisting in the troubleshooting for their business unit
- Promoting users contacting the call center when there are issues that cannot be resolved on-site
- Assisting with the validation of enterprise knowledge portal production fixes
- Participating in regression testing for new releases of enterprise knowledge portal functionality
- Serving as a key contact for enterprise knowledge portal functional specifics
- Assisting with enterprise knowledge portal enhancements, upgrades, and fixes
- Reviewing impacts of new enterprise knowledge portal implementations and helping to correct any issues

Call Center Representatives (Second-Level Support)

Call center representatives are responsive with a basic knowledge of the enterprise knowledge portal. They are familiar with the call tracking system. They possess management, communication, and problem-solving skills. Call center representatives do not work on the support and competency center team. Responsibilities include:

- Receiving calls from enterprise knowledge portal users
- Resolving basic requests (e.g., log-in, passwords, navigation)
- Documenting as much information as possible on the problem ticket according to appropriate severity and other indicators

Support and Competency Center Manager (Third-Level Support)

The support and competency center manager has leadership, project management, call center management, and communication skills. This person has strong working relationships with information technology and the enterprise knowledge portal program management team. Responsibilities include:

- Defining and evolving the enterprise knowledge portal services
- Defining and evolving the enterprise knowledge portal support strategy
- Owning the resource budget and forecast
- Developing and maintaining client relationships with business units
- Coordinating and allocating appropriate resources to handle support and maintenance issues
- Owning the work processes that identify, create, test, communicate, and migrate all enterprise knowledge portal changes to the production environments
- Working with enterprise knowledge portal project teams and developers to recognize the impacts between production fixes and new development
- Participating in communication with other corporate initiatives
- Updating the support and competency center procedures with lessons learned

Support and Competency Center Problem Ticket Coordinator (Third-Level Support)

The support and competency center problem ticket coordinator requires basic understanding of the enterprise knowledge portal and a high level of knowledge around business unit work processes. This individual has an excellent understanding of the support and competency center work processes. Communications, project management, decisiveness, and problem solving are several skills needed by the support and competency center problem ticket coordinator. Responsibilities include:

- Analyzing the problem ticket queue and assigning user incidents to members of the support and competency center
- Providing additional measurements in addition to the information technology service level reporting
- Managing the customization of problem tickets to facilitate support and competency center work processes (e.g., automatic queries, macros)

Identity Management Administration (Third-Level Support)

The identity management administration has extensive knowledge of the organization's internal controls. They have strong security and communications skills. They are not members of the support and competency center. Responsibilities include:

- Administering the enterprise knowledge portal security processes
- Owning security issues
- Changing user identification information and passwords
- Ensuring enterprise knowledge portal production incidents are addressed and closed within the time frames aligned with the problem-tracking work processes

Support and Competency Center Representatives (Third-Level Support)

The support and competency center representatives have a strong understanding of the enterprise knowledge portal and a high level of knowledge around business unit work processes. These individuals have high-level configuration skills and problem-solving skills of the enterprise knowledge portal. They have a complete understanding of the support and competency center work processes. Communications, project management, and responsiveness are additional required skills. Responsibilities include:

- Owning assigned problem tickets
- Resolving informational service requests and submitted problems
- Identifying scope and expertise needed to resolve complex problem tickets (e.g., configuration change, interface defects, work process problems)
- Assisting in prioritization of problem ticket resolution
- Assessing impacts of potential production fixes to business units and enterprise knowledge portal users
- Ensuring production incidents are resolved and closed in a timely manner
- Following problem management and change control work processes
- Validating that all production fixes have been fully tested
- Communicating with enterprise knowledge portal users in order to close trouble tickets
- Executing the change control work processes for production fixes, maintenance, and enhancements
- Ensuring that resolutions adhere to enterprise knowledge portal standards, best practices, and guidelines

- Executing appropriate test plans for fixes targeted for the enterprise knowledge portal production environment
- Reviewing learning and other communications to ensure that they correctly document the impacts of the production fix

Business Analysts (Third-Level Support)

Business analysts have a basic understanding of the enterprise knowledge portal and strong working knowledge of the business units work processes. These individuals have leadership, communications, problem-solving, and work process design skills. Business analysts do not work on the support and competency center team. Responsibilities include:

- Owning business unit work processes
- Coordinating assignment of business analysts to resolve business unit work processes trouble tickets
- Assisting in the prioritization of enterprise knowledge portal enhancements requests
- Communicating with business unit management and employees

Information Technology (Expert)

Technical leads from information technology have a strong understanding of the enterprise knowledge portal infrastructure and a basic working knowledge of the business units work processes. These individuals have leadership, communications, problem-solving, and enterprise knowledge portal configuration skills. Technical leads do not work on the support and competency center team. Responsibilities include:

- Developing the enterprise knowledge portal architecture and infrastructure strategy and support
- Developing and implementing release schedules for the enterprise knowledge portal
- Maintaining platform and systems management integrity for the enterprise knowledge portal
- Owning enterprise knowledge portal system changes based on the release schedule
- Owning work processes and procedures to maintain consistent configuration across the enterprise knowledge portal environment

Enterprise Knowledge Portal Librarian (Expert)

The enterprise knowledge portal librarian has a strong understanding of portal objects and the enterprise knowledge portal services and a basic working knowledge of the business units work processes. This individual has leadership, communications, and documentation skills. Responsibilities include:

- ❐ Owning the enterprise knowledge portal library and the enterprise knowledge portal design documentation
- ❐ Owning communication plan and reuse of portal objects
- ❐ Ensuring consistency across use and implementation of portal objects
- ❐ Administering the processes to communicate information from the enterprise knowledge portal project teams and enterprise knowledge portal program management team to the support and competency center team

Learning Team (Expert)

Learning team members have a strong understanding of the enterprise knowledge portal infrastructure and a basic working knowledge of the business units work processes. These individuals have distributed learning, communications, and training material development skills. Learning team members do not work on the support and competency center team. Responsibilities include:

- ❐ Developing electronic learning opportunities for the enterprise knowledge portal with the enterprise knowledge portal project teams and the support and competency center
- ❐ Assisting in creating and maintaining enterprise knowledge portal training and learning material
- ❐ Creating communications for availability and changes to enterprise knowledge portal training and learning material

Enterprise Knowledge Portal Operations (Expert)

Operations team members from information technology have a strong understanding of the enterprise knowledge portal environment and a basic working knowledge of the business units work processes. These individuals have problem-solving, infrastructure, and enterprise knowledge portal configuration skills. Operations team members do not work on the support and competency center team. Responsibilities include:

- Monitoring enterprise knowledge portal system performance based on criteria established in the service level agreement
- Owning performance and availability for the enterprise knowledge portal

Enterprise Knowledge Portal Infrastructure Support (Expert)

Infrastructure support team members from information technology have a strong understanding of the enterprise knowledge portal environment and a basic working knowledge of the business unit work processes. These individuals have problem-solving, infrastructure, and enterprise knowledge portal configuration skills. Infrastructure support team members do not work on the support and competency center team. Responsibilities include:

- Coordinating and communicating scheduled enterprise knowledge portal downtime (e.g., production system maintenance, backups, upgrades)
- Defining and implementing work processes for managing, communicating, and escalating nonscheduled enterprise knowledge portal downtime issues (e.g., disaster recovery)

Key Points

Once the enterprise knowledge portal has been deployed, the support and competency center will take over the day-to-day maintenance of services. The maintainability issues of the enterprise knowledge portal are covered in detail as a collection of services. This type of organization allows you to break up the enterprise knowledge portal solution into subsets of activities, best practices, and guidelines for more effective management, support, and maintenance. The enterprise knowledge portal services are owned by the support and competency center. The standards, service levels, best practices, and guidelines to establish include:

Presentation Services

- Usability standards, best practices, and guidelines
- User interface standards, best practices, and guidelines
- Standard user interface templates

Information Services

- Content network
- Content registry

Infrastructure Services

- Platform standards, best practices, and guidelines
- Systems management standards, best practices, and guidelines
- Service-level agreements
- Operational level agreements

Identity Management Services

- User profiles
- Role and group definitions
- Directory structure
- Single sign-on strategy

Administration Services

- Delegated management
- Certification of enterprise knowledge portal objects
- Registration of enterprise knowledge portal objects

Access and Integration Services

- Enterprise application integration standards, best practices, and guidelines
- Connectivity standards, best practices, and guidelines
- Access and integration enterprise knowledge portal objects

Content Services

- Knowledge organization system standards, best practices, and guidelines
- Federated search standards, best practices, and guidelines
- Enterprise knowledge portal library standards, best practices, and guidelines

Collaboration Services

- Discussion forums standards, best practices, and guidelines
- Subscription standards, best practices, and guidelines
- Alert and notification standards, best practices, and guidelines

Development Services

- Programming standards, best practices, and guidelines
- Quality assurance standards, best practices, and guidelines

The enterprise knowledge portal support and competency center staff requires a significant number of skills and people to provide seamless end-to-end support processes for users. They will leverage the current support and help desk structure in your organization. There will be several levels of support established. The first level will be the knowledge expert community to answer questions in their own business units. They will review work processes and explain data, reports, and usability of the enterprise knowledge portal. The second level will be the call center, where all queries and problems will be recorded, resolved, or escalated to the enterprise knowledge portal support and competence center. The third level of support will be the support and competency team to resolve problems that were promoted from the second level. The fourth level of support will be enterprise knowledge portal experts throughout the organization. They might reside in the support and competency center or on enterprise knowledge portal project teams. This collection of corporate experts will work with the support and competency center to resolve the issue.

The roles identified are not necessarily full-time activities. The roles ensure that the skill sets and responsibilities are well defined. These clear definitions of what is needed to fill the role assists the support and competency center's management in synchronizing the skills of the team members to get the job done effectively. It consists of the following core team roles:

- Knowledge expert community (first-level support)
- Call center representatives (second-level support)
- Support and competency center manager (third-level support)
- Support and competency center problem ticket coordinator (third-level support)
- Identity management administration (third-level support)
- Support and competency center representatives (third-level support)

- ❒ Business analysts (third-level support)
- ❒ Information technology (expert)
- ❒ Enterprise knowledge portal librarian (expert)
- ❒ Learning team (expert)
- ❒ Enterprise knowledge portal operations (expert)
- ❒ Enterprise knowledge portal infrastructure support (expert)

The material covered throughout this book is a compilation of the material and tasks identified to create the enterprise knowledge portal map, the enterprise knowledge portal program, and the enterprise knowledge portal project methodology. MyCompany is a fictitious presentation for you to use as an example. You will want to replace or enhance the material and templates presented with those deliverables that are more specific to your organization as you begin to map your knowledge management objectives into the enterprise portal, establish how the resulting enterprise knowledge portal can be integrated into your business strategy, and outline a design methodology to create your work process-centric enterprise knowledge portal.

V

Appendixes

Appendix A: Knowledge Management Resources

Harvard Business Review. *Harvard Business Review on Knowledge Management*. Boston, MA: Harvard Business School Publishing, 1998.

Huang, Kuan-Tsae, Yang W. Lee, and Richard Y. Yang. *Knowledge Power: Quality Information and Knowledge Management*. Paramus, N.J.: Prentice Hall, 1998.

Koulopoulos, Thomas M., Carl Frappaolo, and Tom M. Koulopoulos. *Smart Things to Know About Knowledge Management*. Mankato, MN: Capstone Press, 2001.

Krogh, Georg Von, Kazuo Ichijo, and Ikujiro Nonaka. *Enabling Knowledge Creation: How to Unlock the Mystery of Tacit Knowledge and Release the Power of Innovation*. Oxford, UK: Oxford University Press, 2000.

Liebowitz, Jay. *Building Organizational Intelligence: A Knowledge Management Primer*. Boca Raton, FL: CRC Press, 2000.

Liebowitz, Jay. *Knowledge Management Handbook*. Boca Raton, FL: CRC Press, 1999.

Tidd, Joe, and Joseph Tidd. *From Knowledge Management to Strategic Competence: Measuring Technological, Market and Organizational Innovation*. River Edge, NJ: World Scientific Publishing Company, Incorporated, 2001.

Tiwana, Amrit. The Knowledge Management Toolkit: Practical Techniques for Building a Knowledge Management System. Paramus, N.J.: Prentice Hall, 1999.

Tiwana, Amrit, and Miles Williams. *The Essential Guide to Knowledge Management: E-Business and CRM Applications*. Paramus, N.J.: Prentice Hall, 2000.

APPENDIX B: ENTERPRISE KNOWLEDGE PORTAL RESOURCES

Collins, Heidi. *Corporate Portals: Revolutionizing Information Access to Increase Productivity and Drive the Bottom Line*. New York: AMACOM, 2000.

Davydov, Mark M. *Corporate Portals and E-Business Integration*. New York: McGraw-Hill Professional Publishing, 2001.

Liautaud, Bernard, and Mark Hammond. *E-Business Intelligence: Turning Information into Knowledge into Profit*. New York: McGraw-Hill Professional Publishing, 2000.

Vering, Matthias, Grant Norris, Peter Barth, James R. Hurley, Brenda MacKay, and David J. Duray. *The E-Business Workplace: Discovering the Power of Enterprise Portals*. New York: John Wiley & Sons, 2001.

APPENDIX C: RECOMMENDED READING

Business Intelligence

De Ville, Barry. *Microsoft Data Mining: Integrating Business Intelligence for E-Commerce and Knowledge Management*. Woburn, MA: Butterworth-Heinemann, 2001.

Sullivan, Dan. *Document Warehousing and Text Mining: Techniques for Improving Business Operations, Marketing, and Sales*. New York: John Wiley & Sons, 2001.

Collaboration and Communities

Cohen, Don, and Laurence Prusak. *In Good Company: How Social Capital Makes Organizations Work*. Boston, MA: Harvard Business School Publishing, 2001.

Davenport, Thomas H., and Laurence Prusak. *Working Knowledge*. Boston, MA: Harvard Business School Publishing, 2000.

Davis, Julie L., and Suzanne Harrison. *Edison in the Boardroom: How Leading Companies Realize Value from Their Intellectual Assets*. New York: John Wiley & Sons, Inc., 2001.

O'Dell, Carla, and C. Jackson Grayson. *If Only We Knew What We Know: The Transfer of Internal Knowledge and Best Practice*. New York: Simon & Schuster Trade, 1998.

Senge, Peter M. *The Fifth Discipline: The Art and Practice of the Learning Organization*. Garden City, NY: Doubleday & Company, Inc., 1994.

Senge, Peter M., Charlotte Roberts, Richard B. Ross, and Bryan Smigh. *The Fifth Discipline Fieldbook: Strategies and Tools for Building a Learning Organization*. New York: Bantam Doubleday Dell Publishing Group, 1994.

Content Management

Bannan, Joan. *Intranet Document Management: A Guide for Webmasters and Content Providers*. Reading, MA: Addison Wesley Longman, Inc., 1997.

Nakano, Russell. Web Content Management: A Collaborative Approach. Reading, MA: Addison Wesley Longman, Inc., 2001.

Learning

Rosenberg, Marc J. *E-Learning: Strategies for Delivering Knowledge in the Digital Age*. New York: McGraw-Hill Professional Publishing, 2000.

Project Management

Forsberg, Kevin, Howard Cotterman, Hal Mooz. *Visualizing Project Management: A Model for Business and Technical Success*. New York: John Wiley & Sons, 2000.

McConnell, Steve. *Software Project Survival Guide: How to Be Sure Your First Important Project Isn't Your Last*. Redmond, WA: Microsoft Press, 1998.

Murch, Richard. *Project Management: Best Practices for IT Professionals*. New York: Prentice Hall, 2000.

Information Technology

Janczewski, Lech. *Internet and Intranet Security Management: Risks and Solutions*. Hershey, PA: Idea Group Publishing, 2000.

Northcutt, Stephen, Donald McLachlan, and Judy Novak. *Network Intrusion Detection: An Analyst's Handbook*. Indianapolis, IN: New Riders Publishing, 2000.

Zwicky, Elizabeth D., Simon Cooper, D. Brent Chapman, and Deborah Russell. *Building Internet Firewalls (Second Edition)*. Cambridge, MA: O'Reilly & Associates, 2000.

BIBLIOGRAPHY

Andrews, Whit. "Portals and E-Commerce: Different Goals, Parallel Projects." *Gartner Research Note* (June 2001).

Applehans, Wayne, Alden Globe, and Greg Laugero. *Managing Knowledge: A Practical Web-Based Approach*. Reading, MA: Addison Wesley Longman, Inc., 1999.

Bachman, John E., John R. Devereaux, Christopher M. Neenan, Jonathan M. Peacock. "Value Transformation: Driving Shareholder Value Throughout the Organization." PricewaterhouseCoopers, 1997.

Batchelder, Robert, and David Smith. "Instant Messaging: The Sleeping Giant." *Gartner Research Note* (August 2001).

"Best Practices for mySAP Supply Chain Management." Walldorf, Germany: SAP AG (2001).

Black, Andrew, Philip Wright, and John E. Bachman. "In Search of Shareholder Value." Pitman, 1998.

"Business Portals: The New Media for E-Business Interchange." Boston, MA: The Delphi Group, Inc. (February 2001).

Beyer, Hugh, and Karen Holtzblatt. *Contextual Design: Defining Customer-Centered Systems*. San Francisco, CA: Morgan Kaufmann Publishers, Inc., 1998.

Collins, Heidi. *Corporate Portals: Revolutionizing Information Access to Increase Productivity and Drive the Bottom Line*. New York: AMACOM, 2000.

Connelly, Ph.D., Richard, Robin McNeill, and Roland Mosimann. *The Multidimensional Manager: 24 Ways to Impact Your Bottom Line in 90 Days*. Ontario, Canada: Cognos Inc., 1999.

Drakos, Nikos, Jim Duggan, Mark Gilbert, Benoit Lheureux, Debra Logan, Mark Nicolett, Victor Votsch, and Alan Weintraub. "The Elements of a

Content Management Strategy." *Gartner Research Note* (February 2000).

"Electronic Business Strategies." Stamford, CT: META Group, Inc. (2000).

"Embedding KM: Creating a Value Proposition." Houston, TX: American Productivity and Quality Center (May 2001).

Fleming, M. "Measuring the Value of Knowledge Content." *Gartner Research Note* (January 1999).

Fritz, Ph.D., Roger. *Think Like a Manager: Everything They Didn't Tell You When They Promoted You*. Shawnee Mission, KS: National Seminars Publications, Inc., 1994.

Gartner Research. *Dealing in Web Currency*. Stamford, CT: Gartner, Inc., 2001.

Gassman, Bill. "Enterprise Portals: Can They Be Managed?" *Gartner Research Note* (May 1999).

Gilbert, M., A. Weintraub, V. Votsch, B. Lheureux, M. Nicolett, N. Drakos, D. Logan, and J. Duggan. "The Elements of a Content Management Strategy." *Gartner Research Note* (February 2000).

Gilbert, M., V. Votsch, and A. Weintraub. "Content and Process Intersect in Web Publishing." *Gartner Research Note* (March 2001).

Gold-Bernstein, Beth. "EAI Market Segmentation." *EAI Journal* (2001).

"Groove Product Backgrounder." Beverly, MA: Groove Networks, Inc. (2001).

Harris, Kathy, and Wildir Arevolo De Azevedo Filho. "Communities: Sociology Meets Technology." *Gartner Research Note* (July 2001).

Harvard Business Review. *Harvard Business Review on Knowledge Management*. Boston, MA: Harvard Business School Publishing, 1998.

"The Hidden Power of Communities." Houston, TX: American Productivity and Quality Center (January 2000).

Kaplan, Robert, and David Norton. "The Balanced Scorecard—Measures That Drive Performance." *Harvard Business Review* (1992).

Keen, Peter G. W. "Ready for 'new' B2B?" *Computer World* (September 2000).

Kiechel, Walter. "Sniping at Strategic Planning." *Planning Review* (May 1984).

King, John, and Frank Ashton. "ValueTech: Making the 21st Century Financial Management System a Reality Today." PricewaterhouseCoopers, 1998.

"Key Roles in the Success of Communities of Practice." Houston, TX: American Productivity and Quality Center (June 2001).

Knox, R., M. Gilbert, J. Ingalls, J. Lundy, and A. Weintraub. "The Content Space." *Gartner Research Note* (April 2000).

Knox, R. "Publishing and the Content Enabled Infrastructure." *Gartner Research Note* (February 1999).

Kotter, John. *Leading Change*. Boston, MA: Harvard Business School Press, 1996.

Latham, L. "Web Content Management and Portals: Who's Doing What?" *Gartner Research Note* (July 2001).

Letson, Russell. "A Closer Look at Portals and EAI." *Transform Magazine* (July 2001).

Leonard, Ph.D., Allenna. "A Viable System Model: Consideration of Knowledge Management." *Journal of Knowledge Management Practice* (August 1999).

"Leveraging Dynamic Content to Create a Powerful e-Business." Pleasanton, CA: Documentum, Inc. (2000).

Logan, Debra. "Content Management Meets Knowledge Management." Gartner Research Note (February 2001).

"Measurement for Knowledge Management." Houston, TX: American Productivity and Quality Center (February 2001).

Mintzberg, Henry. "The Rise and Fall of Strategic Planning." *Free Press*, 1993.

"Mobile Computing." Walldorf, Germany: SAP AG (2000).

"myKGN: A Return-On-Investment Study." Stamford, CT: META Group, Inc. (2001).

"mySAP.com Security." Walldorf, Germany: SAP AG (2000).

"mySAP.com Workplace." Walldorf, Germany: SAP AG (2000).

"mySAP.com Workplace–External Community Portals." Walldorf, Germany: SAP AG (2000).

Najjar, L. J. (1996). "Multimedia Information and Learning." *Journal of Educational Multimedia and Hypermedia,* 5, 129-150.

Norton, David. "Building a Management System to Implement Your Strategy." *Renaissance Solutions*, 1996.

Phifer, Gene. "Best Practices in Deploying Enterprise Portals." *Gartner Research Note* (July 2000).

Phifer, Gene. "How Does One Get an Intranet Portal?" *Gartner Research Note* (December 1998).

Phifer, Gene. "How Portals Will Help Slow the 'Infoflood.'" *Gartner Research Note* (May 2001).

Phifer, Gene. "Multiple Portals in Your Enterprise? Count on It." *Gartner Research Note* (April 2000).

Phifer, Gene, and Tom Berg. "'Portal': The Most Abused Term in IT." *Gartner Research Note* (September 2000).

Phifer, Gene. "Portals into the Software Ecosystem." *Gartner Research Note* (February 2001).

Porter, Michael. "What is Strategy?" *Harvard Business Review* (December 1996).

"SAP Travel Management." Walldorf, Germany: SAP AG (2000).

Rappaport, Alfred. "Creating Shareholder Value." Free Press, 1998.

Rigby, Darrell. "Management Tools and Techniques: 1998," Boston, MA: Bain & Company, 1998.

"SAP Strategic Enterprise Management—Translating Strategy into Action: The Balanced Scorecard." Walldorf, Germany: SAP AG (1999).

Senge, Peter. *The Fifth Discipline*. New York: Doubleday, 1990.

Shaw, Rochelle. "Portals: An Introduction." *Gartner Technology Overview* (May 2000).

Shegda, Karen. "Integrated Document Management Software: Perspective." *Gartner Technology Overview* (April 2001).

Stewart, Thomas. *Intellectual Capital*. London: Nicholas Brealy, 1998.

Vering, Matthias, Grant Norris, Peter Barth, James R. Hurley, Brenda MacKay, and David J. Duray. *The E-Business Workplace: Discovering the Power of Enterprise Portals*. New York: John Wiley & Sons, 2001.

Votsch, V. "The Challenges of Web Content Transformation." *Gartner Research Note* (March 2001).

INDEX

access
  as enterprise portal feature, 124
  to information, 14, 30
  user, 63–64, 66
access and integration services, 390
activities
  assignment to, 245, 248
  focus area diagrams of targeted, 295–300
  identification of, 242–245
  organization of, 243, 245–247
  and tasks, 247–252
  work process maps of targeted, 290–295
administration services, 389
administrative resources, centralized, 72
administrators, server, 379
agendas, sample
  for architecture and infrastructure kick-off, 233
  for architecture and infrastructure report, 239
  to management objectives review, 117
  for portal maps, 110
  for portal requirements kick-off, 207
  for portal requirements report, 213
  for program review, 255
  for strategy kick-off, 220
  for strategy report, 225
Anderson, Philip
  on group communication, 384
  on success of corporation, *xi*
AOL, 35, 82
API (application programming interface), 390
application and integration services (layer five), 375–376
application developers, 381
application development team, 270–271
application hosting services, 371
application integration, 69, 70, 375
application programming interface (API), 390
applications and systems (layer six), 376–377
approval, executive, 249, 253–256
architects, Web access, 378
architecture and infrastructure, *xvii–xviii*, 225, 228–242
  chief technology office interviews for, 230, 232–234
  report for, 233–242
  template for, 229–231
architecture and infrastructure team, 271–272

Arquilla, John, on networks vs. hierarchies, 259
assets, *xii*, 5, 341
audioconferencing, 129
auditing, work processes, 13–14
authentication, 370
authority files, 53

behavior, *see* culture and behavior
best practices, 285
bookmarks, 64
Boolean search, 56
Brown, John Seely, on innovation in corporations, 171
budgets, 177, 190, 194, 195
Building a Learning Organization (David Garvin), 3
business analysts, 398
business intelligence, 120
  documentation of applications of, 132, 133, 135, 136
  horizontal portal support of, 34
  as IT-enabling framework feature, 124–125
  in user interface, 41, 42
business object context, 310–318
  business rules as, 315–318
  and presentation filters, 312–315
  user context as, 311–313
business objectives support
  by knowledge management, 4, 18–20
  as questionnaire section, 100
business objects, 289–301
  focus area diagrams as, 295–301
  in methodology, 289–301
  work process diagrams as, 290–295
business rules, 315–318
business-to-business integration, 376
buyers, 35

caching, 371
call center representatives, 395
categorization schemes, 54
category search, 56
cellular phones, 35
centralized administrative resources, 72
certification, 389
change management plan
  charter documentation of, 177, 196, 199–202
  template of, 200
  in value proposition, 174
charter (enterprise knowledge portal program), 175–202
  benefits of portal defined in, 177, 187–189
  budgets/funding documented in, 177, 190, 194, 195
  change management plan documented in, 177, 196, 199–202
  communication plan documented in, 177, 194, 196–198
  risks with portal defined in, 177, 189–193
  scope and objectives documented in, 176, 177, 179, 180
  strategic relationships defined in, 177, 185–187
  team members and stakeholders identified in, 176, 179–186
  template for, 177, 178
chief technology office, 230, 232–234, 234
classifications and categories (knowledge organization systems), 53–54
classification schemes, 54
collaboration and communities, 120
  documentation of applications of, 135, 137, 138
  horizontal portal support of, 34
  as IT-enabling framework feature, 126–127
  in user interface, 41–43
collaboration services, 391–392
collaborative commerce, 127
collapsible windows, 46
Collins, Heidi, on methodology, 283
color, use of, 323

The Coming of the New Organization (Peter Drucker), 365
commerce server, 39
communication, knowledge expert community
  about approval of program, 254, 256
  about architecture and infrastructure, 232, 234
  about architecture and infrastructure report, 235, 242
  about interviews, 110, 112, 206–208, 219–221
  about objectives report, 114, 119
  about requirements report, 209, 216
  about strategy report, 224, 228
communication and collaboration integration, 55
communication facilitation
  constraints on, 13
  enterprise portals for, 31–32
  by knowledge management, 10–15
  as questionnaire section, 98–99
communication plan, 177, 194, 196–198
community(-ies)
  applications of, 135, 137, 138
  as collaboration and communities feature, 127
  customer, 37
  employee, 36–37
  partner, 37
  supplier, 37
  user, 35–37
competitive advantage, 172, 174
competitiveness, 8
complexity, removal of, 28
component integration, 375
computers, 365
computing resources, 73
concept-based search, 56, 60–62
confidentiality issues, 14
connectivity standards, 390
content elements, 301–309
  content networks as, 303–304
  enterprise entities as, 304–307
  information owners as, 307–309
content management, 55, 120, 121
  documentation of applications of, 137, 139–141
  horizontal portal support of, 34
  as IT-enabling framework feature, 127–129
  in user interface, 42, 44
content networks
  as content elements, 303–304
  and support and competency centers, 387
content page
  in storyboards and scripts, 322–324
  in user interface, 47–49
content page tabs
  in storyboards and scripts, 324
  in user interface, 46
content registry, 387
content-relevant information
  in storyboards and scripts, 326–328
  in user interface, 48
content services, 390–391
content windows
  in storyboards and scripts, 324–326
  in user interface, 46, 47, 49
controls, positioning, 323
corporate innovation, 171
Corporate Portals (Heidi Collins), 283
cost savings, 347–349
CRM (customer relationship management), 34
culture and behavior, 275–277
  and business objectives, 18–19
  and change management plan, 199
customer community, 37
customer relationship management (CRM), 34

data filtering and analysis, 54
data mining, 125
decision cycle, 30
decision making
  by employees, 32
  multi-repository support for, 67–69
decision support, 124
delegated management, 389

demilitarized zone (DMZ), 369–370
development services, 392–393
dictionaries, 53
differentiation, 77
digital identity, 64
directory and security services, 38
directory structure, 388–389
discussion groups, 127
discussion threads, 47
DMZ, *see* demilitarized zone
documentation
  of business intelligence applications, 132, 133, 135, 136
  of collaboration and communities applications, 135, 137, 138
  of content management applications, 137, 139–141
  of enterprise portals applications, 131–134
  of existing applications/systems/services, 130–143
  of learning applications, 139, 142, 143
document management, 127, 128
drilling into reports, 49, 50
Drucker, Peter, on computers, 365
dynamically built content, *xiii*
dynamically retrieved content, *xiii*

EAI, *see* enterprise application integration
early adopter advantages, 175
e-business portals, 34–35
e-commerce portals, 34–35
efficiency, 73
electronic commerce, 128
electronic messaging management, 126
electronic performance support systems, 129
employees
  as community for enterprise portals, 36–37
  and enterprise portals, 26–28
  involvement of, 32
  in support and competency center, 393–400
  see also information technology staff
enterprise application integration (EAI), 377, 390
enterprise entities, 304–307
enterprise information portals, 33–34
enterprise knowledge portal maps, 140, 142, 144–161
  IT-enabling framework on, 144, 146–150
  knowledge management objectives on, 142, 144, 145
  prioritizing features with, 151, 156–167
  prioritizing knowledge management objectives with, 146, 151–155
enterprise knowledge portal program, *xv–xvi*, 169–279
  architecture and infrastructure for, 225, 228–242
  charter for, 175–202
  executive approval for, 249, 253–256
  organization of, 259–279
  outline of, 171–258
  plan for, 235, 238, 239, 242–252
  requirements for, 201, 203–216
  strategy for, 209, 212–228
  value proposition for, 172, 174–175
enterprise knowledge portals (layer four), 77–168, 373–375
  benefits of, 28
  definition of, 77
  documentation of existing functions for, 130–143
  features of, 151, 156–167
  IT-enabling framework for, 114, 116, 117, 119–140
  knowledge management objectives for, 86–114
  maps for, 140, 142, 144–161
  market overview for, 82–86
  MyCompany case study of, 80, 82
  structure of, *xiii*

enterprise portals, 26–76, 120
application integration feature of, 69, 70
architecture of, 38–39
considerations for, 83, 84
documentation of applications of, 131–134
functionality of, 41–66
integration features of, 66–73
as IT-enabling framework feature, 122–124
for knowledge management objectives, 29–32
market overview for, 82–86
multi-repository support feature of, 67–69
peer-to-peer computing feature of, 72–73
process integration feature of, 69–71
services of, 37–41
types of, 32–35
user communities of, 35–37
vendors of, 83–85
Web services feature of, 70–72
enterprise portal team, 180
enterprise resource planning (ERP), 34, 376, 390
environment, information technology, *see* information technology environment
ERP, *see* enterprise resource planning
exact phrase search, 55
Excite, 35
exclude (search feature), 60
executive approval (for enterprise knowledge portal program), 249, 253–256
executive sponsors, 181
importance of, 260
process and governance role of, 262–264
expandable windows, 46
expert knowledge community, *see* knowledge expert community
experts
content window list of, 47
subject matter, 274–275
of support and competency center, 398–400
extensible markup language (XML), 371
extensible stylesheet language transformation (XSLT), 371
extranet and Internet (layer one), 368–369
extranet portals, 34–35

favorites, 64
feedback, 32
filters, presentation, 312–315
financial metrics, *xvii*, 341–361
and change management plan, 199
cost savings section of, 347–349
human resources information section of, 343–345
labor savings section of, 345–347
project costs section of, 350–354
return on investment section of, 353–359
revenue section of, 349–351
Finkelstein, Sydney
on group communication, 384
on success of corporation, *xi*
firewall (layer two), 369–370
first-level support staff, 394–395
flow charts, organizational, 261, 262
focus area diagrams, 289–290, 295–301
as business objects, 295–301
of targeted activities, 295–300
of user roles, 300, 301
format, publishing, 31
forward links, 47
functional areas, 261, 262
functionality, enterprise portal, 41–66
knowledge organization systems feature of, 49–55
personalization and roles feature of, 63–66
presentation feature of, 43–52

functionality, enterprise portal (*continued*)
search and index feature of, 55–63
funding, 177, 190, 194, 195
future focus
of knowledge management, 4, 15–18
as questionnaire section, 99–100

Garvin, David A., on learning organizations, 3
gazetteers, 53
glossaries, 53
Google, 35
governance, *see* process and governance
graphic navigation buttons, 65
group communication, 384
group definitions, 388

Harvard Business Review, 77
hierarchies, networks vs., 259
horizontal portals, 33–34
human resources
and financial metrics, 343–345
and innovation, 20–21

identity management administration, 396–397
identity management services, 388–389
images, use of, 323
In Athena's Camp (John Arquilla and David Ron), 259
index, *see* search and index
information
accessibility of, 14, 30
road map to available, 8
timeliness of, 66
information brokering, 55
information library services, 272–274
information mining, 55, 125
information owners, 307–309
information retrieval, 127
information services, 386–387
information technology environment, 367–377
application and integration services layer of, 375–376
applications and systems layer of, 376–377
enterprise knowledge portal layer of, 373–375
extranet and Internet layer of, 368–369
firewall layer, 369–370
intranet layer of, 370–373
information technology staff, 377–381
application developers on, 381
multimedia coordinators on, 381
server administrators on, 379
site managers on, 378–379
of support and competency center, 379–380, 398
support and competency center on, 379–380
technical analysts on, 380
user interface designers on, 381
Web access architects on, 378
infrastructure, *see* architecture and infrastructure
infrastructure services, 387–388
infrastructure support team, 400
initiatives, objectives and, 87–98
innovation (in corporation), 171
innovation promotion
by knowledge management, 4, 20–22
as questionnaire section, 100–101
installation, portal, 39–40
integration, 66–73, 124
Intellectual Capital (Thomas Stewart), 341
intellectual growth, 174
Internet, *see* extranet and Internet
Internet portals, 35
interviews, knowledge expert community
with chief technology office, 230, 232–234

and knowledge management objectives, 107–112
as program requirements, 204, 206–208
in program strategy, 217, 219–221
intranet (layer three), 370–373
invitations, sample
for architecture and infrastructure kick-off, 233
for architecture and infrastructure report, 239
to management objectives review, 117
for portal maps, 110
for portal requirements kick-off, 207
for portal requirements report, 213
for program review, 255
for strategy kick-off, 220
for strategy report, 225
involvement, employee, 32
ISO9000, 83
IT-enabling framework (for enterprise knowledge portals), 114, 116, 117, 119–140
business intelligence feature of, 124–125
collaboration and communities feature of, 126–127
content management feature of, 127–129
enterprise portal feature of, 122–124
features added to technologies, 121–130
identification of primary technologies for, 119–121
learning feature of, 129–130
on maps, 144, 146–150

keyword search, 55
kick-off meetings
for architecture and infrastructure, 230, 232, 233
for portal maps, 109–110
for portal requirements, 206, 207
for strategy, 219
knowledge assets, 5, 341
knowledge-creating organization maintenance
by knowledge management, 5, 22–23
as questionnaire section, 101
knowledge expert community, 102, 107–112
communication with, *see* communication, knowledge expert community
identification of, 102, 107, 108
interviews with, *see* interviews, knowledge expert community
process and governance role of, 266–267
on support and competency center staff, 394–395
as team members, 181–183
knowledge maintenance, 4, 10–15, 98–99
knowledge management, 3–25
business objectives supported by, 18–20
definitions of, *xiii–xiv*, 3–4
future focus of, 15–18
innovations promoted by, 20–22
knowledge-creating organizations maintained by, 22–23
knowledge maintained/communication facilitated by, 10–15
work processes organization of, 6–10
knowledge management conceptual model, 22–23
knowledge management deliverables, 174
knowledge management objectives, 86–114
enterprise portals for, 29–32
and expert community identification, 102, 107, 108
and expert community interviews, 107–112
on maps, 142, 144, 145
and mission/initiatives, 87–98
questionnaire creation for, 88, 94, 98–107

knowledge management objectives (*continued*)
  report for, 112, 114–119
  template for, 110, 112, 113
knowledge organization systems
  benefits of, 54–55
  characteristics of, 51
  classification and category type of, 53–54
  as enterprise portal feature, 123
  as enterprise portal functionality feature, 49–55
  relationship list type of, 54
  term list type of, 53
  types of, 53–55
knowledge workers, 5–6
  autonomy of, 10–11
  and business processes, 6–7
  and communication, 11–12
  needs of, 6

labor savings, 345–347
LANs (local area networks), 370
leadership, 31
learning, 121
  documentation of applications of, 139, 142, 143
  horizontal portal support of, 34
  as IT-enabling framework feature, 129–130
  in user interface, 42, 43, 45
learning management systems, 129
learning organizations, 3
learning team, 399
letters, welcome, *see* welcome letters
librarian, support and competency center, 399
libraries, 48–49, 50–53
library services, information, 272–274
links
  and multipart documents, 66
  selecting, 49, 52
link search (search feature), 60
local area networks (LANs), 370
long-term knowledge expert community, 102
Lotus Notes, 130, 131
management
  and communication, 13
  delegated, 389
  network, 370
  program, 267–269
  project, 285
  and value added work processes, 12
  Web applications, 370
  and work processes, 11
  work processes audited by, 13–14
managers
  site, 378–379
  of support and competency center, 395–396
Managing Professional Intellect (James Quinn, Philip Anderson, and Sydney Finkelstein), *xi*, 384
maps, *xiv*
  for accessing information, 8
  enterprise knowledge portal, *see* enterprise knowledge portal maps
  in knowledge organization systems, 50
  site, 66, 67
  of targeted activities into work process, 290–295
market overview, 82–86
match all (search feature), 60
match any (search feature), 59
maximizing windows, 47
meetings, kick-off, *see* kick-off meetings
Merrill Lynch, Inc. (Shilakes and Tyleman), 26
metadata search, 56, 62–63
methodology, *xvi–xvii*, 283–340
  business object content in, 310–318
  business objects in, 289–301
  content elements in, 301–309
  MyCompany case study of, 288–289
  storyboards and scripts in, 317–340
metrics, *see* financial metrics
Microsoft Outlook, 122

Microsoft SharePoint Portal Server, 130–131
minimizing windows, 47
mission
  and business objectives, 18–19
  and knowledge management objectives, 87–98
  questionnaire about, 88–94
mission and task management, 55
mobile commerce portals, 35
MSN, 35
multimedia coordinators, 381
multipart documents, 65–66
multi-repository support, 67–69
MyCompany case study
  of architecture and infrastructure template, 230, 232, 234–235
  of benefits of program, 188–189
  of budgets/funding, 194
  of business object context, 311–312, 314, 317
  of change management plan, 201
  of communication plan, 196
  of content networks, 303–305, 307
  of cost savings, 348–349
  of documentation, 131
  of enterprise knowledge portal features, 151, 160
  of enterprise knowledge portals, 80, 82
  of focus area diagrams, 295, 299–301
  of human resources information, 345
  of IT categories, 120–121
  of IT-enabling framework map, 146
  of IT features added, 122
  of knowledge expert community interviews, 109–110, 206–207, 219, 220
  of knowledge expert community recruitment, 102, 107
  of knowledge management categories, 101–102
  of knowledge management objectives map, 144
  of knowledge management objectives prioritization, 146, 151
  of knowledge management objectives report, 114
  of labor savings, 347
  of methodology, 288–289
  of mission and initiatives, 88
  of plan activities/tasks assignment, 245
  of plan activities/tasks identification, 243
  of plan activities/tasks organization, 245
  of plan activities/tasks relationships, 249
  of program review, 253–254
  of program strategy, 216, 217
  of program strategy report, 221, 224
  of projected costs, 353
  of requirements for program, 204
  of requirements report, 208–209
  of return on investment, 359
  of revenue, 350
  of risks with program, 190
  of scope and objectives, 179
  of storyboards, 329–333
  of strategic relationships, 185–187
  of team members and stakeholders, 183, 185
  of work process diagrams, 293–295

navigation, 66
navigation buttons, 65
navigation schemes, 54, 56
network management, 370
network resources, 73
networks, hierarchies vs., 259

objectives
  business, *see* business objectives support
  charter documentation of, 176, 177, 179, 180
  knowledge management, 86–114
ontology, 54
open standards, 40

operational level agreements, 388
operational managers, 12
operations team, 399–400
organization, work processes, *see* work processes organization
organizational flow charts, 261, 262
organization (enterprise knowledge portal program), 259–279
  culture and behavior in, 275–277
  process and governance in, 261–275
owners, information, 306–309

pagers, 35
partner community, 37
partnership development, 174–175
payback period, 342
PDAs (personal data assistants), 35
peer-to-peer computing, 72–73
performance, technical architecture, 40
performance-based metrics, 19, 32, 124, 125
performance management programs, 21–22
personal data assistants (PDAs), 35
personalization
  as enterprise portal feature, 124
  as enterprise portal functionality feature, 63–66
  in user interface, 46
personalization server, 38–39
plan (enterprise knowledge portal program), 235, 238, 239, 242–252
  activity and task identification in, 242–245
  assignment of resources/roles/team members in, 245, 248
  relationship of tasks/activities determined in, 247–252
  task list outline in, 243, 245–247
platform integration, 375
platforms, server, 39
plug and play, 123
portal banners, 44, 46, 320
portal component server, 38
portal menus, 46, 321–322
portal metadata repository, 39
portal object library, 39
portal objects, 389, 390
portals
  enterprise information, 33–34
  horizontal, 33–34
  vertical, 34
portal servers, 38–39
portal technologies, 119–130
Porter, Michael, on differentiation, 77
positioning (of controls), 323
presentation
  as enterprise portal feature, 123
  as enterprise portal functionality feature, 43–52
presentation filters, 312–315
presentation services, 385–386
prioritization
  of features, 151, 156–167
  of knowledge management objectives, 16–17, 146, 151–155
problem ticket coordinator, 396
process and governance, 261–275
  application development team's role in, 270–271
  architecture and infrastructure team's role in, 271–272
  executive sponsor's role in, 262–264
  expert knowledge community's role in, 266–267
  information library services' role in, 272–274
  program management's role in, 267–269
  stakeholders' role in, 265–266
  steering committee's role in, 264–265
  subject matter experts' role in, 274–275
  support and competency center's role in, 269–270
process integration, 69–71, 375–376
productivity, 28
profiling, 124

program, enterprise knowledge portal, *see* enterprise knowledge portal program
program management, 267–269
project costs, 350–354
project management, 285
property definitions, 64
proprietary information, 14
proximity (search feature), 60
proxy server software, 370

query system, 58
questionnaire (for knowledge management objectives), 88, 94, 98–107
  business objectives support section of, 100
  future focus section of, 99–100
  innovation promotion section of, 100–101
  knowledge-creating organization maintenance section of, 101
  knowledge maintenance/communication facilitation section of, 98–99
  mission, 88–94
  work processes organization section of, 94, 98
Quinn, James Brian
  on group communication, 384
  on success of corporation, *xi*

readability, 323
real-time collaboration, 126
refresh feature, 47
registration, 389
relational database management system, 128
relationship lists, 54
relationships, strategic, 177, 185–187
replication, 371
reports
  for architecture and infrastructure, 233–242
  drilling into details of, 49, 50
  for knowledge management objectives, 112, 114–119
  of program requirements, 207–216
  of program strategy, 220–228
representatives, support and competency center, 397–398
request, submitting, 49, 51
requirements (for enterprise knowledge portal program), 201, 203–216
  expert community interviews as, 204, 206–208
  report of, 207–216
  template for, 203–205
Research That Reinvents the Corporation (John Seely Brown), 171
resource assignment, 245, 248
responsibilities, 199, 261, 262
return on investment (ROI), 188, 342, 353–359
revenue, 349–351
reward systems, 18
risk management, 55
risks
  and business objectives, 19
  charter definition of, 177, 189–193
rituals, 20–21
ROI, *see* return on investment
role definitions, 388
roles
  and change management plan, 199
  as enterprise portal functionality feature, 63–66
  focus area diagrams of, 300, 301
  of information technology staff, 378–381
  plan assignment of, 245, 248
  of support and competency center, 394–400
  see also personalization and roles
Ron, David, on networks vs. hierarchies, 259
rules, business, 315–318
rules server, 38

sales force automation (SFA), 34
sample agendas, *see* agendas, sample

sample invitations, *see* invitations, sample
scalability, 40
SCM (supply chain management), 34
scope, 176, 177, 179, 180
scripts, *see* storyboards and scripts
scrolling, 65
search and index
  Boolean search feature of, 56
  category search feature of, 56
  concept-based search feature of, 56, 60–62
  as enterprise portal feature, 123
  as enterprise portal functionality feature, 55–63
  exact phrase search feature of, 55
  formats of, 58
  keywork search feature of, 55
  metadata search feature of, 56, 62–63
  standard search features of, 56, 59–61
second-level support staff, 395
security, 14, 38
  of enterprise portal technical architecture, 41
  and firewalls, 369–370
selecting links, 49, 52
self-service, employee, 27
semantic networks, 54
server administrators, 379
server platforms, 39
servers, 38–39
service-level agreements, 387
services
  of enterprise portals, 37–41
  portal server, 38–39
  of support and competency center, 384–393
SFA (sales force automation), 34
Shilakes and Tyleman, 26
short-term knowledge expert community, 102
simplicity, 323
single sign-on strategy, 389
site managers, 378–379
site maps, 66, 67
site search (search feature), 60
space, white, 323
sponsors, executive, 181
staff, *see* employees
stakeholders
  charter identification of, 176, 179–186
  process and governance role of, 265–266
  as team members, 181, 183–186
standards
  alert and notification, 392
  connectivity, 390
  discussion forum, 392
  knowledge organization, 391
  library, 391
  platform, 387
  programming, 393
  quality assurance, 393
  search, 391
  subscription, 392
  usability and interface, 386
standard search features, 56, 59–61
statistical approach (to concept-based search), 61–62
steering committee, 264–265
Stewart, Thomas A., on knowledge assets, 341
storage resources, 73
storyboards and scripts, 317–340
  content page in, 322–324
  content page tabs in, 324
  content-relevant information in, 326–328
  content windows in, 324–326
  frame of, 328–340
  in methodology, 317–340
  portal banner in, 320
  portal menu in, 321–322
strategic plans, 16
strategic relationships, 177, 185–187
strategy (enterprise knowledge portal program), 209, 212–228

expert community interviews in, 217, 219–221
report of, 220–228
template for, 213, 216–218
subject headings, 53–54
subject matter experts, 274–275
submitting requests, 49, 51
success factors, 31
success (of corporation), *xi*
suppliers, 35, 37
supply chain management (SCM), 34
support and competency center, *xvii–xviii*, 384–403
access and integration services of, 390
administration services of, 389
business analysts of, 398
call center representatives of, 395
collaboration services of, 391–392
content services of, 390–391
development services of, 392–393
enterprise knowledge portal infrastructure support team of, 400
enterprise knowledge portal librarian of, 399
enterprise knowledge portal operations team of, 399–400
experts of, 398–400
first-level support staff of, 394–395
identity management administration of, 396–397
identity management services of, 388–389
information services of, 386–387
on information technology staff, 379–380
information technology staff of, 398
infrastructure services of, 387–388
knowledge expert community staff of, 394–395
learning team of, 399
manager of, 395–396
presentation services of, 385–386
problem ticket coordinator of, 396
process and governance role of, 269–270
representatives of, 397–398
second-level support staff of, 395
services of, 384–393
staff of, 393–400
third-level support staff of, 395–398
syndication, 371

tasks
assignment to, 245, 248
identification of, 242–245
organization of, 243, 245–247
relationship of activities to, 247–252
taxonomies, 54
team-based collaboration, 126, 127
team information management, 55
teams/team members
charter identification of, 176, 179–186
enterprise knowledge portal, *xv*
enterprise portal, 180
executive sponsors as, 181
expert knowledge community as, 181–183
plan assignment of, 245, 248
technical analysts, 380
technical architecture, enterprise knowledge portal, *xvii–xviii*, 365–383
information technology environment of, 367–377
information technology staff of, 377–381
technical architecture, enterprise portal, 38–41
administration of, 41
enterprise portal architecture of, 38–39
installation of, 39–40
performance of, 40
scalability of, 40
security of, 41
server platforms of, 39
standards of, 40–41
technical support
as business intelligence feature, 125

technical support (*continued*)
as collaboration and communities feature, 127
as content management feature, 129
as enterprise portal feature, 124
as learning feature, 129
technologies, portal, 119–130
IT-enabling framework addition of, 121–130
IT-enabling framework identification of, 119–121
template(s), *xiv*
for application integration, 69
for architecture and infrastructure, 229–231
for charter, 177, 178
for communication plan, 197
for knowledge management objectives, 110, 112, 113
for portal requirements, 205
as program requirements, 203–205
for program strategy, 213, 216–218
for risks, 191
for work process, 291–293
term lists, 53
thesauri, 54
thesaurus approach (to concept-based search), 61
third-level support staff, 395–398
third-party management software, 235, 238
third-party search tools, 57
timeliness, 66
title search (search feature), 60
toolbars, 322–323
training coordinators, 12

URL search (search feature), 60
user access, 63–64, 66
user communities, 35–37
user context, 311–313
user interface, enterprise knowledge portal, 41–45
business intelligence in, 41, 42
collaboration and communities in, 41–43
content management in, 42, 44
learning in, 42, 43, 45
presentation of, 41–52
user interface designers, 381
user profiles, 388

value proposition, 172, 174–175
vendors, enterprise portal, 83–86
vertical portals, 34, 35
videoconferencing, 129
vision, 15–16

WANs (wide area networks), 370
Web access architects, 378
Web applications management, 370
Web browsers, 28
Webcast, 110, 111
Web content management, 127, 128
Web phones, 35
Web services, 70–72
welcome letters
to knowledge expert community, 107, 108, 181–183
to stakeholders, 181, 184
white space, 323
wide area networks (WANs), 370
wildcards (search feature), 60
wireless personal data assistants, 35
work flow management, 55
work process diagrams, 289, 290–295, 291–294
work processes
and future focus, 15–16
management audits of, 13–14
work processes organization
dynamic entry to/exit from, 12
of knowledge management, 4, 6–10
as questionnaire section, 94, 98

XML (extensible markup language), 371
XSLT (extensible stylesheet language transformation), 371

Yahoo, 35, 82